1972

UNIVERSITY OF WASHINGTON PUBLICATIONS ON ASIA

SPONSORED BY THE FAR EASTERN AND RUSSIAN INSTITUTE

COURT AND CONSTITUTION IN JAPAN

Selected Supreme Court Decisions, 1948-60

By JOHN M. MAKI

With translations by Ikeda Masaaki,
David C. S. Sissons, and Kurt Steiner

Seattle   UNIVERSITY OF WASHINGTON PRESS   1964

*This book is published with the assistance
of a grant from the Ford Foundation.*

PREFACE

MORE by chance than by design I discovered in the supplementary
volume of *Nihonkoku Kempō* ("The Constitution of Japan")
by Professor Miyazawa Toshiyoshi, Japan's most distinguished constitutional scholar, a selection of the constitutional decisions of
the Supreme Court of Japan. They not only dealt with constitutional problems in the narrow sense but with such important matters as the land reform, changing attitudes toward the family, new
relationships among the branches of government, the nature of
the new freedoms guaranteed under the Constitution, the rights of
the individual before the law, and the relationship between individual freedom and society.

Not only because they shed light from a different angle on the
fascinating changes wrought in the fabric of Japanese society by
both the occupation and the Japanese themselves but also because
they reflected the attitudes of Japan's most distinguished jurists
toward the contemporary problems of their society, these decisions
were the source of considerable intellectual excitement. In addition, they revealed the operation of the Supreme Court itself, a
new and exceedingly significant judicial institution in Japan. The
more I read and thought about the decisions the more regrettable
it seemed that only those who could read Japanese had access to
them. Therefore, I decided to translate a limited but representative selection from the whole body of the Court's constitutional
decisions.

v

From the beginning my aim in preparing this volume was a simple one: to introduce to the English-reading world a representative group of the constitutional decisions of the Supreme Court of Japan. I have rigorously avoided analytical comment on any of the decisions, but have tried to present as accurate a translation as possible, leaving it to the knowledgeable reader to provide his own critical comment and draw the appropriate conclusions.

Although I lacked some of the ideal qualifications for the task, such as an intimate knowledge of Japanese law and of the legal system, a thorough knowledge of at least one foreign legal and judicial system, and research experience in comparative law, I did have the basic advantages of a working knowledge of the Japanese language and a considerable familiarity with Japan's constitutional problems. My will to get on with the job was not dampened by a subsequent discovery that the Supreme Court itself had made several translations of important decisions, because its principles of selection and its objectives differed from mine.

During the 1958–59 academic year I was fortunate to receive both a Fulbright research professorship and a sabbatical leave granted by the University of Washington. The combination made this study possible, for it enabled me to go to Japan for a year of uninterrupted work.

Not long after my arrival in Japan I learned that the three scholars who became associated with me had already translated some Supreme Court decisions for other purposes but had no plans for their publication. Coincidentally, some of these decisions were on my original list. Professor Ikeda Masaaki, now of the Faculty of Law of Rikkyo (St. Paul's) University in Tokyo, had translated either in full or in summary form some fifteen decisions, ten of which appear in this volume. Mr. David C. S. Sissons of the Department of International Relations of the Australian National University was then at the Institute of Social Science, Tokyo University, working on the topic of fundamental human rights under the new Constitution. He has made eight of the translations. He also called attention to an article by Professor Kurt Steiner of Stanford University, which had obviously been based on an extensive translation of the Fukuoka Patricide Decision. Professor Steiner has contributed that decision, certainly one of the more interesting ones.

It was most fortunate that all three men agreed to join in the project. Their contributions not only lightened the work I had been considering but, more importantly, widened the scope of the selection. I most gratefully acknowledge their cooperation. As editor I must assume full responsibility for infelicity of language or possible inaccuracy in translation.

The source of all decisions included in this volume is the *Saikōsai-bansho Hanreishū* ("Collection of Supreme Court Precedents"). It was my original intention to present each decision exactly as it appeared in the *Hanreishū*, including all such material as names of parties involved in the case, courts of first and second instance, summary of the decision, the point at issue in the case, and the names of all participating justices. I decided to eliminate such material because it contributes nothing to an understanding of the decisions themselves. However, all other material, except the titles, is drawn from the decisions as they appear in the *Hanreishū*. Since the titles in the original are, for the most part, highly technical, more descriptive ones have been substituted. Where appropriate the popular titles by which they are known have been added.

Between 1947 and 1957 the Supreme Court handed down just under 1,100 constitutional decisions, representing only about 3 per cent of all decisions; the rest dealt with matters of criminal and civil law not bearing directly on the Constitution. Excluded from consideration was one group of constitutional decisions, numbering several hundred, dealing with questions of constitutionality arising out of legislative or executive actions taken as a result of occupation orders. Since all concerned actions of a government that was not free and sovereign because of the occupation, the constitutional decisions dealing with them fell into a special and ephemeral category. Many other constitutional decisions were excluded from consideration because of extreme brevity, similarity to other more interesting or more significant decisions, or their highly technical nature. After having scanned all in a preliminary screening, I read about 10 per cent of the constitutional decisions before making the final selection. I had originally planned to limit the selection to the first ten years (1947–57) of the Court's work, but included several subsequent decisions of especial significance.

The criteria used for the selection of the twenty-six decisions in this volume were: the importance of the decision; the nature of the issue dealt with; and the light that each could shed on the opinions of the Court and the individual justices. These criteria are all related to the stated purpose of this volume—the introduction of the Court's work to those who do not read Japanese. If there is a bias in the selection, it has arisen from a desire to show the thinking of the Court on broad social issues, and not alone on relatively narrow problems of jurisprudence. This collection includes most of the more famous decisions of the Court. Notably missing are several that were made into great political issues on the ground that the accused had been legally victimized because they were members of labor unions. These decisions were not included because the basic constitutional issues, as far as I could see, were relatively minor, and had been considerably inflated by the controversy.

I am confident that, although the twenty-six decisions in this volume are only a small fraction of the total number of the Court's constitutional decisions, they present a reasonably accurate picture of the thinking of the Court.

I should like to make a few comments about certain problems of translation:

1. Every effort has been made to avoid the use of technical legal language, except where it seems required. The assumption is that the lay reader would find it difficult to follow technical language, while the expert reader will not be misled by the use of nontechnical language.

2. The Japanese system of appeal is a matter of some technical complexity, described briefly in the Introduction (see p. xxv). Although the original text specifies the type of appeal, the translations do not because this knowledge is not necessary for an understanding of the decisions.

3. Paraphrase and summary have been rigorously avoided, although on occasion they would have eased the burden of translation without distorting the meaning of the original.

4. In a few places the language of the original has been perfectly clear, but the meaning has not. There I have taken the liberty of adding explanatory footnotes for the guidance of the reader.

5. With a few exceptions I have used the exact text of existing translations of Japanese laws (see Bibliography). This practice accounts for certain minor differences in style between the translations of laws and the translations of decisions.

6. All footnotes are mine, unless attributed to the translator. Parentheses appear as in the original; all bracketed material has been supplied by either the translator or the editor.

7. Repetitious material has not been eliminated, for to do so would give a misleading impression of the original.

8. Some sections of the translations read clearly and smoothly while others seem rough and opaque. In almost every instance this reflects the nature of the original. In a number of places I was tempted, either as translator or editor, to recast unclear or tortured passages into clearer and perhaps more graceful language, but this would have been misleading. Of course, I must assume blame for any awkwardness or infelicity not traceable to the language of the original.

9. Japanese personal names are given according to the Japanese order: surname first, personal name second.

I have already expressed my appreciation of the work of my colleagues. In addition, I wish also to express my thanks and appreciation to the following:

Professor Miyazawa Toshiyoshi, dean of the Faculty of Law of Rikkyo University and professor emeritus of Tokyo University, for his wise counsel, so generously and kindly given, in the planning stages of this study.

Dr. Kaya Seiji, president of Tokyo University, for approving my research affiliation with his University.

Professor Suzuki Takeo, then dean of the Faculty of Law of Tokyo University, for making the arrangements for my association with Professor Miyazawa.

Professor Kawashima Takeyoshi of Tokyo University, to whom both Professor Steiner and I are indebted for assistance on the Fukuoka Patricide Decision.

Judge Naitō Yorihiro, Deputy Secretary-General of the Supreme Court of Japan, for his great kindness in both locating and making available to me much invaluable material and for arranging for me to observe Japanese courts in action.

Mr. Nishimura Iwao, Executive Secretary of the United States Educational Commission in Japan, for introducing me to many of those who were of such great assistance, and to both him and his staff for their great efficiency and kindness in assisting my family and me in our living arrangements in Tokyo, thereby contributing indirectly but substantially to the ease and speed with which I was able to pursue my research.

Professor Okudaira Yasuhiro of Nagoya University and Professor Kubota Kinuko of Rikkyo University, whose conversations gave me considerable insight into the work of the Supreme Court.

Professors Robert Fletcher, Arval Morris, and Cornelius Peck of the University of Washington School of Law for reading a number of the decisions.

Professor Dan F. Henderson, also of the School of Law, for reading and commenting on the Introduction, a task for which he is eminently well qualified because of his membership in the Japanese bar, a distinction shared by few foreigners.

The members of the Modern Japan Project of the Far Eastern and Russian Institute of the University of Washington for a fruitful discussion of the Introduction.

Professor George E. Taylor, director of the Far Eastern and Russian Institute, both for advice during the planning of this study and for approving a grant-in-aid from the Institute which enabled me to enjoy the leave necessary for its completion.

The International Educational Exchange Program for the grant of a Fulbright research professorship.

The Board of Regents of the University of Washington for granting the sabbatical leave and subsequent leave of absence that gave me the time to work on this study.

The Agnes Anderson Research Fund of the University of Washington for providing a partial publication subsidy.

Mr. Sissons wishes to add a note of appreciation for the assistance of Professor Okudaira and of Mr. Tokikuni Yasuo of the Supreme Court Secretariat.

The strength of this study comes in great part from the contributions of my colleagues and of those whose assistance I gratefully acknowledge. However, I alone must be held responsible for any of its weaknesses and defects. All opinions stated in the Introduction are, of course, my own.

I have learned much from this study and hope to share my knowledge with others. My efforts will be more than rewarded if they lead a specialist in comparative jurisprudence or in comparative judicial systems to undertake the comprehensive study of the Supreme Court of Japan that remains to be done.

JOHN M. MAKI

June, 1962
Seattle, Washington

CONTENTS

INTRODUCTION

THE Supreme Court of Japan possesses broad powers of control over the realm of Japanese jurisprudence. Not only is it the court of last resort with the power of constitutional review, but it administers the entire judiciary, is responsible for the training of all who enter the legal profession, and possesses the rule-making power relating to procedure in litigation and to the internal discipline of the courts. This volume concentrates on the problem of constitutional review. However, it is the purpose of this Introduction to present in broad outline a description of the structure, the functions, and the work of the Court, and to describe the nature of the Constitution of Japan and the manner in which the Court has approached the main problems of constitutional review.

Japan's Constitution, promulgated on May 3, 1947, created the Supreme Court and vested it with functions and powers new to the Japanese judiciary. The Court came into existence on August 4, 1947, and, like every major Japanese governmental and political institution of the democracy that has been created since World War II, it owes its existence to the occupation. It is equally significant that, like most of the other institutions, the Court was built on a nondemocratic predecessor which collapsed under the weight of war, defeat, and occupation. Japan's former highest court was the *Daishinin* or Court of Cassation.[1] It was frequently

1. Little has appeared in English on the Court of Cassation. Professor Harold S. Quigley's *Japanese Government and Politics* (New York: The Century Company, 1932) has a chapter on

termed in English the "Supreme Court," but the appellation was somewhat misleading and would be even more so now because of the great differences between the *Daishinin* and the present Supreme Court. It was the final court of appeal and stood at the apex of the judicial system. Originally established on April 14, 1875, when an early and important reorganization of the newly emerging Japanese central government took place, it assumed its final form on February 10, 1890, the date on which the Court Organization Law went into effect, just a year less one day after the promulgation of Japan's first modern written constitution, the so-called Meiji Constitution, in 1889. Under the Court Organization Law, the Court of Cassation was the "highest court." It was the final court of appeal in both civil and criminal cases and possessed original jurisdiction over crimes involving rebellion and offenses by members of the Imperial Family. Though it was the highest court, its powers were circumscribed, especially in comparison with those of its successor.

The Constitution of 1889 did set forth the principle of the separation of powers in the sense that the executive, legislative, and judicial branches of government were recognized as having separate and distinct areas of function and responsibility. However, it fell far short of enacting the principle as it is commonly understood, and certainly there was completely lacking the system of checks and balances that gives the separation of powers its true meaning in a system of democratic government. The fundamental principle of the 1889 Constitution was the idea of imperial sovereignty, as stated in Article 4: "The Emperor is the head of the Empire, combining in himself the rights of sovereignty." In accordance with this principle, the Constitution dealt with the executive, legislative, and judicial branches of government simply as if they were three aspects of the unitary imperial sovereign power. This was clearly brought out in Article 57 of the Constitution of 1889 and the official commentary on it. That article reads as follows: "The Judicature shall be exercised by the Courts of Law according to law, in the name of the Emperor." Prince Itō

the old judicial system with a few remarks on the Court of Cassation. Good brief accounts of it can be found in *Waga Kuni ni okeru Saibansho Seido no Enkaku* ("The Development of the Court System in Our Country"), published by the Secretariat General of the Supreme Court (October, 1957), and in *Saibanhō* ("Trial Law") by Professor Kaneko Hajime (Tokyo: Yuhikaku, 1959).

Hirobumi, the principal drafter of the Constitution, in his official commentary made the following remarks about the meaning of this article:

But the Sovereign is the fountain of justice, and His judicial authority is nothing more than a form of the manifestation of the sovereign power. Therefore judgments shall be pronounced in the name of the Emperor, the judicial authority in this respect representing Him in His sovereign power. . . . The judicature is combined in the sovereign power of the Emperor as part of His executive power . . . the judiciary is only a part of the executive, and the executive, strictly speaking, is made up of two parts the judiciary and the administrative, each performing distinct services.[2]

However outlandish the Prince's reasoning may appear to one schooled in the idea of the separation of powers and the system of checks and balances, the fact remains that both the Meiji Constitution and the Prince's commentary thereon established the pattern of Japanese government that prevailed to the end of World War II. It is abundantly clear from the quotations above that there was no room under the previous Japanese system for a truly independent judiciary.

Perhaps the most serious limitation on the independence of the courts was that they were all under the direction of the Ministry of Justice, an executive agency. Since under law the Ministry controlled judicial budgetary and administrative matters, including appointment and promotion, the weight of executive pressure on the courts was great. Although some critics maintain that the courts remained independent in their exercise of the judicial power, that is to say, in the handing down of judicial decisions involving the interpretation of law, others aver that some judges, at least, tended to think of themselves more as bureaucrats than as judges.

Conspicuously absent from the powers of the Court of Cassation was jurisdiction over problems of constitutionality. The Meiji Constitution was a fundamental law that permitted no room for interpretation in the true sense. It was presented to the Japanese as a gracious gift from the Emperor himself; it was not an instrument wrested from a reluctant ruler by a people clamoring for democratic rights and freedoms. The document, flowing directly from the source of sovereignty itself, was regarded as the supreme

2. See pp. 100–104 in Itō Hirobumi, *Commentaries on the Constitution of the Empire of Japan,* trans. Miyoji Itō (Tokyo: Igirisu Hōritsu Gakko, 1889).

expression of the imperial sovereign will. Given these premises, it would have been illogical and in contravention of the concept of imperial sovereignty for the courts—clearly only the mouthpieces of the sovereign—to have been empowered to rule on the meaning of the Constitution.

"Advice" on constitutional issues could be made to the Emperor only by the Privy Council, his most important advisory organ, which had also been established by the 1889 Constitution. Although on several occasions the Privy Council rendered advice on the meaning of certain provisions of the Constitution, it handled no cases of constitutional review as that phrase is understood under the Constitution of 1947.

However ably and efficiently the forty-five justices of the Court of Cassation may have handled their business, it was clear in the early stages of the occupation that though it was the highest court of the land, it could not be preserved intact under the new systems of government and of law that were being instituted.

The occupation in its fostering of the revision of the existing constitution, in its shifting of the basis of Japanese law from the historical models of French and German law to the unfamiliar and untried principles of Anglo-American law, and in its desire to bring about a thoroughgoing alteration in the nature and status of the legal profession and the judicial system, had two aims: to eliminate the nondemocratic features of the preoccupation system and to introduce what were regarded as desirable democratic features of law and justice and their administration.[3] Therefore, the seven articles of Chapter VI of the Constitution of 1947 deal with the judiciary and especially with the Supreme Court, a striking contrast to the complete absence of mention of the Court of Cassation in the Meiji Constitution.

Now "the whole judicial power" is vested in the Supreme Court and "in such inferior courts as are established by law" (Article 76). The Supreme Court also possesses "the rule-making power

---

3. The following two articles, written by Americans closely associated with the immediate postwar legal and judicial changes, are extremely useful: Thomas L. Blakemore, "Postwar Developments in Japanese Law," *Wisconsin Law Review*, Vol. 1947, pp. 632–53; and Alfred C. Oppler, "The Reform of Japan's Legal and Judicial System under Allied Occupation," *Washington Law Review*, XXIV, 290–324. See also Oppler's "Japan's Courts and Law in Transition," *Contemporary Japan*, XXI, Nos. 1–3 (June, 1952), 241–63, for an excellent survey of developments to approximately the end of occupation.

under which it determines the rules of procedure and practice, and of matters relating to attorneys, the internal discipline of the courts and the administration of judicial affairs" (Article 77). It is further stipulated in Article 77 that public prosecutors are subject to the rule-making power of the Court. Although judges of the inferior courts are to be appointed by the cabinet, such appointments must be made from a list of nominees provided by the Supreme Court (Article 80). Finally, the Constitution provides that the Supreme Court "is the court of last resort with power to determine the constitutionality of any law, order, regulation or official act" (Article 81). Constitutionally, therefore, the Supreme Court possesses very broad judicial power. In spite of its obvious importance, the rule-making power will not be discussed here. The administration of the judicial system will be dealt with to show the relation between the Supreme Court and the rest of the system and to indicate how it adds to the pressure of the Court's business. Constitutional review is, of course, the main theme of this study.

Although the whole judicial power is vested in the Supreme Court and the inferior courts and the principle of the separation of powers is followed in the Constitution, it is necessary to observe briefly the nature of the constitutional relationship between the judiciary and the executive branch. The only direct constitutional link between the Supreme Court and the cabinet is in the process of appointment. The Constitution requires the formal appointment by the Emperor of the chief justice, who is to be designated by the cabinet (Article 6). Such appointment is only a formality, for the Constitution specifically states that the Emperor shall have no "powers related to government" (Article 4) and that he shall perform only certain "acts in matters of state on behalf of the people" (Article 7). Imperial appointment of the chief justice is designed to give him the same prestige as the prime minister, who is also an imperial appointee. The fourteen other justices (the number having been established in the Court Organization Law,[4] passed April 16, 1947, and effective as of May 3, 1947) are all appointed directly by the cabinet. The chief justice is *primus inter pares.* He differs from his fellow justices only in title, manner of appointment, salary, and the fact that he presides over the Court.

4. An English translation of this law appears in *The Constitution of Japan and Criminal Statutes* (Tokyo: Ministry of Justice, 1958).

What are the stated qualifications for men aspiring to positions on the bench of the Supreme Court? What kind of men served as justices in the first twelve years of the Court's existence?

General qualifications for appointment to the Supreme Court, as provided in the Court Organization Law, include only the attainment of the minimum age of forty and "broad vision and extensive knowledge of law." In addition, the law provides that at least ten of the justices must have either ten years' experience as presidents of high courts or as judges in such courts, or twenty years' experience as judges of summary courts, or as public prosecutors or lawyers, or as professors or assistant professors "in legal science in universities which shall be determined elsewhere by law."

There is one curious constitutional provision that originated with the occupation concerning the appointment of the justices of the Supreme Court that requires comment. The second paragraph of Article 79 of the Constitution reads as follows:

> The appointment of the judges of the Supreme Court shall be reviewed by the people at the first general election of members of the House of Representatives following their appointment, and shall be reviewed again at the first general election of members of the House of Representatives after a lapse of ten years, and in the same manner thereafter.

This is a manifestation of the principle of popular sovereignty, guaranteeing that the people have a voice in the appointment of Supreme Court justices even though the right of appointment is lodged in the cabinet. It seems to carry the principle of popular sovereignty to an almost ridiculous extreme.

On every occasion when this popular review has been made, the justices concerned have received overwhelming votes of approval. However, following the general election of 1949, the first in which this right was exercised by the people, one citizen challenged the constitutionality of the law that created the arrangements for the review. The law provides that those who wish to vote against the confirmation of an appointment place an "X" on the ballot after the name of the justice. The plaintiff charged that this provision of the law violated the freedom of conscience of many, because a blank ballot would be counted as approval even though it might mean either an abstention because of ignorance of the qualifications of the justice, or an unwillingness to express an opinion. Therefore, he argued, to interpret a blank ballot as approval meant that there might be attributed to a voter an opinion that he did not hold, thereby violating his freedom of conscience. The Supreme Court held against the plaintiff.[5]

It is difficult to see what useful purpose this constitutional provision serves. Other laws provide that a justice can be retired for reasons of age or mental or physical incompetence or that he can be impeached if he "has swerved from his duty, neglected his duty or degraded himself." In any situation in which it appears likely that the people will vote a justice off the bench, other remedies could be applied. As long as this provision remains, there will be the possibility, however slight, that political considerations may sway the opinions of individual justices.

Between the creation of the Court on August 8, 1947, and January 1, 1959, two chief justices (Mibuchi Tadahiko, who served from August 8, 1947, to his retirement because of age on March 2, 1950, and his successor, Tanaka Kōtarō) and twenty-seven justices had been appointed.

Of the twenty-nine justices [6] no fewer than twenty-one were graduated from Tokyo Imperial University (now simply Tokyo University). Three others were graduates of Kyoto Imperial University. The remaining five came from Waseda, Meiji, Hōsei, Nihon, and Chūō, private universities in Tokyo. All were graduates of faculties of law. Of those on whom I have data regarding specialization within law, nine studied German law, three French, two English, and one political science. In addition, no fewer than fourteen had traveled abroad to study or observe foreign systems of law or courts.

Prior to their appointment to the Supreme Court four justices had been professors of law, eleven lawyers, ten judges, two public prosecutors, one a diplomat, and one a bureaucrat. The diplomat had once been the chief of the Treaty Bureau of the Ministry of Foreign Affairs, and the bureaucrat had been the director of the important and influential Bureau of Legislation of the cabinet. Thus, all twenty-nine justices had careers intimately related to law or the administration of justice. Among the twenty-nine some had worked in fields other than their professional careers: eleven as lawyers, four as lecturers in universities, two as public prosecu-

5. This decision is to be found in *Hanreishū*, VI, No. 2, 122 (Civil).
6. See Appendix II for brief biographical sketches of the justices.

tors, and two as judges. One (Chief Justice Tanaka) also served briefly as a postwar minister of education. In addition, eleven had from two to twenty-four years of experience as judges of the Court of Cassation.

The long experience of the justices in the area of jurisprudence was undoubtedly one of the principal reasons why the Court was able to handle new and unfamiliar legal and constitutional concepts as effectively as it did after its creation only two years after the end of World War II. Many observers—Japanese and foreign alike—had feared that it would be a number of years before the Court would be able to deal effectively with the issues presented by the new Constitution.

That the justices were able to shift from the old to the new so rapidly and smoothly was a remarkable achievement. All of them had dealt in a professional capacity with a system of law and courts completely different from the one they had to administer after 1947; only two had been educated in a system of law, English law, related to the new system, and those two presumably had not dealt professionally with that system for a number of years. Thorough competence and long experience in the field of law, an understanding of the spirit of the new Constitution and the battery of laws relating to it, and an undoubted will to operate the new system effectively and to make it permanent were the major elements in the success of the Supreme Court.

The Supreme Court's organization [7] is designed to enable it to carry out its three principal functions: as a court; as the body responsible for the administration of the Japanese judiciary; and as the organ responsible for the training of those entering the legal profession. At this point I shall discuss only the organizational features of the Court; later there will be a discussion of the nature of these three functions. As we have seen, the Constitution delineates the general powers, functions, and structure of the Supreme Court and all lower courts. Specific organizational details are covered for the entire judiciary in the Court Organization Law. Book II of this law, consisting of Articles 6 through 14, deals only with the Supreme Court, but the following articles also touch on

7. For an organization chart of both the Supreme Court and the entire judicial system see pages 108–10 of *Gyōsei Kikō Zu* ("Charts of Administrative Organization"), 1958 ed., compiled by the Administrative Management Bureau of the Administrative Management Agency.

Court matters: Article 39, appointment and dismissal of justices; Article 41, qualifications for appointment; Article 50, retirement; Articles 53 through 56, officials other than justices attached to the Supreme Court; and Articles 66 through 68, judicial apprentices as appointed and directed by the Supreme Court. Other laws deal with such matters as establishment and location of lower courts, authorized personnel, maintenance of order in courts, impeachment and dismissal. Also the "Regulations Concerning the Conduct of Business by the Supreme Court" were promulgated by the Court itself on November 1, 1947. Its fifteen articles deal with the internal affairs of the Court, with special reference to the organization of the Grand Bench and the petty benches and the relations between them. The following discussion of the Supreme Court is based largely on the Court Organization Law and the Regulations.

The Supreme Court as it functions as a court consists of a Grand Bench and three petty benches. The Grand Bench is the full court over which the chief justice presides. Nine members constitute a quorum for the Grand Bench. When it holds any law, ordinance, regulation, or action to be unconstitutional, at least eight justices must share the opinion. Under law only the Grand Bench can render decisions in cases involving the constitutionality of any law, ordinance, regulation, or disposition. However, a petty bench may decide a constitutional case for which there is a Grand Bench precedent. In addition, the Grand Bench must render a decision in any case wherein there is a tie vote in a petty bench. The Grand Bench also handles any cases deemed proper for its consideration (see below).

There are three petty benches, designated simply as the first, second, and third. Each consists of five justices, three of whom constitute a quorum. Under Supreme Court regulations the Judicial Assembly (see below) determines each December which justices will sit on which petty bench and what types of cases are to be allotted to each bench. Although neither regulation nor law touches on the issue, in practice one bench is assigned criminal cases, one civil cases, and the other administrative cases, i.e., those dealing with ordinances, regulations, and administrative actions. All cases presented to the Supreme Court are referred initially to a petty bench, which decides whether they must be handled by the Grand Bench. In civil cases, even those that the Grand Bench has decided, petty benches are empowered to render decisions concerning extension or cancellation of detention, or suspension of compulsory execution.

The chief justice and his fourteen associates are also responsible for the administration of the judiciary. In carrying out this responsibility, they sit not as the Grand Bench but as the Judicial Assembly (*saibankan kaigi*). However, as is pointed out in the discussion of judicial administration, the Judicial Assembly does not directly administer all inferior courts.

The principal internal administrative organ of the Court is the Secretariat General. It has ten sections, divisions, and bureaus: Secretariat Section, Information Section, Court Division, General Affairs Bureau, Personnel Bureau, Accounting Bureau, Civil Bureau, Criminal Bureau, Administrative Bureau (dealing with cases involving administrative law), and Domestic Court Bureau. The Secretariat General serves the Court in both areas, pure judicial work and judicial administration.

Also under the jurisdiction of the Supreme Court are three institutes: the Legal Training and Research Institute, which is of major importance and is discussed in some detail below, the Research and Training Institute for Court Clerks, and the Institute for Family Court Probation Officers.

The Supreme Court also has ten committees: four advisory committees on making rules (civil, criminal, general, and domestic court); an investigative committee on the court reporters' system; a deliberative committee on court expenses; and four general committees, one each on Supreme Court statistics, the Supreme Court Library, examinations for family court probation officers, and precedents. The total personnel authorized for all operations of the Supreme Court as of February 1, 1958, was 1,056.[8]

In turning to the strictly judicial function of the Supreme Court, it should be noted initially that, as pointed out above, the broad boundaries of the Court's judicial activities are well defined in the Constitution. However, the Court Organization Law touches only lightly on the specific issue of the jurisdiction of the Court. Article 7 of that law reads simply: "The Supreme Court

8. *Ibid.*, p. 108.

shall have jurisdiction over the following matters: (1) Appeal (*jōkoku*); (2) Complaint (*kōkoku*) prescribed specially in codes of procedure." On the basis of this article, it is clear that the Supreme Court can be regarded as a purely appellate court; yet the Court itself has had to define more accurately the scope of its jurisdiction.

In two judgments contained in this collection (see No. XXIV, "The Suzuki Decision" and No. XXV dealing with the power of the cabinet to dissolve the House of Representatives) the Court further clarified its position in the judiciary by making the following points: (1) it is not a constitutional court with the power to determine abstract questions of constitutionality; (2) it has no power of original jurisdiction even in constitutional cases; and (3) it can decide only cases involving concrete legal disputes. The role of the Supreme Court is further defined indirectly in the chapters on appeals in the Code of Criminal Procedure and the Code of Civil Procedure. Here it is necessary to examine briefly and in broadest outline the system of appeals as it sheds light on the work of the Supreme Court.[9]

In the Japanese judicial system there are three forms of appeal: [10]

1. *Koso: Koso* appeal may be lodged against first instance judgments of district courts, family courts, or summary courts. Since this type of appeal cannot be carried to the Supreme Court, it will not be discussed in detail here. In criminal cases such appeals can be made on the following grounds: procedural irregularities; mistakes in construction, interpretation, or application of law, provided that they are material to the judgment; improper or unjust determination of the punishment; and errors in finding of facts material to the judgment. In civil cases grounds include procedural or jurisdictional error and "unjustifiability" of the original judgment.

2. *Kōkoku:* A *kōkoku* appeal is a complaint made against a ruling rendered by a court. This type of appeal in criminal cases asks rescission or alteration of court rulings in such matters as: dismissal of a motion for challenge; decisions relating to detention, release

---

9. See Book III, Appeal, in both codes.

10. There are no suitable English equivalents for these three types of appeal; consequently, the general practice is to use the three Japanese terms as adjectives modifying *appeal*. As stated in the Preface, I have used only the single word *appeal* in the translations because in no case is the type of appeal relevant to an understanding of the decision.

on bail, seizure or restoration of confiscated articles; and impositions of nonpenal fines or orders for compensation for costs for such things as witness fees, expert witnesses, interpreters, or translators. They can also be made against dispositions in criminal procedure carried out by public prosecutors, assistant public prosecutors, and judicial police officers. In civil cases *kōkoku* appeal is possible only against "a ruling or order turning down a motion relating to litigation procedure" or against a ruling or order regarding matters "which could not be adjudicated by ruling or order." Ordinary *kōkoku* appeal cannot be filed with the Supreme Court in either criminal or civil cases. However, the law provides that "special *kōkoku* appeal" can be filed with the highest court, but this type of appeal is in effect *jōkoku* appeal.

3. *Jōkoku:* In criminal cases *jōkoku* appeal can be made to the Supreme Court against a judgment of a high court in the first or second instance if such a judgment involves either (1) violation of the Constitution or an error in construction, interpretation, or application of the Constitution; or (2) incompatibility with judicial precedents established by the Supreme Court (Article 405 of the Code of Criminal Procedure). However, Article 406 of the same code provides that in cases not falling within Article 405 the Supreme Court "as the court of *Jōkoku* appeal" may admit "any cases which it deems involve an important problem of the construction of law or ordinance." The special *kōkoku* appeal referred to in the preceding paragraph can be made only if an alleged violation of the Constitution or an incompatibility with precedent has been claimed.

Article 411 of the same code further provides that the Supreme Court can quash an original judgment by means of a judgment, even if no grounds under Article 405 exist, under any of the following conditions: when there exists any mistake of construction, interpretation, or application of law or ordinance material to the judgment; when the punishment has been imposed with gross injustice; when there is a gross error in finding facts that are material to the judgment; when there is any reason supporting reopening of procedure; or when the punishment has been abolished or changed, or a general amnesty has been proclaimed. In civil procedure *jōkoku* appeal can be made only if there is a misinterpretation of the Constitution or any other contravention of the

Constitution, or if "there exists such contravention of laws and orders as affect clearly the judgment." Also under civil procedure it is possible to make *jōkoku* appeal to a high court against a summary court judgment. Appeal against a high court judgment involving *jōkoku* appeal can be made only if there is a constitutional issue.

To summarize the above discussion: the jurisdiction of the Supreme Court extends over only those cases involving concrete legal disputes that come to it from inferior courts as a result of *jōkoku* appeal or special *kōkoku* appeal, which has, in effect, become *jōkoku* appeal. But these jurisdictional limitations have not kept the Supreme Court from being confronted with a flood of cases. The most serious single problem confronting the Supreme Court is the great volume of cases brought before it and the consequent delay in the administration of justice. This is a problem for all levels of the Japanese courts, as will be indicated below.

In 1957 the Supreme Court received 1,619 civil cases, disposed of 1,557, and had a total of 1,927 still pending.[11] Between 1951 and 1957 the number of civil cases received varied from a low of 1,301 to a high of 1,982, while the number of cases disposed of ranged from 1,254 to 1,753, with the backlog ranging from 1,600 to 1,983. Also in 1957 the number of criminal cases received amounted to 5,875 and the number disposed of was 7,236; but a backlog of 3,296 pending cases still remained. Between 1950 and 1957 the number of criminal cases received ranged from 5,875 to 9,994, the number disposed of from 4,198 to 11,279, and the backlog of pending cases from 3,294 to 7,688, the high in the last category coming in 1952.

The Supreme Court must handle every case that comes before it by a judgment, a ruling, or an order, the last being rare. Occasionally, cases are withdrawn before action is taken by the Court. As we have seen, cases may be handled either by the Grand Bench or by one of the three petty benches. In 1957 judgments were handed down in about 72 per cent of all civil cases and rulings in a little more than 21 per cent. The remainder was accounted for by withdrawals and miscellaneous actions. In the same year less than 12 per cent of the criminal cases were handled by judgments

11. These statistics are taken from pages 498–99 and 502–3 in the *Japan Statistical Yearbook: 1958* (Tokyo: Bureau of Statistics, Office of the Prime Minister, 1959).

and almost 80 per cent by rulings. Special *kōkoku* appeal accounted for almost all the civil case rulings, for such appeals can be settled only by rulings. The high percentage of rulings in criminal cases is to be accounted for by the fact that rulings are handed down when there has been a procedural irregularity in the case and when it is deemed that the grounds for *jōkoku* appeal are not sufficiently supported by reasons required by law.[12] The Court Organization Law requires that the opinion of every justice be expressed in a written decision (Article 11). Opinions of justices in Grand Bench judgments, as will be seen from those given in this volume, may appear in any of the following forms: unanimous opinions, majority opinions, individual or group supplementary opinions, and individual or group minority opinions (occasionally referred to as dissenting opinions). Selected judgments and rulings are published in the *Saikōsaibansho Hanreishū* ("Collection of Supreme Court Precedents"), which has as its English subtitle for the first seven volumes, *Supreme Court Reports*. A seven-justice Committee on Precedents decides which judgments and rulings are to be published. There is at least one number a month, and all the numbers for a calendar year constitute a volume.

The number of cases and the way they must be handled place a considerable burden on each justice. A comparison of the case load of each justice with that of his predecessor in the Court of Cassation shows the great increase in cases handled by the Supreme Court justices.[13] The former Court of Cassation had a total of 45 judges. Between 1932 and 1941 each justice was assigned an average of 57.6 new civil cases per year and made an average of 61.1 decisions in such cases. He was also assigned an average of 46.4 new criminal cases and made an average of 46.3 decisions in such cases. Thus each judge was given an average of 103.9 new cases a year and rendered an average of 107.4 decisions, the difference being accounted for by the number of cases held over from earlier years.

Comparable averages for the fifteen justices of the Supreme

12. For the material in this paragraph I am greatly indebted to Judge Naitō Yorihiro, Deputy Secretary-General of the Supreme Court, who supplied it in a personal communication.

13. See Table 12, p. 111, in *Saikōsaibansho Kikō Kaikaku Mondai Shiryō*, I ("Materials Relating to the Problem of the Reform of the Organization of the Supreme Court"), compiled by the Secretariat General of the Supreme Court (Tokyo, June, 1957—April, 1958). Referred to below as *Saikōsai Kikō*.

Court for the 1947–56 period provide a striking contrast. Each justice was assigned an average of 53 new civil cases and made an average of 40.9 decisions. On the other hand, he was assigned an average of 304.4 new criminal cases and made an average of 284.6 decisions in such cases. Thus each judge was given an average of 357.4 new cases a year and rendered an average of 325.5 decisions. Consequently, the average work load for each Supreme Court justice was slightly more than triple that of his predecessor in the Court of Cassation.

The delay of justice has been the one serious fault of the Supreme Court on which there is complete agreement among its friends, its critics, and even the Court itself. We have already seen that the Court is confronted with a heavy load of cases. The following statistics, released by the Supreme Court, indicate clearly the extent to which justice has been delayed. An examination of the average of 1,166 decisions per year made in civil cases in 1953, 1954, and 1955 revealed that 10.8 per cent had been made within three months, 10.6 per cent in three to six months, 16.1 per cent in six to twelve months, 57.2 per cent in from one to three years, and 5.3 per cent in "more than three years." In an average of 8,177 criminal case decisions per year in the same period, 2 per cent were made within a month, 11.2 per cent in one to three months, 36.9 per cent in three to six months, 22.6 per cent in six to twelve months, 24.4 per cent in one to two years, and 2.9 per cent in "more than" two years.[14] Some cases in the "more than" categories had to wait five or six years for a decision.

Since the petty benches have a far heavier burden of cases than the Grand Bench, it is there that the greatest backlog of cases accumulated. For example, on January 1, 1954, of the cases awaiting decision in the Supreme Court, 249 were before the Grand Bench (of which 148 dealt with criminal violations of various ordinances relating to the occupation), 1,327 before the first petty bench, 1,533 before the second petty bench, and 2,045 before the third petty bench.[15]

The situation has been neither viewed with complacency nor accepted with resignation. No one was more aware of the seriousness

14. *Ibid.*, Table 6, pp. 102–3.
15. *Ibid.*, Table 14, p. 113.

of the problem than Chief Justice Tanaka Kōtarō.[16] On a number of occasions he spoke of the need for speeding up the course of justice on all levels, and the Court itself, undoubtedly under his leadership, has issued formal statements on the problem. The reasons for this delay in the administration of justice are many, but Justice Tanaka and others have listed as among the major ones: a general lack of familiarity with the new system of law and its administration; a general unfamiliarity with the basic concept of the rule of law; a still underdeveloped sense of proper procedure in the courtroom; a certain inexpertness in the preparation of cases by attorneys, especially the older ones who began their careers under the prewar system; a tendency on the part of some judges in the lower courts not to make clear decisions in cases that they assume will end in appeal to the Supreme Court; and an obvious willingness on the part of the defense attorneys to discover and to take full advantage of any possible constitutional pretext as the basis of an appeal.

Several proposals have been made concerning a revision of either the structure or the responsibilities of the Court in order to expedite its handling of cases. These have included doubling the number of justices to a total of thirty; creating a new Grand Bench which would sit only on constitutional cases; reducing the number of justices to nine or eleven; and establishing a new judicial organ to handle certain types of appeal. However, all these suggestions seem to be nothing more than temporary palliative measures.

If these and similar causes were the true ones, it would seem that time itself would be the best solution to the problem, for presumably as the members of the legal profession become more skillful and as the public learns more about the nature of the new system and the spirit of the new laws, the happy result will be the speeding up of justice on all levels.

Judicial administration is the second of the major functions of the Supreme Court. I have been able to find no study of the impact of this administrative task on the purely judicial function of the Court. However, the Court itself has released figures on the

16. See pp. 14–17 in *Kempō Chōsa Kai Dai Jūrokkai Sōkai Gijiroku* ("Minutes of the Sixteenth General Meeting of the Commission on the Constitution"), (Tokyo: Printing Bureau of the Ministry of Finance, April, 1958) for his testimony before that commission, and the Tokyo *Asahi Shimbun*, March 16, 1959 (evening edition) for a summary of his remarks on the delay of justice to a gathering of high and district court judges.

meetings of the Judicial Assembly in the 1954–56 period. It will be recalled that the Judicial Assembly is responsible for judicial administration. In 1954 there were forty-four meetings, lasting a total of about fifty-eight hours; in 1955, thirty-five meetings, lasting about thirty-eight hours; and in 1956, forty-seven meetings, lasting about sixty-one hours. Personnel matters were the most frequent item of business.[17]

Although, the organization of the lower courts lies outside the scope of this study, I shall describe it in some detail at this point because it sheds some light on the Supreme Court's problem of judicial administration and because the lower courts constitute the bulk of the judicial structure of which the Supreme Court is the summit. The inferior courts are all national courts, operating as a single, unified system under the over-all supervision of the Supreme Court.

Japan does not have a jury system. Under a law passed in 1923 a jury system was established and came into operation in 1928.[18] However, it was rarely utilized, partly because there was no tradition of trial by jury, partly because there were limitations in the law (especially the provision that certain types of appeal could not be resorted to if the trial had been by jury), and partly because of a lack of confidence and trust in the system. At any rate, it was not retained in the postwar reconstruction of the judiciary.

Japanese courts are organized as either collegiate courts or single-judge courts. As we have seen, the Supreme Court is a collegiate court. High courts are also collegiate courts, three members are the normal number but five-member courts are required for cases involving the crime of insurrection. District courts sit either as single-judge courts or as collegiate courts consisting of three judges. Collegiate courts are required in the following situations: when it is specified in law that a case must be heard by such a court; when the case being heard involves severe penalties; when appeals from the decisions of summary courts are being heard. Domestic courts are single-judge courts except when the law provides that a collegiate court, consisting of three judges, must sit. Summary courts are all single-judge courts.

17. See Table 18, p. 122 in *Saikōsai Kikō*.
18. See Professor Kaneko's *Saibanhō*, p. 54, for a brief account of the jury system.

There are eight high courts,[19] located in Tokyo, Osaka, Nagoya, Sendai, Hiroshima, Fukuoka, Sapporo, and Takamatsu. There are also six branches: Kanazawa (under the Nagoya High Court), Okayama and Matsue (both Hiroshima), Miyazaki (Fukuoka), Akita (Sendai), and Hakodate (Sapporo). The high courts are essentially appellate courts. However, they hold jurisdiction in the first instance over the crime of insurrection and of the crimes of preparing, plotting, and assisting insurrection.

District courts number 49. However, they have a total of 235 branches and one local office, which can handle only cases involving arbitration. The 235 branches fall into two categories: 78 "A" branches, which are collegiate courts, and 157 "B" branches, which are single-judge courts.[20] District courts have jurisdiction over actions in the first instance, except crimes involving insurrection and matters handled by the summary courts. District courts also hear appeals from judgments, rulings, and orders of the summary courts.

The 570 summary courts have jurisdiction over misdemeanors, minor offenses, and claims of less than ¥100,000. The summary courts are prohibited from handing out prison sentences or heavier punishment. Cases in which a summary court judge deems such sentences appropriate must be transferred by him to the appropriate district court.

In general, the organization of the family courts, a postwar innovation in the Japanese judicial system, parallels that of the district courts, there being 49 with 235 branches, divided similarly into 78 "A" branches and 157 "B" branches. However, there are 65 local offices which handle only cases of arbitration and mediation. The family courts have jurisdiction over the following matters: judgment and conciliation in family cases; protection of juveniles; and jurisdiction in the first instance over crimes by adults against juveniles involving smoking, drinking, labor, welfare, and education.

The total number of courts (including the Supreme Court) is just under 1,220. At the end of 1960, the entire judiciary had an

19. On the number and location of lower courts see laws and regulations relating to their establishment in *Genkō Nihon Hōki* ("Complete Collection of Laws, Statutes, and Ordinances of Japan"), VIII (*Shihō* [Judiciary], No. 1), 45 ff.

20. On the definition of "A" branches and "B" branches, see "Regulation Establishing Branches of District and Domestic Courts," *ibid.*, pp. 141 ff.

authorized personnel consisting of 2,387 judges and 20,043 others who assisted in the operation of the courts (excluding public prosecutors and their aides). The breakdown of the number of judges is as follows: chief justice of the Supreme Court, 1; Supreme Court justices, 14; high court presidents, 8; judges (for high, district, and family courts), 1,152; assistant judges, 512; and summary court judges, 700.[21] The difference between the number of courts and the number of judges is explained by the collegiate court system, and the fact that some judges are exclusively engaged in administrative tasks.

In 1957 (the last year for which statistics were available when this was written) the entire judicial system received a total of 795,730 civil cases and handed down some 772,639 decisions. There were some 208,612 civil cases still pending in the courts. Of the cases decided almost 500,000 were handled in the summary courts and about 280,000 in the district courts. The courts also mediated in almost 79,000 civil suits. Also in 1957 the courts received some 2,703,696 criminal cases and handed down 2,701,842 decisions, leaving 100,589 cases still unsettled. Summary courts received some 2,330,000 cases and district courts just under 350,000. Domestic courts in 1957 received 314,082 cases and disposed of 311,618, leaving an accumulated backlog of 23,410. They also settled 42,450 cases of mediation out of a total of 43,358.[22]

Besides its own judicial function and the administration of the national judiciary, the Supreme Court is also responsible for the training of all those who enter any branch of the legal and judicial professions. The importance of this function of the Supreme Court cannot be overestimated. All judges, lawyers, public prosecutors, court clerks, and probation officers attached to family courts may be appointed only if they have successfully completed courses of study in institutes under the direction of the Supreme Court. Thus, not only the quality of the members of the legal profession, in its widest meaning, but also the whole system of the law and the courts are directly influenced by the manner in which the Supreme Court carries out this major function.

University graduates of faculties of law who wish to pursue

---

21. Figures on personnel are taken from *Saibansho Shokuin Teiin Hō* ("Law on Authorized Strength of Court Personnel"), Law No. 164, December 26, 1960, *ibid.*, p. 28 (5).

22. See footnote 11 above.

careers in the courtroom must pass a stiff judicial examination; only about one in twenty-two candidates passed in the six years between 1952 and 1957. The successful candidates are then appointed to positions as "judicial apprentices" by the Supreme Court. These judicial apprentices, who under law receive compensation from the government, though they are not classed as government employees, constitute the student body of the Supreme Court's Legal Training and Research Institute.[23] This institute manages affairs relating to research, the training of judges and other court officials, and the education of judicial apprentices. In the area of research it compiles, publishes, and distributes much material dealing with both the Japanese and foreign legal and judicial systems.

Under the Institute's training system all judicial apprentices must have at least eight months' in-service training in a court, four months' training in a public prosecutor's office, and four months' training under the direction of a bar association. At the end of two years, the balance of the time being taken up by research and study, the apprentice must take another difficult examination, set up and administered by the Judicial Apprentices' Examination Committee, which is responsible to the Supreme Court. The examination is both written and oral, and covers civil and criminal judgments and criminal and civil practice and prosecution. If successful in this examination, the apprentices are eligible for assignment as assistant judges, public prosecutors, or attorneys. Few apprentices fail this examination, undoubtedly because of the high standards for initial selection and the soundness of the training program. The total system, from entrance into a university to initial appointment, seems ideally designed to select persons of superior intellectual capacity, to train them widely in law in general, to give them practical experience in jurisprudence, and to assign them on the basis of demonstrated interest and ability.

The Research and Training Institute for Court Clerks manages affairs relating to "research and training of court clerks and court stenographers and to their education." The Institute for Family

23. For an excellent discussion of the Institute see "The Japanese Legal Training and Research Institute," *American Journal of Comparative Law*, VII (1958), Summer, No. 3, 366–79, by Matsuda Jiro, a judge of the Tokyo High Court and the Institute's president. In the article he states that the Institute's title, as given in the article's title, is the authorized English translation. Elsewhere it is frequently referred to as the Judicial Research and Training Institute.

Court Probation Officers performs similar functions. Thus, the Supreme Court is responsible for the training of court personnel on all levels in every judicial activity, and as a result is responsible for the excellence, or lack thereof, of the entire judicial system.

Before presenting a brief and impressionistic critique of the work of the Supreme Court in the area of constitutional interpretation, I shall outline the principal features of the 1947 Constitution, passing by such interesting problems as its origins under the occupation and the highly controversial issue of revision, which are not directly relevant to constitutional review.

The three basic principles of the 1947 Constitution are the renunciation of war, popular sovereignty, and the guarantee of fundamental human rights. The first has presented only a minor problem to the Supreme Court, the second has raised only a few issues, but the third has been the source of many of the decisions that the Court has rendered on constitutional problems.

The renunciation of war as set forth in Article 9 is perhaps the most famous and most controversial article in the entire instrument. It was written into the Constitution because of the desire of the United States government, which was principally responsible for the occupation, to make certain that Japan would never again become a threat to the peace and security of the world. Although Japan's armed forces had been soundly defeated in the field and although the occupation in its early months had effectively completed the demobilization of all armed forces and the destruction or neutralization of all war materiel, it was felt that to write a renunciation of war into the fundamental law of the land would add the final barrier to a possible future resurgence of Japan as a military and aggressive power. However, the Japanese people themselves certainly welcomed Article 9 at the time the Constitution was promulgated, and their continuing antiwar sentiment weakened little in the following years. Nevertheless, the exigencies of world politics in general and the situation on the Asiatic continent just across from Japan led the Japanese government, with the encouragement of the occupation and because of its own reading of the problem of national security, to establish new armed forces.[24]

24. For a general discussion of this problem see John M. Maki, *Government and Politics in Japan: The Road to Democracy* (New York: Frederick A. Praeger, 1962), pp. 102–4 and 144–45.

This created a problem of constitutional interpretation, since Article 9 provided for the renunciation of "land, sea, and air forces and all other war potential." Nevertheless, both in the final months of the occupation and after its end, the Japanese government maintained successively a National Police Reserve, a Security Force, and a Self-Defense Force, thus avoiding by verbal means the difficulties that would have arisen had they been called the "army, navy, and air force." This obvious violation of the spirit of Article 9 has not brought about a crisis in Japan's new constitutional system, although it has led to bitter controversy. The extremely interesting Sunakawa Decision, given in this volume, is the only one in which the Supreme Court dealt directly with Article 9; however, it did not touch on the crucial issue of the constitutionality of Japan's own self-defense forces, but properly concentrated on the issue of the constitutionality of United States bases in Japan.

As important as the theory of popular sovereignty is in the Constitution, it does not lend itself directly to interpretation by the Supreme Court. However, it pervades every major constitutional issue, such as rights and freedoms, legislative supremacy, and the separation of powers. A close reading of the decisions given here will reveal that the Court has consistently used the concept as one of its basic premises in interpreting a wide range of issues. It does not regard the theory itself as a matter of controversy or even as one requiring interpretation; it is the basic premise, in the view of the Court, which must be accepted if the Constitution is to have any meaning at all either as a fundamental law granting a wide range of rights and freedoms to the people or as one establishing a certain form of government and creating a democratic structure of political activity.

The third principle, the guarantee of fundamental human rights, has provided the Supreme Court with many problems of interpretation. Chapter III of the Constitution, entitled "Rights and Duties of the People," includes Articles 10 through 40. Articles 10 through 30 deal with a wide range of rights, freedoms, and responsibilities, while Articles 31 through 40 cover the rights of the individual before the law. This long list of rights and immunities did not evolve in Japan. The occupation insisted that they appear in the Constitution largely because they did not exist or were not effectively realized under the previous system of justice.

Not only did the occupation feel that they had to be included in the Constitution if Japan were to enjoy a democratic system and the specific benefits of democratic laws, but also many Japanese, who had either suffered under the old system or had observed its oppressive operations, wanted the benefits that would accrue from this system, non-Japanese in origin and development but clearly of benefit to the Japanese people.[25]

The great majority of the Supreme Court's decisions in constitutional cases fall within the area of rights and freedoms. Consequently the fact that twenty-two of the twenty-six decisions given in this volume deal with interpretations of rights and freedoms is a fairly accurate reflection of the Court's work in this important area.

In addition to the basic principles, there are two secondary constitutional questions that have been significantly dealt with by the Supreme Court: the first is local autonomy, and the second is legislative supremacy. Both stem from popular sovereignty: the first because it is designed to give the people control over the local governmental bodies under which they live and to provide them with freedom from central government control; and the second because the elected members of the National Diet are the direct representatives of the sovereign people and should therefore enjoy the supreme position within the government.

From 1870 to the end of World War II the Japanese government had strong central control over the affairs of prefectures, cities, towns, and villages. The drafters of the new Constitution considered desirable the elimination of what they thought was an unhealthy overcentralization. As a result the Constitution established the principle of local autonomy, under which local public entities have a considerable amount of control over their "property, affairs, and administration" and the right to enact their own regulations. However, it is also provided that "regulations concerning organization and operations of local public entities shall be fixed by law." The Local Autonomy Law, passed by the National Diet in 1947, establishes throughout the country a system of local government and covers all operations of units of local administration. The most important constitutional issues in local

25. For a brief description of the abuses possible under the old system see Blakemore, "Postwar Developments in Japanese Law," pp. 649–52.

government controversies concern the so-called public safety ordinances (see the Niigata Ordinance Decision and the Tokyo Ordinance Decision) that empower local government bodies to control the right of assembly in certain situations. The Aomori Assembly Decision also raised certain important questions regarding the relations between a prefectural assembly and the central government.

The principle of legislative supremacy is clearly enunciated in the constitutional provision that the National Diet "shall be the highest organ of state power, and shall be the sole law-making organ of the State" (Article 41). It is reinforced by the further provision that the cabinet in the exercise of executive power "shall be collectively responsible to the Diet" (Article 66, paragraph 3). As was implied in the earlier discussion, there is no explicit statement regarding the relation between the Supreme Court and the Diet. Clearly, however, the "highest organ of state power" provision places the Diet over the Court.

The principle of legislative supremacy gives a peculiar cast (to the American observer at least) to the doctrine of the separation of powers, which is clearly developed in the Constitution, and to that of checks and balances, which is not. Later I shall return to this issue, but here I shall only point out that the question of legislative supremacy has been dealt with and upheld in a number of the principal constitutional decisions of the Supreme Court with the important qualification that the Court is vested with "the whole judicial power."

As "the sole law-making organ of the State," the National Diet was, of course, responsible for enacting all the new legislation required by the new Constitution; however, the executive branch was responsible for drafting the legislation. Great care was taken by the Japanese and by the occupation that all the new laws should reflect faithfully the letter and the spirit of the new Constitution. The close linking of this legislative task with the Constitution automatically eliminated a number of problems that might have arisen had the law evolved normally within a developing framework of constitutional government. The structure of the Japanese system of law itself has further reduced the area of conflict between statutory law and the Constitution.

Since the National Diet is the "sole law-making organ of the

State," all national laws have been passed by the Diet itself and all local laws, that is, those enacted by the assemblies of local public entities, have come into existence under authority granted by Diet-enacted legislation. Ordinances and regulations issued by executive bodies, national or local, have effect only if they have been authorized by duly enacted legislation. Whatever area of discretionary action any executive body possesses has been created by legislative act. Thus, the supreme legislative position of the National Diet and the resulting structure of national and unified law covering the entire nation likewise reduce somewhat the area of conflict in matters of legal and constitutional interpretation.

Following the promulgation of the Meiji Constitution in 1889, Japan developed the system of codified law. The six codes, then and now, are the Constitution, the Criminal Code, the Code of Criminal Procedure, the Civil Code, the Code of Civil Procedure, and the Commercial Code. These six codes were all enacted between 1889 (the Constitution) and 1907, when the final version of the Criminal Code was approved. Thus, before the wholesale revision of Japanese law under the occupation, the Japanese had had about fifty years of experience in living under and dealing with a system of carefully codified law, based mainly on the French and German systems with a few modifications required by Japanese social tradition.

The present 1,044-article Civil Code, the 805-article Code of Civil Procedure, the 264-article Criminal Code, the 506-article Code of Criminal Procedure, and the 851-article Commercial Code were enacted in 1947 and 1948.[26] These are buttressed with many additional laws on related matters. Closely related to the Constitution are such laws as the National Diet Law, the Court Organization Law, the Cabinet Law, and a host of others dealing with the organization, structure, and functions of government. Finally, there are the broad areas of social and economic legislation, covering such matters as labor standards, social insurance, unemployment, public housing, labor unions, monopoly control, atomic energy, and education. Almost without exception these laws have specific provisions tying them directly to appropriate sections of the Constitution.

I approach my own limited critique of the work of the Supreme

26. See Bibliography under "Translations of Laws" for English translations of these codes.

Court in the area of constitutional review by stating the two major criticisms that have been directed at it by both Japanese and foreign observers: first, it has not fought valiantly and aggressively for the protection of individual rights and freedoms guaranteed in the Constitution; second, it has not effectively utilized its right of constitutional review to check the power of the executive and legislative branches, particularly the former. Even a casual reading of the decisions in this volume will reveal that there is abundant ground for both criticisms. I do not deny their justice. However, both are based on the assumption or the expectation that the Supreme Court of Japan should follow the pattern of the Supreme Court of the United States on which it was modeled, particularly in respect to the key power of constitutional review.

It seems to me that the work of the Supreme Court of Japan in the vital area of constitutional interpretation can only be understood within the context peculiar to Japanese history, government, politics, and law. Its constitutional decisions have been molded both by its existence in that context and by the views that the justices hold on the whole context and its parts, whether they are—to quote examples from some of the decisions in this volume—the concept of the Japanese family system, a philosophical and psychological analysis of the nature of obscenity, or finely spun interpretations of narrow points of law.

To return to the criticism that the Court has not functioned effectively as the guardian of constitutional freedoms, it should be noted that it has had neither to create the concept of freedom under democratic, constitutional government nor to build up the meaning of freedom through the development of a large body of precedent. The Japanese people were given freedom in general and a wide range of specific rights, freedoms, and immunities under the Constitution of 1947, which embodies every significant democratic right and freedom that has been developed in the West. The older freedoms such as those of speech, religion, assembly, and association and the newer ones such as academic freedom and the freedom of labor to organize and to bargain collectively were all incorporated into the Constitution of Japan without having developed within Japanese society. The Supreme Court—to say nothing of other organs or branches of the Japanese government—had no role to play in such vital political, social, and economic developments as the emancipation of women, specifically the extension to them of political, social, and economic rights; the creation of standards for labor; the control of monopolistic practices; and the development of a broad program of social welfare.

All the above rights and freedoms and political, social, and economic developments were introduced into Japan by the occupation. Consequently the Supreme Court had no role in creating the concept of freedom, establishing the basic rules governing the relation between the state and the people, or in defining the nature of specific freedoms. The Court did not have to fight to create freedom or to defend individual liberty against the state. Moreover, all legislation that had an actual or a potential restrictive effect on constitutional rights and freedoms was provided with safeguards that at least retarded the development of that effect.

The response of the Japanese people to the occupation-sponsored reforms that led to the rapid creation of a working system of democracy was immediate, favorable, and impressive. One result has been a society that is truly free, where the standard freedoms of democracy are widely enjoyed and freely exercised. The circumstances of the introduction of democratic freedoms and of their subsequent enjoyment have therefore considerably curtailed the potential positive role of the Supreme Court as the guardian of the Constitution. Nevertheless, the Court has played a prominent role in the interpretation of the meaning of freedom under the Constitution, a role that has provided many of the Court's critics with grounds for maintaining, not altogether fairly in my opinion, that it has tended to undermine the new freedom and liberty. That role has been in the reconciliation of the doctrine of the public welfare with the guarantee of fundamental rights and freedoms.

The Court has consistently supported the view that the public welfare can be used as the justification for placing limited restrictions on the exercise of fundamental freedoms. No article of the Constitution deals solely with the problem of the public welfare, defining the conditions under which it is operative. However, certain key articles contain the phrase as a limitation on the enjoyment or exercise of freedom: Article 12 states that the people in their enjoyment of all freedoms and rights guaranteed in the Constitution are "responsible for utilizing them for the public welfare"; Article 13 states that the people's right to "life, liberty, and the pursuit of happiness" shall be "the supreme consideration in legislation and other governmental affairs to the extent that it does not interfere with the public welfare"; Article 22 guarantees the right to choose occupation "to the extent that it does not interfere with the public welfare"; and Article 29 states that the definition of property rights by law shall be "in conformity with the public welfare."

Using these provisions as a basis, the Court has consistently taken the view that the public welfare, that is, the general good of all the members of the society, cannot be interfered with by the unrestricted exercise of a constitutionally guaranteed freedom by an individual or a group. The reasons why the Court has taken this course are fairly clear. First, the doctrine of the public welfare is clearly stated in the Constitution and explicitly related to the exercise of freedom. Thus, the Court is resorting to a constitutionally recognized restriction on freedom in its use of the doctrine. Second, the problem of establishing the boundary beyond which individual freedom cannot go without infringing on the freedom of others or without undermining the order necessary for the normal functioning of society is not a problem of constitutional government or interpretation in Japan alone; it is a problem of any free society. Third, the Court developed its use of the doctrine at a time of great stress in Japanese society in the early postwar years of occupation. Disturbed economic conditions, extremist political activity, social dislocation, and the resort by attorneys to an extremely broad interpretation of the new freedoms combined to create a situation in which the Court was virtually forced to resort to the doctrine to balance the new freedoms of the individual against the requirement of social order.

However, the Court has upheld the doctrine only as it is applied under specific legislation in specific situations or has itself applied it in similarly specific situations. The danger inherent in the concept of the public welfare will be realized only if the courts (or other branches of the Japanese government) apply it generally and indiscriminately in the absence of specific enabling legislation to the exercise of all freedoms. It is precisely this danger that fills politically conscious Japanese with considerable uneasiness because, although the explicit doctrine of the public welfare was unknown in prewar Japan, one of the foundations of the old ultranationalism was the glorification of the society at the expense of the individual, an attitude that justified the imposition of restrictions on all freedoms so that in practice they did not exist.

However disquieting the Supreme Court's utilization of the concept of the public welfare may be to many Japanese, the fact remains that it has not resulted in the practical abridgement of the exercise of any constitutionally guaranteed right or freedom. Although this is not a positive contribution to constitutionalism by the Supreme Court, it is, nevertheless, a far cry from a betrayal of its role as guardian of the Constitution.

If its interpretation of the doctrine of the public welfare has been its most important contribution to the emerging idea of freedom in Japan, the Supreme Court's interpretation of the principle of legislative supremacy has been its most significant contribution to the development of the working relationships among the branches of the new government. We have already observed the constitutional basis for legislative supremacy; the Supreme Court has been scrupulous in its adherence to it. The position of the Court can be described as follows: though the legislative power is supreme, each of the three powers, executive, legislative, and judicial, is independent in its own area; the judicial power must not be interfered with by either of the other two powers; but, in turn, the judicial power should not intervene in the legitimate spheres of the other two.

One striking result, from the standpoint of the American observer, is that until 1961 the Supreme Court had never found a Diet-enacted law or an executive action to be unconstitutional. Although a number of decisions were handed down upholding pleas of unconstitutionality, they all dealt with cases involving cabinet orders issued as a result of directives from occupation headquarters. On the other hand, the Court has never been the object of executive pressure, and only once has the National Diet attempted to interfere with court activity. In 1948 the Judicial Committee of the House of Councillors, exercising the right of legislative investigation guaranteed by the Constitution, investigated a criminal trial in a district court. It held that the punishment inflicted by the court was too mild, and that there had been improper finding of facts. In 1949 the Supreme Court firmly rejected this unique attempt at legislative interference with the judicial process on the principal ground that the Constitution reserves the judicial power exclusively to the courts.[27]

The Court's refusal to act as a checkrein on either the legislative or the executive process has been regarded as a weakness in that it is taken to be a refusal to exercise power, particularly the power of constitutional review, granted to it by the Constitution. However, the Supreme Court in the development of its position on the separation of powers has never held that the legislative and executive branches of the government are to be responsible to no one in their exercise of power. Notably in the Sunakawa Decision it held that the executive and legislative branches of the government are politically accountable to the electorate for their acts. Such political accountability, the Court declared, is to the "sovereign people." This, too, is soundly grounded on a basic principle of the Constitution. It can be argued that this concept of political accountability to the people in general elections comes closer to the realization of the principles of democratic, responsible government than does the concept of judicial supremacy, exercised through the right of constitutional review.

Thus, under the Supreme Court's conception of the separation of powers, it has never become involved in struggles with either the National Diet or the cabinet. This has obviously robbed the Japanese political scene of the spectacle of dramatic and perhaps edifying conflict between the judiciary and the other branches of the government, but it has also meant that the Court has concentrated its full attention on the problems of justice and law which are its own under constitutional mandate.

If the Supreme Court can be fairly criticized for failing to act as an active guardian of individual freedom and for failing to challenge the power of the other two branches of the government, then I believe that the criticism can be fairly answered by pointing out

27. For a brief discussion of the general problem of judicial-legislative relations and of this incident see pp. 466–67 in *Nihonkoku Kempō* ("The Constitution of Japan") by Professor Miyazawa Toshiyoshi (Tokyo: Nihon Hyōron Shinsha, 1955). The supplementary volume contains the text of the statements by the Supreme Court and the Judicial Committee, pp. 303–8.

that these failures to act have not produced an erosion of freedom or a disruptive imbalance in the powers of the three branches of government. Yet this criticism and the answer thereto do not touch on the positive contributions of the Supreme Court.[28]

As a result of the research that has gone into this volume, I have come to the conclusion—valid, I believe, even though it is that of a nonspecialist in the field—that the two main contributions of the Supreme Court in the field of constitutional review are that it has given meaning to the content of the Constitution and that it has consistently striven to establish the rule of law under democracy in Japan.

The Court's insistence that it can exercise the right of constitutional review only when there is a concrete legal dispute has obviously meant that in its constitutional judgments, however controversial they may be on political or even legal grounds, constitutional provisions have been concretely applied to actual legal cases. The result is that the Constitution has not been a dead document but has been related directly to many political, economic, and social problems in Japanese society. Although the Court has provided only a legal link between the fundamental law and the people under it, this legal link has been supplied by the supreme judicial authority carrying out its own constitutional responsibility of applying, interpreting, and construing the nation's fundamental law.

The Court's emphasis on the rule of law may seem to indicate that the justices place a far higher value on the letter of the law than they do on either individual freedom in the abstract or on its constitutional guarantee. However, it seems fairer to conclude that the Court takes this position because it honors the constitutional principle of legislative supremacy based on popular sovereignty, and that the justices clearly believe that law, duly enacted by a legislative assembly, is the foundation for both social order in general and Japanese democracy in particular. Further, the Court has made it clear that it does not believe that the corpus of the law is sacred and immutable. As can be seen in some of the

---

28. The best discussion of the work of the Supreme Court from a comparative point of view is Professor Nathaniel L. Nathanson's "Constitutional Adjudication in Japan," *American Journal of Comparative Law*, VII (1958), Spring, No. 2, 195–218.

key decisions in this collection, the Court believes that the sovereign people can and should change the laws by which they are ruled if they are dissatisfied with them.

The Supreme Court of Japan has, then, made its own significant contribution in its proper sphere of the law and the judiciary to the successful operation of Japan's new system of constitutional democracy. It has not been alone in the task of establishing and operating this system; that the system was created so rapidly and has operated so effectively is due to the massive and combined efforts of countless individuals and groups within Japanese society. But the Supreme Court's contribution to the task has been both great and unique: the bringing together of law and liberty under the Constitution.

COURT AND CONSTITUTION IN JAPAN

SELECTED SUPREME COURT DECISIONS, 1948–60

Hanreishū, XI, No. 3, 997 (Criminal)

EDITORIAL NOTE: The accused, a reputable publisher and a prominent novelist, were arrested on the charge of selling an obscene publication after a translation of the work in question had become a best-seller (about 80,000 copies of the first volume and 70,000 copies of the second having been sold in about ten weeks) in the spring and early summer of 1950.

The court of first instance found the publisher guilty and fined him ¥250,000, but found the translator not guilty. The court also held that the book was not obscene, but that certain passages closely resembled pornography. The defense then appealed on the ground that the publisher had been wrongly convicted, and the prosecution appealed on the ground that the translator also should have been found guilty.

The Tokyo High Court reaffirmed the verdict of guilty for the publisher and upheld his fine, and also found the translator guilty and fined him ¥100,000. Both then appealed to the Supreme Court.

It should be noted that Justices Mano and Kobayashi argue a point of criminal procedure in respect to the High Court's verdict of guilty for the translator that is perhaps of greater significance than the nature of obscenity.

Grand Bench decision, March 13, 1952: Dismissed.

REFERENCES

Criminal Code. ARTICLE 175. A person who distributes or sells an obscene writing, picture or other object or who publicly displays the same, shall be punished with imprisonment at forced labor for not more than two years or a fine of not more than 5,000 yen [1] or a minor fine. The same applies to a person who possesses the same for the purpose of sale.

Criminal Code. ARTICLE 38, paragraph 1. An act done without criminal intent is not punishable except as otherwise specially provided by law.

Constitution of Japan. ARTICLE 21. Freedom of assembly and association as well as speech, press and all other forms of expression is guaranteed.

No censorship shall be maintained, nor shall the secrecy of any means of communication be violated.

Constitution of Japan. ARTICLE 76, paragraph 3. All judges shall be independent in the exercise of their conscience and shall be bound only by this Constitution and the laws.

Publications Law (Law No. 15 of 1893). ARTICLE 27. When a writing or drawing which disturbs public peace and order or which corrupts public morals is published, the author and publisher are to be punished with imprisonment without hard labor of not less than eleven days or more than six months or a fine of not less than ten yen or not more than one hundred yen.

Code of Criminal Procedure. ARTICLE 400. When the original judgment is to be quashed on any ground other than the grounds mentioned in the two preceding Articles [Article 398, "on the ground that the original court illegally pronounced itself incompetent or illegally dismissed the public action"; Article 399, "on the ground that the court illegally considered itself competent"], the case shall be either sent back to original court or transferred to another court in the same class as the original court by means of a judgment. However, if the court recognizes that it may immediately render a judgment on the basis of record and evidences

---

1. It will be noted that the fine imposed on the accused, Koyama, is fifty times the maximum here stated. Approximately a year after the enactment of the Criminal Code, the National Diet passed the Law for Temporary Measures Concerning Fines, which raised the maximums stated in the Criminal Code by a factor of fifty because of the postwar inflation.

already made and examined by the original court or the court of appeal, it may render the judgment for the case.

FORMAL JUDGMENT

The appeal in the present case is dismissed.

REASONS. The main points of the respective appeals presented by Masaki Hiroshi, Tamaki Naoya, and Tamaki Shoichi, counsel representing the accused, Koyama Kyūjirō, and the accused, Itō Hitoshi, are as recorded below. The judgment of the present Court in respect to these matters is as follows.

I. The translation and publication of *Lady Chatterley's Lover* and Article 175 of the Criminal Code.

Lady Chatterley's Lover is a long novel by D. H. Lawrence, who is well known in the field of English literature; it is a work of rather high repute from the artistic standpoint. The author's artistic talents can be judged from the development of the plot, the analysis and depiction of nature, society, and the personality of the characters, and the dialogue, rich in humor and irony, which also reveals the breadth of the author's culture. In addition, this novel also contains a number of problems relating to the criticism of ideas and civilization. In respect to these the author, generally speaking, frankly reveals his own rebellious and advanced ideals respecting traditional and, especially in England, dominant concepts.

The story begins with the life in midland Rugby of the young peer Clifford, who had lost his sexual powers as a result of a wound suffered during World War I, and his wife Connie, a life both unnatural and dull for her. Before long both love and carnal relations sprang up and grew between Connie and Mellors, a woodsman, separated from his wife and living on Clifford's property as an employee. Finally, the two shook off the restraints of society and entered into a new life based on love with the dissolution by divorce of a marriage considered to be unnatural. This is a rough outline of the structure of the novel, which is fleshed with themes dealing with thought, economics, and society. The ideas criticize the atmosphere of the aristocratic class, the destruction of the beauty of nature by industrialization, the influences on the lives of the people in farming villages, the tragic circumstances of workers in the coal mines, the desolation in men's minds, and the actualities of dehumanization. In addition, the novel also suggests the author's social ideas and what he himself regards as a life with true value. The most important themes, which run through the entire novel, are the primacy of the complete satisfaction of sexual desire and the philosophy of life that recognizes in love the perfection of humankind and the significance of human life.

With this philosophy of life the author denies the traditional (or what he calls puritanical) code, morality, and concept of sex that are approved not only in his own country but all others as well, and affirms the freedom of extramarital sexual relations; but at the same time he is critical of the sexual tendencies in the erratic new age. That he also affirms a new sexual code and a morality that respects the harmony and equality of the spirit and the flesh can be inferred from the content of the present work, the author's own introduction, and his other writings and correspondence cited in the original decision. That the present book, viewed thus, is a work of art different in nature from pornography is recognized in the decisions of both the court of first instance and the court of appeal. However, whether or not the sexual code and world view advocated by Lawrence should be affirmed is a question relating to the areas of morality, philosophy, religion, education, and such matters, and even though the conclusion is reached that they are antimoral and unedifying, it is impossible for that reason alone under existing law to punish the sale and distribution [of the book]. This must be recognized as relating to the area of freedom of expression and publication. The problem is whether or not there are included in the present work elements that fall within the purview of "obscene writing" of Article 175 of the Criminal Code. If it is so affirmed, then the acts of distribution and sale of the present book fall under the heading of the crimes set forth in Article 175 of the Criminal Code.

Even so, what is the meaning of "obscene writing" (and "picture or other object") as set forth in the provision of the Criminal Code previously cited? The precedent stated by the Court of Cassation (see the decision of the Second Division dated June 10, 1918) was: ". . . It designates writings, pictures, or any other objects which stimulate or arouse sexual desire or could lead to its gratification, and, accordingly, such obscene objects necessarily are those that produce the sense of shame or disgust in human beings." In addition, the present Supreme Court has held (First Petty Bench decision, *Hanreishū*, V, No. 6, 1026 ff.) that ". . . [obscene matter] is that which wantonly stimulates or arouses sexual desire or offends the normal sense of sexual modesty of ordinary persons, and is contrary to proper ideas of sexual morality." Now, we recognize as proper the original decision, which was made in accordance with the above precedents of the Court of Cassation and of the Supreme Court itself, and we also approve these precedents.

In essence, according to the above precedents, in order for a writing to be obscene it is required that it cause the arousal and stimulation of sexual desire, or offend the sense of shame, or run counter to proper concepts of sexual morality.

As a general rule, the possession, irrespective of differences of civilization, race, clime, and history, of a sense of shame is a fundamental characteristic that sets man apart from the beasts. Shame, compassion, and reverence are the most fundamental emotions that man possesses. As man possesses the emotion of compassion for things on an equal footing with him and the emotion of reverence for things above him, so does he possess the sense of shame toward offensive things around him. These emotions constitute the foundation of universal morality.

The existence of the sense of shame is especially striking in respect to sexual desire. Sexual desire in itself is not evil; it is the instinct with which man is provided for the preservation of the species, that is, for the continuation and development of the family and of human society. That men possess this in common with other animals is a natural aspect of mankind. Consequently, the spirituality existent in man, namely, his nobility, is conscious of a feeling of revulsion toward it. This is, of course, the sense of shame. This emotion is not to be discerned in animals. There may be situations in which it is lacking or rare in certain spiritually undeveloped or ill individual human beings or in certain special societies, but it exists beyond question, if one observes humanity in general. For example, even in uncivilized societies the custom of complete exposure of the sexual organs is extremely rare and, again, there is no such thing as the public performance of the sex act. In short, the nonpublic nature of the sex act, which characterizes man alone, is a natural manifestation of the sense of shame that has its origin in human nature. This sense of shame must be respected, and any rejection of it as a form of hypocrisy runs counter to human nature. Thus, the existence of the sense of shame, in company with reason, controls the sexual life of man, which is difficult to restrain, so that it will not fall into licentiousness and, no matter how uncivilized a society may be, contributes to the maintenance of order and morality in respect to sex.

Because an obscene writing stimulates and arouses sexual desire and clearly makes known the existence of the animal side of man's nature, it involves the sense of shame. It paralyzes conscience in respect to matters of human sex; it ignores the restraint of reason; it comports itself wildly and without restraint; and it contains the danger of inducing a disregard for sexual morality and sexual order. Naturally, law is not burdened with the duty to maintain all morality and good customs. Such a duty pertains also to the fields of education and religion. Law incorporates into itself only "the minimum morality," namely, the morality which alone possesses a considerable significance for the maintenance of the social order it is designed to achieve. What each provision of the Criminal Code mentions as a crime is, in short, something that can be recognized as a type of conduct in violation of this minimum morality. Likewise, in respect to sexual morality it is the duty of the law to provide for the maintenance of that minimum. Thus, the prohibition of the sale and distribution of obscene writing, as crimes in Article 175 of the Criminal Code, arises from this idea.

Then, does *Lady Chatterley's Lover*, which is the problem in the present case, fall under the heading of obscene writing as in Article 175 of the Criminal Code? What must be made clear here as the preliminary issue is that the judgment to be made is one involving the interpretation of law, namely, that it relates to a legal value judgment and is not a question of determination of fact.

As for the facts of the distribution and sale of the literary work in the present case, and the cooperation of the translator, and such items as the number and method of publication and the motive for distribution and sale, there was suitable testimony from witnesses in relation both to the constituent elements of the crime and the circumstances relating thereto. Also, the hearing of the opinions of expert witnesses concerning the position of the author in the world of letters and the literary value of the work in question was both valuable and necessary. However, the judgment as to whether or not the work itself falls under the purview of Article 175 of the Criminal Code as an obscene writing is not a problem of the establishment of fact in relation to the work in question but is a problem of the interpretation of law. The work in question actually exists, and the court need only interpret and apply the law. This matter differs in no way from instances involving the interpretation of provisions relating to the constituent elements of individual crimes set forth in each provision of the Criminal Code. For this reason the court must make the judgment [of obscenity] no matter how much this work stimulates or arouses the average reader or awakens his sense of shame.

The standard for the court when it makes such a decision is the good sense operating generally through the society, that is, the prevailing ideas of society. These, as the original decision puts it, "are not the sum of the understanding of separate individuals and are not a mean value of such understanding; they are a collective understanding that transcends both. They cannot be rejected by separate individuals who hold to an understanding opposed to them." The judgment of what the prevailing ideas of society are is, under our present system, entrusted to judges. The fact that, as with separate individuals in society, there is no necessary unanimity of ideas among judges, either on different levels or on the same level among those who make up collegiate courts, is the same as in the other situation: the interpretation of law. This exists not only when there is a judgment as to obscenity in writing; hence, it cannot be denied that courts have the authority to determine what constitute the prevailing ideas of society. Accordingly, a judgment of whether the present book falls under the heading of obscene writing is unavoidable, even though it may not be in accord with the opinions of some of the nation's people. The fact that the judge in this situation must decide in accordance with his conscience what the prevailing ideas of society are does not differ from all situations in which the law is interpreted. Similarly, particular problems arise when there is to be interpretation of general provisions regarding what good morals are or of the comprehensive concepts that lay down general laws and ordinances. In these situations the courts confront concrete cases and make judgments; the accumulation of these constitutes case law.

The prevailing social ideas in respect to sex generally differ according to time and place; changes take place even in the same society. In contemporary society, for example, pictures and sculptures may be exhibited which previously were banned from public display or, again, novels which earlier were not approved for publication may appear and not be generally regarded as unusual. Also at the present time freedom is widely recognized in respect to co-education and social intercourse between men and women. As a result, a modification of the traditional concepts relating to the two sexes has become necessary. It is a fact that eventually taboos in existence since ancient times will gradually disappear. However, notwithstanding the fact that changes in such prevailing concepts regarding sex have taken place or are taking place, it cannot be denied that in every society it is recognized that there are limits that must not be overstepped and that there are norms that must be generally observed. One is the previously described principle of the nonpublic nature of the sexual act. Only in respect to this point can it be admitted that there has not been such a striking change in the prevailing social ideas that what was previously regarded as obscenity is now not generally recognized as such. To yield a point for the moment, even though the ethical sense of a substantial majority of the people were paralyzed and truly obscene matters were not recognized as obscene, the courts would have to guard society against moral degeneration in accordance with the norms of the prevailing social ideas, which are the ideas of sound men of good sense. After all, neither the courts nor the law must always and necessarily affirm social realities, they must confront evil and corruption with a critical attitude and must play a clinical role.

Now on examining the translation in the present case, the portrayal of the sexual scenes therein, amounting to some twelve as pointed out by the public prosecutor, must be recognized as possessing artistic characteristics that differ from pornography, but nevertheless, the portrayal is fairly bold, detailed, and realistic. These scenes run counter to the principle of the nonpublic nature of the sex act and offend the sense of shame to the extent that one would be reluctant to read them aloud in a public meeting, to say nothing of a family gathering. Also in respect to their effect on both individuals and society, it must be recognized that they are of an order to arouse and stimulate sexual desire and to run counter to good concepts of sexual morality. In short, the portrayal of sexual scenes in the present translation must be regarded as going beyond the limits recognized by the prevailing ideas of society. Accordingly, the original decision, which held that the translation in the present case is obscene writing as set forth in Article 175 of the Criminal Code, is proper; the points of the appeal that attack the court for disregarding the prevailing ideas of society and the verdict as having been determined by an arbitrary decision of the judges are improper.

Next we consider the second and third points of the decision regarding the obscene nature of the present translation.

The present book as a whole is an artistic and thoughtful work and as described above it has consequently enjoyed a rather high reputation in the world of English literature. The artistic nature of the present book is apparent not only in the work as a whole, but also in those sections dealing with the depiction of sex, some twelve passages as pointed out by the public prosecutor. However, artistry and obscenity are concepts that have different dimensions; they can exist side by side. If it is said that obscene things cannot be called true art and that true art cannot be obscene, then we are faced with a question of concepts. This resembles the problem of whether we can recognize a bad law as law. As in cases where the content of positive law can be ethically evil, there are cases where what we ordinarily recognize as an artistic composition does possess the character of obscenity. Because what is generally regarded as pornography is largely lacking in artistic qualities, the fact that the translation in the present case, having such qualities, cannot be recognized as pornography was decided in the court of first instance. However, the obscene character of the work cannot be denied on the grounds that it is an artistic composition and not pornography. The reason is that even though from the standpoint of art it is an outstanding composition, it is not impossible for it to be appraised as possessing obscenity from the legal and moral standpoints, which are of a different order. We cannot approve the principle of the supremacy of art, which emphasizes only the artistic nature of a composition and rejects criticism from the standpoint of law and morality. Even though a composition may have high artistic merit, it does not necessarily follow that its obscene nature is thereby dissipated. Though it be art, it has no right to present obscene matters publicly. The artist, too, in the pursuit of his mission must respect both the sense of shame and moral law and he must not act contrary to the duties borne by the people at large.

Approximately the same circumstances can be recognized in regard to scientific and educational books dealing with sex as have been described above in respect to artistic matters. However, artistic creations differ from scientific works, which describe matters objectively and dispassionately; and because they appeal strongly to the senses and emotions, it cannot be said that obscenity is dissipated because they are artistic or, on the contrary, that the arousal or stimulation arising from them is not strengthened.

The existence of obscenity must be determined objectively and, in the final analysis, from the composition itself; it is not something that can be influenced by the subjective intent of the author. Counsel defines obscene writings as follows:

Writings of evil intent dealing with sex that are designed exclusively to appeal to the curiosity of only adolescents whose spontaneous powers of judgment are undeveloped, or that are designed to deny or make one forget the human function of sex as a racial instinct, or that make real the dissolute pleasures of the flesh, or that cause injury, difficult to repair, to the minds and bodies of the adolescent. . . .

and on the grounds that the translation in the present case is possessed of sincerity, he denounces the decision. However, according to this definition, any publication whatsover that possesses an artistic, academic, or other aim must be excluded from the category of obscene literature, no matter how extreme its obscenity, and obscene writing must be limited only to pornography. It does not follow that the sincerity of a work necessarily dissipates its obscene nature. Accordingly, we cannot accept this argument of the appeal.

Next, the argument asserts that the translation in the present case was made "with the aim of warning the world," denies the existence of criminal intent in the accused, and on those grounds assails the original decision.

However, in respect to the establishment of criminal intent in the crime set forth in Article 175 of the Criminal Code, it is sufficient if there is a recognition of the existence of the passages in question and of their distribution and sale; recognition that the writing containing such passages is obscene, as defined in the same article, is not necessary. For example, even though one sells a writing that one believes, subjectively, does not fall under obscene writing in Article 175 of the Criminal Code, if it does objectively possess the character of obscenity, it must be said that that [subjective belief], as a legal mistake, does not rule out criminal intent. Regarding obscenity, whether there was complete or only partial recognition of it, or no recognition at all are only questions of circumstances under the provisos of Article 38, paragraph 3 of the Criminal Code [2] and are not related to the establishment of criminal intent. Consequently, the original decision, which accepts this point, is proper and the argument cannot be accepted.

The argument for appeal holds in respect to obscene writing that it is necessary that it appeal to the curiosity only of immature adolescents and that it cause injury, difficult to repair, to the adolescent mind and body. Because the spread of obscene literature has a bad effect on the adolescent mind and body, its prohibition is naturally of very great significance as far as adolescents are concerned. However, the question of what constitutes obscene writing cannot be considered only in terms of the influences brought to bear on one specific class of readers. It is necessary that its influence on general readers throughout society be considered. The argument for appeal that holds that the relevant class of readers is limited only to adolescents is arbitrary and cannot be accepted.

II. Article 175 of the Criminal Code and Article 21 of the Constitution.

The appeal brief (counsel Tamaki Shoichi) pleads as follows: The guarantee of freedom of expression in Article 21 of the Constitution is almost unrestricted; for example, even if restriction in the name of the "public welfare" is permissible, the basis for deciding permissibility must be clear before the fact. Accordingly, under the new Constitution, which prohibits a system of censor-

2. "An ignorance of the law cannot be deemed to constitute a lack of intention to commit a crime. . . ."

ship, whether or not there may be a violation of the "public welfare" must be left to the independent judgment of each person.
Thus, it is argued, because the original decision accepted an error
of independent judgment in respect to the translation in the present case and held the accused guilty, it violated Article 21 of the
Constitution.

However, because the basis for judging the permissibility of the
translation in the present case lies in the prevailing ideas of society
or in the good sense that is prevalent throughout society, it cannot
be said that it was not clear before the fact. Also, whether there is
an offense against the public welfare must be determined objectively; it is not something that can be entrusted to the independent judgment of each person. Consequently, it is impossible for
this point to be used in the argument.

The appeal brief (counsel Tamaki Naoya) argues that because
the freedom of expression guaranteed in Article 21 of the Constitution does not explicitly involve the possibility of restriction
as in the case of other fundamental human rights set forth in Articles 21 and 29 of the Constitution, it is absolutely unrestricted
and cannot be limited even for the public welfare. However, notwithstanding the fact that each provision of the Constitution
does not expressly set forth the possibility of restriction of individual fundamental human rights in the Constitution, the present court has frequently held [eight citations omitted] that the
abuse of such rights is prohibited by the stipulations of Articles 12
and 13 of the Constitution, that they stand under restriction for
the public welfare, and that they are not absolutely unlimited. If
this principle be applied to freedom of publication and other expression—a type of freedom that is extremely important—it must
nevertheless be recognized that it, too, can be restricted for the
public welfare. Thus, because there is no room to doubt that the
protection of a sexual code and the maintenance of a minimum
sexual morality are to be considered parts of the public welfare,
the original decision, which held that the translation in the present
case should be regarded as an obscene writing and that its publication was against the public welfare, is proper. The argument is
groundless. Moreover, the argument presented from the above
standpoint, that if there are situations in which Article 175 of the
Criminal Code is to be applied, they must, from all points of view,

involve both harmful and useless matters—for example only pornography—is also groundless.

The appeal brief (counsel Masaki Hiroshi) conceives of the public welfare only from the point of view of the respect for fundamental human rights, treats the present book as in conformity with the public welfare because it deals with the problem of sex seriously, and attacks the original decision, which held that a crime was constituted under Article 175 of the Criminal Code. However, this argument rests on an arbitrary opinion that differs with the previously quoted precedents respecting the fact that fundamental human rights are not unlimited and can be restricted for the public welfare. In addition, even though it is said that the translation in the present case is sincere and its content is in accord with the public welfare, that does not offset or dissipate its obscenity. For this reason the argument is groundless.

The appeal brief (counsel Masaki Hiroshi) attacks the appeal decision by utilizing the fact that the Publications Law under the old Constitution was abolished and that "a writing or drawing that corrupts public morals" as referred to in Article 27 of the said law is not the object of punishment at the present time. The fact that, as the appeal brief asserts, the previous Publication Law existed, that writings corrupting morals were punished under it, that this was also done in conformity with the Publications Law in respect to the publication of obscene writing, which is included under that heading, and that the application of Article 175 of the Criminal Code [to writings which corrupt public morals] has been eliminated makes possible the acceptance of this argument. However, the matter is one involving the relation of the two laws, one ordinary and the other special, concerning obscene writing. Under present conditions in which the Publications Law, which was a special law, has been abolished, it must be recognized that the publication of obscene writing has fallen under the application of Article 175 of the Criminal Code. Accordingly, the argument is groundless.[3]

3. The text here is not clear, both because of the extreme brevity of the summary of the argument and because of the terseness of the decision. Counsel's argument seems to have been as follows: The phrases, "obscene writing" and "writing corrupting public morals" are not identical. Therefore, since the Publications Law which dealt with the latter was abolished and because the phrase does not appear in the Criminal Code, the translation cannot be regarded as "a writing corrupting public morals," and its distribution cannot be regarded as a criminal act.

The appeal brief (counsel Tamaki Shoichi), relying on the fact that Article 21 of the Constitution prohibits censorship, asserts that it is impossible to know before the fact what is impermissible in the name of the public welfare and that the original decision, which found the accused guilty on the grounds of errors in judgment concerning a matter that they should have judged independently, was in violation of Article 21 of the Constitution. However, on the basis of the fact that the Constitution prohibits prior censorship one cannot conclude that prohibition of the distribution and sale of obscene literature has likewise become impossible. Because it is clear that the prohibition of obscene literature is in conformity with the public welfare and because what constitutes obscene literature is to be judged on the basis of the prevailing ideas of society, there is no unconstitutionality in the original verdict as the argument contends.

III. Article 76, paragraph 3 of the Constitution and the original decision.

The appeal brief (counsel Masaki Hiroshi) asserts that the original decision is in contravention of Article 76, paragraph 3, of the Constitution, because it is unconscionable, being based on a wrongful judgment made with deliberate disregard of and deviation from the rules of logic. However, it has been recognized in an earlier decision of the Court (Grand Bench decision, November 17, 1948) that "judges . . . in the exercise of their conscience" in the said article means the exercise of their internal good sense and moral views without submission to either tangible or intangible external pressure or inducement. The argument amounts to no more than an attack on the judge in the original trial as being without conscience simply because the original decision differs from the opinion of counsel. Consequently, it must be stated that the assertions in the argument of a violation of Article 76, paragraph 3, of the Constitution, and, of course, of all other claims of unconstitutionality are groundless.

Accordingly, the decision is as in the formal judgment in accordance with Article 408 of the Code of Criminal Procedure.[4]

This decision is the unanimous opinion of the Justices except for

4. *Code of Criminal Procedure.* ARTICLE 408. Where the court of *Jokoku* appeal finds, after examining the statement of reasons for *Jokoku* appeal and other documents, that the appeal is not sustainable, it may dismiss the appeal, by means of a judgment, without holding the oral proceedings.

the opinions of Justice Mano Tsuyoshi and Justice Kobayashi Shunzō, recorded below.

* * *

The opinion of Justice Mano Tsuyoshi in the present case follows.

I. I agree in general both with the majority opinion relating to the appeal of Koyama Kyūjirō and with the reasons therefor except for what I set down below.

In the present case the most important problem is whether or not the translation in question falls under the heading of obscene writing as stated in Article 175 of the Criminal Code. I believe that what constitutes obscenity is by nature neither absolute nor immutable nor constant, but that it varies according to differences in time, in peoples, and in social customs, manners, traditions, morality, popular consciousness, popular feeling, religion, education, and other matters and, in addition, as historical changes gradually accumulate. Speaking from the standpoint of justice, this is ultimately a problem that judges must decide in accordance with their reading of the prevailing ideas of society; also these prevailing social ideas must necessarily alter in accordance with the changes and transitions in the society that is their basis. Consequently, it is not necessary to dwell at length on the fact that, as a necessary result, what constitutes obscenity is a shifting, flowing concept that varies according to time and place. Nevertheless, the majority opinion expresses it as if there were two stages or two forms of obscenity, one that changes with time and place and one that is unchanging and transcends both time and place. The point expressed in the opinion that the descriptions in the translation in this case belong to the second category is unscientific and I am completely unable to agree with it.

In the marriage manners and customs revealed in such ancient Japanese literary classics as the *Kojiki, Nihon Shoki, Manyōshū,* and *Fūdoki* the methods by which men and women selected spouses were quite free and the complete reverse of the extreme formality under feudalism in later ages. Of special note is the ancient custom of *kagai,* in which large groups of young men and women hand-in-hand would climb mountains commonly believed to be holy, and after great merrymaking—eating, drinking, singing, and dancing—would perform the sexual act publicly or even *en masse* and enter into a state of ecstasy. It is said that not only unmarried men and women but married ones as well would take part in these rites. In the *Manyōshū* in regard to this *kagai* it was even sung that wives would be exchanged. However, this was a practice carried out with the permission of the gods on holy ground and was not something that should be measured by today's feelings about simple eroticism or obscenity. It can be regarded on the one hand as revealing a marriage custom based on group feelings and group consciousness that transcends eroticism and obscenity and, on the other hand, as being rich in the coloring of a religious and agricultural rite. Only on the basis of this single fact, without presenting ostentatiously any examples from various foreign countries, the manner of thinking in the majority opinion that attempts to establish absolute limits for obscenity going beyond both time and people, cannot escape criticism as an abstract argument that ignores authoritative historical fact. Not only that, but it must also be termed an argument completely unnecessary for the judgment of this case. In my opinion, what constitutes obscenity must be regarded as a question to be judged according to the prevailing ideas of a society, which are always relative to its historical period. In respect to similar cases in the United States it is noteworthy that Judge Hand has said that he feels it really inconceivable that the sense of shame may prevent forever the adequate portrayal of the most beautiful and important aspects of human nature.

According to the protocol signed November 12, 1947—a revision of the international convention concluded at Geneva on September 23, 1923—for the purpose of prohibiting traffic in and circulation of obscene literature, the problem of whether to determine internationally a definition of obscenity arose; but an international determination of such a definition was treated as troublesome and unnecessary because of differences in customs, moral standards, popular consciousness, and so forth, in each country. This will probably help to make clear the impossibility of a fixed and unchanging [definition of] obscenity that is above time and peoples and society.

Generally speaking, thoughts, ideas, feelings, and emotions about sex accompany changes in external society and also produce individual changes. These changes come rapidly or frequently, but they are not fixed. Especially at the present time when the world is becoming smaller and there is a tendency toward change—not only because there are many more opportunities for the customs of different peoples and societies to come into contact, to interact, and to exert mutual influences on each other, but also because there is rapid advance in scientific research in sex—there is the possibility that social changes regarding sex can occur much more rapidly than in earlier periods of history.

In proceedings involving literature, as in the present case, obscenity can be reduced, purged, purified, or swept away where literary and artistic claims, thoughts, values, and sincerity exist. This is an important factor, which must be considered, but cannot always be regarded as decisive. Accordingly, if we conclude that the revelation of sexual sensations is excessive in view of the social ideas prevailing in our country, then the degree of the presentation and description of the sexual scenes, which are the so-called hot part [in original] of the present translation, properly falls within the purview of the legal definition of obscenity, and we may disregard those actual social conditions that might be tolerant of them. Therefore it is proper to conclude that the present translation is an obscene writing.

Here I believe I must speak about two or three points in the majority opinion with which I find it difficult to agree.

The majority opinion argues:

However, notwithstanding the fact that changes in such prevailing concepts regarding sex have taken place or are taking place, it cannot be denied that in every society it is recognized that there are limits that must not be overstepped and that there are norms that must be generally observed. One is the previously described principle of the nonpublic nature of the sexual act.

It was held by the majority opinion only that the sense of shame

. . . exists beyond question, if one observes humanity in general. For example, even in uncivilized societies the custom of complete exposure of the sexual organs is extremely rare and, again, there is no such thing as the public performance of the sex act. In short, the nonpublic nature of the sex act, which characterizes man alone, is a natural manifestation of the sense of shame that has its origin in human nature.

However, the aforesaid "nonpublic nature of the sex act" signifies no more than that the sex act is not performed in public. "The principle of the nonpublic nature of the sex act" has a really grand ring to it, but its content is no more than what I have just stated. The majority opinion on the one hand holds that the prevailing ideas of society regarding sex ". . . generally differ according to time and place; changes take place even in the same society . . ." and on the other hand states that the "principle of the nonpublic nature of the sex act" is a universal norm that transcends time and place and society and sets "limits that must not be overstepped" when changes in the prevailing ideas of society occur.

Then on this premise the majority opinion holds, ". . . on examining the translation in the present case, the portrayal of the sexual scenes therein, amounting to some twelve as pointed out by the public prosecutor, . . . is fairly bold, detailed, and realistic. These scenes run counter to the principle of the nonpublic nature of the sex act. . . ." However, I am compelled to say that this kind of judgment is not only extremely illogical, but also confused.

Because the "principle of the nonpublic nature of the sex act" as expounded by the majority opinion has no more significance, as I have already pointed out, than saying that the sex act is not performed publicly, the violation of the principle of the nonpublic nature of the sex act amounts to no more than the public performance of the sex act. (Because the present translation is naturally not a living thing, the translation itself cannot perform the sex act, either publicly or privately.) The description of the sexual scenes in the present translation does not depict the public performance of the sex act. Thus, in any meaning of the phrase, it must be held that there is no violation of the principle of the nonpublic nature of the sex act.

Again, because it is stated in the first part of the majority opinion that the principle of the nonpublic nature of the sex act is a universal norm that does not change with time, place, or society, to say that the description of the sexual scenes in the present translation is a violation of the principle of the nonpublic nature of the sex act amounts to saying, in other words, that there is a violation of a universal norm that does not change with time, place, or society. How in the world such an extreme statement can be made is something that is completely beyond my understanding. At present in France the original and a complete translation are in print; in Italy the original and in Germany a complete translation have been published. It is a well-known story, but ten persons in the trial of first instance of the present case testified that the work is not obscene, six others that it is unclear whether it is obscene or not, and eight others that it does reach the level of obscene literature. [Names given in original on pages 1017–18 are omitted here.] I believe that those parts of the majority opinion that declare that the descriptions in the present translation possess an obscenity transcending time and people and unchanging in character should be stricken.

Next the majority opinion states, ". . . the judgment as to whether or not the work itself falls under the purview of Article 175 of the Criminal Code as an obscene writing is not a problem of the establishment of fact in relation to the work in question, but is a problem of the interpretation of law." In a number of subsequent places it also uses the phrase "interpretation of law," but this is also an expression extremely jarring to the ear.

Applying it to the present case, Article 175 of the Criminal Code provides for the punishment of ". . . a person who sells . . . an obscene writing." In the present case the meaning of "obscenity" is the issue directly confronting us, and the decision makes clear the content of that meaning as ". . . that which wantonly stimulates or arouses sexual desire or offends the normal sense of sexual modesty of ordinary persons, and is contrary to proper ideas of sexual morality." To this point it is a question of the interpretation of law.

But now to decide whether the description itself in the work is one that can be clearly determined by such an interpretation of law, and accordingly to decide whether it fits into the category of obscene writing does not require proof from witnesses and other sources but must be decided according to a legal value judgment by the judge. Consequently, the judgment of whether or not the work is an obscene writing is a question of legal application, fitting a law to the concrete facts, and is not a problem of legal interpretation as the majority opinion states it. The interpretation of the law and the application of the law are different in character in the judicial process, and the distinction between the two is important (see Article 394 of the Code of Civil Procedure [providing for appeal to the Supreme Court "only on the ground that there exists misinterpretation of the Constitution or any other contravention of the Constitution in the judgment or that there exists such contravention of laws and orders as clearly affect the judgment"], Article 405, paragraph 1, of the Code of Criminal Procedure [providing for appeal to the Supreme Court "on the ground that there is a violation of the Constitution or an error in construction, interpretation or application of the Constitution"], and Article 406 of the Code of Criminal Procedure [providing that the Supreme Court may admit cases under certain conditions that "involve an important problem of the construction of law or ordinance"]). Only because there is a process of mutual interaction between the interpretation of law and the application of law are there occasional situations when the application of the law in the wide sense includes both. For example, Article 380 of the Code of Criminal Procedure in its reference to "a mistake in the . . . application of law or ordinance" includes both, that is, a mistake in the application of a law or ordinance in the narrow sense or in the interpretation of a law or ordinance. On the other hand, it may or may not be possible for the phrase, "interpretation of the law" to include the application of the law. Again, in using the terms "breach of the law" or "violation of the law" there are occasions when both mistakes in the interpretation and in the application of laws and ordinances are included (see Article 394 of the Code of Civil Procedure, Article 458 of the Code of Criminal Procedure [dealing with quashing "when the original judgment was in violation of law or ordinance" or "when any procedure was in violation of law or ordinance"], Article 409 of the former Code of Criminal Procedure [providing for appeal in the event of violation of a law or ordinance], and Article 520 of the last code [providing for certain types of appeal in the event of a violation of law or ordinance in an original judgment]). The phrase "violation of law or ordinance" is also used in cases of extraordinary appeal, and in regard to this matter the decision of the Grand Bench was that it involves only a mistake in the interpretation of the law and not a mistake in the application of the law (*Hanreishū*, VI, No. 4, 685). I wrote in considerable detail on the impropriety of that point in a minority opinion at the time and received considerable support later on, but judging from such instances, I believe that it is necessary always to have a clear recognition of the difference between the interpretation of the law and the application of the law. Consequently, I am unable to approve, as it stands, the majority opinion in its handling of the aforementioned problem of the interpretation of the law in the present case.

Generally speaking, it is an extremely difficult task to nail down a correct interpretation that will make clear the content and meaning in law of obscenity. In the decision of second instance, in its attempt to determine a definition of what constitutes obscenity, to decide whether the concrete passages that had become the issue really could be interpreted as falling under that definition was an even more difficult task for the judge. It was not a matter that the judge could decide as an individual on a purely subjective basis; it was something he had to decide with objectivity according to the prevailing ideas of society, which are based on the good sense of normal, healthy members of society. It was a matter that could be decided by neither pure subjectivity nor pure objectivity (as in the determination of facts), but by what could be termed the subjective objectivity of the judge.

The majority opinion declares,

. . . even though the ethical sense of a substantial majority of the people were paralyzed and truly obscene matters were not recognized as obscene, the courts would have to guard society against moral degeneration in accordance with the norms of the prevailing social ideas, which are the ideas of sound men of good sense. After all, neither the courts nor the law must always and necessarily affirm social realities, they must confront evil and corruption with a critical attitude and must play a clinical role.

This relates not only to this single case, but possesses a surpassingly great significance in that it touches on both the mission of justice and the mental attitude of judges in all cases. To deal with matters regarded as true obscenity under law as obscene matters under justice is entirely natural, but beyond this, the manner of thinking in such phrases as "would have to guard society against moral degeneration" and "must confront evil and corruption with a critical attitude and must play a clinical role" constitutes the wrong course for justice to take. I reflect on this problem almost every day. The mission of the judge is to interpret and to apply the law honestly, dispassionately, and impartially. This is the proper and most important attitude for the judge to take. This is what the Constitution means when it says that judges are bound by the law. However, in many cases in which the objectivity necessary to proper justice should be respected, the dispensing of judgments with the fervent intention of playing the role of the guardian of morality and of good and beautiful customs may, as pointed out above, lead to the evil—easily fallen into—of disposing of cases with either strong or pure subjectivity, differing greatly from individual to individual. On the other hand it may lead to the deciding of cases according to a dogmatic or easygoing intuition that has been given individual prejudice arising from the seeking of an objective lying outside the law. I feel strongly that this is precisely the case in questions of thought, morality, and customs. In regard to this erroneous course, in criminal cases in which perfect consideration must be given to the protection of the fundamental human rights of the accused and when the execution of the law places even greater emphasis on the necessity for discipline, the most serious consideration must be given to the possibility of entry into any wrong course that might lead to a disregard or slighting of the principle of legality [*nullum crimen sine lege, nulla poena sine lege*] (see *Hanreishū,* IV, 1988; VII, No. 7, 1591 ff.).

II. I oppose the conclusion of the majority opinion regarding the appeal of Itō Hitoshi. The original decision in respect to the said person is in grave error as shown below. Because it is clear that there will be a striking violation of justice if the appeal decision is not quashed, it is proper that it be quashed under the authority of Article 411, paragraph 1, of the Code of Criminal Procedure [which provides for quashing "when there exists any mistake of construction, interpretation, or application of law or ordinance which is material to the judgment"] and that the case be returned to the court of appeal without a judgment of the substance of the appeal.

In a case in which the court of first instance has handed down a verdict of not guilty without establishing the existence of the facts of the crime and with the crime not proved, it is not permissible for the court of appeal to quash the previous decision; to establish directly the existence of the facts of the crime only on the evidence taken in the court of first instance and on the record of the proceedings, without instituting any investigation into the facts; and to hand down a verdict of guilty. This is based on an interpretation of Article 400 of the Code of Criminal Procedure and has already been shown in many decisions of the Grand Bench (decision of July 18, 1956, *Hanreishū*, X, No. 7, 1147; Grand Bench decision, September 26, 1956, *Hanreishū*, X, No. 9, 1393). Under the heading of reasons in these decisions it is stated that in the event of a verdict of not guilty as charged in the court of first instance,

. . . in case there is appeal against the decision by the prosecutor, even though the case is pending in the court of appeal, the accused enjoys the rights guaranteed in Articles 31 and 37 of the Constitution. The said appeal trial must be declared to be one to which the principles of oral proceeding and of direct examination are applied in open court as in the case of trial in first instance. Accordingly, the legal procedures for the taking of evidence in open court before the accused must be followed, and the accused must be afforded the opportunity to present his pleas and opinions in respect to the said evidence; if not, then it must be said that he enjoys the rights of not being held guilty and of not having the facts constituting the crime established. For this reason decisions in which, as in this one, the court of first instance pronounced a verdict of not guilty without establishing the facts constituting the crime of the accused, and then the court of appeal quashed the verdict of the first instance, established directly the facts constituting the crime of the accused only on the basis of evidence taken in the trial of first instance and the record of the proceedings thereof, and handed down a verdict of guilty, must be declared to be impermissible in accordance with the provisos of Article 400 of the Code of Criminal Procedure, because the aforesaid constitutional rights of the accused have been impaired and because the principles of oral proceedings and direct examination have been violated.

Moreover, the same decisions in respect to this conclusion expressly point out, "Previous decisions relating to the provisos of Article 400 of the Code of Criminal Procedure, to the extent that they run counter to the above interpretation, are to be considered altered." The relationship between this interpretation of the provisos of Article 400 of the Code of Criminal Procedure and Article 31 and others of the Constitution has been a topic of considerable discussion for some time; but even more thought has been devoted to it since the occasion of the Mitaka Incident.[5] As a result, in respect to the establishment of the facts constituting a crime anew in the court of appeal, the attitude of earlier decisions was changed and the precedent of the Grand Bench as recorded above was established.

5. This was a famous case involving the trial and conviction of men accused of wrecking a train and killing a number of people in the Tokyo suburb of Mitaka in the course of a labor demonstration. In the trial, one of the major issues was whether the infliction of a heavier penalty in the appeal court was proper.

However, in the present case Itō Hitoshi was held not guilty in the court of first instance and the facts of guilt were not established. In the establishment of the facts of the decision of the court of first instance the following is recorded: "Koyama Kyūjirō planned the translation and publication of *Lady Chatterley's Lover* written by Lawrence . . . and obtained a Japanese translation thereof by requesting Itō Hitoshi to do it." But the court of appeal found that there were several means of cooperation on the part of the translator, that there were also situations that constituted the crime of abetment because of the cooperation, and also that there were instances constituting collaboration in the principal offense. Thus, the original decision, without any investigation, established the facts constituting the collaboration in the original offense by Itō Hitoshi only with evidence taken in the court of first instance, the records of the court of first instance, and the records of the proceedings. In respect to this point the present case coincides exactly with the situation discussed in the Grand Bench decision set down above; and because there is illegality arising from violation of the provisos of Article 400 of the Code of Criminal Procedure, the appeal decision in respect to this point should be quashed.

In addition, because it is clear that Itō Hitoshi was held not guilty in the court of first instance and was fined ¥100,000 in the court of second instance, the appeal decision should be quashed for reasons set down below.

I think that in cases in which a new penalty is imposed that is heavier than that in the first instance, one must reach exactly the same conclusions for exactly the same reasons as those in the decision of the Grand Bench set down above. Namely, I believe that the imposition by the court of appeal, in respect to a prosecution, of a sentence heavier than that handed down by the court of first instance without examination of the facts and only on the evidence taken in the court of first instance and on the trial proceedings, is impermissible under the interpretation of the provisos of Article 400 of the Code of Criminal Procedure.

Moreover, the majority opinion in a Grand Bench decision handed down in a different case but on the same July 18 (*Hanreishū*, X, No. 7, 1177), in respect to a case in which a decision postponing the execution of sentence in a court of first instance was set aside and an actual punishment inflicted by the court of appeal held:

When the court of appeal examines the propriety of a sentence passed by the court of first instance on the basis of an appeal by the public prosecutor, which holds that the punishment inflicted in the decision of first instance is improper, it need not always carry out its own investigation of the facts. When it recognizes an improper weighing of the offense on the basis of evidence produced in the first instance and of the record of the proceedings, it cannot be said that there was an error in the interpretation of the provisos of Article 400 of the Code of Criminal Procedure, even though it hands down a sentence heavier than that of the court of first instance without carrying out its own investigation of the facts.

The Grand Bench decision mentioned earlier, which deals with the new determination of the facts of a crime, presented in detail the reasons for its view. In contrast, this decision, which deals with the weighing of the offense, is extremely simple as seen above, and in regard to the reasons why there should be a difference between the determination of the facts of the crime and the handling of the meting out of punishment it remains silent, uttering not a word. Consequently, there is no particular way to come to grips with it. I believe that there is a grave defect in this decision because it is clearly in contradiction of the earlier decision which sets forth reasons in some detail.

The reasons previously stated for the decision in respect to the determination of the facts of the crime are essentially that in the court of appeal, too, the accused possesses the rights provided for in Articles 31 and 37 of the Constitution, and that the trial must be subject to the principles of direct examination and oral testimony in open court just as in the trial of first instance. Article 31 of the Constitution provides, "No person shall be deprived of life or liberty, nor shall any other criminal penalty be imposed, except according to procedure established by law." This article guarantees proper procedure in respect to punishment, that is to say, trial procedure based on the principles of direct examination and oral testimony, which are the basic principles of existing criminal procedure. In other words, this guarantee has been provided in respect to penalties. Therefore, "the infliction of penalty" in judicial proceedings on the one hand requires the establishment of the facts of the crime and on the other hand the weighing of the offense. Establishment of fact and weighing of offense are closely linked elements of punishment, and it is impossible for it to be based on one alone. (On rare occasions, although there may be the establishment of guilt in the verdict, there may not be the meting out of punishment. Such is not to be termed true punishment. For example, the judgment of second instance in the Placard Case returned a verdict of guilty, but aquitted the prisoner because of a general amnesty.[6] <*Hanreishū*, II, No. 6, 607.>) Because Article 31 of the Constitution expressly provides for a guarantee with respect to the infliction of penalty, it is proper that both the establishment of facts and the weighing of the offense, the two elements of punishment, fall under the guarantee of the said article. Thus, the reasons of the previous decision, which explained in detail the guarantee of the said article in respect to the establishment of facts, must be considered to be applicable to the weighing of the offense.

Possibly there may be the feeling that the establishment of the facts is an important problem, whereas the weighing of the offense is a minor one. To be sure the establishment of the facts of guilt comes first, and then the necessity for the determination of the penalty arises. If there is no establishment of guilt, then the problem of weighing the offense does not arise. However, these must not be treated discriminatorily on the basis of the hasty conclusion that because the establishment of facts is more important it falls under the guarantee of Article 31 of the Constitution, whereas because the weighing of the offense is minor it does not fall under the guarantee of the said article. This is a completely abstract way of thinking. It is well to take a broad and searching view of the following hard facts. That the number of accused found guilty is overwhelmingly greater than the number found innocent, and that the accused who meekly accept the charges against them in open court greatly outnumber those who deny and contest them, are facts to which judicial statistics all over the world eloquently attest. This shows that the serious concern in court of the great majority of the accused is not the establishment of facts, but in reality the weighing of the offense. It is said that the weighing of

---

6. This famous case in 1947 concerned a man found guilty of carrying a placard in a demonstration over the distribution of food, which carried a phrase judged to involve *lèse majesté*.

the offense is the judicial issue that requires the greatest consideration. In view of this real situation, under an administration of justice that is inclined to the one-sided view that the establishment of facts falls under the guarantee of Article 31 of the Constitution and that the meting out of punishment does not, it cannot be said that the fundamental rights of the people are adequately guaranteed. For example, if it is said that it is impermissible to establish the facts of the crime of pocketpicking in a court of appeal on the basis of documentary examination, but permissible in a case like the Mitaka Incident for the court of appeal to change a verdict of life imprisonment in the court of first instance to the death penalty on the basis of documentary examination, then this is an extremely unbalanced way of handling the matters, and it must be stated that it is an extremely regrettable defect in the guarantee of human rights.

Also, it is said that a reason for the difference in the handling of the establishment of facts and the weighing of the offense is that the former is a search for true facts where there is no room for discretion, and the latter is a matter in which there is room for wide discretion, but I cannot agree with this view. In it there are two defects: (1) that the establishment of the facts is a matter in which there is no room for discretion; and (2) that because the weighing of the offense is a matter of discretion the problem of illegality never arises.

However, (*a*) the establishment of the facts is also done on the basis of discretion, and (*b*) the weighing of the offense is a matter of discretion. Therefore when the court of second instance imposes a heavier penalty, it is required to exercise discretion in respect to the weighing of the offense in accordance with the principles of direct examination and oral proceedings and in conformity with the requirements of Article 31 of the Constitution; and if there is a violation of this, then the method of exercising discretion becomes illegal. I would like to describe this relationship in somewhat more detail.

The establishment of the facts of a crime is, of course, a matter of the search for and discovery of true facts as in the case of historical facts, but from this it is impossible to jump directly to the hasty conclusion that the establishment of facts is "a matter in which there is no room for discretion." To the extent that the human intellect has not advanced to the point that there are exact scientific methods, for example, a precise mechanical means, for recreating freely and precisely past historical facts (even in a specific recent past), and to the extent that procedures for judicial evidence have been developed by judges at present, then, by ignoring the problem of competency in respect to human evidence and inanimate evidence, the worth of evidence becomes the objective of a value judgment, and the upshot is that it must be entrusted to the discretion of the judge (in situations in which there is no problem of the violation of the rules of experience). Because the value judgment of evidence is thus left to the discretion of judges, what is termed trial by evidence—the establishment of facts ascertainable as reality by a selection of proof based on a value judgment of evidence—is in the final analysis left to the discretion of the judges. In general, the statement that the establishment of facts is the exclusive prerogative of the judge who is examining them has the above significance. The point of view that holds that the establishment of facts is the search for the truth and that there is no room for discretion consists of a confusion of ends and means. The establishment of facts has as its primary aim the discovery of the truth. However, to achieve that aim the taking of evidence is required; the making of value judgments in the selection of evidence is required; and in the final analysis the value judgment of evidence requires the exercise of discretion by judges. Under the present system of judicial evidence, except for the fact that the rules of the competency of evidence and the rules of experience must not be violated, it is clear that the establishment of facts is a matter left to the discretion of judges.

Thus, the meting out of punishment must, in the same way and as a matter of principle, be left to the discretion of judges. The establishment of facts and the meting out of punishment naturally differ in objective; but not only are they the same in means, that is, discretion, but also such discretion is the same [in both cases] in that it uses the judge's value judgment of evidence as its basis. (There is only the difference that under the present Code of Criminal Procedure it is required that the evidence in a finding of guilt be presented in the verdict, but in the setting of sentence it is not required.) Thus, in respect to both the establishment of facts and the setting of sentence the discretion of the judge must be based on his value judgment of the evidence by means of the principle of direct examination and the principle of oral testimony, the fundamental principles of our existing Code of Criminal Procedure; and it is not permissible, as a principle, to exercise discretion simply on the basis of his value judgment of evidence in written documents. Article 31 of the Constitution certainly has this meaning; the principles of direct examination and oral testimony, fundamental in existing criminal procedure, and built up by the experience and age-old struggles of mankind, are also guaranteed in the Constitution; and it must be understood that the infliction of punishment only according to such proper procedures is also guaranteed as a fundamental human right.

More often than not a value judgment of evidence made on the basis of direct examination and oral testimony differs from one made simply on the basis of examination of written documents. To mention one example, the judge who interrogates a witness by means of direct examination and oral testimony can observe directly and minutely such things as the manner of speaking and changes in expression, voice, eyes, and color of the witness, as well as the content of his testimony; and since he can make a value judgment of the content of the statement by combining all these things, even though the content of such testimony may be to all appearances perfectly consistent and in order, he may immediately perceive perjury or recognize that the testimony is worthless as evidence. On the other hand, the content of testimony may change somewhat according to the interrogation, but that may be due to an unclear memory of what took place originally, the progress of the interrogation may gradually awaken memories, and it may turn out in the end that the final statement may have sufficient value as proof—an account which accords with the true facts. In this case the judge has heard living testimony and this is what forms his convictions. But if in the court of appeal there is a value judgment of evidence on the basis of only the written record and the creation of a sense of conviction only by means of viewing testimony lying dead on paper, the judge may perceive in the value of the evidence in the protocol only the consistent and the orderly and he may not perceive the changes that may have taken place in the testimony. Herein lies the fundamental reason why it is strongly urged, as a matter of human reason, that the principles of direct examination and oral argument must be present in trials, especially criminal trials.

*   *   *

The supplementary opinion of Justice Kobayashi Shunzō follows.

I side with the majority opinion; but because I believe that there are illegal sections in the trial procedure of the court of appeal, because there were points not touched on in the argument set down above, and because there is a danger of misunderstanding, I would like to add my own private opinion.

The trial procedure in the court of appeal was illegal only in respect to the accused, Itō Hitoshi. Namely, the court of first instance handed down a decision of not guilty in respect to the above accused, but the appeal court in its own hearing quashed the original verdict of not guilty and handed down a decision of guilty only on the basis of an examination of the written record, without any examination of the facts and without hearing the opinion or the plea of the accused. I believe that this procedure, finding the defendant guilty for the first time in the court of second instance, is impermissible under the Code of Criminal Procedure and is in violation of the substance of the precedents of the Grand Bench set down below. Nevertheless, the appeal makes no reference to this point. The fact that the aforesaid majority opinion did not touch on this point does not mean that it approved of the procedure in the court of appeal, but only perhaps that it recognized that there was no need to judge it. However, because in my opinion there was a serious violation, as pointed out above, in the procedure of the court of appeal, I think that this Court should have dealt with this problem under its official power (Article 411 of the Code of Criminal Procedure [see p. 24 above]) and decided it, though the result might have been the same.

First of all, if for the time being we adopt as a premise the view contained in the majority opinion that the procedure in the court of appeal is acceptable, then if the facts sufficient to establish guilt in the conduct of the accused were objectively ascertained in the trial of first instance and if the trial of second instance recognized guilt on the basis of those already ascertained facts, the handing down of a verdict of guilty only on the basis of the written record is not in contravention of the law, and it may be that the meaning of the precedent of the Grand Bench given below does not include cases of this kind. However, I interpret this case, in which the accused was found not guilty in the first instance, as one in which it cannot be admitted that, no matter to what degree the facts had been established, "the facts constituting guilt" by means of "strict proof," which are the minimum requirements for the finding of guilt in a criminal court, were established.

For example, in a situation in which a verdict of not guilty in the first instance has been produced solely as a result of an error of application or interpretation of a penal provision and the conduct of the accused has been judged to be nothing more than a simple objective fact, it may be possible, according to one's point of view, to say that that "objective fact" was established. However, in my opinion, even in such a case what is established is never "the facts constituting guilt." The acts of a person differ from the facts of the simple external world and are all related to his intentions. Particularly since the appeal decision in the present case requires the existence of "criminal intent" and in this differs from the decision of the first instance, it is perfectly reasonable that in the establishment of these facts it is necessary to go through the process of establishing strict proof all over again (see below). Thus, even after the court had established the outward existence of the facts constituting the crime and after it had gone through an investigation for grounds for the negation of illegality [of the acts] and had made doubly sure of every point, finally it would examine the circumstances and hand down a verdict of guilty that would for the first time constitute a decision involving concrete punishment. Consequently, it is a natural surmise that since in this case in which the court of first instance denied that the facts of the arraignment had been established in respect to the accused Itō, it probably did not undertake an examination or a study of grounds for the negation of illegality. However, if the interpretation is that only in the court of second instance can a verdict of guilty be reached merely through a study of the written record without examining in any way the above points, then the existence of criminal trials and instances that do not go into the above points may be approved, and it goes without saying that this ends in absurdity.

The appeal decision in the present case, in addition to setting

down the opinion of first instance on the grounds of error, and
deciding that the translation in the present case constitutes obscene
writing under Article 175 of the Criminal Code, also held in respect to the accused Itō Hitoshi that the criminal intent required
in order to establish the crime of the sale of obscene literature was
sufficiently established by the existence of the passages of sexual
description at issue in the present translation and by the publication and sale thereof. Using the evidence examined in the trial of
first instance and now in the record of the present case, it also held
that there was nothing lacking for the necessary criminal intent
in the establishment of the crime of Itō Hitoshi and that there was
nothing to prevent the presumption of a sharing of both intent and
acts of joint complicity with Koyama Kyūjirō. However, because
the decision of first instance held that the translation in the present
case could not in itself be termed an obscene writing, but because
it was in accord with the view that it could be regarded as obscene
in some respects, it stated in regard to the accused Itō that ". . . in
regard to the fact that certain circumstances were created and
fostered [by the other accused] it must be held that the accused
did not, under law, assist in the crime, and this cannot be regarded
as complicity under the Criminal Code." The original decision
differed in legal character in respect to the issue of criminal intent
required to establish a crime in the present case and consequently
did not carry out the establishment of the "facts constituting
guilt" required for such a decision. Of course, because both the
person involved and the objective facts were the same, it is natural
that among these individual facts there are certain areas of mutual
interaction, but the issue is the problem of the appellate court's
establishing anew the necessary criminal intent, and because its
own determination of guilt or innocence depends on the existence
of the said intent, the court must carry out its own investigation
of the facts relating to the establishment of the necessary criminal
intent; after the determination of the facts it can for the first
time hand down its own verdict of guilty. To use facts that were
investigated as "facts constituting guilt" in the court of first instance in order to meet completely different requirements and
that were superfluous to a verdict of not guilty as the basis for a
verdict of guilty in the second instance, cannot escape censure,
for it has treated certain extraneous facts as being identical with

those that would make the acts of a person a crime. Situations such as that in the present case are naturally included in the precedents of the Grand Bench of the present Court given below, which hold that a court of second instance cannot hand down a decision of guilty, reversing a verdict of not guilty in the court of first instance, without itself carrying out an investigation of the facts. I am confident that there are no grounds for making the present case an exception. Accordingly the appeal decision must be regarded as being in contravention of the meaning of the precedents of the Grand Bench. (See decision of July 18, 1956, *Hanreishū*, X, No. 7, 1147; and decision of September 26, 1956, *Hanreishū*, X, No. 9, 1391.)

In addition to what is set down above, I should like to point out that the procedure of the appellate court in respect to the meting out of punishment contains undeniable illegalities.

Because the court of first instance returned a verdict of not guilty only in respect to the accused, Itō Hitoshi, it was natural that there was no examination of the circumstances surrounding him and that there was no necessity for it. However, the appeal decision, while adopting an opinion different from that of the court of first instance in respect to what constitutes obscene writing and the crime of its sale, handed down a sentence of guilty on the basis only of the documentary material produced in the first instance; and as the court of second instance it carried out no examination of the facts in relation to the accused and did not even hear his plea. In addition, the court of second instance held that because the translation in question is obscene literature, the court of first instance had already made an erroneous assumption of facts in its original premise by taking a different view, and that his recognition of whether or not the translation in question was obscene was not related to the existence of a crime on the part of the accused, Itō, but it was related to the question of mitigation. While holding in its conclusion that the court of first instance on this point had made an erroneous assumption of fact that influenced its decision, the appeal judgment also established the decisive fact, which gave added weight to the circumstances [of the crime], namely, that the accused, Itō Hitoshi, necessarily possessed knowledge that the translation in question had the quality of obscenity. The court did this without any investigation of its own and simply on the basis of documentary materials. I am completely unable to believe that there are any grounds for thinking that such arbitrary decisions in relation to the circumstances are permissible only in cases involving a verdict of guilty in the court of second instance. I do not deny that what are termed the circumstances can be determined to the extent that there are materials in the record, but the most important thing is that the judge himself who administers justice attend to the direct plea of the accused with his own eyes and ears and that this constitutes his actual living conviction [in respect to the case]; herein lies also the principle of direct oral examination. If the view is established that only in decisions of guilty in the court of second instance is it sufficient for the examination of the circumstances to include only material from the written documents, and because there may also be cases, as pointed out earlier, in which in the court of first instance there was also absolutely no examination of the [directly relevant] circumstances, then we must accept the conclusion that verdicts of guilty in the court of second instance are possible without the examination of any of the circumstances. That this is unreasonable requires no argument. In order to justify such unreasonableness either the court of second instance must act as an ex post facto court or [we must assume] the judge of the second instance is able adequately to determine the circumstances on the basis of written documents. Either course of action would mean the sacrifice of important principles of criminal procedure for the sake of simplifying procedure, or the maintenance of the legal fiction of a certain special supremacy, with no real basis, in the judgment of judges of second instance. Such would be no more than hypocrisy. We cannot accept the existence of criminal trials that inflict punishment without the guarantee of Article 31 of the Constitution.

As shown above, the procedure of the appellate trial is illegal, but as I have shown earlier, neither the accused nor his attorneys made any assertion in the appeal brief that is critical of this point. Thus, it must be recognized that the accused had no objection regarding it. In my opinion the aforementioned illegality, because it is in contravention of the precedent of the Grand Bench, might properly be taken up by this Court under the competency granted by Article 411 of the Code of Criminal Procedure [which grants

the power to quash earlier judgments on the grounds of illegality]
and to render a decision thereon, but considering the above attitude
of the appeal brief and what was also pointed out in the appellate
decision, I do not believe it can be recognized that there would be
a striking miscarriage of justice even though the appellate decision
is not quashed. Accordingly, I am in accord with the gist of the
decision rejecting the appeal.

Here I also cite my opinion in the Third Petty Bench decision of
June 8, 1954 (*Hanreishū*, VIII, No. 6, 821) and the Grand Bench
decision of June 22, 1955 (*Hanreishū*, IX, No. 8, 1219).

(TRANSLATED BY J. M. MAKI)

II: THE RIGHT OF A REPORTER TO REFUSE TO DIVULGE A SOURCE OF NEWS AND THE DUTY TO TESTIFY IN COURT

Hanreishū, VI, No. 8, 974 (Criminal)

EDITORIAL NOTE: A newspaper reporter refused to be sworn in court to testify as to a source of information (see the decision under point 3 of the argument for appeal for particulars), and was later found guilty of violating Article 161 of the Code of Criminal Procedure, which makes it a crime for anyone to refuse to be sworn or to testify "without due reason," and was fined ¥3,000. He lost on appeal and then carried his case to the Supreme Court.

Grand Bench decision, August 6, 1952: Dismissed.

REFERENCES

Constitution of Japan. ARTICLE 21. Freedom of assembly and association as well as speech, press and all other forms of expression are guaranteed.

No censorship shall be maintained, nor shall the secrecy of any means of communication be violated.

ARTICLE 38, paragraph 1. No person shall be compelled to testify against himself.

Code of Criminal Procedure. ARTICLE 146. A person may refuse to answer any question which may tend to incriminate himself or herself.

ARTICLE 147. A witness may refuse to answer any question which may tend to incriminate the following persons:

(1) The spouse, a relative by blood within the third degree of relationship or a relative by affinity within the second degree of relationship of the witness, or a person who was in any of such relationships to the witness;

(2) The guardian, supervisor of guardianship or curator, of the witness;

(3) A person of whom the witness is the guardian, supervisor of guardianship or curator.

ARTICLE 226. When a person who apparently possesses information essential to the investigation of a crime refuses to appear or disclose such information voluntarily at the examination in accordance with Paragraph 1, Article 223, the public prosecutor may request a judge to interrogate him as a witness, only before the first date fixed for the public trial of the case.

[ARTICLE 161. (1) Any person who refuses to be sworn or to testify without due reason shall be punished with a fine not exceeding 5,000 yen or penal detention.

(2) In the case mentioned in the preceding paragraph, both fine and penal detention may be imposed according to the circumstances. (*Note:* This article does not appear in the original decision, but is included here for reference because it was this that the defendant was convicted of violating.)]

FORMAL JUDGMENT

The appeal in the present case is dismissed.

REASONS. Concerning the first point in the argument for appeal: Article 143 of the Code of Criminal Procedure provides as follows: "Except as otherwise provided in this law, a court may examine any person whomsoever as a witness." Thus it imposes on all the people the duty to testify. Appearance in court as a witness may be a great sacrifice for an individual. Sometimes he may have to testify about things that he would like to keep secret according to his personal moral convictions and, by so testifying, he may make enemies, create animosity, or be charged with bad faith. Although a concrete case requiring testimony is a matter between the litigants, the reason such a sacrifice is required of a witness is that the mission of a judicial hearing is to achieve the proper realization of the intent of the law by discovering the empirical truth, and compelling witnesses to testify is indispensable for the accomplishment of that mission. Accordingly, the duty to testify must be regarded as extremely important, essential to the people's cooperation in the proper execution of judicial hearings.

Therefore, the law establishes as a general principle the people's duty to testify, and cases involving exemption therefrom are regarded as exceptional. For example, Articles 144 through 149 of the Code of Criminal Procedure [1] list such cases, and in quite recent legislation a regulation to the same effect can be found in Article 59 of the Offenders' Rehabilitation Law.[2] Among the regulations concerning the duty to testify, Article 146 of the Code of Criminal Procedure is also an exception that was enacted in order to realize the constitutional guarantee set forth in Article 38, paragraph 1, of the Constitution; but all other regulations that recognize exceptions involving the refusal to testify are cases recognized as proper because of considerations of legislative policy. Thus, as a reflection of the extreme importance of the people's duty to testify, cases that recognize the right to refuse to testify are extremely limited and exceptional. Therefore it is natural that the above regulations concerning exceptions be few and that they not be applied by analogy to other cases.

Whether a reporter's right to refuse to testify concerning a source of news can be approved is a question to be considered by legislative policy; there are examples of legislation that have recognized a reporter's right to refuse to testify. Nevertheless, because our existing Code of Criminal Procedure does not include reporters among those who have the right of refusal, it is obvious that the above provisions concerning doctors and others enumerated in Article 149 of the Code of Criminal Procedure cannot by analogy be applied to reporters. It cannot be doubted that our existing

1. Exceptions not mentioned in Article 147 include: doctors, dentists, midwives, nurses, practicing attorneys, patent agents, notaries public, government officials, and members of the National Diet. However, these have the right to refuse to testify only in regard to certain matters, e.g., the secrets of other persons and affairs in which disclosure of information would be "prejudicial to important interests of the State."

2. This article provides that officials involved in rehabilitation work may refuse to testify regarding the secrets of other persons if they believe that such testimony "may hinder the rehabilitation" of such other persons.

Code of Criminal Procedure and, of course, the former one do not give reporters the right to refuse to testify.

However, the argument for appeal contends that because newspapers under democratic government present material that constitutes the basis for sound understanding by the people, they are not therefore merely profit-making enterprises, but possess the characteristics of public organs of society. Thus, because general freedom of expression is guaranteed by Article 21, paragraph 1, of the Constitution, in order for that guarantee to be realized, a reporter's methods of acquiring information must also be free.

Again, the argument contends, it is necessary to maintain secrecy of the source of information in order to maintain the freedom of acquisition of information, and therein lies the reason for the belief that maintaining the secrecy of the source of information is part of the code of ethics of the reporter and is also his right. Thus, to maintain the secrecy of the source of information is not only a moral responsibility to the supplier of the information, but in reality is also an absolutely necessary means of protection for the freedom of expression of newspapers; such is newspaper ethics the world over.

Therefore, the argument continues, because the secrecy of the source of information must be regarded as being guaranteed by Article 21, paragraph 1 of the Constitution, which guarantees freedom of expression, cases in which a reporter refuses to testify concerning his source of information must be considered as falling under the "due reason" clause of Article 161 of the Code of Criminal Procedure. Consequently, the argument for appeal contends, the original decision, which held that a reporter's refusal to testify does not fall under the due reason clause, is in violation of Article 21 of the Constitution, which guarantees freedom of expression.

However, the above constitutional provision guarantees the freedom of expression equally to all the people; it does not provide reporters with any special guarantee. Consequently, if we were to adopt the logic of the appeal, then all the people would be guaranteed the freedom of sources under Article 21, even in the drafting of articles and essays, and, as a result, they would end by having the right to refuse to testify concerning the sources used. Constitutional guarantees impose considerable restrictions on the legislative power of the National Diet by making it impossible to easily restrict such guarantees, even by Diet-enacted legislation; but such guarantees are not open to infinitely wide interpretation, as in the argument for appeal.

The guarantee of the above constitutional provisions means that everyone must be allowed to say what he wishes to the extent that it does not interfere with the public welfare. This absolutely cannot be interpreted as a guarantee of the right to refuse—even before one has decided what he wishes to write—to testify regarding a source of material that will be used later on, thus sacrificing the duty to testify, indispensable to the proper operation of the judicial process, which is of the highest importance to the public welfare.

The appeal emphasizes the special mission and position of reporters, but the above constitutional guarantee is recognized as applying equally to all the people and, as pointed out, does not grant special privileges to reporters. Whether or not specially designated persons among the people shall be guaranteed special rights in consideration of their special position or mission must be left to legislation; it is not a problem of Article 21 of the Constitution. Accordingly, the argument attacking the original decision on the basis of the above article is groundless.

Concerning the second point in the argument for appeal: This argument has as its premise the statement that Articles 146 and 147 of the Code of Criminal Procedure are based on Article 38, paragraph 1, of the Constitution. Article 146 is based on the above constitutional provision as has already been explained. However, the word "himself" in the above constitutional provision should be limited to the deponent and should be interpreted not to include near relatives as stipulated in Article 147 of the Code of Criminal Procedure. Accordingly, the stipulations of Article 147 of the Code of Criminal Procedure do not fall within what is guaranteed in Article 38, paragraph 1, of the Constitution, but by legislative policy they have been recognized as appropriately granting the right to refuse to testify because of the intimate ties among close relatives, such as those existing between a witness and those specially related to him. Therefore, the section of the argument for appeal concerning unconstitutionality that deals with Article 147 of the Code of Criminal Procedure is improper because of its premise.

Meanwhile, because, as has been shown, Article 146 of the Code of Criminal Procedure is based on Article 38, paragraph 1, of the Constitution, if to force a witness to testify under Article 226 of the Code of Criminal Procedure in a case in which the suspect is unspecified violates Article 146 of the Code of Criminal Procedure, then it [Article 226] can also be declared in violation of the above constitutional provision. However, as the original decision pointed out, a witness can judge for himself how the content of the testimony that is required may or may not involve the possibility of criminal proceedings or a conviction for him; thus the matter can be presented as a general principle and not simply as a concrete case in the present instance. Accordingly, the original decision, which held that the right to refuse to testify under Article 146 of the Code of Criminal Procedure is not operative in cases in which the suspect is unspecified, is of course proper, and the argument for appeal is groundless in respect to this point.

Concerning the third point in the argument for appeal: Because under the process of investigation as set forth in the Code of Criminal Procedure the right to use coercion in investigation is not recognized in principle, the investigating officer, in situations in which it is deemed necessary to examine witnesses in order to achieve the objectives of the investigation, must make a request to that effect of a judge through the public prosecutor, as set forth in Article 226 of the Code of Criminal Procedure. In cases in which the judge who has received such a request deems it proper, it becomes possible to examine a witness and, of course, a witness who has received a summons then assumes the obligation to testify. In the case of the suspect in the present case, subsequent investigation revealed that there were not sufficient grounds for him to be charged with a crime and no action was instituted. Even if the accused in the original case was found not to have committed a crime or found not guilty for lack of evidence, it is clear that the witness could not refuse to testify on the grounds that there were no objective facts concerning the suspected crime, because on tracing back the manner in which the evidence was compiled there was no illegality or invalidity to be found.

Consequently, in order for a public prosecutor to request a judge to examine a witness under Article 226 of the Code of Criminal Procedure there need only be enough facts regarding the suspected crime to give the investigative organ reason to believe that the crime has occurred. As has been pointed out in the original decision, the objective existence of the facts of the suspected crime is not a necessary condition [for the request]. Naturally, if an investigative organ deliberately fabricates a set of imaginary facts, opens an investigation, and requests the examination of a witness under Article 226 of the Code of Criminal Procedure without having any basis for believing that a crime has been committed, then this must be clearly regarded as an abuse of official duties under the pretext of investigation. However, in the present case the original judgment held as below, to wit:

On April 24, 1949, a judicial police officer of the police station of the city of Matsumoto requested a judge of the Matsumoto Summary Court to issue a warrant of arrest for one Seki Itarō, an official of the Matsumoto Tax Office, on charges of suspected corruption, etc. On the 25th, the following day, at about 10:00 A.M. he did obtain the said warrant. But on the same day at about 3:00 P.M. the accused [in this case], Ishii Kiyoshi, a reporter of the Matsumoto branch office of the *Asahi Shimbun* appeared before Kaida Takehira, the chief of the investigation division of the said police station, informed him that he knew that the police intended to issue a warrant for the arrest of Seki Itarō, and asked him how the case was progressing. However, the latter [Kaida] replied that he knew nothing about it, but because it appeared that the facts concerning the above warrant for arrest had leaked out he altered the plan and executed the arrest at about 9:00 P.M. on the same day.

However, the Nagano edition of the *Asahi* under the dateline of the 26th, the following day, published the facts concerning the request for the said warrant and the suspicion of the crime as recorded in the warrant. The fact that the arrangement of the text of the said report resembled that of the warrant was clearly established in the testimony taken in the trial of first instance.

Thus, because the leaking of the facts concerning the request for and the issuance of the warrant made its execution difficult and, even more, because it presented a grave obstacle to the investigation itself, it is clear that secrets were divulged that had been acquired in the course of official duties, as set forth in Article 100 of the National Public Service Law, by a public service official working on the task of the request for, the compilation, and the issuance of the warrant for arrest.

Thus, combining the above facts and other evidence, it is clear that someone in the machinery of investigation, either in the Matsumoto Summary Court or in the police station of that city, had revealed to a third party secrets acquired in the course of his official duties. Thus, there was sufficient reason to open an investigation of the circumstances that caused a suspicion that the National Public Service Law had been violated. Not only is it impossible to state, as the argument contends, that the facts for the suspicion of a crime were nothing more than rumor and did not even reach the level of suspicion, but it is also completely impossible to accept the alleged fact that the request for the interrogation of the witness in the present case, which was recognized as being necessary to the investigation of the suspect, constituted an abuse of official duties.

Therefore, the judgment of the original decision that the request for the interrogation of the witness in the present case was not in contravention of Article 226 of the Code of Criminal Procedure is, of course, proper; and it cannot be said, as the argument does, that there is anything unconstitutional about it.

Again, the argument maintains that if Article 226 of the Code of Criminal Procedure has a purport that is the same as the interpretation in the original judgment, the said article contravenes Article 13 of the Constitution. However, the judgment is proper, as has already been pointed out, and because it cannot be said that the provisions of Article 226 of the Code of Criminal Procedure are unconstitutional, it is completely impossible to accept the argument for appeal under discussion here.

Concerning the substance of counsel Ashikari's argument: Because it has already been shown that to require testimony regarding a reporter's source of information is not a violation of the freedom of expression guaranteed in Article 21, paragraph 1, of the Constitution, the argument concerning unconstitutionality is groundless. The argument for appeal contends that the matters in the present case did not constitute a crime, and consequently the request for the interrogation of a witness, based on Article 226 of the Code of Criminal Procedure, which has as a premise the fact that the said matters did constitute a crime, is invalid;

but this argument is groundless because facts for the suspicion of a crime did exist in respect to the request for the interrogation of the witness in the present case, and the said request was not invalid, as has already been explained in regard to the previous argument.

Thus, it cannot be recognized that Article 411 of the Code of Criminal Procedure is applicable to the present case.[3]

Consequently, the Court decides as stated in the formal text of the decision in accordance with Article 408 of the Code of Criminal Procedure.[4]

The above is the unanimous opinion of the Justices.

Because Justice Hasegawa Taichirō had retired he did not participate in the deliberations.

(TRANSLATED BY IKEDA MASAAKI)

---

3. *Code of Criminal Procedure*. ARTICLE 411. Even where there exists no ground [constitutional violation or incompatibility with precedent] as prescribed by any one of the Items in Article 405, if the court of *Jokoku* appeal deems it incompatible with justice not to quash the original judgment because of the existence of the following causes, it may quash it by means of a judgment:

(1) When there exists any mistake of construction, interpretation or application of law or ordinance which is material to the judgment;

(2) When the punishment has been imposed too unjustly and improperly;

(3) When there exists a gross error in finding facts which is material to the judgment;

(4) When there exists any reason which would support reopening of procedure (*Saishin*);

(5) When the punishment has been abolished or changed, or a general amnesty has been proclaimed after the rendition of the original judgment.

4. See footnote 4, p. 16.

Hanreishū, X, No. 7, 785 (Civil)

EDITORIAL NOTE: Both the plaintiff and the defendant in the original suit were candidates for the House of Representatives in the election of October, 1952. The defendant asserted in several campaign radio broadcasts that the plaintiff had accepted a considerable sum of money in connection with the purchase of electrical equipment while he was vice-governor of Tokushima Prefecture.

The plaintiff brought suit on the ground of injury of reputation as provided in the Civil Code; and the defendant was found guilty and sentenced to publish in several newspapers and to broadcast for three consecutive days a detailed public apology. The defendant lost on appeal and then carried his case to the Supreme Court, using as his principal argument the claim that the original verdict violated his freedom of conscience because of the detail he was forced to go into in his apology.

Grand Bench decision, July 4, 1956: Dismissed.

REFERENCES

Code of Civil Procedure. ARTICLE 733. 1. In the case of Article 414, paragraph 2 or paragraph 3, of the Civil Code [see footnote 6] the first filing court in the first instance shall, upon motion, render ruling in accordance with the provisions of the Civil Code.

2. The obligee may, at the same time, apply for the pronouncement of a ruling to cause the obligor to pay in advance the costs defrayable in undertaking the said act: Provided, that this shall not preclude the right to demand later the costs defrayed more than the above due to the performance of the said act.

Civil Code. ARTICLE 723.   If a person has injured the reputation of another, the Court may, on the application of the latter, make an order requiring the former to take suitable measures for the restoration of the latter's reputation either in lieu of or together with compensation for damages.

Constitution of Japan. ARTICLE 19.   Freedom of thought and conscience shall not be violated.

FORMAL JUDGMENT

The appeal in the present case is dismissed. The cost of the appeal is to be borne by the appellant.

REASONS. Concerning the first reason for appeal in the argument of the representative of the appellant, Agawa Junichi (including the reason for appeal appearing in the petition for appeal) : [1] Article 21 of the Constitution does not guarantee the freedom of expression unconditionally. Thus, in the present case, the publication of baseless facts in regard to the actions of another person, as established in the original trial, and the injury of such person's reputation are abuses of the freedom of expression. Even though a candidate publish such facts during an election for the House of Representatives to criticize an office-holder on an occasion such as the statement of his platform, it is impossible to recognize this publication as falling within the limits of freedom of expression guaranteed in the Constitution. Consequently, the original verdict, which held that the conduct of the appellant in the present case was illegal because it injured the reputation of another, was in no wise in violation of Article 21 of the Constitution. The argument is groundless.

Concerning the second reason for appeal: [2] The conduct of the

1. The reason referred to was that the freedom of speech guaranteed by the Constitution was to be interpreted particularly widely on occasions such as elections, both because candidates should be criticized and because the final judgment as to the rightness or wrongness of the criticism lies with the voters.

2. This argument maintained that since the action in question had occurred during an election, the case should have been tried, not under private law respecting libel, but under public law governing elections.

appellant in the present case in respect to the respondent is related only to private law. Even though from one point of view it does possess a character that would bring it under the regulations of the election law, which is in the area of public law, it is only natural in regard to the aspect relating to private law that the Civil Code be applied. The argument is only a personal view and is insufficient to be accepted.

Concerning the third reason: [3] The ordering of a wrongdoer to publish a notice of apology in a newspaper under Article 723 of the Civil Code, which reads in part, "If a person has injured the reputation of another, the Court [may require] the former to take suitable measures for the restoration of the latter's reputation," has been approved by past theory and precedent. In addition, in our country the order to publish notices of apology in newspapers has been carried out.

In a judgment that orders a notice of apology it is proper for its publication in a newspaper to be left to the voluntary decision of the one apologizing. It is also proper that performance in a situation in which such a notice has been ordered be accomplished by indirect compulsion based on Article 734 of the Code of Civil Procedure [4] as [an act of] nonexecution by substitution done only voluntarily by the obligor. On occasion, to enforce this may result in disregard of the personality of the obligor, or striking injury to his honor, or improper limitation on his freedom of voluntary decision or his freedom of conscience; if so it may become a case not suitable for compulsory execution. However, if it involves no more than the revelation of the true facts of a situation and an expression of an intention to apologize, then it must be said that compulsory execution is possible in accordance with the procedures of Article 733 of the Code of Civil Procedure,[5] as execution by substitution.[6]

3. This reason stated that the original verdict, in its demand for extreme detail in the content of the public apology, violated the appellant's freedom of conscience.

4. Article 734 provides that if the nature of the obligation permits "compulsory performance," the court of first instance may order the obligor to pay damages if he does not perform the obligation within a stated period. The order to pay damages constitutes the indirect compulsion.

5. See the text of Article 733 under "References" above, and note particularly the reference to Article 414 of the Civil Code, which states in paragraph 1, "If an obligor does not voluntarily perform his obligation, the obligee may apply to the Court for compulsory performance thereof. . . ."

6. Note that execution by substitution is provided for in paragraphs 2 and 3 of Article 414 of the Civil Code. The key passage in paragraph 2 is, "If, where the nature of the obligation

Thus, the original plea of the respondent [plaintiff], which was approved in the original decision, called for the appellant in respect to the objective facts, which had been published abroad, on the designated date and in designated broadcasts and newspapers under his name to address the respondent as follows: "The above broadcasts and articles were contrary to fact, injured your reputation, and caused you much trouble. I hereby announce my apology." In the long run, the decision amounts to a demand that the appellant proclaim through the media of public information that the previously published facts were falsehoods and improper. Thus, the original decision, which ordered that such a notice of apology —at the very least of the above type— be published in the newspapers, cannot be interpreted as having inflicted a humiliating or onerous hardship on the appellant or as having required a violation of his freedom of conscience or ethical will; and since, in addition, it must be regarded as a suitable measure as set forth in Article 723 of the Civil Code, the argument cannot be accepted.

Accordingly, the Court decides as in the formal judgment in accordance with Articles 401 and 89 of the Code of Civil Procedure.[7]

This decision is the unanimous opinion of the Justices except for the supplementary opinions of Justices Tanaka Kōtarō, Kuriyama Shigeru, and Iriye Toshio and the dissenting opinions of Justices Fujita Hachirō and Tarumi Katsumi in respect to the third reason in the argument for appeal of representative Agawa Junichi.

*　　*　　*

The supplementary opinion of Justice Tanaka Kōtarō in respect to the third reason for appeal presented by appeal representative Agawa Junichi follows.

The argument for appeal is, in essence, that ordering the appellant to publish an apology in the newspaper is in contravention of both the spirit and the letter of Article 19 of the Constitution since it infringes on the freedom of conscience of the appellant

does not admit of compulsory performance . . . the obligee may apply to the Court to cause it to be done by a third person at the expense of the obligor. . . ."

7. Article 401 of the Code of Civil Procedure is the equivalent of Article 408 of the Code of Criminal Procedure (see footnote 4, p. 16). Article 89 provides that court costs shall be borne by the losing party.

because he "even now is firmly convinced that the content of the speech was the truth, and that his utterance was for the good of the people."

However, the majority opinion did not enter into the problem of the meaning of what is termed "conscience" in Article 19 of the Constitution. It only recognizes a number of things in the content of the judgment ordering a notice of apology, among them that the performance thereof does not fall under compulsory execution, which improperly limits the freedom of conscience and of voluntary decision, disregards the personality of the obligor, and strikingly injures his honor; regarding the content of the original decision in the present case, it goes no further than to recognize the possibility of execution by substitution under the procedures of Article 733 of the Code of Civil Procedure, and that it cannot be interpreted as demanding an injury to the appellant's freedom of conscience or ethical will.

In my opinion there are a number of gaps in this logic. Regarding this problem, in respect to the content of the decision, the question whether, depending only on the wish of the obligor, compulsory performance as an act of nonexecution by substitution is proper, or whether execution by substitution is possible, is not of importance in determining whether the content of the decision in the present case is in contravention of the provisions concerning freedom of conscience in Article 19 of the Constitution. On the other hand, in the present case it would seem that indirect compulsion is the method for the restoration of reputation here called for. Whether a notice of apology is indirect or compulsory leaves unchanged the question whether the ordering of such a notice of apology in itself is unconstitutional. Or to put it another way, because a judgment, as an order of the state, must be obeyed by the one on whom it is imposed, the question remains even though the problem of compulsory enforcement is regarded separately.

I interpret what is termed "conscience" in Article 19 of the Constitution not to include moral sincerity or reflection that serves as the basis for an expression of an intent to apologize. And, again, it is not, for example, the same as the concept of "conscience" that appears in Kant's moral philosophy. The foreign terms "conscience" and *Gewissen,* which correspond to "conscience" in Article 19, have been used historically, in relation to the guarantee of freedom in a constitution, in the same sense as religious faith. However, today these terms are not limited to religious faith, but must be regarded broadly as depicting a world view or doctrine or thought or declaration. The freedoms of thought, conscience and religion, and academic freedom provided for in the Constitution must be considered as essentially overlapping and in harmony with each other.

In essence, preferential treatment of religion (or matters that must be treated as such, as pointed out above) by the state through the granting of patronage or special rights or through coercion resulting from prohibition, punishment, or prejudicial action violates Article 19 or in certain situations violates the principle of equality in Article 14, paragraph 1, of the Constitution, because it leads to interference in matters in which every individual freely holds to a certain religion, thought, or the like, according to his conscience. That Article 19 of the Constitution arose from such an idea is perfectly clear if we examine the provisions of various foreign constitutions that apply to this point.

That Article 19 presents thought and conscience side by side is to be recognized by noting on the one hand their objective content as objects of the guarantee and on the other their subjective formalistic nature. But the notice of apology which is the problem here is not a case of that kind. Of course, because the state by means of a verdict has demanded of the person in question an action possessing an ethical meaning, that is, an apology, the state considers that the person who has been so commanded not only must not refuse to comply for moral considerations but must regard apology as desirable. This must be considered reasonable from the standpoint of the harmony between law and morality. However, at the present time such harmony does not necessarily exist and there are many occasions when the person so ordered obeys the decree while detesting it. If, in such situations, one says that his freedom of conscience is being impaired, then it becomes impossible to punish a person guilty of a criminal act [if he claims moral justification for it], and all duties that naturally arise from morality (such as the duty to support others) and the performance and enforcement of all other obligations would also become impossible. Again, in extreme cases, it would have to be concluded that these [obligations] are against the freedom of conscience and in contravention of the Constitution, even in the case of laws which, in accordance with the principles of a certain legal theory, would attach to declarations of intention a legal effectiveness that differs from that which those concerned desire.[8] And, again, it must also be said that to make those who deny in general the legal system obey the law is a violation of their freedom of conscience.

In a notice of apology, the law wishes, of course, that it be accompanied by morality (*Moralität*) [in original]; however, we must be satisfied for the time being, because of the nature of law, which differs from morality, if legality (*Legalität*) [in original], namely, behavior, coincides with what the law orders externally, apart from the state of one's inner feelings. Unless it springs from one's innermost heart, what is demanded [in the way of apology] is impossible even with the power of the law. In this sense, violation of the conscience is impossible. It is possible to say the same about "apology in a public session of the assembly," which is recognized in both the National Diet Law and the Local Autonomy Law (Article 122, item 2, National Diet Law; Article 135, paragraph 1, item 2, in the Local Autonomy Law) as a form of disciplinary action.

Though there be a notice of apology not accompanied by the intent to apologize, it still has meaning in the realm of the law for the one injured. That is because reputation is a social concept, and thus this type of notice of apology can be recognized as a sensible and valid method for the restoration of the reputation of the injured person. In this sense there is no distinction between a simple retraction and an apology. If one accepts the interpretation of conscience given in the argument for appeal, then a forced retraction violates freedom of conscience because it opposes the strong faith that one has in one's actions.

In addition, in improper situations in which a method of apology imposes on the offender a humiliating or enslaving obligation,

8. The terseness of Justice Tanaka's language here is confusing, although the meaning would undoubtedly be clear to a Japanese legal expert. The meaning is probably somewhat as follows: "The legal effectiveness of declarations of intention can be determined either by the content of the declaration itself as an expression of the inner feelings of the declarer or by inference from the actual conduct of the declarer growing out of his stated intention. The law generally supports the latter view, which would be negated if we followed the rigid interpretation of freedom of conscience." On this point see also "3. Concerning law and morality," in Justice Tarumi's dissenting opinion.

then it must be regarded as a violation of Article 13 of the Constitution regarding respect for the individual; it is not related to Article 19 of the Constitution, which deals with freedom of conscience.

In essence, the present case is unrelated to Article 19 of the Constitution, and for this reason this point in the argument for appeal must be rejected. In the interpretation of the Constitution it is necessary to take the broad view and come to grips with the spirit of the system and the law and to make decisions on the basis of its phraseology and the meaning of its concepts. It must not be forgotten that both the theory and the concepts of private law and of other special areas of law must be sought for in the Constitution, and judgments must be rendered on a broad basis.

* * *

The opinion of Justice Kuriyama Shigeru in respect to the third reason for appeal of appeal representative Agawa Junichi follows.

The majority opinion has rendered a judgment in respect to the argument for appeal that a violation of Article 19 is involved, but because I believe that this case does not give rise to the problem of a violation of the said article, I supplement below the reasons given in the majority opinion.

The argument for appeal asserts that the original sentence is in contravention of the said article on the mistaken assumption that the "freedom of conscience" of Article 19 means the freedom of ethical feelings. However, the freedom of conscience of Article 19 is a translation of the same English phrase, and the fact that "freedom of conscience" means the freedom to select one's faith (below referred to as "freedom of faith") is clear from examples from various foreign constitutions that are given below.

To glance at the Constitution of Ireland first, Article 44 of the said constitution under the heading of religion provides that the freedom of conscience (the freedom of faith), and the free practice and following of religion are guaranteed to each citizen to the extent that they do not violate public morality and order. Next, in the United States of America the Constitution of the State of California (Article 1, section 4), while guaranteeing freedom of religion, also provides that no person shall be disqualified either as a witness or a juror on the ground of his opinions concerning religious beliefs and that the freedom of conscience (freedom of faith) thus guaranteed should not be interpreted as justifying immoral conduct or conduct that would impair the peace and security of the state.

This phrase, freedom of conscience (freedom of faith), is not limited as a term only to the constitutions of Christian countries. Article 25 of the Constitution of India, under the express title of "The Right to Freedom of Religion" stipulates that all persons shall enjoy equally freedom of conscience (freedom of faith) and the right freely to follow a religion, to hold religious celebrations, and to proselytize. Also the Constitution of Burma under the heading of "Rights regarding Religion" in Article 20 stipulates that all the people possess the right of equal freedom of conscience (freedom of faith) and also the right freely to follow and to practice a religion. Article 13 of the Constitution of Iraq, after proclaiming Islam as the state religion and guaranteeing freedom of ritual to the different sects of Islam, guarantees complete freedom of conscience (freedom of faith) and freedom of worship. (Peasley, *The Constitutions of Nations of the World*, II, 219, noted as the official English translation.) The English "freedom of conscience" is the French *liberté de conscience*. In France in Article 1 of the law of 1905 separating church and state, it was provided that the Republic guarantee *liberté de conscience* (freedom of faith). That this is a guarantee of freedom of choice of faith is clear from the body of the law itself. Léon Duguit holds that *liberté de conscience* is the freedom either to believe or not to believe in one's own inner heart in a religion (see page 415 in Volume V of his treatise on constitutions, 1925 edition).

It can be seen from the above examples from different constitutions that freedom of faith is set forth as one aspect of freedom of religion in the broad sense. This does not provide for a freedom of thought differing from that in the Constitution of Japan. The Constitution of Japan was set up in accordance with the conditions of the Potsdam Declaration (paragraph 10 of the Declaration providing that freedom of thought and religion, and respect for fundamental human rights be established), and it must be interpreted as having provided in Article 19 for both freedom of thought and the original freedom of faith related to it, and in the succeeding Article 20 as having provided for the freedom of religion in the narrow sense, which was not included in the freedom of faith.

Because this kind of freedom of faith is both freedom of thought and freedom of religion, the Universal Declaration of Human Rights (Article 18), which has been adopted by the United Nations, and the draft covenant of human rights (Article 13) of UNESCO combine the three things and provide that all persons shall have the right to enjoy freedom of thought, faith, and religion. As shown above, in the Constitution of Japan freedom of faith is separated from the freedom of religion of Article 20, and is provided for in combination with the freedom of thought of Article 19. I believe it should not be interpreted—for the reason that it has been translated as "freedom of conscience"—to mean that only the Constitution of Japan for some odd reason has provided for the freedom of ethical feelings.

As Article 97 of the Constitution states, "The fundamental human rights by this Constitution guaranteed to the people of Japan are fruits of the age-old struggle of man to be free . . . ," so the "freedom of conscience" of Article 19 should be understood as a legal term that enjoys that some historical background. Nevertheless, the argument for appeal states, "To force the publication in a newspaper of an apology whose content is as set forth in the original sentence is a violation of the appellant's freedom of conscience and is contrary to the provisions of Article 19 of the Constitution"; but that is an assertion that mistakenly interprets "freedom of conscience" of Article 19 and does not create in the original verdict the problem of the violation of "freedom of conscience" of Article 19, as the appellant states.

* * *

The opinion of Justice Iriye Toshio concerning the third reason of appeal of appeal representative Agawa Junichi follows.

In respect to the dismissal of the appeal in the present case, my conclusion is the same as that of the majority opinion, but because I differ in regard to the reason for dismissing the third reason in the above appeal, I shall express my own opinion in order to make my views clear.

1. The third reason for appeal, in essence as given in the decision in the present case, is that the appellant was forced to publish in

the newspapers a notice of apology with a certain content, that this constituted a violation of the appellant's freedom of conscience, and that it was in contravention of Article 19 of the Constitution. However, I interpret the decision in this case to be an executory judgment but, for reasons described below, one in which compulsory execution is not permissible. If so, the content of the decision in the present case cannot be realized except by the voluntary performance of the appellant; consequently, because it did not come about that the appellant was forced by the present decision to publish the notice of apology in a newspaper, the assertion of unconstitutionality cannot be accepted because of the lack of that premise in the argument. I believe that the third argument for appeal must be rejected for the above reason.

2. The majority opinion says that the claim of the respondent [the original plaintiff] in the present suit, admitted by the original decision, amounted to a demand that the appellant should announce in the media of public information that the facts he previously disseminated were either falsehoods or inaccurate, and that it cannot be interpreted as requiring the infliction of a humiliating or enslaving hardship on the appellant or violating his freedom of conscience or of voluntary decision. Finally, on the premise that the decision in the present case can be carried out by compulsory performance in accordance with the procedures for execution by substitution of Article 733 of the Code of Civil Procedure, the majority opinion adjudges that it is not unconstitutional.

However, I believe that the content of the decision in the present case is not as the majority opinion holds, but must be interpreted as follows: the actions of the appellant, carried out earlier, constituted misconduct that injured the honor of the other party and caused him much trouble and must be regarded as requiring the announcement of a formal voluntary statement by the appellant requesting the pardon of the other party for it. If such a notice of apology is published in a newspaper in the name of the appellant, regardless of his true feelings, then it is a recognition of the fact that the appellant regards his own actions as misconduct just as if it were his true feeling, and it is perfectly clear that this would end by being generally accepted as a plea for the forgiveness of the other party. To put it in other words, it must be said that the publication of a notice of apology of this kind must be regarded as producing the effect (the effect of the expression itself) that what was published must itself be treated as the expression of the true feelings of the appellant. If the recognition that one's own actions are misconduct and a plea for forgiveness by the other party do not constitute an ethical judgment in accordance with one's conscience, what are they? Therefore, if the appellant announces such an intention voluntarily in accordance with the decision in the present case, there is no problem; but to force the appellant by means of compulsory execution, regardless of the fact that the appellant is in a mental state in which he cannot, after consulting his conscience, submit to such a decision, to announce matters as if they really reflected his own conscience, even though they might be different, and to force by public power a formation and manifestation of an ethical judgment to which he cannot submit, produce a result that otherwise would not be chosen and must be regarded as a violation of the freedom of conscience clause of Article 19 of the Constitution and a disregard of the individual personality clause of Article 13 of the Constitution.

3. Of course, the liberties in the Constitution are not absolutely unlimited; in situations in which there exists sufficient reason recognized as absolutely necessary for the public welfare or for other constitutional requirements, a limitation thereof up to a certain point would not be considered unconstitutional. However, even in such limitations on freedom, there must be certain differences in method and extent in accordance with the nature of the liberties that are to be subject to limitation. However, the ancients said that a mighty army could be robbed of its commander in times of unrest but a humble man, no matter how weak he might be, could not be deprived of his determination once he made up his mind. Freedom of conscience is the determination that cannot be wrested from a humble man, and it is truly one of the basic liberties that constitute the foundation of the respect for the individual which must be stressed in any democratic society. Thus, even supposing that a situation existed in which the state decided that from its standpoint an individual was in error in respect to certain matters of conscience in which he sincerely believed, what can be done by public power is to bring out factual relationships that the state has decided to be true, but only within the limits not related to the freedom itself, which is what the individual embraces in his heart

as an ethical judgment relating to good and evil. I believe that it is probably impossible to discover any basis whatsoever for the admissibility of anything deviating from the above, for example, the compulsory execution of the judgment in this case under which the person concerned is forced to express something from within his own conscience and to which he does not really submit.

In England, America, Germany, France, and other countries, judgments requiring a notice of apology as in the present case do not seem to be recognized as a method of restoring reputation. For example, in Britain and America recovery in libel is based on the principle of damages for injury, and there is nothing resembling spontaneous apology by the wrongdoer except the relief provided by the amount of compensation; and also in France and Germany the recognized methods include the action of the wrongdoer in printing in the newspapers, at his own expense, the text of the verdict in favor of the injured who was the plaintiff in the action for libel, or the publication by the wrongdoer of a retraction in the newspapers. Even in cases involving Article 723 of our Civil Code, in addition to a required notice of apology as in the present case, the following methods are recognized: (1) the publication in the newspapers, at the wrongdoer's expense, of the verdict against him in a civil suit; (2) the publication in the newspapers of the verdict of guilty in a similar suit for criminal libel; and (3) the retraction of the libelous item. If such methods exist, then no question of unconstitutionality is created, because, even though it is said that there has been compulsory enforcement in the verdict that requires the above from the wrongdoer, it neither improperly violates his freedom of conscience nor disregards his individuality. However, a verdict as in the present case, even if such compulsory enforcement is permissible, produces, as has already been shown, a situation in which the appellant is forced by public power to resort to both the formation and the manifestation of an ethical judgment; and since, as was shown above, there are other proper means of restoring reputation as provided for under Article 723 of the Civil Code, if we take those into consideration, it absolutely cannot be recognized that it is impossible to realize the restoration of reputation in the present case by a compulsory execution of the present verdict, as shown above, without striking injury to the individual personality and freedom of conscience.

Namely, if we regard this from the standpoint of comparative benefit [to the plaintiff and defendant both], we cannot discover a basis sufficient to permit approval of this matter. I conclude that as a method for the restoration of reputation it goes too far; and I believe that it cannot escape unconstitutionality, is an improper infringement of freedom of conscience, and disregards the personality of the individual.

(In my opinion, the publication of a retraction is not pertinent to the "apology in open session" as a disciplinary measure in the National Diet and the local assemblies, as described above. The former does involve a text of a retraction, but it has no connection with the freedom of conscience for it is merely an expression of intent uttered only once and is limited to the aim of restoring the original situation by going back to the previous state of affairs; and, again, the latter is not only not recognized as a method of compulsory execution, but in respect to the fact that it is a special disciplinary measure designed to maintain order in relation to a special authority, it must be said to have a character different from a verdict related to the general authority that requires the publication of an apology as in the present case.)

4. As described above, my interpretation is that if the verdict in the present case is treated as permitting compulsory enforcement, it is in contravention of Articles 19 and 13 of the Constitution. Accordingly, I cannot agree with the majority opinion, which holds that the verdict in the present case is not unconstitutional on the premise that compulsory execution can be carried out by the method of substitute execution as provided for in Article 733 of the Code of Civil Procedure.

As I point out below, I interpret compulsory execution in the present verdict to be completely impermissible. On reflection, a claim for an executory judgment and a claim for compulsory execution are completely different matters and, accordingly, an executory judgment must be regarded as usually being an exception to the application of compulsory execution, as was shown in the explanation of the majority opinion (an example of a completely impermissible compulsory execution would be a verdict relating to the obligation of a married couple to live together, even though the judgment is executory). Whether or not the verdict in the present case really corresponds to compulsory execution is a problem requiring re-examination on the basis of the content of the verdict itself. But, among executory judgments there are some in which compulsory execution is not appropriate: (1) cases in which from the nature of the obligation it is impossible to realize a future performance appropriate to the main object of the obligation by means of compulsory execution; and (2) cases in which, from the content of the obligation, compulsory execution would inflict patent injury on the person or the personality of the obligor and could not be recognized as being proper constitutionally or from the standpoint of social concepts in the light of contemporary legal theory. In (1) above it is possible to determine whether or not the character of the obligation is appropriate to compulsory execution, but in (2) above it is necessary to determine whether or not compulsory execution itself is proper in the light of contemporary civilized doctrine.

Thus, because compulsory execution of a verdict like that described in the present case cannot escape being unconstitutional and because it involves improper injury to the freedom of conscience and a disregard of the personality of the individual, it really corresponds to (2) above, and regardless of whether execution by substitution of Article 733 of the Code of Civil Procedure or indirect compulsion of Article 734 is carried out, it is appropriate to interpret it as being completely impermissible compulsory execution. On the other hand, I believe that the decision in the present case as a method of restoring the reputation of the injured party is effective because it requires the wrongdoer to publish in the newspaper a notice of apology, and because the court recognized it as a suitable action as provided for in Article 723 of the Civil Code. I also believe that to declare compulsory execution impermissible in this regard would not make the decision meaningless as an executory judgment.

As I have pointed out above, because the decision in the present case does not recognize compulsory execution [in the strict sense], there is no room for the creation of the problem of unconstitutionality, and the argument for appeal, lacking that premise, cannot escape dismissal.

*   *   *

The dissenting opinion of Justice Fujita Hachirō in respect to the third reason in the argument for appeal of appeal representative Agawa follows.

It is perfectly clear that the essence of the plea of the respondent [the original plaintiff] in the present case and the gist of what the original verdict approved in respect to it were to the effect that the earlier actions of the appellant, as pointed out in the verdict, constituted misconduct that damaged the reputation of the respondent and caused him trouble, and that in respect to it the appellant was ordered to express the intent of apology by means of the publication in the newspaper of a notice of apology. However, the appellant did not believe that his earlier action was a misdeed that damaged the reputation of the respondent, and it is also perfectly clear from the course of the entire proceedings in this case that he did not have the slightest intention to apologize to the respondent.

The state ordered the appellant, by means of an exercise of authority called a trial, to announce publicly both an ethical judgment in respect to his own conduct, namely, that it constituted a misdeed, and also the moral intent of an apology or a plea for pardon. This is a violation of the "freedom of conscience" of Article 19 of the Constitution. After all, the freedom of conscience of Article 19 of the Constitution is not simply the inward freedom to make distinctions between right and wrong; it must be understood to include the freedom to announce or not to announce to the outside world one's judgments in regard to distinctions between right and wrong. Even in respect to the freedom of religion of Article 20 regarding this matter, the Constitution does not stop with merely guaranteeing an internal freedom of religion, but it also guarantees the freedom to announce or not announce publicly one's feelings about religion. That the Constitution of course does not permit of the forced outward expression through the exercise of state power of one's conception of religion, against one's will, such as our country's former practice of *fumi-e* [forcing those who were suspected of being Christians to tread on a holy picture or a crucifix as a demonstration of their nonbelief], must be considered to be along the same line. Consequently, there is no doubt but that forcing someone, as in the present case, to announce to the outside world against his real feelings his judgment concerning the rightness or wrongness, or goodness or evil of things, and to order him to utter an apology that he did not really feel, is truly a violation of the outward freedom of conscience guaranteed in Article 19 of the Constitution.

Previously, in our country as is pointed out in the majority opinion, there was the practice of ordering, through a judgment in respect to the parties in a suit, the publication in a newspaper of a notice of apology as a means of restoring reputation as provided for in Article 723 of the Civil Code; but it must be understood that a bad custom is not permissible under the new Constitution, which clearly and expressly guarantees the "freedom of conscience."

(Thus, we do not have to concern ourselves with whether such a verdict permits of compulsory execution in legal actions. The very ordering of such a thing through the exercise of state power must be considered a violation of the freedom of conscience. More precisely, even though the fact of the conclusion of a marriage contract be recognized, to order the parties by a court decision to execute it—that is, to get married—must be construed, from the viewpoint of the nature of marriage, to call forth the illegality of the decision itself, not withstanding the permissibility of compulsory execution, and to be similarly impermissible.)

Accordingly, the argument for appeal is reasonable on this point and the part of the original judgment that ordered the appellant to announce his intent to apologize in the form of a notice of apology and to admit that his own action was a misdeed must be reversed.

*　　*　　*

The dissenting opinion of Justice Tarumi Katsumi in respect to the third argument for appeal of appeal representative Agawa Junichi follows.

I believe that the part of the original verdict that orders the announcement of the intention of apology and plea for pardon violates Article 19 of the Constitution and that the original verdict should be reversed.

1. The verdict and the thoughts of the party concerned: A court in a situation in which it orders, by means of a trial, a litigant to announce a certain intention, cannot know what thoughts,

principles, or conscience a litigant may possess inside his heart; these are also not matters that can be investigated. It is, of course, the same with respect to the verdict ordering the notice of apology in the present case or one's judgment as to whether it should be approved. That is to say, in respect to whether such a judgment should be made, it must be anticipated that in certain cases to make such an announcement might appear undesirable to the appellant for the reason that it might be against his thoughts, faith, or conscience. It is possible that there are persons in the world who would say the following: "Today in many countries of the world the great majority of the people are deprived of the fruits of their labor by the few, and endure a life unworthy of human beings. Because this results from the capitalistic organization of the state that recognizes the private ownership of the means of production, countries that have such a system must be swept from the face of the earth. Because the legal means of constitutional revision to achieve that aim is virtually hopeless, it is permissible to struggle for it by any means, legal or illegal, peaceful or violent, and to use any of them against such a state, its laws, its organs, and its courts, and against the reactionary enemies. We must not submit. This is our faith, our morality, our conscience." Or, on the other hand, there may also be those, such as some religious believers or anarchists, who think that no person should be subjected to the oppression and control of others and who adopt the attitude, at least as far as is possible, of nonsubmission to the state and to law because they depend on force to control men. What Articles 19 and 20 of the Constitution guarantee is that the freedom of inward thought, faith, and conscience of such people be not impaired even by the law, state power, or trial.

Some disputants may say, "Superstitions and ideas that are not widely accepted as valid are neither thought nor religion, and lie outside the guarantees of the Constitution." But who judges what is superstition or what is widely accepted as valid? A system of a single religion and a single ideology rejects other religions and ideologies as being superstition or falsehood. But the free and lively expression, discovery, and discussion of all varieties of thought and belief are the very means by which contributions can be made to the perfection of individuality and the spiritual development of both the individual and mankind in general. It is also the fundamental spirit of our liberal Constitution. The special characteristic of a free constitution can be found in the struggle of thought against thought without the denial of the opportunity of expression even to thoughts that attack the Constitution.

2. On the assumption that the appellant is the possessor of beliefs set forth in the previous paragraph, do not both the apology and the request for pardon in the verdict in the present case violate his beliefs and force him to express an intention against his wishes? In reaching a judgment of this point it is necessary first of all to determine the meaning of both apology and request for pardon. Generally, the expressions of intent such as "I am wrong," "Please forgive me," "the begging of pardon," and "regret," are related to such perceptions as: (1) the recognition of an error in one's conduct or attitude (of commission or omission) in respect to religion, social morality, custom, or principles (that is, impermissible violations of norms that were evil, unjust, erroneous, or wrongful—that is, not good or just or righteous or correct) or, in other words, a denial of the correctness of one's own conduct; (2) a recognition, after reflection, of wrongness in one's own ideas (including beliefs) as a source of conduct or, to go further, a revelation of a shortcoming in one's character or even of inferiority; or (3) a change in the ideas of the performer of the act and an avowal not to repeat a similar error in the future. Still further, it is the retraction of an utterance or statement. But in respect to the latter it means not only simple correction, but also a denial of the correctness of the original because of defects or improprieties in one's own statements or utterances.

The public notice in the present case involved the modification with a considerable amount of care of the text of the apology as requested by the respondent; but because the original trial either deliberately or through error went no further than to recognize libel through an illegal act and did not recognize criminal libel, the fact that the public notice in the present case used the expression "apology," which must be interpreted as meaning the admission of an offense, probably is undesirable from the standpoint of the beliefs of the appellant. In addition, in the verdict in the present case, the part which, under the heading of "Apology" in the notice, uses the phrase "I wish to express herewith my apology," is against the principles of the person involved and requires that he publicly announce an intention that may be undesirable to him; and this must be said to be in contravention of Article 19 of the Constitution. Moreover, the same article also guarantees the right of silence to those who, as a matter of principle, wish to be silent.

Someone may raise the following question: "If this is true, and since it may not be possible to know what kind of principles the person involved may have, might it not become impossible for the courts to issue any kind of decision that would order any person to express an intention (such as a request for registration)?" Of course, that is not the case. The courts can order matters that must be regarded as responsibilities in the realm of law. However, because a verdict orders such things as the expression of an apology— which is impossible unless the person concerned admits that his own conduct is an offense that is a violation of a rule in religion, moral customs, or principles—it enters into a problem of an inner world that from its very nature lies beyond the realm of law, even assuming that the court recognized it as a proper method for restoring a reputation in accordance with Article 723 of the Civil Code.

3. Concerning law and morality: Law consists of compulsory norms that deal with the conduct of men and depends on the public authority of the state; conduct is an outward expression of intent. The thoughts of men once outwardly expressed, or when they reach the point of being recognized as conduct (either of commission or omission), cannot be disregarded by either society or the state. The law ordains that conduct be defended as authorized conduct; or that it not be interfered with, as conduct that should be left alone; or that it be punished as a crime or as an abuse of the freedom of expression (whether actually carried out or not); or that restitution be made or execution carried out in the case of illegal conduct or the nonexecution of an obligation. In such cases the law gives careful consideration to whether the conduct was based on intent and what the intent was.

Of course, morality is the basis for a fairly large portion of the laws under the Constitution. I readily affirm that such important concepts as "respect for the individual," "the public welfare," "the abuse of rights," "truthfulness and sincerity," "public order and good morals," "just reason," and "proper conduct" have already become legal concepts because an immediate understanding is impossible if they are omitted from such a basis.

However, even in cases in which law becomes involved with the conditions of these inmost feelings or in which it inquires into a legal significance derived from the morality of such conduct, the law, of course, goes no further than to pose the question of the conditions of one's inmost feelings that can be grasped from external acts within the necessary limits for the determination of the merit of such outward conduct. In respect to the perception of specific conduct as that carried out under conditions of specific intent, which the law requires, the law does not concern itself with the kind of principle under which it was done. The intent of the performer with respect to stealing or murdering is treated as a problem, but no account is taken of the kind of idea from which it may have arisen. Even though an anarchist denounces the system of taxation and even though he may not wish to make a declaration of income, the law forces him to make such a declaration and to pay taxes, without regard to his theories. The law is thus effectively applied to acts of commission or omission and by this means brings about or does not bring about a certain result and thus deals with such acts.

4. The content of the notice in the present case: There is no reason why a verdict should be constitutional that orders a person who has no intention to apologize to issue a notice of apology. After all, an apology originates in an internal judgment of right and wrong in matters of religion, morality, or principle, apart from the realm of law, and has worth only when the person admits from within that his own conduct was wrong. First of all, in cases in which the court recognizes that the appellant has committed the act at issue and that the said act is equivalent to libel, which is illegal conduct, it can, of course, then determine the existence of a responsibility without taking into account the principles of the appellant; there is also no doubt that the court can also force the appellant against his will to publish a notice to the effect that it has been established that he did commit such acts and that they are equivalent to libel. I think that there is nothing that would prevent the court, without violating Article 19 of the Constitution, from issuing an order to publish a notice such as the one in

the present case simply under the heading of "Public Notice," and with contents reading as follows: "What I published [on the occasion of the election of] October 1, 1952, was inexcusable, and why I did it I do not know, but the broadcast and the statements differed from fact and I injured your reputation and caused you much trouble." (To assert positively that he was made to recognize that "it differed from the facts" and that he had caused harm constitutes a discharge of the legal responsibility to assert that "I have caused you much trouble.") But the section in the verdict in this case that used the phrases "apology" and "I express my intent to beg your pardon" was vigorously contested by both parties. So, can it be said that the responsibility for thus expressing the intent to apologize has the character of having been produced both from "the custom of goodness" as a legal concept and from the libelous act of the appellant in the present case? Or, again, can the following be said? "Such an expression of an intention to apologize is appended to the recognition of libel and goes no further than a formal, social, and gentlemanly civility that respects the honor of both parties in the present case. Thus, because even though it is no more than a formal utterance not coming from the heart, it has the character of something that should be accepted as such both by the injured and the public at large, and the appellant should accept it in the same manner." I cannot but doubt both. It must be regarded as improper to judge this matter by considering such a civility only from the standpoint of its effectiveness in restoring the reputation of the injured party, without taking into consideration the fact that it was a forced expression of intent against the principles of the person who did not wish, as a matter of principle, to make the said apology.

I believe that the original verdict—in which the phrases "apology" and "I wish to express my intent to beg your pardon" appear in the notice and which orders something done that the appellant is unwilling to do as a matter of principle—because of its very character, violates the freedoms of thought and conscience of the appellant and also contravenes Article 19 of the Constitution. In respect to this, I should like to add still another reason.

On the point that the verdict in the present case can set up compulsory execution by the method of substitute enforcement as stated in Article 733 of the Code of Civil Procedure, one view holds that even though the verdict in the present case is an executory judgment, it is not permissible to carry out compulsory enforcement, just as in the case of a verdict ordering husband and wife to reside together. If it is self-evident that to carry out compulsory enforcement is impossible, as in the case of a decision ordering husband and wife to live together, then it is as argued above. But the verdict in the present case in regard to the public notice, which is presented separately from the reasons for the verdict, does not state that compulsory enforcement is impermissible, and it is possible to interpret the decision itself as permitting it. Thus, when the public notice in the present case was published in the newspapers, the reader had no way of knowing that it was so ordered in a verdict in a civil case and that there was no way to avoid carrying it out; also there would be much room for the mistaken impression that the appellant was doing it of his own will. Thus it ends as a case of the publication of a notice of apology in the name of the appellant, but against his principles and not from his intention; and it can be seen that in the end it differs in result from the situation of a verdict ordering husband and wife to reside together, which is impossible to enforce without the willing submission of both parties.

Thus, the argument is sound and the parts of the original decisions that ordered the publication of the phrases "Apology" in the title of the text of the public announcement and at the end "I announce my intention of begging your pardon" violate Article 19 of the Constitution, and therefore the original decision must be reversed.

(TRANSLATED BY IKEDA MASAAKI)

IV: LICENSING OF PUBLIC GATHER-
INGS (THE NIIGATA ORDINANCE
DECISION)

Hanreishū, VIII, No. 11, 1866 (Criminal)

EDITORIAL NOTE: (See also "Editorial Note" on next decision.) On April 7, 1949, about thirty Koreans were arrested in Takada, Niigata Prefecture, on a charge of illicit brewing. The next day a crowd of several hundred people gathered before the police station and demanded their release. The two accused, the secretary of the local district committee of the Communist party and the former vice-chairman of the Korean Democratic Youth Alliance of Japan, led the demonstration, which included speeches against the government, the singing of communist and Korean patriotic songs, and some scuffling. They had not obtained a license for the demonstration and so were arrested on the charge of violating Niigata Prefectural Ordinance No. 4 of 1949, which required such a license. They were tried, found guilty, and given short jail sentences, one of three months and the other of four. They lost on appeal to the Tokyo High Court and then took their case to the Supreme Court.

Grand Bench decision, November 24, 1954: Dismissed.

REFERENCES

Constitution of Japan. ARTICLE 12. The freedoms and rights guaranteed to the people by this Constitution shall be maintained by the constant endeavor of the people, who shall refrain from any abuse of these freedoms and rights and shall always be responsible for utilizing them for the public welfare.

ARTICLE 21. Freedom of assembly and association as well as speech, press, and all others forms of expression are guaranteed.

No censorship shall be maintained, nor shall the secrecy of any means of communication be violated.

ARTICLE 28. The right of workers to organize and to bargain and act collectively is guaranteed.

ARTICLE 98. This Constitution shall be the supreme law of the nation and no law, ordinance, imperial rescript, or other act of government or part thereof, contrary to the provisions hereof, shall have legal force or validity.

The treaties concluded by Japan and established laws of nations shall be faithfully observed.

ARTICLE 92. Regulations concerning organization and operations of local public entities shall be fixed by law in accordance with the principle of local autonomy.

ARTICLE 94. Local public entities shall have the right to manage their property, affairs, and administration and to enact their own regulations within law.

Ordinance concerning Parades, Processions, and Mass Demonstrations (Niigata Prefectural Ordinance No. 4, March 25, 1949).

ARTICLE 1. Parades, processions, and mass demonstrations (anything that involves marching in, or the exclusive use of, a place that the public can freely traverse on foot or by vehicle such as a road or a park; hereafter the same) shall not be conducted without obtaining a license from the public safety commission which exercises jurisdiction over the area concerned.

Parades and processions involving only students, pupils, or children and carried out for educational purposes as prescribed in a course of study and under the direction of a responsible person of the school concerned do not require a license.

ARTICLE 2. When taking out the license provided for in paragraph 1 of the preceding article, the sponsor or the representative of the sponsoring organization shall file a written application with the public safety commission which exercises jurisdiction over the area concerned seventy-two hours in advance of the time when the march or demonstration is to be held.

ARTICLE 3. The following particulars shall be stated in the written application referred to in the preceding article:

1. Date and time of the parade or demonstration.

2. Address, occupation, full name, and date of birth of the sponsor. (For an organization, its name, the location of its office, and the address, full name, and date of birth of its representative.)

3. Purpose and type of parade or demonstration.

4. Route of parade and place of demonstration.

5. Names of participating organizations, the anticipated number of participants, and number of vehicles of each organization.

Article 4. The public safety commission shall, in cases wherein it recognizes that the parade or demonstration concerned involves no threat of a disturbance to public order, grant a license twenty-four hours in advance of the time when such parade or demonstration is to start.

In granting the license mentioned in the preceding paragraph, the public safety commission may impose certain conditions, as it deems necessary, to protect the general public against disorderly or violent group acts.

The public safety commission shall, in cases wherein it does not grant a license in accordance with paragraph 1, promptly report the reasons therefor in detail to the legislative assembly of the local public entity to which the said public safety commission is attached.

In cases wherein the public safety commission which receives the written application mentioned in Article 2 does not announce an intention either to refuse a license or to impose conditions twenty-four hours in advance of the time when the parade or demonstration is to be held, it may be carried out as if a license had been granted.

Article 5. Those to whom any of the following items apply may be sentenced to not more than one year's imprisonment or a fine of not more than ¥50,000:

1. Those who violate the provisions of Article 1, paragraph 1.

2. Those who make false statements in the written application for a license as mentioned in Article 2.

3. Those who violate conditions imposed by the public safety commission in accordance with Article 4, paragraph 2.

Article 6. This ordinance shall not be construed to ban or restrict in any manner whatsoever any public assembly other than parades, processions, and mass demonstrations, or to give to the public safety commission, any police officer, or other public official the authority to supervise or to censor public assemblies, political movements, placards, publications, or other documents or drawings.

ARTICLE 7. This ordinance shall not be construed to infringe upon the laws and regulations concerning election of public officers or to require a license for speeches or assemblies during election campaigns.

[Not translated here is "Procedure for the Enforcement of the Ordinance concerning Parades, Processions, and Mass Demonstrations." This is based on the ordinance and contains nothing relevant to an understanding of the decision.]

Code of Criminal Procedure. ARTICLE 335. 1. In pronouncing the accused guilty, the facts constituting the offense, an inventory of the evidence, and the application of laws and ordinances shall be indicated.

2. When an allegation has been made as to legal grounds barring the formation of the offense, or as to facts by reason of which the punishment should be aggravated or commuted, a decision thereon shall also be indicated.

Local Autonomy Law. ARTICLE 14. An ordinary local public entity can, to the extent that it does not violate laws or ordinances, enact ordinances relating to the matters set forth in Article 2, paragraph 2 [see below].

An ordinary local public entity must determine the management of administrative matters by ordinance, except for those matters covered by special regulations in laws or ordinances.

Prefectural governments can establish by ordinance the necessary rules for administrative matters in cities, towns, and villages, except for matters covered by special regulations in laws or ordinances.

When city, town, and village ordinances relating to administrative matters contravene the prefectural ordinances established under the preceding paragraph, the said city, town, and village ordinances shall be invalid.

An ordinary local public entity can, in regard to violators of ordinances, establish provisions in those ordinances setting punishments of penal servitude up to two years, confinement, fines of not more than ¥100,000, detention, light fines, and confiscation, except for matters covered by special regulations in laws or ordinances.

Cases involving the penalties set forth in the previous paragraph fall under the jurisdiction of the national courts.

ARTICLE 2, paragraph 2 and paragraph 3 (*a*). Ordinary local public entities manage their public affairs and, in addition to those vested in them by existing laws and ordinances and by future laws or cabinet orders, those administrative matters within their borders not pertaining to national affairs.

Examples of the matters mentioned in the preceding paragraph are in general as follows. However, cases especially provided for in law or ordinance are excepted.

1. Matters pertaining to the maintenance of local public order and to the preservation of the safety, health, and welfare of residents and visitors.

FORMAL JUDGMENT

The appeal in the present case is dismissed.

REASONS. Concerning the first point in the appeal of the attorneys for the defendants: The appeal decision argued as follows: Ordinances are legislative formalities of local public entities as recognized directly in Article 94 of the Constitution. Their validity is determined within law in accordance with the same article, and in addition there is no special constitutional limitation in regard to matters that can be determined by ordinance. Because everything is based exclusively on what is enacted in law, it therefore cannot be argued that the establishment of penal provisions by ordinance in conformity with law is prohibited by the Constitution.

It cannot be recognized that, as the argument for appeal holds, the original decision sets forth the view that ordinances under the mandate of law have the unlimited power to inflict penalties or that they have the unlimited power to regulate any matter whatsoever. The argument for appeal, on an assumption not in accord with the assertions in the original decision, claims that it [the original decision] is erroneous in its interpretation of Article 94 of the Constitution; the argument cannot be accepted.

Concerning the second and third points of the argument for appeal: It is against the intent of the Constitution and impermissible to place prior restraints upon parades, processions, and mass public demonstrations (hereafter referred to simply as "such activities") under an ordinance that provides for a general system of licensing rather than a system of simple notification, because the people have the basic freedom to demonstrate unless the purpose and manner of the demonstration are improper and against the public welfare. However, even if regulations are established by ordinance that might prohibit such activities in situations as below, or require a license or notification concerning the place and procedure under reasonable and clear criteria in order to maintain public order and to protect the public welfare against serious harm from such activities, they cannot be interpreted as placing improper restrictions on freedoms of the people directly guaranteed by the Constitution because, after all, the provisions of such ordinances do not have the effect of restricting such activities in general, but only constitute recognition of the fact that there may be occasions, as indicated above, when restrictions may be placed on specific places or procedures.

Furthermore, if the regulations provide that in respect to such activities a license need not be granted or a prohibition may be enforced, if it is foreseen that they may involve a clear and present danger to the public safety, such a procedure cannot be interpreted as placing improper restrictions on freedoms of the people directly guaranteed by the Constitution.

With regard to Article 1 of the Niigata Prefectural Ordinance (hereafter referred to as the "present ordinance"), it requires that without a license from the public safety commission such activities cannot be carried out. But because the "parades, processions, and mass demonstrations" are interpreted parenthetically to involve "marching in, or the exclusive use of, a place that the public can freely traverse on foot or by vehicle such as a road or a park," the present ordinance can be recognized as being intended to designate matters relating to specific places or procedures, as indicated above, in reference to activities requiring a license. Also under Article 1, paragraph 2, and Articles 6 and 7, certain activities that, because they are similar to or closely related to those dealt with in the ordinance, might easily be made the objects of said ordinance are excluded from its application. In addition, if paragraphs 1 (*b*), 2, and 4 of Article 4 are considered—together with the fact that there are stipulations that strictly warn against making activities described above the objects of control—it can be seen that the ordinance, in respect to the activities that require a license under Article 1, deals only with specific areas and procedures as described above. And, again, in respect to even such activities, the ordinance adheres to the general principle that they must be licensed, unless there is a specific reason for not doing so.

Nevertheless, the view expressed (parenthetically) in Article 1 of the present ordinance has quite general aspects, and paragraph 1 (*a*) of Article 4, especially, sets forth an extremely abstract standard. Thus, there is the danger that the area of discretion of the public safety commission might be interpreted to be very broad. It may be desirable to revise the ordinance into clearer and more concrete terms; but if the general intent of the ordinance is considered as a whole, even if the present ordinance uses the word "license," it is reasonable to interpret it as not intending to control all such activities by means of a general system of licensing, but only as stipulating that there may be occasions to restrict specific places and procedures from the point of view described above. Therefore, the present ordinance is not in contravention of Articles 12, 21, 28, 98 or any other provision of the Constitution as contended in the argument of appeal. Accordingly, the original decision is not illegal and the argument for appeal is groundless.

(However, even though licensing is accepted to be the basic principle of Article 4, paragraph 1, because of that article's extremely general and abstract condition—"in cases wherein it recognizes that there is no threat of a disturbance of public order" —then the opposite interpretation must also be accepted, and "in cases wherein it recognizes that there is a threat of disturbance to public order," licenses will not be granted. If it is decided not to grant a license on the basis of that condition alone, then there is the danger that such activities will be subjected to improper limitation at the discretion of the public safety commission. Accordingly, if the present ordinance used such a general and abstract standard as the only basis for decision, then it would have to be stated that it was not in accord with the spirit of the Constitution. However, the limitation on such activities cannot be interpreted as being unconstitutional according to the conclusion of the argument given above, since it was logically reached on the basis of the above interpretation and application of the law—not on the single standard described above, but on the basis of the organic whole consisting of all the provisions of the ordinance and of the subsidiary regulations.)

Concerning the fourth point of the appeal:[1] This argument does not conform with the reasons for appeal to the Supreme Court stated in Article 405 of the Code of Criminal Procedure,[2] not only because it was not presented at the original trial and was not there judged, but also because it is no more than a claim that the original judgment is a violation of the statutes. (Nevertheless, the courts by virtue of their authority bear the responsibility for examining statutes pertinent to matters on trial, and ordinances are included among these, as the argument for appeal states. However, because, as a matter of principle, those statutes are not subject to the taking of evidence, there is no need either to examine them or to hand down decisions concerning them, except in cases of special necessity. Accordingly, it cannot be said that the proceedings in the original trial were illegal because they did not elucidate the point raised by the argument for appeal in respect to the present ordinance. In addition, the present ordinance did make clear the fact that it was proclaimed on March 25, 1949, and became effective on the same day.)

Concerning the fifth point of the argument for appeal:[3] This argument does not conform with the reasons for appeal to the Supreme Court as stated in Article 405 of the Code of Criminal

1. The fourth argument for appeal was to the effect that the court of first instance did not establish the date of the legal proclamation of the ordinance and that this failure might have had an adverse effect on its decision.

2. *Code of Criminal Procedure.* ARTICLE 405. *Jokoku* appeal may be lodged against a judgment in first or second instance rendered by a high court in the following cases:

(1) On the ground that there is a violation of the Constitution or an error in construction, interpretation, or application of the Constitution;

(2) On the ground that a judgment has been formed incompatible with the judicial precedents formerly established by the Supreme Court;

(3) In cases for which there exist no judicial precedents of the Supreme Court, on the ground that a judgment has been formed incompatible with the judicial precedents formerly established by the former Supreme Court (*Dai Shin In* [sic]) or by the high court as the court of *Jokoku* appeal, or, after the enforcement of this code, by the high court as the court of *Koso* appeal.

3. The argument in the fifth point was that since one of the accused was a resident of Nagano Prefecture, the Niigata ordinance did not apply to him.

Procedure, not only because it was not presented at the original trial and was not there judged, but also because it is no more than an assertion that the original judgment is a violation of the statutes and that the weighing of the offense was improper. (Ordinances enacted by local public entities are based <Article 92> on the principle of local autonomy constitutionally guaranteed as an essential element of a system of democratic government; and they are municipal enactments recognized as [arising from] a power within law as provided directly in Article 94 of the Constitution. Accordingly, although neither the power to enact ordinances nor their validity can go beyond the limits established by law, the said validity, on the principle that it exists within the limits of the law, must be interpreted as arising from the territorial jurisdiction of the local public entity. Therefore, the present ordinance must have binding force within the boundaries of Niigata Prefecture and must apply to anyone entering that area. Such validity is recognized, except where special provisions are enacted in statutes or ordinances or where it is clear from the special nature of the ordinance that it applies only to residents, but such intent cannot be recognized in the present ordinance. Therefore, even though the accused in the present case is a resident of Nagano Prefecture, he cannot escape liability in the territory of Niigata Prefecture for actions to which the penal provisions of Article 5 of the present ordinance apply. Consequently, it cannot be recognized that there was a violation of statute in the original decision.)

The argument that there was an improper weighing of the offense does not conform with the reasons for appeal to the Supreme Court stated in Article 405 of the Code of Criminal Procedure.

The Court decides as stated in the formal judgment and in accordance with Article 408 of the Code of Criminal Procedure.[4]

This judgment is the unanimous opinion of the Justices, except for the minority opinion of Justice Fujita Hachirō.

*   *   *

The minority opinion of Justice Fujita Hachirō follows.

I am in accord with the part of the majority opinion that holds

4. See footnote 4, p. 16.

that it is against the intent of the Constitution and impermissible to place prior restraints upon parades, processions, and mass demonstrations under an ordinance that provides for a general system of licensing rather than a system of simple notification of the authorities, because the people have the basic freedom to demonstrate unless the purpose and the means of demonstration are improper and against the public welfare. Also I am in accord with the parts of the majority opinion that hold that Article 4, paragraph 1, stipulating that the public safety commission must grant a license in "cases wherein it recognizes that there is no threat of a disturbance to public order" as a necessary condition, is extremely general and abstract; that if it is decided not to grant a license on that condition alone there would be danger that parades, processions, and mass demonstrations would be subject to improper limitation at the discretion of the public safety commission; and that if the present ordinance used such a general and abstract standard as the only basis for decision, then it would have to be recognized as not being in accord with the spirit of the Constitution.

However, the majority opinion, while approving the principle above, held the present ordinance to be constitutional solely on the ground that it does not have the intent to restrict the above mass demonstrations by a general system of licensing, but only provides that there may be "occasions for restricting specific places and procedures of demonstration." It is clear that the phrase "restricting specific places and procedures" refers to the parenthetical statement in Article 1, namely, "anything that involves marching or the exclusive use of a place that the public can freely traverse on foot or by vehicle such as a road or a park."

Every parade, procession, or mass demonstration that will cause dispute will involve marching or exclusive occupation of a road, park, or other place that the public can freely traverse on foot or by vehicle, and it is not an exaggeration to say that mass activity using any other place or procedure would never become a problem. To apply the licensing system to all mass activity carried out in places or by methods indicated in the above ordinance is nothing more than a general and abstract restriction on such activity, and treating it as a localized restraint involving specific designation of area and procedure cannot escape the criticism that it is being termed something other than it really is.

The majority opinion points out that Article 1, paragraph 2, and Articles 6 and 7 exclude from the application of the ordinance certain activities that, because they are similar or closely related to activities dealt with in the ordinance, might easily be made its objects. This is offered as evidence that the present ordinance is not a general restraint. However, Article 1, paragraph 2, contains only the following stipulation: "Parades and processions involving only students, pupils, or children and carried out for educational purposes as prescribed in a course of study and under the direction of a responsible person of the school concerned do not require a license." Needless to say, this is not sufficient grounds to claim that there is no general restraint, for it excludes only this type of activity. Rather, this stipulation has the powerful opposite effect of making it abundantly clear that all mass activities other than such educational ones must be licensed.

The stipulations of Articles 6 and 7 are no more than indications of legislators' arbitrary interpretations of the meaning of the ordinance—for example, that it must not be interpreted as giving to any public official the right to control or supervise any public assembly or as requiring licenses for public speeches—and it is perfectly clear from an examination of the language of these passages that they add nothing at all to what is termed the "specific places and procedures" in the majority opinion.

On the whole this ordinance requires that all parades, processions, and mass demonstrations that are held in parks or on roads, except for educational travel, and the like, as provided for in Article 1, paragraph 2, must always be licensed beforehand by the public safety commission and if carried out without such a license be subject to a fine of not more than ¥50,000 or imprisonment of not more than a year. Also, Article 4 provides that the "public safety commission shall in cases wherein it recognizes . . . no threat of a disturbance of public safety, grant a license . . . ," and this means, in the language of the majority opinion, that "the opposite interpretation must also be accepted, and 'in cases wherein it recognizes that there is a threat of disturbance to public order,' licenses will not be granted." Thus, the decision of whether there is a threat to public safety in such activity is left to the extremely broad—particularly since no standards were set up—discretion of the public safety commission.

Naturally, this group activity is closely related to the freedoms of expression and assembly guaranteed by the Constitution, and as the majority opinion points out, any general prohibition of such activity or the delegation of licensing to the broad discretion of a public safety commission is not in accord with the spirit of the Constitution; and yet, as I have explained, the majority opinion has not offered any convincing proof that this ordinance does not involve a general prohibition of such activity.

Because I cannot agree with the majority opinion, which holds that there is no general prohibition, I must conclude that this ordinance is unconstitutional, although I agree with the major premise of the majority opinion.

*   *   *

The supplementary opinion of Justices Inouye Nobori and Iwamatsu Saburō follows.

The Constitution guarantees the freedom of individuals, but this guarantee is not unlimited. There can, of course, be cases in which the free conduct of one person is obstructed by the free conduct of another. In such cases, needless to state, if both parties are left to take their own free courses, conflict may occur between them, thus threatening a disturbance of public order. In these cases, therefore, it may be necessary to impose certain proper restrictions on freedom by law and regulations to maintain public order; this should be permitted without being deemed unconstitutional. Since it is apprehended that parades, processions, or mass demonstrations as stipulated in the present ordinance have considerable effect on the passage and other free acts of the general public, control thereof to a certain extent by prefectural ordinances and the like under the necessity of maintaining order (the public welfare) should not be regarded as unconstitutional.

Since to exercise such control it is necessary to know beforehand by what method and in what place these activities are to be held, a notification that states the place, the procedure, and other particulars is required. Further, if activities in certain places or by certain procedures seem to threaten the public welfare, either a prohibition or an appropriate limitation may be necessary and permissible. Such being the case, it may safely be said that the prohibition of activities conducted without notification or punishment (of course, within the limits permitted by law) of those violating the prohibition may be allowed in order to make effective such a system of notification. Some hold that the present ordinance is not permissible because it is based on the license system, not the notification system. The present ordinance uses the term "license," but it specifically prescribes cases wherein license will not be granted and provides that license must be granted in cases not falling under the preceding limitation (Article 4, paragraph 1), and further it states that the same effect as licensing will be given unless a manifestation of intention not to grant license is specifically made (Article 4, paragraph 4). Therefore, the term "license" is used, but the essence of its meaning differs not at all from prohibition for just cause under a system of notification.

Accordingly, it is meaningless to state that a "notification" system is permissible but that the present ordinance is impermissible, by seizing only on the word "license." Of course, Article 4, paragraph 1, of the present ordinance may be interpreted, on the other hand, to mean that a public safety commission, in cases where it recognizes that there is danger of disturbance of public order, may not grant a license. Therefore, in cases in which the said commission does not grant a request for a license because of a mistaken recognition of a threat to public order, there may be some room for a question of unconstitutionality involving Article 1 of the ordinance and the denial of the license.

However, because the present case deals with proceedings in the court of first instance in which there was no request for a license, it cannot be said that there was unconstitutionality involved in the original judgment, which concerned the sentencing of the accused without reference to the possible unconstitutionality of Article 1 under discussion here. After all, using license in the sense pointed out above, the ordinance cannot be regarded as unconstitutional simply because it requires an application for license and provides for the punishment of those who violate the requirement. Since the present decision held that Article 1 was constitutional simply by way of precaution and since this matter can be used as a guide for many cases pending in the lower courts involving violations of similar ordinances, it cannot be said that, in this sense, the decision recorded an unnecessary matter; however it [the constitutionality of Article 1] was a superfluous factor in the judging of the present case. Therefore, it is reasonable to uphold the present judgment regardless of whether the above Article 1 is constitutional.

(TRANSLATED BY IKEDA MASAAKI)

V: LICENSING OF PUBLIC GATHER-
INGS (THE TOKYO ORDINANCE
DECISION)

Hanreishū, XIV, No. 9, 1243 (Criminal)

EDITORIAL NOTE: In the initial stage of the occupation the Japanese government was required by the occupation authorities to repeal existing legislation that restricted freedom of expression and association. After the middle of 1948, however, at the suggestion of the American military government detachments, Japanese prefectural and municipal assemblies enacted local ordinances imposing on persons proposing to hold assemblies or demonstrations the duty to notify the local public safety commission, and empowering the latter, in certain circumstances, to refuse permission. By 1960, sixty-nine local authorities throughout the country had enacted some such regulations.

The Supreme Court on November 24, 1954, found the Niigata ordinance constitutional (see preceding decision) and subsequently applied the same reasoning to find the Saga, Saitama, and Tokuyama ordinances constitutional. In June, 1958, and October, 1959, however, the Tokyo District Court ruled the Tokyo ordinance unconstitutional. Moreover, in November, 1959 (when the demonstrations against the revision of the U.S.–Japan Security Treaty were beginning), the Tokyo District Court, arguing that the ordinance was unconstitutional, refused to authorize the detention of demonstrating students arrested by the police.

In these circumstances the Supreme Court, at the request of the Tokyo district prosecutor, agreed to deal with three cases simultaneously as a matter of urgency: an appeal directly to the Supreme

Court from a decision of "unconstitutional" by the Tokyo District Court, and appeals against the Hiroshima and Shizuoka High Courts' decisions of "constitutional" and "unconstitutional," respectively.

Of the three cases, the Court selected the Tokyo case as the most suitable for giving its reasoning in detail. The decision that emerged was received with dissatisfaction by many Japanese academic lawyers. In particular, they criticized (as does Justice Fujita) the Court for reversing its line of reasoning in the Niigata decision without explaining its reasons for so doing.

Grand Bench decision, July 20, 1960: Decisions set aside; retrial ordered.

REFERENCES

Ordinance Concerning Assemblies, Processions, and Demonstrations (Tokyo Ordinance No. 44 of 1950). ARTICLE 1. When intending to conduct assemblies or processions on roads or in other public places, or demonstrations in any place whatsoever, the consent of the public safety commission must be received; provided that this shall not apply to the following:

(i) excursions and travel by students, physical training, and sport;
(ii) the normal ceremonies connected with coming of age, marriage, death, religion, etc.

ARTICLE 2. The application for consent containing the following shall be tendered in triplicate through the police station in whose area of jurisdiction the event will take place, by the individual or the representative of the organization sponsoring it, at least seventy-two hours before the assembly, procession, or demonstration is to take place:

(i) name and address of the sponsor;
(ii) where the sponsor lives outside the ward . . . city, town, or village where the event is to take place, the name and address of a person concerned and responsible there;
(iii) the time of the assembly, procession, or demonstration;
(iv) the route or place of the assembly, procession, or demonstration, and a sketch map;
(v) the name of the organizations that intend to participate and the names and addresses of persons representing them;

(vi) the number of persons intending to participate;
(vii) the object and name of the assembly, procession, or demonstration.

ARTICLE 3. The public safety commission, when it receives the application prescribed in the preceding article, must give its consent except where it is clearly recognized that the carrying out of the assembly, procession, or demonstration will directly endanger the maintenance of public peace; provided that it may attach necessary conditions with respect to the following:

(i) the prevention of interference with the business of public offices;
(ii) restricting the carrying of firearms, offensive weapons, and other dangerous articles and the prevention of danger arising therefrom;
(iii) preserving the flow of traffic;
(iv) maintaining the orderliness of the assembly, procession, or demonstration;
(v) the maintenance of quiet at night;
(vi) changes in the route, place, or time when unavoidable for the preservation of public order or public health.

The public safety commission, having given its consent, shall endorse one copy of the application to that effect, and unless there are special reasons shall return it to the sponsor or the person concerned and responsible, at least twenty-four hours before the assembly, procession, or demonstration is to take place.

The public safety commission, notwithstanding the preceding paragraph, may revoke its consent or change the conditions attached, when it becomes clearly recognized that there is urgent need to preserve public order.

The public safety commission, when it refuses permission under the first paragraph of this article, or when it revokes consent according to the preceding paragraph, shall promptly report to that effect, enclosing its detailed reasons, to the local government assembly of the area to which the public safety commission belongs.

ARTICLE 4. A police chief in order to maintain public order may warn or stop the actions of persons participating in an assembly, procession, or demonstration that is being held in contravention of: Article 1; the matters contained in the application pursuant to Article 2; the conditions attached pursuant to the proviso to Article 3, paragraph 1; or Article 3, paragraph 3. In addition, he may take the requisite steps, to the extent necessary, to rectify such breaches.

ARTICLE 5. A sponsor whose application under Article 2 contains a falsehood, or any sponsor, leader, or inciter of an assembly, procession, or demonstration held contrary to: Article 1; the matters contained in the application pursuant to Article 2; the conditions attached pursuant to the proviso to Article 3, paragraph 1; or Article 3, paragraph 3, shall be sentenced to a maximum of one year's imprisonment or a fine of not more than ¥50,000.

ARTICLE 6. No provision of these regulations shall be interpreted as conferring on any public safety commission, police officer, or police employee, or any other prefectural or municipal official or employee, any authority to prohibit or restrict the holding of meetings other than meetings, processions, and demonstrations prescribed in Article 1, or to supervise meetings or political movements, or to censor placards, publications, or other documents or drawings.

ARTICLE 7. No provision of these regulations shall be interpreted as conflicting with legislation concerning elections to public office or as requiring prior notification in the case of political meetings or speeches during election campaigns.

Constitution of Japan. ARTICLE 21. 1. Freedom of assembly and association as well as speech, press, and all other forms of expression are guaranteed.

2. No censorship shall be maintained, nor shall the secrecy of any means of communication be violated.

FORMAL JUDGMENT

The part of the judgment appealed against that relates to the defendants [holding them not guilty] is set aside. Case to be retried in the Tokyo District Court.

REASONS. Regarding item I in the Statement of Appeal tendered by Mr. Okazaki representing the Tokyo District Prosecutor's Office: Freedom of assembly, association, publication, and all other kinds of expression, as provided in Article 21 of the Constitution, are among the eternal and inviolable rights, namely, the fundamental human rights. That they be completely guaranteed is one of the fundamental principles of democratic government. That this is the most important feature that distinguishes democracy from totalitarianism goes without saying. The people, however, may not abuse these freedoms, but have a responsibility at all times to exercise them for the public welfare; in this respect they do not differ from other fundamental rights (see Article 12 of the Constitution). Accordingly, under the Japanese Constitution the task of the courts in dealing with individual concrete cases is to protect freedom of expression and, at the same time, by preventing its abuse and by striking a balance between it and the public welfare, to draw a proper boundary between freedom and the public welfare.

In this case the Tokyo Metropolitan Ordinance Concerning Assemblies, Processions, and Demonstrations (Ordinance No. 44 of 1950, hereafter referred to as "the ordinance") is in dispute. To decide whether it conforms with the Constitution is to decide whether it improperly restricts the freedom of expression guaranteed by the Constitution by exceeding the requirements set forth in the Constitution that prohibit the abuse of freedom and enjoin the maintenance of the public welfare.

The subjects of the controls in the ordinance are assemblies or processions on roads or in other public places and mass demonstrations in any place whatsoever. (Such activities shall hereafter be referred to as "collective activities.") The basic question is whether such collective activities must be left completely unfettered or whether in the interests of the public welfare (in the present case, the maintenance of public peace) they may be subjected to some type of legal regulation.

Collective activities (with the exception of school excursions and tours, and so forth, and ceremonies connected with coming of age, marriage, death, festivals, and the like) generally involve the expression of thoughts, contentions, or feelings regarding politics, economics, labor, and so forth, or concerning one's basic philosophy, in order to appeal to the general populace. In this respect, of course, collective activity contains essential elements that, as freedom of expression, should be guaranteed by the Constitution. As a means of expressing thoughts, collective activities,

however, differ from mere speech or writing: they are characterized by the fact that they are supported by the might of a large
number of people actually assembled together in a body, a type
of latent physical force. Such latent force by its nature can be
set in motion very easily, whether in accordance with a preconceived plan or unexpectedly as a result of incitement or excitement
either from within or from without. In such circumstances there
is the danger that even a quiet crowd will sometimes become
caught up in a vortex of excitement and anger, and in extreme
cases it will turn suddenly into a mob whose own momentum im-
pels it toward the violation of law and order, a situation in which
both the crowd's own leaders and the police are powerless. So much
is clear from the laws of crowd psychology and from actual experience. Therefore, even though Article 21, paragraph 2, of the
Constitution prohibits censorship—previous restraint—of publication that can be called "expression" in the strict sense, it is, after
all, unavoidable that local authorities, in due consideration of both
local and general circumstances, adopt prior to the fact the minimum measures necessary to maintain law and order and to guard
against unforeseen situations by means of what are termed "public
safety ordinances," but only in respect to expression by means of
collective action.

Accepting this, what level can be approved as minimum and
necessary? This cannot be determined merely by reference to concepts or terms—problems of whether the ordinance requires the
sponsors of collective activities to obtain "a license" or whether
it merely requires them to give prior "notification." Moreover, in
determining this we must consider the spirit of the ordinance
as a whole, not superficially, but as a functional entity.

When we come to examine the ordinance, we see the permission
of the public safety commission is required for collective activities
(Article 1). However, the commission must give such permission
except "where it is clearly recognized" that the carrying out of
the collective activity "will directly endanger the maintenance of
public peace" (Article 3). That is to say, it has a duty to give
permission; the circumstances in which it can refuse are strictly
limited. Thus, although the ordinance, so far as the wording of its
provisions is concerned, adopts a licensing system, this system in
essentials nowhere differs from one of notification. The pre-

requisites for collective activities, whether license or notification, are immaterial so long as freedom of expression is not thereby improperly restricted. Naturally, "where it is clearly recognized that the maintenance of public peace will be directly endangered" license will not be given. This, however, is unavoidable in view of the fact that local authorities have a responsibility to the inhabitants to maintain law and order. That it is within the discretion of the public safety commission to decide, when granting or refusing permission, whether such a situation exists, follows naturally from the fact that these are matters of such a nature that they should be decided by concrete study and consideration of the various factors operating in the particular situation. We cannot straightway find the ordinance unconstitutional and void merely because we can visualize situations where a decision not to grant permission would be improper; nor can we do so on the ground that the applicant is provided with no means of redress when the appointed day arrives and the decision is still deferred.

In the ordinance there is no provision that the collective activity may take place as if permitted, when the public safety commission has given no indication of refusal by a certain time before its scheduled commencement. From this the original decision made the interpretation that to carry out the collective activity in such circumstances is prohibited and that if the sponsors, and so forth do so they will be punished; it inferred that the ordinance is a general prohibition on collective activities; and it accordingly concluded that it is unconstitutional. However, in holding that in the absence of such a provision the meaning of the ordinance is to restrict freedom of expression by means of a licensing system, and that, accordingly, the ordinance is unconstitutional *in toto,* the conclusion of the original decision mistakenly evaluates the problem and is quite wrong.

Then, the original decision, dealing with the places in which collective activities subject to control take place, criticizes the restrictions as ill-defined and lacking in concreteness because the ordinance sets up general or almost general restrictions in such phrases as "in streets and other public places" with respect to assemblies and processions and "in any place whatsoever" with respect to mass demonstrations. However, once it is agreed that there is the need to place a legal limit on collective activities, then one must either list with some degree of generality the places where collective activities can be held, or provide that the ordinance applies to such activities wheresoever occurring. One cannot say that because it does not set forth a somewhat more detailed standard (e.g., "a place that the public can freely traverse . . . such as a road or park") as can be seen in other ordinances, it is unconstitutional and invalid. Furthermore, even though it be admitted that mass demonstrations are subject to a general restriction in that the ordinance applies to them "in any place whatsoever," it is inconceivable from their nature that they will be held in places utterly unused by the public; to debate this is completely profitless.

To sum up, the subject matter of the ordinance, collective activity (and particularly mass demonstrations), comprises material force. A dangerous attribute of material force is that it may exceed the bounds of the exercise of pure freedom of expression (which should comport itself peacefully, respecting order) and disturb the peace, developing into violence. Hence, it cannot be denied that some degree of legal regulation is necessary. The state and society must, of course, accord the maximum respect to freedom of expression. However, it must be acknowledged that the authorities should know in advance of activities that, in the guise of freedom of speech, may disrupt peace and order by collective activity or that contain such tendencies, and that they should be able to prepare against unforeseen situations and take proper action. Nevertheless, it cannot be said that the ordinance is entirely free from the danger that it may be used in such a way as to violate the guarantee of freedom of expression provided in Article 21 of the Constitution. It goes without saying that a public safety commission in applying the ordinance must use the utmost care to ensure that it does not abuse its powers and, under the guise of maintaining the peace, repress peaceful and orderly collective activities. However, it is improper to hold the ordinance unconstitutional by saying that there is the possibility of abuse.

For the above reasons the contentions of the appellant are correct, and the original decision, which held the ordinance unconstitutional and invalid, must be set aside.

Accordingly, judgment is given as in the formal judgment in accordance with Articles 410(i), 405(i), and 413 of the Code of

Criminal Procedure.[1] This judgment is unanimous save for the dissenting opinions of Justices Fujita Hachirō and Tarumi Katsumi.

*   *   *

The dissenting opinion of Justice Fujita Hachirō follows.

As the majority opinion states, the complete guarantee of freedom of expression provided in Article 21 of the Constitution is one of the most important of the basic principles of democratic government, and the state and society must accord the maximum respect to freedom of expression. Moreover, the precedents of this Court have long indicated that the guarantee of freedom of expression under the new Constitution differs from that under the old: it cannot be arbitrarily restricted even by legislation. The majority opinion acknowledges that "assemblies and processions on roads or in other public places, and mass demonstrations in any place whatsoever," the subject matter of the Tokyo Metropolitan Ordinance, all possess essential elements of freedom of expression, which is guaranteed by the Constitution. (However, both because "freedom of assembly" is directly and explicitly guaranteed by Article 21 of the Constitution and because the present case, inasmuch as it concerns collective activities, does not deal directly with "freedom of assembly," I omit here the question of whether a system that subjects the Constitution's "freedom of assembly" to licensing is constitutional.) This Court, however, has already held that freedom of expression in the new Constitution must be regulated in accordance with the public welfare, since fundamental human rights, though ensured in the Constitution, may not be abused by the people, who have a responsibility to use them for the public welfare. Such being the case, ". . . it is, after all, un-

---

1. *Code of Criminal Procedure.* ARTICLE 410, paragraph 1. The courts of *Jōkoku* appeal shall quash the original judgment, by means of a judgment, if it finds out that there exists any of the grounds for quashing provided by each item of Article 405. However, this shall not apply if the existence of the ground does not affect the judgment at all.

On Article 405, paragraph 1, see footnote 2, p. 77.

Code of Criminal Procedure. ARTICLE 413. When the original judgment is to be quashed on any ground other than the grounds mentioned in the preceding article ["that the court illegally considered itself competent"], the case shall be either sent back to the original court or the court of first instance, or transferred to another court in the same class as these courts, by means of a judgment. However, if the court of *Jōkoku* appeal recognizes that it may immediately render a judgment on the basis of record and evidence already made and examined by the original court or court of first instance, it may render the judgment for the case.

avoidable that local public authorities, in due consideration of both local and general circumstances, adopt prior to the fact the minimum measures necessary to maintain law and order and to guard against unforeseen situations by means of what are termed public safety ordinances," and whether or not the Tokyo Metropolitan Ordinance, which is at issue in the present case, is constitutional will depend on whether the provisions set forth in the ordinance are permissible as "the necessary, unavoidable minimum restriction" on the freedom of expression guaranteed by the Constitution.

The fifteen justices of the Grand Bench of the Supreme Court, when they earlier considered the constitutionality of the Niigata Prefectural Ordinance, were unanimous that it

. . . is a proper interpretation to say that it is against the intent of the Constitution and impermissible to place prior restraints upon parades, processions, and mass demonstrations . . . under an ordinance that provides for a general system of licensing rather than a system of simple notification, because the people have the basic freedom to demonstrate unless the purpose and manner of the demonstration are improper and against the public welfare.

Thus, the Court made clear the basic principles relating to this type of freedom and to restrictions on it (*Hanreishū*, VIII, No. 11, 1866 <Criminal>, November 24, 1954). This should be understood as a clear declaration that any system is incompatible with the nature of freedom of expression and is constitutionally impermissible if it subjects activities of this kind concerning freedom of expression to over-all licensing by administrative agencies so that this freedom can be enjoyed only if there has been an administrative act permitting it, while in the absence of permission such activities are punishable as unlawful. It means that since a notification system, on the other hand, does not wait on the acts of administrative agencies but merely requires of those who wish to express themselves that they should give notice, it does not violate the essence of freedom of expression, although it enables steps to be taken in advance, in response to the notification, to prevent the emergence of unforeseeable situations. Hence, it means that this degree of control is unavoidable under present conditions.

(The Grand Bench in another decision on November 24, 1954, held in dealing with the constitutionality of legislation relating to the regulation of moneylending that since anyone who gives noti-

fication may freely carry on the business of moneylending, whereas
a person who does so without making notification is punished
under such legislation, this cannot be considered the improper
suppression of his freedom to choose his occupation.)

The fundamental principles relating to liberty and restrictions
on liberty set forth in the Grand Bench decision on the Niigata ordinance must always be adhered to, for they are based on a thorough understanding of the fundamental human rights that the
Constitution guarantees. We cannot reject them as dealing with
mere concepts or terms. It is because such principles must be adhered to that West German, French, and Italian legislation has, in
regulating such activities, adopted notification systems, not licensing systems. This also, no doubt, is the starting point of the doctrine underlying the decisions in which on many occasions over
the years the United States Supreme Court has held to be unconstitutional state laws and municipal ordinances that adopted licensing for conduct involving freedom of expression. I cannot believe
that today the majority opinion means summarily to alter the
basic principles set forth in the Grand Bench decision on the
Niigata ordinance.

The majority opinion however comments as follows on Article
3 of the Tokyo Metropolitan Ordinance:

The [public safety] commission must give such permission except "where it is
clearly recognized" that the carrying out of the collective activity "will directly
endanger the maintenance of public peace." That is to say, it has a duty to give
permission; the circumstances in which it can refuse are strictly limited. Thus,
although the ordinance, so far as the wording of its provisions is concerned,
adopts a licensing system, this system in essentials nowhere differs from one of
notification.

It is obvious, however, that one cannot say, just because there is a
duty to give permission and the circumstances in which there can
be refusal are strictly limited, that such a system of licensing, in
essentials, nowhere differs from a system of notification. Apart
from differences in doctrine concerning the nature of this freedom,
once a public safety commission is given discretion to give or withhold permission for the activity itself we can, of course, no longer
consider it the same as a notification system. In dealing with the
point that "in the ordinance there is no provision that the collective activity may take place as if permitted, when the public safety

commission has given no indication of refusal by a certain time before its scheduled commencement," the majority opinion argues that "holding that in the absence of such a provision the meaning of the ordinance is to restrict freedom of expression by means of a licensing system . . . mistakenly evaluates the problem. . . ."

To decide whether the content of a particular piece of legislation is unconstitutional, however, requires, of course, not only an over-all consideration of the meaning of the legislation, but also a careful examination, article by article, of the individual provisions of which the legislation consists. Accordingly, I consider that the presence or absence of such a provision is a vital factor in determining whether, although the ordinance by its wording adopts a licensing system, it can be said to be in essentials no different from a notification system. One of the important factors that caused the majority in the Niigata ordinance case to hold that, although it constituted a licensing system, it was nevertheless constitutional, was that it contained such a provision and that they considered the various provisions of that ordinance as "the organic whole." This is readily apparent if one compares the majority opinion and the supplementary opinions. The presence of such a provision is to be regarded as the *sine qua non* that enables us to regard the system as the equivalent of a notification system, while being a licensing system. There is no such provision in the Tokyo Metropolitan Ordinance.

In the ordinance the standard to be used in deciding whether to give or refuse permission is whether or not it is clearly recognized that the maintenance of the public peace will be directly endangered. This indicates that granting or refusal is not based on considerations of traffic control or on the necessities of administering buildings in public places (there is other legislation regulating these matters), but is based solely on the necessity of maintaining public order. The determination whether there is a clear and present danger to public order is to be made before the event, at the latest twenty-four hours before it is due to commence. It is entrusted solely to the discretion of the public safety commission on whose decision freedom to indulge in such activity is to depend. Thus, in this system there is no safeguard against the dangers of previous restraint. The majority opinion states that ". . . it cannot be said that the ordinance is entirely free from the danger that it may be used in such a way as to violate the guarantee of freedom of expression provided in Article 21 of the Constitution." Nevertheless, it continues, ". . . it is improper to hold the ordinance unconstitutional by saying that there is the possibility of abuse." The decision whether or not legislation is constitutional, however, largely depends on whether there are in the legislation itself provisions sufficient to prevent its abuse. Furthermore, in the case of legislation restricting freedom of expression, the greatest possible consideration must, of course, be given in the content of the regulations themselves to prevent such abuse. To blame the way a piece of legislation is applied is to disregard its normative nature. Insofar as the ordinance adopts a system of previous restraint, it cannot be said that in providing the aforementioned standard the maximum consideration has been given to preventing abuse. It is absolutely impossible to treat the licensing system in this case, on the basis of this standard, as essentially no different from a notification system. (In addition, I can readily concur in the lower court's observations that the licensing system embodied in the ordinance cannot be considered the same as a notification system.)

For the above reasons I, together with the lower court, am unable to accept the licensing system of the ordinance as the minimum, necessarily unavoidable restriction on freedom of expression. I must conclude that it does not accord with the meaning of the Constitution.

The majority opinion, like the prosecutor's, stressed that such activities are easily set in motion and are likely to cause unforeseeable disasters. One must not, however, be so obsessed with the necessity of regulation as to lose sight of the essential nature of freedom guaranteed by the Constitution. One must not easily lapse into controls; one must adopt an attitude of vigilance when considering the great precepts of the Constitution. Justice Roberts of the Supreme Court of the United States said in *Hague* v. *Congress of Industrial Organizations* (1939), "But uncontrolled official suppression of the privilege cannot be made a substitute for the duty to maintain order in connection with the exercise of the right." Furthermore, in *Saia* v. *New York* (1947), the majority held that, "Courts must balance the various community interests in passing on the constitutionality of local regulations of the character involved here. But in that process they should be mindful to keep the freedoms of the First Amendment in a preferred position."

These should be heeded. Since the ordinance, even when considered from the standpoint of measures to maintain public order, contains provisions that are obscure, it cannot be expected to be effective in operation.

I consider that what is urgent today is to meet the situation by providing regulations whose constitutionality is beyond question.

* * *

The dissenting opinion of Justice Tarumi Katsumi follows.

I.

Because of the presence of the phrase "in any place whatsoever" referring to demonstrations (but not to other types of collective activity) in Article 1 of the ordinance and because it contains no clause like Article 4 of the Niigata Ordinance (i.e., "In cases wherein the public safety commission that receives the written application . . . does not announce an intention either to refuse a license or to impose conditions twenty-four hours in advance of the time when the parade or demonstration is to be held, it may be carried out as if the license had been granted"), the provisions in the ordinance that subject mass demonstrations to a licensing system and that punish the sponsors, and so forth, of mass demonstrations that have taken place without a license or contrary to the conditions attached to such a license, are, in my opinion, contrary to Article 21, paragraph 1, of the Constitution.

I consider "in any place whatsoever" to mean parks, and the like, "provided for public use" and roads "provided for general thoroughfare" and, at the most, such places as privately owned areas similar to these (e.g., parking areas and vacant lots). Furthermore, it is not clear whether the meaning of the majority opinion is that, if by a particular time there has been no determination whether permission is given or withheld, the applicants and their organizations are at liberty to carry out their mass demonstration (in the manner stated in their application). If this is its meaning, it is not impossible to understand. However, since this meaning is not clearly indicated in the text of the ordinance, ordinary citizens will abandon mass demonstrations whenever they do not receive permission. Moreover, if mass demonstrations do take place in such circumstances, there is no guarantee that the police will not frequently deal with them as unlawful, unlicensed demonstrations and make arrests.

In actual fact when we come to examine the cases in which the Tokyo Public Safety Commission granted licenses on the single day, June 1, 1957, we see that the following meetings were sanctioned after applications had been lodged pursuant to Tokyo Metropolitan Ordinance No. 44 of 1950 (the subject of the present case): a social held by the film club of an insurance company (this was held in the Tokyo Electric Company's Ginza Building); a film preview in a temple compound sponsored by a Tokyo adult education society; the reunion of Class IIId of a high school held in a city office building; a lecture on nutrition sponsored by the Honjo District Health Center at a private home; a film evening of a social club sponsored by an individual and held in his garden. (These facts are accepted on the basis of the evidence by the 4th Division <Criminal> of the Tokyo District Court in its judgment of October 13, 1959, in another case brought against Shiokawa, one of the accused in the present case, and one other in which Shiokawa was found not guilty.) Is there anyone who is not alarmed at this state of affairs? We must not be blind to this.

Where the ordinary man has been deceived into thinking that a road has been blocked, this will prevent many people from passing along it. It is not right later to say to the people who gave up their plan to pass along it, "You could have passed." This is to bewilder the public. Even though, after the opportunity to hold the proposed demonstration has been lost, one tried to take to court the failure of the authorities to make a decision either way, permitting or refusing to permit the demonstration, the suit would be rejected for the reason given by the Grand Bench in its decision of December 23, 1953 (*Hanreishū*, VII, No. 13, 1561): "The suit for the annulment of the decision refusing the use of the Imperial Palace Plaza on May Day, 1952, contains no legal interest requiring adjudication, since the day in question has passed." There is no means of redress. Accordingly, I consider that it is proper to regard the provisions of the ordinance that relate to mass demonstrations as contrary to Article 21 of the Constitution because

they set indefinite standards that make it possible by licensing to
suppress the freedom to demonstrate. In those cases where no decision permitting or refusing the application has been made within
the prescribed time limit, yet the scheduled demonstration has still
taken place, if you ask me, the reason why the leaders are not to be
punished is that the ordinance is defective and unconstitutional.
Inasmuch as we are dealing with the restriction of freedom of expression, it is wrong to go so far as the majority opinion and interpret the ordinance as constitutional. The above-mentioned
provisions, which limit freedom of expression, need to be amended
and made definite.

What worries me more than this is that the majority opinion in
deciding the ordinance constitutional, may have cast away its
strict standard [for allowing restriction only] "where it is clearly
recognized that [the carrying out of the collective activity] will
directly endanger the maintenance of public peace." In other
words, have they not introduced a new and broad standard that
is abstract and open to wide interpretation? When the majority
say "to guard against unforeseen and emergency situations" (I
suppose they mean unexpected and unforeseeable), they are using
a much wider concept than "where it is clearly recognized that
[the carrying out of the collective activity] will directly endanger the maintenance of public peace." The same goes for their
"necessary to maintain law and order" and "activities that
[. . .] may injure peace and order [. . .] that contain such
tendencies." The majority would probably not say that they are
making a new standard out of these. If, however, such a standard
is adopted, then freedom of expression by groups will be capable
of almost any curtailment by laws and ordinances and the majority would thereby be at variance with Article 21 of the Constitution and close to the Meiji Constitution's "Japanese subjects
shall, within the limits of law, enjoy the liberty of speech, writing,
publication, public meetings and associations." I hope that I am
mistaken in my interpretation of the majority opinion, and that I
am too apprehensive. As the majority opinion states, the people
are always responsible for using for the public welfare the freedoms and rights guaranteed by the Constitution (Article 12 of the
Constitution). Freedom of expression, however, may not be restricted by the abstract yardstick "for the public welfare," but by

a reasonable and definite standard appropriate to each type of expression: in the case of group expression, appropriate to group expression. Freedom of expression is so vital under the Constitution that it differs from other rights and freedoms.

I consider that the provisions in the ordinance relating to mass demonstrations are contrary to Article 21, paragraph 1 of the Constitution and that as a consequence the court of first instance was correct in holding that the ordinance was unconstitutional and in not applying it to the acts of Itō, Matsunaga, Shiokawa, and Ogawa whom it accordingly found not guilty. Hence, I consider the appeal [of the prosecution] to be without grounds.

I wish next to set forth briefly the reasons that have led me to the above conclusions.

II. Basic Positions

Whereas all men may engage in intellectual or physical work according to their talents and ability, and may receive adequate moral and physical sustenance, none may exploit the fruits of another's labor and eat without toiling. We must eliminate the situation in which men end their lives in misery and poverty. Today this is the principle set forth in all the constitutions of mankind throughout the world and in the "Universal Declaration of Human Rights." However, it is natural that the people, aware that this is a noble principle not to be infringed by individuals, should consider that no matter how fully they are endowed with material happiness (and even with some types of spiritual happiness), a society robbed of freedom (particularly intellectual and political freedom) can barely be said to be alive. The soul of the Japanese Constitution is that one of the most vital of the basic freedoms of which no man may be deprived and which may not be transgressed is freedom of expression.

What is that soul? It is that each individual is an object worthy of pride and respect. Every citizen may freely meditate and freely express his meditations on what is truth, what is good, and what is beautiful in the realms of religion, belief, morals, scholarship, and philosophy, and in every field: society, politics, economics, culture, art, and so forth. Furthermore, he is entitled to know the views of other people differing from his own. When thought is deepened and refined by vigorous and free mutual discussion without physical violence and by exchange of artistic expression, then every man can by developing, maturing, and refining his individuality, perfect himself and lead a significant and noble life. Moreover, this provides a legacy to future generations and a great contribution to the progress of all mankind. Provided that the law and the government do not place discussion under control but recognize free competition in expression, truth will finally prevail and "a hundred flowers will bloom together and bear fruit." This is the rejection of absolute conformity. If free competition in discussion and expression is suppressed or controlled, the very spirit of the people will harden into orthodoxy, will atrophy and stagnate like a world in which all sports contests have been forbidden and no new records can be expected.

Moreover, every citizen must inquire abroad of the events of the day and must be told the truth. It is only by the people's hearing the voice of the inner feelings of the many—by hearing outspoken advice and reports of grievous events—that there can be enlightened government founded on reality and complying with the will of the people. Where there is not sufficient information, the people can be deceived by rumors and by false reports. If the people are given only limited news as in an official gazette, they will very soon become blind and deaf; and if it is so contrived that discussion in open meeting is reduced, the people will become submissively obedient mutes. In the field of history, also, the people must tell and be told the truth. There must be no control whereby they are told history selected in accordance with a particular ideology in which some facts are obliterated and others exaggerated. At the same time, it is vital that every individual should have the freedom not to express something, and not to see or hear something. Therefore, under our Constitution there is a general freedom to spread abroad any religion or belief; or anarchism, communism, or dictatorship—each of which advocates abolishing the present Constitution; or inequality of the sexes. This is both the weakness and the strength of a liberal constitution. Hence, the Constitution guarantees that this freedom will not be oppressed either by legislation or administrative action irrespective of the ideology or policy of government, Diet, or local assembly, and provides that if it is suppressed such suppression will be held unconstitutional and invalid by the courts.

The following, I suppose, are the essentials of communism and communist socialism: land, buildings, factories, transport and communications, and all other important means of production are to be taken from private individuals and placed under social ownership; production is to be carried on not in accordance with individual freedom, but according to plan and by the labor of all; each person's share of material and spiritual life must also be according to plan. The ultimate aim is to bring about such a socialist system, making the whole world a single unit. Communism in one country is denied; the destiny of the state is that, like the feudal system, it should eventually wither away out of the historical necessity for mankind to advance. Nevertheless, a violent revolution (involving the wholesale destruction or seizure of life, limb and freedom of many people and of almost all important property) by the oppressed classes is the only method of achieving total confiscation and social ownership (or, at the outset, national ownership). This is because under the capitalist state today the capitalist class is exploiting the workers (i.e., the proletariat) and is unlikely to agree (even by the method of constitutional amendment) to the confiscation of its property. After the dawn when this revolution has been completed throughout the world, an eternally peaceful society will endure, without war, without nations, and without class struggle. The forces that aim at eternal peace are the progressive peace-loving forces that are opening the way for the destined advance of mankind. The people who oppose this are reactionaries. The wars waged by the capitalist class (irrespective of who fires the first shot) are all wars of aggression. The peace-loving forces must not sheath the sword until the world revolution has been completed and the counterrevolution utterly crushed. Even before the revolution they must discredit the capitalist legal system and bureaucratic authority, and, regardless of the means, must bring about the situation in which the revolution will take place. Is this not what they say?

If this is their teaching, it is patently contrary to the doctrines of our Constitution. Nevertheless, the freedom to propagate or listen to this teaching is guaranteed in the Constitution and it should be adequately heard. This is the toleration of thought which we find in liberal constitutions.

But if in the postrevolutionary society the system is one in which freedom of occupation and freedom to change one's residence are oppressed and, worse still, freedom of person, freedom of religion, academic freedom, freedom of assembly, association, discussion, publication, and all other types of freedom of expression are suppressed, and there is no freedom to speak in open meeting and the people are made ignorant of the truth, and expression and thought are controlled by force, then how in such a social situation can the people (comprising a large number of alert individuals rich in the spirit of independent self-respect) consider such a society worthwhile? That every man alike should suffer in poverty or be blessed with abundance is certainly an excellent thing. But if, however, men are robbed of their freedom of expression and all the people must submit to an iron discipline (these must be the new iron chains) concerning the political decisions and actions not only of the distinguished leaders at the summit but also of the host of petty leaders (who will have many faults because they are human beings), then will they not yearn for the liberal world on the shore opposite communistic socialism? For all this we cannot allow the Constitution to be changed other than by the procedure for constitutional amendment, nor can we allow it to be disregarded. Our people, and especially the judges, must protect the liberal Constitution, just as judges in countries whose ideology differs from ours must protect their constitutions.

Naturally the majority opinion does not deal with these points. The reason why I set down my own ideas is, however, not because I want to conjure up views different from theirs, but because I want to show the starting point of my views.

III. Restrictions on the Freedom of Expression by the Public Power

The object of Article 20 of the Constitution ("No religious organization shall receive any privileges from the State. . . . The State and its organs shall refrain from religious education or any other religious activity") and Article 21, paragraph 2 ("No censorship shall be maintained") is that neither the state nor its organs, by laws or ordinances, nor officials, by the public power, may maintain or restrain a religion or impose prior censorship on the expression of thought, and that on the other hand, the freedom of private persons to believe in or to maintain a religion or to reject it, and the freedom of private educational establishments to provide religious education will be guaranteed.

(However, just as the Constitution permits laws which do not confer the franchise on minors <Article 44> ["The qualifications of . . . electors shall be fixed by law"], I do not think that it affirms the freedom at governmental educational establishments, when teaching young people what is true, what is good, what is beautiful, to deny the ideals of the present Constitution, the spirit of democratic freedom, and the provisions of the Constitution.)

Under this freedom, private newspaper or magazine companies or private broadcasting stations are free, of course, to "censor" in advance news or the contents of broadcasts, omit and select material, and publish only what they wish. This is not "censorship." The limitation of the freedom of expression of individuals, even by laws and ordinances which are the manifestation of the common will of the citizens and residents, and a fortiori by the discretion of public officials, must be avoided to the utmost. Otherwise, the result will be that we shall have a society in which freedom is oppressed according to the arbitrary whim of officials (even though this may not be malicious). This is what Article 21 means. It means not so much that the Diet and public safety commissions are not to be trusted, but that freedom of expression is so important that it must be safeguarded by some device to ensure that they do not make errors. It is surely evident from the judicial system, in which the judges are firmly bound by the law, that constitutional government seeks to guarantee the rights and liberties of individuals by a system that regulates the acts of the state, its organs, and its officials—and places obligations on them. The Constitution, particularly where freedom of expression is concerned, must not be thought of as merely ensuring that the public power is not abused, but as requiring that there be provided a safeguard in the form of standards as reasonable and definite as possible to prevent officials from making errors of fact and law. This is because you cannot, when the freedom of the people to express their views and ideas is suppressed, have a democratic, politically free society in which the individual citizens and residents decide to make their own laws and ordinances in accordance with their own wishes, and in which such laws are to be obeyed by administrative agencies, by officials, and by themselves.

IV. The Meaning of Collective Activities

By "assembly," "speech," and "all other forms of expression" in Article 21 of the Constitution are meant things by nature peaceful in which no other elements are included. Hence, essentially, they refer only to peaceful activity. Similarly, Article 16 requires that "petition" shall be "peaceful." When one discusses "collective activities" one must above all recognize this. (See the First Amendment to the United States Constitution, "the right of the people peaceably to assemble, and to petition"; the West German Fundamental Law, Article 8, and the Italian Constitution, Article 17, "the right to assemble peacefully without arms.") Some people, interpreting collective activity accompanied by trespass, wounding, violence, by obstruction to trains and streetcars, by interference with officials in the course of their duties, by damage to buildings, and the like, to be demonstration in the proper sense, may insist that it is legitimate "use of force," whereas others, conversely, may consider that all collective activity may be regulated. Both groups are wrong. Nevertheless, you cannot say that an assembly is not peaceful merely because it is "boisterous and noisy." (This is clear when you compare such things as the uproar at festivals and the noise made by spectators at sporting events.)

Furthermore, economic activities in markets or squares [or "open areas"], such as buying and selling, soliciting employment, publicity and advertising, are excluded from "expression" as defined in Article 21 of the Constitution. Economic freedom may be restricted more rigorously than freedom of expression. Generally speaking, welcome or farewell groups, students traveling or going to school together, sports meetings, recreational groups, and collective activity connected with one's occupation (e.g., fire brigade practices) cannot be regarded as "expression." On the other hand, gatherings for musical recitals, drama, or the cinema pertain to artistic "expression."

In short, "assembly" as used in the Constitution means a gathering of people somewhere in order to exchange beliefs, information, emotions, views, hopes, or thoughts, to express these to the assembled listeners, and to appeal for their support. "Mass demonstrations" and "processions" in the ordinance, like assemblies, are essentially the expression of the thought of a peaceful group of people. Such expression, however, is not the mutual exchange of thoughts among members of the group, but the external expression of the agreed ideas of the group as a whole on a specific issue. Its purpose is to express their hopes, opposition, protest, agreement, or complaints about conditions to the government, the people, a segment thereof, or a particular person, thereby attracting the sympathy of the government, of various interests, and of people in general, and securing the fulfillment of the group's wishes. Moreover, although mass demonstrations sometimes do not move from a fixed place, they frequently operate like processions by moving through places provided for public use such as parks, squares, roads, or places provided for general thoroughfare. At such demonstrations and processions flags and placards are carried and there is shouting; sometimes loud-speakers are used. Processions are by foot or vehicle, by horse or by boat. In *jiiundō* [demonstration] the second ideograph [the *i* following the *ji*] is not to be given the connotation it has in the word *iryoku* [threat] which appears in Articles 234 and 96 (3) of the Criminal Code and in Article 1 of the "Law Relating to Violence, etc."; it has the same connotation as in *ikō* [authority], *ifū* [dignity], and *keni* [prestige]. *Jii* [*Ji*, to show; *i*, influence] means "influential." Therefore, *jiiundō* [*undō* means "movement," hence, *jiiundō* is literally "an influential movement" or "a movement to influence"] has the same meaning as the English word, "demonstration." One must not lose sight of this.

Because mass demonstrations and processions have the objects we have mentioned above, it is natural that they should often be held in places like parks and streets where they can be seen and heard by the ordinary citizen. Hence, it is conceivable that there may be competing demonstrations at the same time and place with opposing views or that the antipathy of numerous third parties will be aroused.

Furthermore, groups are assemblies of people who, as living organisms, have volume, weight, and energy and, in accordance with prearranged plans, following the orders of their leaders, can organize and concentrate their physical force using it either effectively, in a proper fashion, or destructively. Again, as the majority opinion states, one cannot say that there is absolutely no general danger that this will "be set in motion very easily . . . as a result of incitement or excitement either from within or from without," and that sometimes it will be "caught up in a vortex of excitement or anger," or fall into confusion which it itself cannot control, and that eventually there will be damage to life, limb, liberty, property, and so forth. If a large number of automobiles are used in the demonstration, the danger becomes all the greater.

Thus, if a group championing some cause or demand uses its volume of physical force to occupy or pass through a park or street where the general public may enter or pass, then you cannot say that the distant general danger is absolutely nonexistent, but that—depending on the scale of the collective activity, its object, its methods, and other factors—there may arise either by design or spontaneously, damage to life, limb, freedom, or property (this includes disasters where we cannot tell who was negligent). It is the same with assemblies. This must be said to be a special feature of activities of this nature wherein they differ from expression by newspapers, publication, radio, and the like, which do not use public property like parks and roads. They also have a special character distinguishing them from such things as excursions, publicity and advertising processions, and funerals that are "non-expression." You may say, "When we form a procession with our vehicles along the road, if our object is sightseeing, it is sufficient that we obey the traffic regulations, but if we do the same thing to seek the amendment of a law then, in addition to this, we must get permission. This means that because it is 'expression' we are subject to this additional restriction. Surely, this is topsy-turvy." But that collective activities should be able to be held freely, irrespective of time and route, irrespective of whether there are tens of thousands or hundreds of thousands of participants, is clearly against the dictates of logic and common sense. Herein lies the reason why collective activities may be lightly regulated by means of a notification or licensing system based on reasonable and clear standards.

In short, collective activities, as one would expect from their essential form, are normally carried out peacefully. Nevertheless, depending on internal (particularly psychological) and external conditions, there is the danger that there will be violence and damage to or from outsiders or within the group. To determine either by legislation or by the public power whether this probability (danger) is clear and imminent and, when it is decided that such is the case, to subject the collective activity to prior control or prohibition, and to that end to adopt a notification or licensing system, is not contrary to Article 21 of the Constitution, so long as the standard is reasonable and clear. Such a system is indeed necessary for the public welfare.

V. Limits as to Place

(1) Places for Use by the General Public. Under the National Property Law "property provided for public use as parks or squares or designated to be so provided (Article 13)" is under the control of the finance minister or his deputy. Under the Roads Law, among "roads" "provided for general traffic" (Articles 2 and 3), national roads are under the control of the minister of construction or the governor, prefectural roads are under the control of the prefectural authorities, and city, town, and village roads are under the control of those local authorities (Articles 12 to 16). All of these roads were opened with the object of serving the public or for general traffic. Accordingly, ordinary local public entities [2] can be permitted, in accordance with circumstances within their areas and the ideals of the residents, to regulate, by means of ordinances, the rights of the general public to use these roads and parks, provided that the object of the roads and parks, which is public use, is kept in mind and that the rights of the controlling authority are not impaired. However, the method and the extent of the control of collective activities in such places raises the problem of Article 21 of the Constitution. The Local Autonomy Law provides that "ordinary local public entities . . . maintain local public order, protect and preserve the safety, health and welfare of the inhabitants and visitors" (Article 2, paragraph 3, item 1), and may deal with certain affairs. For example, they are empowered "to establish and manage parks, playgrounds, open spaces, greens, roads, bridges, rivers, canals, reservoirs . . . and to regulate the rights to use them" (Article 2, paragraph 3, item 2). The same applies here. But if one should include in parks, playgrounds, roads, and the like, places that are not unrestrictedly thrown open to public use (e.g., recreation

2. For the meaning of the term "local public entities," see footnote 2 on p. 391.

grounds for which an admission fee is charged), then there is a limit on the methods which can be used to regulate the right to use such places for collective activities and this becomes generally the same as in the case of privately owned places, as described below.

(2) Privately Owned Places. May collective activities be held on land or in buildings owned by, or whose use is vested in, private persons (including the parking areas and roofs of offices, factories, department stores, private educational establishments, hospitals, gymnasia, and so forth)? Since the owner or user has the right to determine this (in restricting the collective activities of employees on the premises, however, he may not impair their rights as workers), to restrict such activity by ordinance or to make it subject to a licensing system would be to disregard the rights of the private user and would be *ultra vires*, even in cases in which the collective activity was open to the public. The action of giving or refusing license must not be at variance with the wishes of the private person possessing the right of use. The general public possesses no right or freedom to use such places.

The point which must not be overlooked here is that, generally speaking, private educational establishments, hospitals, department stores, and the like, do not provide their premises for public use or for general thoroughfare. This is a question of law and of fact which must be determined in each individual case. In such places members of the general public and individuals whose private or public business takes them there are permitted to enter. Department stores are open even to people who come only to look at the merchandise. None of these places, however, say to outsiders, "Come here; hold sporting contests, meetings, community singing, or what you will." In contrast to public roads and parks the person who possesses the right to use the premises of these establishments can close them whenever and for as long as he likes without injuring the rights or freedoms of the general public, who are outsiders.

Roads owned by private individuals and not used for general thoroughfare may generally be said to belong to this category even though, in actual fact, the public passes along them.

(3) The Premises of Government Offices. Generally speaking, the buildings and grounds of such places as the National Diet, the courts, government offices, and national educational establish-

ments, of which the rights of ownership or use are held by the nation or by local public entities, are not like parks and roads provided for the use of the public or for general thoroughfare. To hold assemblies, to post bills, or to hold demonstrations in such places without permission is, generally speaking, a violation of the rights of administration and use. Such activity may be prohibited and the bills removed and returned to the person who posted them, without resort to ordinance, by virtue of the powers of the administrator of the government building. Such assemblies and demonstrations would probably amount to the offense of trespass. Accordingly, the power to license collective activities in such places resides in the administrator, not in the local public entity which is not the administrator. It is sufficient for the public safety commission to inform anyone who applies for permission to hold collective activities that it does not have the authority to grant permission. (In such circumstances, its failure to give permission or withhold it does not mean that the collective activity may be held.) [3]

(4) The Special Character of Parks and Roads. Parks, squares, and the like provided, as we have stated above, for general thoroughfare are built so that ordinary citizens either singly or otherwise, may freely enter them and pass the time peacefully and pleasantly in such activities as sightseeing, recreation, meetings, social intercourse, chatting, discussion, and the like. Roads provided for general thoroughfare also are there to be used by people, either singly or otherwise, to travel along freely and, like parks and squares, to be used to pass the time in various activities. In passing the time in such places people must, in my opinion, use them properly in the manner prescribed. If people stamp around on tennis courts and flower beds and harm them, this will spoil their use for the people at large, and inflict damage on the park. Accordingly, you cannot say that you may inflict such damage in

---

3. Justice Tarumi's argument here is not entirely clear. That the local public authorities do not have the right to grant permission to use national government buildings or areas situated in a local area is beyond question. What remains obscure is his statement regarding lack of authority by the local public entity to grant permission for collective activities in a locally-owned government office. It seems reasonable to assume that he is making a distinction between the local government authority (for example, a governor or mayor or local assembly), which does not itself administer buildings or property direction, and a subordinate local administrative authority to which the responsibility for administering the office or property has been delegated.

order to carry out demonstrations, because freedom of expression is more important than property.

The presence of a group in the park or on the road will be a nuisance to other people, but, nevertheless, it constitutes the use of the park or road. Everyone would agree that the principle underlying the use of such places is that a person, having used them, should move on; it seems clear that a reasonable prohibition or restriction may be placed on the large-scale exclusive use of parks and roads for a long period, by a body of people whose size exceeds a certain large figure. This reasoning, however, does not apply only to collective activity; it is also reasonable to apply it in many cases to welcome or farewell gatherings, and to processions of large numbers of trucks and busses used for travel, excursions, funeral parties, and transporting freight (i.e., to physical activity of a group irrespective of whether or not the expression of thought is involved). But one cannot say that, such being the case, it is sufficient if collective activities involving expression of thought are also controlled by traffic regulations. I shall deal with this point below.

(5) "In any place whatsoever." Article 1 of the Tokyo Metropolitan Ordinance says that the permission of the public safety commission is required "when it is proposed to hold a mass demonstration in any place whatsoever." Even if we assume that the Chichibu-Tama National Park (of which about 75,000 acres are in Tokyo Metropolis) is a park within the meaning of the ordinance, one would agree that people do not demonstrate in an area with so few signs of life and that if there were people who wanted to do so, they should be given permission and should not be punished. The restriction of demonstrations on the roofs of private buildings in an area where companies, shops, and houses are densely concentrated or in private parking places fronting on roads, is, as I have said above, essentially a matter to be decided by the owner; the passing public does not have the liberty to use the roofs and the parking areas, and, therefore, the question of their liberty being infringed cannot arise. It might be that demonstrations in such places might make a great deal of noise and thus interfere with those engaged in the public service or in their work in the vicinity, or that the demonstration might overflow into the road. The former, however, can be controlled appropriately by the

police if it comes within Articles 5 and 6 of the Police Duties Execution Law [4] and can be punished under Tokyo Metropolitan Ordinance No. 1 of 1954, which deals with noise prevention; in respect to the latter it would be sufficient if it were handled as a demonstration carried out without notice.

The surface of rivers or lakes, and nationally owned land which *de facto* has been made over to general use for a long period of time (e.g., sea-bathing areas or safe open areas behind river dikes [often used as playgrounds]) can probably be considered as different from parks provided for public use (described above) or roads provided for general thoroughfare. According to the ordinance, an assembly or procession of boats on a river or lake would not be open to objection, but if it were a mass demonstration, license would be required.

The administrators of harbors under the Harbors Law are either the local public entities or harbor bureaus established by them. A harbor bureau "shall regulate as necessary the use of harbor facilities" (Article 12, paragraph 4, item 2) but such regulations relating to the special methods of utilizing and administering harbors should be considered as not conflicting with Article 1 of the Tokyo Metropolitan Ordinance; both can exist together.

"In any place whatsoever" cannot be interpreted to extend to the interior of public and private buildings outside the jurisdiction of Tokyo Metropolis or to outdoor areas such as privately owned baseball grounds where admission is charged. I cannot agree with the majority opinion regarding these words.

(Additional remarks.) In our country it is less than a hundred years since parks, squares, roads, and the like, became recognized as places to be used by all the people in a pleasant atmosphere for the appreciation of the scenery, recreation, social intercourse, chatting, and the open expression of political views. From the start of the Kamakura regime (1194 A.D.) to that time the country had been ruled by the feudal autocratic shogunate in accordance with the samurai ethic. Hence, the people could rarely express their views in the public square; to appeal to the public was futile; and there was nothing but secret entreaty to officials. We are different from Western European countries, where since several centuries

4. Articles 5 and 6 empower the police to take emergency actions in situations involving crime prevention or danger to life, limb, and property.

before the Christian era the squares have been used for social intercourse and for the public expression of views. Moreover, in our
country today there are many many people who do not follow
the Buddhist, Christian, Confucian, or any other faith, and many
others who do not yet know the meaning of using squares for
their own pleasure while at the same time respecting the liberties
and privacy of other people. In particular, there are many people
who, deficient in public spirit, indulge in activity that is illegal
and disorderly; and there are many people who wish others to
look after their affairs, and who act apathetically in accordance
with the direction of their superiors. (Here defeat in the war has
also had its influence.) In view of this, one can understand the
argument that there should be rigorous control of disorder. Nevertheless, we must preserve the supreme injunction of the Constitution that restrictions on freedom of expression must not exceed
the minimum degree necessary. If this is disregarded, then there is
the danger that law, justice, and administration will tend toward
totalitarianism.

(6) A Reasonable and Clear Standard

(i) The enactment of laws or ordinances prohibiting or restricting collective activity in a particular category of the places
mentioned in (5) above, "parks or squares provided for public
use" (National Property Law, Article 13), "roads provided for
general thoroughfare" (Roads Law, Article 2), or "harbors"
(Harbors Law), at particular times, by particular methods, or
in a particular form is reasonable and therefore does not contravene Article 21 of the Constitution. (In the case of ordinances,
I mean places with regard to which the local public entity has the
power to make ordinances.)

(ii) Furthermore, it could not, in my opinion, be said to contravene the same provision of the Constitution if laws or regulations were enacted that confined collective activities to one of the
categories of places mentioned above, that specified the time, the
manner, and the method in which they could be conducted,
thereby providing a notification or licensing system, and that
stipulated that where it was anticipated there would be a clear
and imminent danger to public safety, the police could refuse
permission or ban it. (Is this not what the Grand Bench considered
the basic principle in its decision of November 24, 1954?)

Hence, almost everyone would agree that the following provisions are reasonable and clear and generally incontestable: The English Seditious Meetings Act, 1817, Section 23,

It shall not be lawful for any . . . persons to convene . . . any meeting of persons consisting of more than fifty persons in any street . . . or open place in the city . . . of Westminster . . . within the distance of one mile from the gate of Westminster Hall . . . for the purpose or on the pretext of considering of or preparing any complaint, . . . declaration, or other address . . . for alteration of matters in Church or State, on any day on which . . . either House of Parliament shall meet and sit, or shall be summoned or adjourned or prorogued to meet or sit, nor on any day on which his Majesty's Courts of Chancery, King's Bench . . . shall sit in Westminster Hall . . .

the West German Prohibited Areas Law (1955), Article 1, setting the bounds of the Federal Legislature prohibited area in the City of Bonn; the French Law with Respect to Public Meetings (1881), Article 6, stating that meetings may not be held on public streets and may not continue after 11:00 P.M.

It would, I consider, be constitutional to prohibit by laws or ordinances such things as: collective activities from midnight to 4:00 A.M., so that people could sleep undisturbed; marching in groups or columns exceeding a certain width on sections of roads of less than a certain width or without sidewalks; processions consisting of more than a prescribed number of automobiles of a prescribed weight over bridges of a certain strength; collective activity exclusively occupying specified places by large numbers of people and vehicles when it seems likely to prevent traffic entering or leaving (say for more than four hours), in specified squares or roads adjoining stations, wharves, and airports, or in specified squares or roads adjoining other traffic, communication, or power transmission facilities; processions involving melees and occupying the whole width of a roadway for more than forty minutes continuously.

The general public, which has the liberty and right to use or pass through parks, squares, and roads, and the people who work or divert themselves in the neighboring offices (public and private), companies, and shops do not have to put up with unlimited collective activities. When some member of the group or a bystander faints, or someone living in a nearby shop becomes seriously ill, then there is no reason why the ambulance or the doctor should be unable to pass, or why fire engines should be brought to a standstill.

It is constitutional to enact laws and ordinances providing the above standards forbidding certain things in order to prevent damage to the lives, bodies, health, liberty, or valuable property of the members of groups or private individuals using such places.

Next, for the police to decide whether "there is a clear and imminent danger to public safety" is very difficult unless they understand ever-changing, everyday natural and social phenomena (storms, floods), the tendencies and psychological condition of groups, the groups opposing them, and third parties. Hence, even if the content of "clear and pressing danger" is not spelled out in more detail, the law or ordinance would not, in my opinion, be unconstitutional; I doubt whether this can be avoided.

However, if we go into detail, the following crimes, as specified in the Criminal Code, are violations of rights and freedoms: rebellion, treason, crimes relating to foreign relations, interference with judicial proceedings or with public officials in the execution of their duties, forcibly removing a lawfully imprisoned person from jail, riot, arson or negligence with fire, flooding, destruction or damage to means of communication, trespass, sacrilege, collective abuse of authority by officials, killing or wounding, unlawful arrest or imprisonment, threatening, kidnapping, libel (injuring the dignity of the individual), robbery with violence, intimidation, the destruction of buildings or public documents or valuable property, and offenses against the "Punishment of Violence Law." Accordingly, where it is recognized that there was a clear and pressing danger that any of those acts would be committed by group activity, it would, of course, be constitutional for the police to make regulations that did not permit collective activities, but forbade them, and for the police, acting on those regulations, to prohibit them.

In stopping the above crimes, preventive measures are probably permissible both in respect to crimes not resulting from negligence and in certain kinds of crimes where an unlawful result has been caused by negligence. It is the same where there is the clear and pressing danger that death or injury will result from disorder among a large group of people and one cannot tell who is negligent (e.g., the Yahiko Shrine, Nijubashi, and Singing Contest disasters [all three involving panic] in which many were killed and injured). If, during the time that our people do not understand the meaning of using parks, squares, and roads safely, comfortably, and tidily, they should be used with violence from first to last, destructively, and for collective activities without regard for others, then the ideals of the Constitution would be lost.

As I have said above, in collective activities, too, the places where they occur must be used in a proper manner. The occupation of a place by thousands or tens of thousands of people will perhaps injure the lawns and leave litter. This, however, would not be grounds for disapproving the activity. On the other hand, one could hardly say that the complete ruining of flowerbeds, tennis courts, trees, bamboo, and fences conformed to the proper use of such places. Isn't this also to trample under foot the wishes of the citizens and inhabitants who built these places? But the question in this situation is whether this can become a reason for not permitting the activity, even though liability for damages should arise with respect to the results produced.

(TRANSLATED BY D. C. S. SISSONS)

Hanreishū, XII, No. 13, 1969 (Civil)

EDITORIAL NOTE: Early in 1952 the appellant, an economist favoring trade with Communist countries and a former Left-wing Socialist party member of the House of Representatives, applied for a passport to attend an international economic conference in Moscow, but was denied it under Article 13, paragraph 1, item 5, of the Passport Law (see below). He later received a passport to visit Denmark. Although it was endorsed as not valid for travel in Communist countries, he visited Communist China and the Soviet Union en route.

Subsequently, he sued the state for damages for loss of professional opportunities in not being able to attend the economic conference. He did this under the State Redress Law, which provides that "if a public official entrusted with the exercise of public power . . . has, in the conduct of his official duties, inflicted intentionally or through negligence any damages on another person through an illegal act, the State . . . shall be under obligation to make compensation therefor." He lost in the court of first instance and the court of appeal and took the case to the Supreme Court. It was argued for the state that, among other things, the appellant's attendance at the conference in Moscow would weaken Japan's position in the hitherto unsuccessful negotiations with the Soviet Union for a peace treaty and for the liberation of Japanese prisoners of war and fishermen in Soviet hands. The appellant's political views and affiliations did not become issues.

Grand Bench decision, September 9, 1958: Dismissed.

REFERENCES

Constitution of Japan. ARTICLE 22.   1. Every person shall have freedom to choose and change his residence and to choose his occupation to the extent that it does not interfere with the public welfare.

2. Freedom of all persons to move to a foreign country and to divest themselves of their nationality shall be inviolate.

Passport Law. Article 13, paragraph 1.   When a person wishing an ordinary passport or the addition of destinations to one comes under any of the following items, the Minister of Foreign Affairs or a consul may refuse to issue such ordinary passport or to add such destinations:

(5) . . . a person concerning whom the Minister of Foreign Affairs has reasonable grounds for fearing that he may act in a manner markedly and directly harmful to the national interest or security of Japan.

FORMAL JUDGMENT

Appeal in the present case dismissed. Court fees for the appeal to be borne by the appellant.

REASONS. In regard to item 1 in the Reasons for Appeal tendered by counsel (Mr. Morikawa, Mr. Inomata, and Mr. Ono): Their argument is that although Article 13, paragraph 1, item 5, of the Passport Law is in contravention of Article 22, paragraph 2, of the Constitution and must be construed to be void, the appeal decision held valid the action of the minister of foreign affairs, pursuant to the said provision of the Passport Law in refusing the application for a passport and is therefore, they contend, in violation of the above constitutional provision.

It is, however, our opinion that although the "freedom to move to a foreign country" of Article 22 of the Constitution should be interpreted as including freedom to travel to foreign countries for short periods, freedom of foreign travel should not be interpreted as being permitted without limit, but as subject to reasonable restrictions in the interests of the public welfare. Article 13, paragraph 1, item 5, of the Passport Law provides as one of the circumstances in which the issuing of a passport may be refused the existence of "reasonable grounds for fearing that [the applicant] may act in a manner markedly and directly harmful to the national interest or security of Japan." One may consider this as establishing in the interests of the public welfare a reasonable limitation on freedom of foreign travel. One cannot, like the appellant, say that this provides a vague standard and is therefore void. Accordingly, we cannot accept the appellant's contention that the provision of the above Passport Law is unconstitutional.

In regard to item 2 in the Reasons for Appeal: The appellant claims that even if Article 13, paragraph 1, item 5, of the Passport Law were not unconstitutional, the application for a passport in the present case does not come within its scope. Thus, it is argued that the appeal verdict was contrary to law because it erred in the interpretation and application of the said article when it applied it to the present case and found the minister's refusal to issue a passport lawful. It is further contended that the verdict was contrary to law because of an erroneous interpretation of Article 1, paragraph 1, of the State Redress Law when it held that the action of denial [of the passport] was not intentional or negligent within the meaning of that article.

However, as we have stated above, Article 13, paragraph 1, item 5, of the Passport Law is to be interpreted as placing, in the interests of the public welfare, a reasonable restriction on freedom of foreign travel. Moreover, it is clear that situations can arise in which it is necessary to restrict that freedom, even in cases in which there is [only] the possibility that future acts will be performed harmful to the interests and security of Japan. Thus, there are no grounds for the applicant's contention that the provision should apply only to cases where there is a "clear and present danger."

The appeal decision on the basis of its findings of fact—in particular, that in the international situation confronting Japan under the occupation there was the danger that the participation of the appellant in the international economic conference in Moscow would be markedly and directly harmful to the interests and security of Japan—concluded that the minister's action in refusing to issue a passport could not be said to be contrary to law. With this decision we of the present Court are able to concur.

The appellant further contends that he would participate in the conference in his private capacity, that the issue of a passport is merely a simple act of attestation whereby the government neither gives support to the objective of the travel nor assumes any political responsibility, and that, accordingly, no harm to the interests and security of Japan could arise. The underlying argument of the appeal judgment, however, is that even though the appellant attended as a private individual, there was a possibility that such participation at such a time could affect international relations. In this also the conclusions are reasonable.

The remaining arguments advanced by the appellant are no more than criticisms of the appeal decision's findings of fact and, moreover, attacks on its decisions based on premises the reverse of those adopted by that court. These arguments we are unable to accept.

The appeal judgment states that even if the minister's decision not to issue a passport had been a mistake, it would not amount to an "intentional or negligent" act within the meaning of Article 1, paragraph 1, of the State Redress Law. This addition to the reasons underlying the judgment is unnecessary and hypothetical and, irrespective of whether or not it is correct, the over-all decision would be the same. We cannot accept the appellant's contentions on this question either.

For the above reasons, in accordance with Articles 401, 95, and 89 [1] of the Code of Civil Procedure, we give judgment as set forth in the formal judgment.

This is the unanimous opinion of this Court with the exception of Chief Justice Tanaka and Justice Shimoiizaka, who give a supplementary opinion.

* * *

The opinion of Chief Justice Tanaka and Justice Shimoiizaka follows.

In regard to item 1 in the Reasons for Appeal: The majority

---

1. On Articles 401 and 89 see footnote 7, p. 50. Article 95 grants the court authority to make decisions regarding court costs.

opinion interprets "freedom to move to a foreign country," provided in Article 22, paragraph 2, of the Constitution, as including freedom to travel to foreign countries for a short period. With this interpretation we cannot agree. This provision was enacted to provide freedom to move to a foreign country and to divest oneself of Japanese nationality. This has to do with severing legal connections with the state or with removing oneself from the country and living abroad for a long period, serious matters for the individual and the state. To the extent that there is a change in location, moving to a foreign country and travel involving temporary absence from one's country are similar. However, in all other respects they are very different activities.

No matter how one tries to extend its literal meaning, one cannot include travel in "moving to a foreign country." The latter, after all, results in fixed domicile in a particular place; the former requires moving around. In this sense it is conceivable that travel is included in "change" of paragraph 1 of the same article. Here, however, "change" is used in an exact sense, namely, "to shift residence" (in the English phrase, "to change his residence"). This is regarded as meaning a guarantee against banishment. Thus, it cannot be interpreted as including travel because it is essentially different. This provision is to be regarded as providing a freedom inside Japan in contrast with paragraph 2, which is a provision dealing with going to a foreign country. This being the case, it is proper not to apply it to foreign travel. This provision must be interpreted as not embracing cases of domestic travel.

In short, Article 22 of the Constitution does not guarantee freedom of travel in either paragraph 1 or paragraph 2. It does not follow, however, that because there is no provision dealing with it [freedom of travel], there is no guarantee. The list of human rights and freedoms in the Constitution singles out only the more important freedoms recognized in history; it is not exhaustive. It does not follow that other rights and freedoms do not exist or are not guaranteed. We enjoy countless rights and freedoms in our daily lives. These, however, are not known by particular names. They constitute a part of general freedom or the right of the pursuit of happiness. Freedom to travel, the issue in the present case, is one of these.

In reaching the conclusion that the freedom to travel is subject to reasonable restriction in the interests of the public welfare, we do not differ from the majority opinion.

(TRANSLATED BY D. C. S. SISSONS)

VII: ABETMENT OF SLOWDOWN TACTICS AMONG THE POLICE AND FREEDOM OF EXPRESSION

Hanreishū, VI, No. 8, 1053 (Criminal)

EDITORIAL NOTE: On April 2, 1951, the accused handed a policeman in the city of Muroran a mimeographed handbill urging the police of that city to refuse forthwith to obey the orders of the "foreign imperialists and the traitorous government." He was arrested, tried, and sentenced to six months' imprisonment on the charge of violating a provision (see below) of the Local Public Service Law. He eventually appealed to the Supreme Court, mainly on the grounds that the conviction violated his freedom of expression.

Second Petty Bench decision, August 2, 1951: Dismissed.

REFERENCES

Local Public Service Law. ARTICLE 37, paragraph 1.   Personnel must not resort to strikes, slowdowns, or other types of strike action against the people who, as their employer, are represented by the agencies of the local public entity or to such slowdown tactics as will lower the operational efficiency of the agencies of the local public entity. Nor must any person plot such unlawful acts or conspire concerning them or instigate or incite their execution.

ARTICLE 61, item 4.   A person to whom any of the following items applies shall be liable to penal servitude of not more than three years or a fine of not more than one hundred thousand yen.

(4) Any person who has conspired, instigated, incited the perpetration of, or attempted the unlawful acts stipulated in the first part of Article 37, paragraph 1.

Constitution of Japan. ARTICLE 21. 1. Freedom of assembly and association as well as speech, press, and all other forms of expression are guaranteed.

2. No censorship shall be maintained, nor shall the secrecy of any means of communication be violated.

FORMAL JUDGMENT

The appeal in the present case is dismissed.

REASONS. The substance of the appeal on behalf of the accused is that the original judgment is in violation of Article 9 of the Constitution, providing for the renunciation of war, and of Article 21, providing for the freedom of speech and publication, but because the decision in the original judgment involving Article 37, paragraph 1, and Article 61, item 4, of the Local Public Service Law, has no relation to Article 9 of the Constitution, the assertion that there was a violation of the said article has no bearing on the original decision.[1]

Secondly, Article 21 of the Constitution guarantees the freedom of speech and publication, but that the freedom of the said article is not without restriction is clear from the fact that there is no freedom to instigate a crime. The Grand Bench of this Court in a decision upholding the constitutionality of Article 11 of the Foodstuffs Emergency Order held that acts which instigate the nonperformance of important obligations legally imposed upon the people are injurious to the public welfare and go beyond the limits of the freedom of speech. (Grand Bench decision, May 18, 1949; *Hanreishū*, III, No. 6, 839 <Criminal>.)

According to the document involved in the decision of first instance in this case entitled, *An Appeal to the Top Men of the Muroran Police,* which the accused distributed to the police in

---

1. The argument of the appeal in respect to Article 9 can be paraphrased as follows: "The foreign imperialists and the traitorous government" are leading Japan to war. The accused in urging the police to disobey orders was attempting to keep Japan out of war. Therefore, when the court found him guilty it violated Article 9 because its decision was leading Japan to war.

Muroran, it is clear that the contents of the said handbill aimed to instigate the local police officials to resort to the slowdown. Such conduct by the local police is forbidden by law. In the light of the precedent of this Court, quoted above, abetment of this kind must be said to go beyond the limits of freedom of speech as guaranteed by the Constitution. However, it must also be said that such abetment does not constitute a crime in situations in which there is absolutely no danger that such slowdown activity will take place. But the actions of the accused cannot be said to be necessarily without such danger, because an examination of the passages in the document that use threatening language toward those engaged in secret police activities such as surveillance, intelligence gathering, and investigation reveals phrases such as the following: "Each one of these shall be remembered as an enemy of the people and will suffer the harshest punishment in the name of the people on the day which will surely come."

The original judgment, approving the decision of the court of first instance, which considered the acts concerned in this case to be abetment and applied Article 61, item 4, of the Local Public Service Law to them, is therefore proper and the argument for appeal, which holds that Article 21 of the Constitution is violated, is found groundless in view of the judicial precedent cited above.

In addition, since it cannot be found that the provisions of Article 411 of the Code of Criminal Procedure [2] apply to this case, the Court decides as stated in the formal judgment and in accordance with Article 408 of the Code of Criminal Procedure.[3]

The above is the unanimous opinion of the Justices except for the supplementary opinion of Justice Kuriyama, given below.

*   *   *

The supplementary opinion of Justice Kuriyama follows.

Naturally, when freedom of speech is abused and when the order or security of society is violated, it must be permissible from the standpoint of the maintenance of that order and security to take preventive steps without waiting with folded arms for actual harm to occur. But if the proper exercise of the freedom of speech can be made the object of the exercise of authority in the name

2. See footnote 3, p. 46.
3. See footnote 4, p. 16.

of preventive action, the guarantee in the Constitution cannot be perfect. In brief, drawing the line between what is proper preventive action and what is only a pretext is a very delicate problem. At the very least, if what has been uttered presents the danger of inflicting injury on society it can properly be regarded as the equivalent of actual injury and be treated as an abuse of the freedom of expression. And if it is not regarded as the object of proper preventive action the maintenance of social order and security cannot be achieved.

Starting from this premise, the demonstration that there is sufficient danger of positive harm is a matter to be determined by the courts in concrete cases and on the basis of evidence. Again, if the intent of our new laws is to be strictly interpreted, the courts must make the state, that is, the public prosecutor, establish objective proof in demonstrating whether or not there is such sufficient danger. Namely, he must be made to produce circumstantial evidence [of such danger]. Under the new laws it is natural that the court should not escape censure for an arbitrary and tyrannical decision if it concludes that there is such danger without proof and in the absence of an established case by the public prosecutor, but I believe that the court need not on its own authority take evidence and reach a conclusion on the point. In my humble opinion, such a restriction [on the prosecutor] takes note of the important role of freedom of speech under democratic government and is to be regarded as a standard for the taking of evidence to be established by the courts themselves where application of that constitutional guarantee [of freedom of speech] is concerned.

To examine the decision of the court of first instance from the above point of view: notwithstanding the fact that the accused, Takahashi Kaoru, even supposing he is a member of the Japanese Communist party, handed over to a Muroran city policeman, with the injunction to read it, a handbill with the contents already designated and that the said act, as stated in the indictment, constituted incitement to the execution of slowdown tactics as set forth in Article 37 of the Local Public Service Law, it follows according to the interpretation given above that the public prosecutor must present proof that under the objective circumstances the whole of what was uttered by the accused is sufficiently dangerous actually to produce the illegal activity, namely, the execution of slowdown tactics. Moreover, because police officials, both national and local, are forbidden to form employees' associations, the former by Article 98 of the National Public Service Law and the latter by Article 52 of the Local Public Service Law, the objective circumstances that establish the danger of their use of slowdown tactics as strike action must perhaps be even more conspicuous than in the case of ordinary public officials.

Accordingly, on the basis only of the handbill and the testimony of the police official who received the said handbill, which the court of first instance cited among the evidence, we can safely assume the following: that the accused was a member of the Japanese Communist party who underwent the so-called "red purge"; that he had some dozens of the said handbills in his possession; and that the distribution of the handbill was not accidental, but was carried out as part of the campaign of the Japanese Communist party against the police. However, in regard to whether or not there was danger that the slowdown would be executed as described in the closing statement (summing up) of the prosecutor, we cannot know as actually proved whether the Communist party's campaign toward the police took on the color of a struggle against the authorities after the purge of the Japanese Communist party leaders and the suspension of the party organs in July, 1950, and whether their campaign toward the police was intensified after the spring of 1951. (The public prosecutor neither presented evidence on these points nor insisted that they were matters of common knowledge; that is clear throughout the opening statement and the summary of the proof.) Nor is it possible even today to ascertain the degree of harm involved in the antipolice activities of the Japanese Communist party.

Accordingly, in respect to the existence of danger of the execution of the slowdown as indicated above, I can only conclude that the grounds for a decision in the first instance were insufficient and that there was an illegality involved and, in addition, that the original judgment, which tolerated this, also contravened the law.

The majority opinion, as stated previously, contains the following passage:

But the actions of the accused cannot be said to be necessarily without such danger, because an examination of the passages in the document that use threatening language toward those engaged in secret police activities such as surveillance, intelligence gathering, and investigation reveals phrases such as the following: "Each one of these shall be remembered as an enemy of the people and will suffer the harshest punishment in the name of the people on the day which will surely come."

Yet to conclude merely on the basis of that phrasing without proof that there is danger of positive harm to society is to infer the existence of a danger on highly ambiguous grounds.

Nevertheless, that the accused was, as stated above, a person who, as a member of the Communist party of Japan, was engaged in various activities on behalf of the said party, is clear from the records in this case as is the fact that the handbill involved was published in the name of the Muroran District Committee of the party. If we consider together the objective circumstances in all their aspects, such as the wording of the said handbill and other facts of common knowledge, it cannot be concluded that the appeal decision is patently incompatible with justice because of a contravention of a law or ordinance material to the judgment, as stipulated in Article 411 of the Code of Criminal Procedure. Therefore, I end by agreeing with the majority opinion by finding that I must approve of the appeal decision.

(TRANSLATED BY IKEDA MASAAKI)

VIII: FILIAL PIETY, PATRICIDE, AND EQUALITY UNDER THE LAW (THE FUKUOKA PATRICIDE DECISION)

Hanreishū, IV, No. 10, 2037 (Criminal)

EDITORIAL NOTE: On October 31, 1949, the accused severely beat his father about the head in the course of a family quarrel. The father died the following day, and the accused was brought to trial on the charge of inflicting on his father bodily injury resulting in death.

The court of first instance found the accused guilty and sentenced him to three years at forced labor, but with a three-year stay of execution. In the course of the verdict the court held that the section of Article 205 of the Criminal Code that deals with the crime involved and imposes a more severe penalty on those guilty of inflicting bodily injury resulting in death on a lineal ascendant than on others was unconstitutional because it violated the principle of equality under the law. The public prosecutor then appealed the case directly to the Supreme Court.

The opinions in this case bring out clearly the conflict between the traditional concept of filial piety and the new rights granted in the 1947 Constitution.[1]

Grand Bench decision, October 11, 1950: Quashed and returned.

1. Professor Kawashima Takeyoshi gave unstintingly of his time and his advice to this translation. His help is gratefully acknowledged. (Translator's note.)

REFERENCES

Criminal Code. ARTICLE 205.   1. A person who inflicts a bodily injury upon another and thereby causes his death shall be punished with imprisonment at forced labor for a fixed term of not less than two years.

2. When committed against a lineal ascendant of the offender or of his or her spouse, imprisonment at forced labor for life or for not less than three years shall be imposed.

Constitution of Japan. ARTICLE 14.   All of the people are equal under the law and there shall be no discrimination in political, economic or social relations because of race, creed, sex, social status or family origin.

Peers and peerage shall not be recognized.

No privilege shall accompany any award of honor, decoration or any distinction, nor shall any such award be valid beyond the lifetime of the individual who now holds or hereafter may receive it.

FORMAL JUDGMENT

The original judgment shall be quashed. The case shall be returned to the Fukuoka District Court.

REASONS. Regarding the reasons for appeal by the prosecution: The appeal by the prosecution states that the original decision recognized that the accused inflicted on his lineal ascendant an injury resulting in death, yet failed to apply paragraph 2 of Article 205 of the Criminal Code and disposed of the case under paragraph 1 of the same article on the ground that paragraph 2 violates the spirit of Article 14 of the Constitution. The argument for appeal contends that this decision is contrary to law and should be quashed, because it is based on a misunderstanding of the intent of the constitutional provision and because the penal provision that should have been applied was not applied.

The original judgment states in its "Reasons":

The provision of Article 205, paragraph 2, of the Criminal Code, viewed in the light of its origin, fondly preserved under the name of a so-called beautiful custom a matter which derived from the idea of severe punishment for patricide, which was regarded as the equivalent of the murder of one's lord because it was considered to be treachery against a parent who, in respect to the child, was viewed as the family head or as a protector or as a figure of authority. Thus, in the final analysis, this provision, derived as it is from quite feudalistic, antidemocratic, and antilibertarian ideas, runs counter to the grand spirit of the Constitution, which stresses the legal equality of all human beings.

In stating this, the original judgment holds that the said provision is contrary to the egalitarian democratic spirit of Article 14 of the Constitution and is thus unconstitutional.

Article 14 of the Constitution enunciates the principle of equality under the law for the people and provides that there be no discrimination in political, economic, or social relations because of race, creed, sex, social status, or family origin; this states the equality for all men of the value of human personality. Therefore, it is none other than an expression of the great principle that there be neither special rights nor the infliction of especially disadvantageous treatment on the grounds of differences in race, religion, sex, occupation, social status, and so forth. That slavery and special rights of peers are no longer recognized and that under the new Civil Code the incompetency of the wife and the special privileged position of the head of the house are abolished are also due to this principle. But this does not mean that the law is prevented from laying down appropriate, concrete provisions as required by morality, justice, or the specific purposes to be served by the law—taking into consideration within the scope of the principle of equality of the people such circumstances as age, natural qualities, occupation, or special relations with others. The reason for the more severe punishment of murder or injury resulting in death when committed against lineal ascendants as stipulated in the Criminal Code compared with ordinary cases of the same crimes is that the Code attributes special importance to the moral duties of the child toward his parents; the provision is merely a concrete legal provision, based on the requirements of morality.

The original decision points out that such an attribution of importance to the child's moral duties to his parents arose from feudalistic, antidemocratic ideas and that it is allowed to exist only in a familistic society based on ideas such as "the unity of loyalty and filial piety" and "ancestor worship"; but morality, controlling such relations as those between husband and wife, parent and child, or brother and sister is the great fountainhead of human ethics, a universal moral principle recognized by all mankind without regard to past or present or East and West. In other words, it must be said that this principle belongs to what in theory is called natural law. Therefore, with the exception of England and the United States, which are common law countries, we can find many examples of legislation providing more severe punishment for crimes against lineal ascendants than in ordinary cases. Whereas the original decision found that a morality that attaches special importance to the moral duties of children toward parents is feudalistic and antidemocratic, we find that this is a confusion of the natural relations between parents and children with the artificial social family system centering around the head of the house, which is negated under the new Constitution. In short, it [the original decision] indiscriminately rejects existing beautiful customs for the reason that they are feudalistic and antidemocratic and that it makes the same mistake as the present trend of the world, which falls into the evil of "throwing out the baby with the bath water."

Furthermore, by our interpretation of Article 14, paragraph 1, of the Constitution, the relations between parents and children do not fit under any of the categories, such as social status, and so forth, which are mentioned therein as reasons for discriminatory treatment. Also, the provision of the said article and paragraph that states that all of the people must in principle be treated equally in their political, economic, and social relations considers their position in regard to basic rights and duties from their place as subjects of those rights. It does not prohibit treatment of the people that varies according to their respective differences as objects in the several legal relationships applying to them. The original decision states that applying a more severe penalty when the victim is a direct lineal ascendant is tantamount to establishing, in regard to both the protection of human life and to punishment, a distinction among the people between those who are "special" and those who are "ordinary" and that, therefore, giving special protection to lineal ascendants as compared with ordinary people results in an inequality under law. However, it is reasonable to interpret the main object of the legislation as not being focused on the protection of the lineal ascendant who is the victim, but rather on a special consideration of the antimoral character of the descendant who is the assailant, the occasional greater protection thus given to lineal ascendants being merely a reflection of this.

Furthermore, the original decision holds that affection among relatives, as we know it, does not originate in legal provisions and that although family relations can be considered in weighing penalties, this is no reasonable basis to provide for inequality [of punishment] therein by means of law. However, we find that if it is feudalistic and antidemocratic, as the original judgment states, to emphasize the morality of children and parents and if, consequently, a law based on this emphasis is unconstitutional, then it is also unconstitutional to take these circumstances into consideration in weighing penalties when rendering judgment. Or, stated conversely, if one can take these circumstances into consideration constitutionally, then it is also possible constitutionally to go a step further and to objectify them in the form of law.

The original judgment points out that when the victim is a lineal descendant or spouse, paragraph 1 of Article 205 of the Code applies, and it criticizes the imbalance and the resulting inequality between this situation and a case in which the victim is a lineal ascendant. But the definition of the range of relatives who are victims in this kind of crime is a matter of legislative policy. The legislation of various countries is not always in agreement on this point. Therefore, when the original judgment points this [inequality] out in finding the said article and paragraph unconstitutional, it is confusing constitutional issues and legislative issues, just as is stated in point 6 of the Statement of Reasons for Appeal.

Such being the case, the provisions of Article 205, paragraph 2, of the Criminal Code have definitely remained valid from the time the new Constitution came into effect to today; therefore, the original judgment, which rejected the application of this paragraph in spite of the factual finding that the defendant killed his lineal ascendant and disposed of this case under paragraph 1 of Article 205, which deals with injury causing death in ordinary cases, is illegal because it misinterpreted Article 14, paragraph 1, of the Constitution and failed to apply the penal provisions that should have been applied. Thus, the appeal is well founded.

Accordingly, this Court renders judgment as shown in the formal judgment in accordance with Articles 405, 410, and the principal clause of Article 413 of the Code of Criminal Procedure.[2]

All Justices agreed in this opinion except Justice Saitō Yūsuke, who expressed a supplementary opinion as to substantive law and a dissenting opinion as to procedure, and Justices Mano Tsuyoshi and Hozumi Shigeto, who expressed dissenting opinions.

* * *

The minority opinion of Justice Mano Tsuyoshi follows.

The original decision found that the provision of Article 205 of the Criminal Code relating to injury causing death of a lineal ascendant is unconstitutional and null and void. Against this judgment the prosecution lodged an appeal, contending that the said article is in accord with the Constitution. As I believe, in conclusion, that the decision of unconstitutionality in the original judgment should be accepted, I find that the appeal of the prosecution in this case should be dismissed. The outline of my reasons is as follows:

1. The Constitution declares in Article 14 that "all of the people are equal under the law." Over the front entrance of the building of the Supreme Court of the United States of America four words are engraved in marble: "Equal justice under law." What do they mean? Needless to say, they extol the great principle of "equality under the law," based on democracy. This principle is also solemnly declared in Article 2 of the Universal Declaration of Human Rights of the United Nations. The basis of democracy lies in the equality of individuals founded on human dignity, in other words, on equality of all personalities. And the basis of the equality of individuals lies in the spirit of independence and self-respect that guides unrestrained and free individuals to act—not from external coercion, but with a spontaneity arising from the profound inner self and, inseparably related to this, with a spirit of self–responsibility. To respect one's own independence and responsibility is at the same time to respect the independence and responsibility of others and to respect humanity. This respect, whether of one's own personality or of someone else's, is not simply a means but always an end. Thus, one necessarily becomes conscious of the equal-

2. See footnote 2, p. 77 for Article 405; footnote 1, p. 92 for Article 410; and *ibid.*, for Article 413.

ity of all personalities. After all, democracy has as its basis the equality among individuals of fundamental human rights. This principle of equality under law is generally recognized as the outcome of a long history, and is clearly proclaimed in Article 14 of the new Constitution.

To make a distinction with respect to Article 205 of the Criminal Code between injury causing death of lineal ascendants and injury causing death of other persons and to impose an especially severe penalty in the former case is obviously inequality of treatment, a violation of the above-mentioned great principle of equality under law, and in contravention of Article 14 of the Constitution. To make this easier to understand we illustrate it in the following charts in which we have A, B, and C as lineal ascendants and A′, B′, and C′ as lineal descendants.

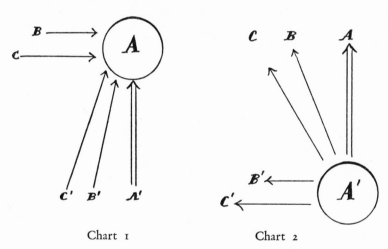

Chart 1   Chart 2

In Chart 1 we view the matter with the victim A at the center. A case in which A suffers an injury resulting in death inflicted by his lineal descendant A′ is distinguished from a case in which the injury resulting in death is caused by B, B′, C, C′ or others; only A′ is subjected to a special, severe penalty. In other words, only in relation to A′ does A receive greater protection. What is this but inequality? In Chart 2 we view the matter with the assailant A′ at the center. A case in which A′ injures his lineal ascendant A causing his death is distinguished from a case in which he injures B, B′, C, C′, or others, causing their death, and he is subjected to a special, severe penalty. Again, what is this but inequality? Nothing could be clearer than that this runs counter to the basic idea of the equality of all personalities and all individuals and thus is also opposed to the constitutional principle of equality under the law.

2. In the second place, Article 14 of the Constitution not only proclaims in general terms the principle of equality under the law as stated above but also provides, as illustrations for the application of the principle of equality, that "there shall be no discrimination in political, economic or social relations because of race, creed, sex, social status or family origin" and that "peers and peerage shall not be recognized." The provision of Article 205 of the Criminal Code that imposes a more severe penalty for injury resulting in death of lineal ascendants falls under the category of the aforesaid examples stipulated in regard to "discrimination in political . . . relations because of . . . social status . . . ," and even in this respect it is unconstitutional. The majority opinion repeatedly emphasizes morality between parents and children and this may easily appeal to those among the masses who do not understand democracy. But what would remain if we subtract from the morality of children toward parents (direct ascendants) the proper democratic morality based on the dignity of man and the respect of personality? There would be only (1) the voluntary obedience and services of children to parents based on natural affection and (2) the duty of obedience and service as return for the *on* [3] which they receive from their parents. These should be left essentially to the free will of the individual, and it is not proper to make them into a relationship of rights and duties under law or to give them other kinds of legal protection. Rather, they belong to a domain in which moral values are to be purified and enhanced under an increasing feeling of freedom in the absence of legal coercion. In a rational, democratic state, as opposed to a primitive society in which moral issues are not distinguished from but are intermingled with legal issues, it is necessary to distinguish rationally between what is properly a moral issue and what is properly a legal issue. Thus, it is necessary to enact laws

3. *On* may be roughly translated as meaning "the benefits for which one is indebted to a superior." For a detailed discussion of *on* see Ruth Benedict, *The Chrysanthemum and the Sword* (Boston: Houghton Mifflin, 1946), pp. 99 ff. (Translator's note.)

consistent with morality after making a critical examination of the peculiar functional differences between law and morality. Through all ages the morality of children toward parents was commonly called filial piety and centered around the duty of absolute obedience and service in gratitude and in repayment for the *on* received from the parents. This *on* was said to be "deeper than the sea and higher than the mountains." The argument that the core of such filial piety is repayment for *on* rests on the same basic principle as the feudal relationship of vassalage, the core of which is a return through service by feudal warriors for a fief, stipend, or allowance bestowed by the lord. This filial piety is a relationship between parents, who hold a superior status, and children, who hold an inferior status in the social organization; in other words, it is a relationship between persons unequal in status and not a relationship between equal individuals. Thus what was called filial piety in the past was the basis of the family system, the foundation of a system of patriarchy that was a kind of relationship of authoritarian control and at the same time had a strong feudalistic coloration. This is indeed an undeniable historical fact. The new filial piety should be a truly voluntary, free, uncoerced, and sound morality based on the principle of equality of personality. As seen above, there has been for a long time a difference in social status between parent and child as superior and inferior. And the provisions of severe punishment for patricide or injury causing death of lineal ascendants, which were established as norms of filial piety arising from this difference of status, are in violation of the examples stipulated in Article 14 of the Constitution.

3. The majority opinion states that the reason for the provisions for more severe penalty for injury causing death of a lineal ascendant in the Criminal Code is that the code attaches importance to the moral duty of the child toward its parents and that

morality, controlling such relations as those between husband and wife, parent and child, or brother and sister is the great fountainhead of human ethics, a universal moral principle recognized by all mankind without regard to past or present or East and West. In other words, it must be said that this principle belongs to what in theory is called natural law.

But if under the name of morality provisions for inequality can be made at random, like bamboo sprouts coming up after a rain, by saying "this is morality between parent and child, that is morality between husband and wife, this is morality between brother and sister, that is morality among relatives, this is morality between teacher and pupil, that is morality among neighbors, and this is such-and-such morality," what will become of the principle of "equality under the law," which is emphatically proclaimed by the new Constitution? I shudder at the thought. The provisions of the Criminal Code governing the murder of lineal ascendants and those governing the crime of inflicting injury on them resulting in death are said to be almost valueless in practice and even harmful at times. This may be proved by statistics. There is no necessary, rational justification for violating the great principle of equality. Therefore, I cannot agree at all with the majority opinion which, even though these provisions clearly involve inequality as pointed out above, vaguely states in the name of morality that they are not in violation of the principle of equality.

4. The majority opinion also states that the principle of equality should be considered from the standpoint of the people's position as the *subjects* of basic rights and duties and that "it [the provision] does not prohibit treatment of the people that varies according to their respective differences as objects in the several legal relationships applying to them." I find it difficult even to understand the meaning of this. As has been illustrated in Chart 1, looking at it from the point of view of the subject, inequality arises according to whether the subject of the criminal act is A' or B, B', C, or C'. Therefore, it seems that there is nothing to do but to recognize a violation of the principle of equality [originating] from this reason in the majority opinion. Moreover, there is no substantial reason for not applying the constitutional principle of equality to the inequality arising out of the difference of the object of the action of A', namely, whether this object is A or B, B', C, or C', as illustrated in Chart 2. After all, the inequality in Chart 1 and the inequality in Chart 2 are the same and are only viewed from a different standpoint. The majority opinion, which sets up a distinction between subject and object, is complete nonsense. Furthermore, to differentiate between degrees of protection according to differences of object is in violation of the principle of equality; is this not clear from the circumstances and developments that arose when offenses against the Imperial House were abolished as discussed later? Was not the fact that this naturally

gave greater protection to the object as compared with ordinary cases treated as inequality under democracy?

5. By the partial amendment of the Criminal Code in 1947 offenses against the Imperial Family were abolished and Articles 73 to 76 were eliminated. The reason was clearly to abolish as discriminatory the special protection of the Emperor in the Code on the premise that Article 14 of the Constitution applies also to the Emperor. Historical observation shows that in our country under the Taihō Code [701 A.D.] the murder of lineal ascendants was called villainy and that the murder of an emperor was called rebellion (whereas infanticide was treated less severely than murder); both were among the eight rebellious offenses, and the most severe penalty was provided for these two offenses. This tradition has been carried on ever since, up to the present Criminal Code. But as a result of the amendment of the Constitution, the provisions concerning offenses against the Imperial Family, which corresponded to the old offense of rebellion, were completely eliminated, as already stated. Logically, the provisions concerning the murder of lineal ascendants and injury resulting in death of lineal ascendants should have been eliminated at the same time. But this comparatively minor problem was left untouched because it was of less political urgency. (On December 27, 1946, the then prime minister sent a letter to the Supreme Commander for the Allied Powers expressing the necessity of retaining the provisions concerning the offenses against the Imperial Family, offering as a reason the fact that the provision regarding the murder of lineal ascendants in the Criminal Code was being retained. But it is said that this was rejected because it was opposed to democratization and the principle of equality.)

*　　*　　*

The minority opinion of Justice Hozumi Shigeto follows.

This case is concerned with Article 205 of the Criminal Code, but the problem originates with Article 200. Therefore, I want to express my opinion on both articles. To begin with I wish to present a critique of these two articles as legislation.

Following upon Article 199 of the Code, which states that "a person who kills another shall be punished with death or imprisonment at forced labor for life or for not less than three years," Article 200 of the Criminal Code provides that "a person who kills one of his or her own or his or her spouse's lineal ascendants shall be punished with death or imprisonment at forced labor for life." In other words, the maximum legal penalty in both cases is death. Therefore, even if the murder of lineal ascendants should be punished by the most severe penalty because of its heinous and wicked nature, it can be achieved through Article 199 and there is no special need for Article 200.

Thus, the difference in the penalties for ordinary murder and the murder of lineal ascendants lies in the minimum legal penalty for each. That is to say, in the former case the penalty may be reduced to three years' penal servitude and the benefit of a stay of execution of sentence may be granted, whereas in the latter case no other penalty but life imprisonment is possible if the death penalty is not imposed. Therefore, even if the penalty is reduced by law and further reduced by extenuating circumstances, it cannot be brought down to less than three years and a half, and accordingly a stay of execution of sentence cannot be granted.[4] The reason for making the distinction between these two cases in the Criminal Code is exactly as expressed in the majority opinion. But just as in the case of ordinary murder a serious case may deserve the death penalty and a light case may be dealt with adequately with a three-year imprisonment that makes it possible to stay the execution of sentence, so there can be similar circumstances, aggravating or extenuating, in the case of murder of lineal ascendants. There are, of course, many cases in which nothing could be more hateful than killing a person who bears the appellation, "parent," but cases may also not be rare in which we may shed tears of sympathy for a person who commits patricide in an extreme situation. Although the amendment of the old Criminal Code took pains to widen the range of the penalty for the crime of murder,[5] it was not reasonable legislation to leave only the old range of penalty for the murder of lineal ascendants. Not only is there no substantial advantage in this, but it is also an inconvenience when it comes to the weighing of penalties.

As regards the crime of "injury resulting in death," specified in

4. Article 25 of the Criminal Code provides that a person who has been sentenced to imprisonment for not more than three years may receive a suspension of execution of sentence.
5. The range was widened through a reduction of the minimum sentences.

Article 205 of the Criminal Code, because the penalty is "limited penal servitude for not less than two years" when the crime is committed against an ordinary person, but "penal servitude for life or not less than three years" when the crime is committed against a lineal ascendant, there are differences established in both the maximum and minimum penalties established by law, and this means that these are special provisions for injury resulting in death to ascendants. However, in respect to the crime of "violence without injury" in Article 208 and the crime of "injury not resulting in death" in Article 204 of the Criminal Code, the Code does not provide lighter or heavier penalties according to a differentiation between ordinary persons and lineal ascendants. If you are to say "it is wicked to lift your hand against a parent," then a more severe penalty should be imposed for the crime of violence against lineal ascendants—and the more so when the violence, committed with the intent of injury, has resulted in such injury. It is not logically consistent for legislation to hold violence against lineal ascendants resulting in injury as not especially serious, but then to impose a severe penalty in a case such as the present one that resulted in death accidentally, although with no clear intent to kill, differentiating it from a case of injury resulting in death to an ordinary person. Moreover, life imprisonment for an act without intent to kill is excessively harsh. Fifteen years, the maximum limited term of penal servitude under Article 205, paragraph 1, of the Criminal Code would suffice.

With respect to the crimes of desertion, Article 218, paragraph 2, of the Criminal Code, and of illegal arrest and confinement, Article 220, paragraph 2, more severe penalties are provided for cases in which such crimes are committed against lineal ascendants. Since these provisions have no direct bearing upon the present case, I shall not comment on them in detail, but the above argument concerning murder and injury applies by and large to them also.

Another noteworthy point is the scope of "lineal ascendants" in Article 200 and Article 205, paragraph 2, of the Criminal Code. It follows the provisions of the Civil Code, but the Civil Code was amended along the lines of the new Constitution, and the scope of "lineal ascendants" has been changed. The parent-child relationship between stepparents and stepchildren which was formerly considered to be like that of direct lineal ascendants and descendants is no longer recognized. Therefore, under the new Civil Code if we apply Article 200 or Article 205, paragraph 2, of the Criminal Code, the murder of stepparents or causing their death is not to be considered murder or injury resulting in death by injury of a lineal ascendant. But the relations of stepparents, and especially of the stepmother, to the stepchild may on occasion be just like those of a real mother or at least more than those of a foster mother in the obligation of *on*. Therefore, as long as patricide is otherwise recognized, there is a considerable imbalance in not charging a killer of stepparents with patricide while charging "a person who kills one of . . . his or her spouse's lineal ascendants," who are in a more distant parental relationship, with the offense of patricide. This, incidentally, reveals a contradiction, namely, that we preserved under the new Constitution the provisions of patricide of the old regime.

Thus, Articles 200 and 205, paragraph 2, of the Criminal Code are, as legislation, without reason and unnecessary and, I think, should have been eliminated when the Criminal Code was partially amended by Law No. 124 of 1947. But today, now that we missed that opportunity and those provisions are still in force, it is quite natural that the question should arise whether these two articles are contrary to the Constitution and therefore null and void. The original decision regarded Article 205, paragraph 2, of the Criminal Code as being in violation of Article 14 of the Constitution and applied paragraph 1 of the same article to the present crime, whereas the majority opinion of this Court, accepting the prosecution's appeal, decided that the said paragraph 2 was not unconstitutional and that therefore this paragraph should be applied to the present crime. But the original judgment and the prosecution's appeal as well as the majority opinion of this Court deal not only with Article 205, paragraph 2, of the Criminal Code, but also with the whole problem of patricide, including Article 200. As this Justice recognizes that the original judgment is correct in its conclusion—although he would have added or eliminated one or the other point of the explanation—he would like to express his opinion on some of the issues in the majority opinion of this Court and in the statement of the prosecution's appeal.

1. The focal point of the problem is Article 14 of the Constitu-

tion. The majority opinion states that this article is "none other than an expression of the great principle," and it "does not mean that the law is prevented from laying down appropriate, concrete provisions, as required by morality, justice, or the specific purposes to be served by the law . . . within the scope of the principle of equality of the people. . . ." However, in regard to the various great principles set forth in the Constitution, I believe that in dealing with the new Constitution, which aims especially at reforming old customs, we must try to preserve its spirit by not narrowing the scope [of the principles] on the basis of this or that so-called requirement. The "principle of equality of all people" in Article 14 of the Constitution is a precious basic idea of the new Constitution. This principle will here and there come into conflict with old ideas across the whole gamut of life—which can be of infinite variety—and this may produce various concrete requirements for exemptions from the principle. There is, therefore, a danger that the basic principle will eventually be emasculated if we listen to this requirement and give in to that one. We must take precautions against this possibility. According to item 4 of the Statement of Reasons for the Appeal, Article 14 of the Constitution "is not designed to prohibit unequal treatment for any cause whatsoever. . . . It must be interpreted to mean that equal treatment is not always required if there is some reasonable cause." But there is a danger that this way of thinking may be misused, resulting in the negation of Article 14 of the Constitution. It is true that reasonable operation of the principle of equality is desirable, but there is no reason at all to approve inequality.

2. The majority opinion states that the provisions of the Criminal Code concerning the murder of parents is exempted from Article 14 of the Constitution because it "is merely a concrete legal provision, based on the requirements of morality." However, Article 14 states that all people are equal "under the law," and by this it proclaims that the law does not provide any discriminatory treatment even in cases when all the people cannot necessarily be viewed as equal under the requirements of morality. The majority opinion also censures the original judgment for finding that "a morality that attaches special importance to the moral duties of children towards parents is feudalistic and antidemocratic." However, I think that the original decision criticized "the idea of a

heavier penalty for patricide," and that it did not deny the morality of filial piety itself. The majority opinion states that "morality controlling such relations as those between husband and wife, parent and child, or brother and sister is the great fountainhead of human ethics, a universal moral principle recognized by all mankind without regard to past or present or East and West." This is completely correct. The question is to what extent such a moral principle can be converted into law, considering the intrinsic boundaries of morality and law. The preamble of the Constitution of Japan states that the provisions of the Constitution are founded upon a "universal principle of mankind," but it does not state that the "universal principles of mankind" should be provided for in law *in toto*. The majority opinion states that because morality governing the relations between parents and children is a universal moral principle of mankind, it "belongs to what in theory is called natural law." From its language it is not clear whether the majority opinion adopts the natural law theory, but I think it unlikely that it is adopting the notion of "morals equal law." The fact that "filial piety is the basis of all virtues" remains unchanged under the new Constitution. But to decree that "children regardless of their age must respect father and mother," as was done in the Napoleonic Code, or to compel filial piety by special provisions of more severe punishment for patricide, as in the articles of the Criminal Code which are here in issue, is [to accept] the notion of the omnipotence of law, which may overstep the boundaries separating it from morality. This impairs the sanctity of the virtue of filial piety. This Justice condemns the legal provisions regarding patricide not because he thinks so little of filial piety, but because he thinks so much of it that he feels that law should not be allowed to touch it.

3. Item 5 of the Statement of Reasons for Appeal says, "The relationship between ascendants and their relatives is still admitted by the new Civil Code." It is true that the Civil Code uses the words *sonzoku* [lineal ascendant] and *hizoku* [lineal descendant] in Articles 729, 736, 793, 887, 888, 889, 900, 901, and 1028 of the Civil Code. But it uses the word *sonzoku* merely for relatives above the line of parents and the word *hizoku* for relatives below the line of children; it does not intend to express the original meaning of *son* [noble] and *hi* [humble] and to provide for dis-

criminatory treatment between them. It would be well if the words *son* and *hi* had been avoided under the new Constitution. Because no proper terms could be thought of, the usage was followed, but only with the meaning of *me-ue* [senior] and *me-shita* [junior]. And the old provision of the Civil Code that gave lineal ascendants first priority to enjoy the right to be supported because of their position was deleted by the reform of the Civil Code in accordance with the new Constitution.

4. The majority opinion states that "by way of interpretation of Article 14, paragraph 1, of the Constitution, the relations between parent and child do not fit under any of the categories such as social status, and so forth, which are mentioned therein as reasons for discriminatory treatment." Item 3 of the Statement of Reasons for Appeal expresses the same idea. This argument takes note of the latter part of the paragraph in question. Apart from whether this is right or wrong, the main point of Article 14, paragraph 1, of the Constitution lies in the phrase of the first part, which states: "All of the people are equal under the law." The latter part is an illustrative explanation of this. Even though the illustrations are comprehensive, the great spirit of the principle of equality in the said article will not be fully realized if we are to exempt anything from the guarantee of equality that does not fall verbatim into one of these illustrative categories. The act of a child killing or injuring his parent is the only aspect of this issue given consideration in the majority opinion. But even considering it in this way, it cannot be admitted that there is absolutely no violation of the principle of equality of Article 14, paragraph 1, of the Constitution when the law differentiates a priori between penalties for the same act according to various types of victims.

5. Furthermore, when it is seen that some victims of the same kind of crime receive the legal benefit of greater protection because they are lineal ascendants than do ordinary people, it is obvious that the provisions of the Criminal Code in question are in violation of the principle of equality of Article 14 of the Constitution. According to the majority opinion,

it is reasonable to interpret the main object of the legislation as not being focused on the protection of the lineal ascendant who is the victim, but rather on a special consideration of the antimoral character of the descendant who is the assailant, the occasional greater protection thus given to lineal ascendants being merely a reflection of this.

But it is questionable where the main object of the legislation lies. That point is not clear in Article 200 of the Criminal Code. However, as I stated before, in case of the offense of violence in Article 208 and in case of the offense of injury in Article 204 of the Code, the offender is not punished more severely on the grounds that he is a lineal descendant; only in Article 205 of the Code, providing for injury resulting in death, is a more severe penalty meted out on the grounds that the victim is a lineal ascendant. Consequently we cannot say that the main object of the legislation is not the legal benefit of protection for lineal ascendants. And since it "may result in greater protection" because the victim is a lineal ascendant, even though this may be a "reflection," we must state that it is really in violation of the principle of equality of Article 14, paragraph 1, of the Constitution.

6. The majority opinion, seizing upon the statement of the original decision that "while family relations can be considered in the area of the weighing of penalties" in individual cases, and assuming that this be so, counterattacks thus:

. . . it is also unconstitutional to take these circumstances into consideration in weighing penalties when rendering judgment. Or, stated conversely, if one can take these circumstances into consideration constitutionally, then it is also possible constitutionally to go a step further and to objectify them in the form of law.

But there is nothing unusual about a statute which, according to the trends in modern criminal law, establishes minimal and maximal legal penalties and leaves the weighing of the penalty to the court in the light of circumstances. Of course it is not objectionable when the court considers the status relationship between offender and victim as one of those circumstances. Only "to go a step further and to stipulate this in the form of law" can be in violation of the constitutional principle of "equality under the law."

7. The appeal states in item 2 that "since the ascendant-descendant relationship . . . exists with respect to any person, we should not necessarily consider it as a recognition of social discrimination against a specific person." This argument is ultimately in-

tended to exclude the relationship between "lineal ascendants" and "lineal descendants" from the category of "social status" in paragraph 1 of Article 14 of the Constitution. But status does not necessarily have to be specific or fixed. It does not matter if it changes in time. At any rate, if it is determined by law that on a specific occasion a person who has the status of ascendant be accorded on the grounds of that status a treatment different from that of one in the status of descendant, then it cannot be said that this is "equality under the law."

8. The Statement of Reasons for Appeal asserts in item 6 that "it is necessary to distinguish rigidly between the question of whether it is necessary as a future legislative problem to establish such special provisions and the question of whether such provisions in force today are constitutional." The majority opinion agrees with the above statement of the appeal and condemns the original judgment as "confusing constitutional issues and legislative issues." I do not think that the original judgment goes quite as far as that in its argument. True, a constitutional question must not be confused with a legislative question. However, as stated above, the unreasonableness of the provisions of Article 200 and Article 205, paragraph 2, of the Criminal Code is manifest; this has been aggravated because they [the provisions] antedate the new Constitution and because of the amendment of the Civil Code which accompanied the enactment of the new Constitution. So one may well wonder whether the said articles did not, in the light of Article 14, paragraph 1, and Article 98, paragraph 1, of the Constitution become null and void at the time of the enforcement of the Constitution. As also stated above, even without these special provisions there is no particular difficulty in punishing unfilial children under the ordinary provisions, and it is not necessarily wrong in discussing the unconstitutionality of these provisions of the Criminal Code to question their propriety and necessity as legislation.

For these reasons this Justice cannot agree with the majority opinion of the Justices of this Court in the present case, and he believes it proper to reject the prosecution's appeal and to uphold the original judgment.

* * *

The opinion of Justice Saitō Yūsuke follows.

In summary, I agree with the majority opinion that the appeal in this case is well founded; but I absolutely disagree with the minority opinion, which particularly misleads morals and the public mind, and I insist that this Court should directly decide the present case.

The reason for providing in paragraph 1 of Article 14 of the Constitution that "all of the people are equal under the law and there shall be no discrimination in political, economic or social relations, because of race, creed, sex, social status or family origin" is to prohibit unreasonable and unfair treatment such as discrimination in the above relations for the aforesaid reasons, but it does not preclude fair but differential treatment based on reasonable grounds, as I pointed out in my opinion in an earlier Grand Bench judgment (*Hanreishū*, II, No. 6, 550 <Criminal>). In other words, equality under this article means reasonable equality in the treatment of citizens as subjects in fundamental legal relationships; it does not mean a spurious physical or a leveling equality. Therefore, it is not necessarily in violation of this article not to give the right to vote to minors under a certain age, who are actually a majority of the whole nation, or to give only to juveniles and adults connected with juveniles the right to trial under the Juvenile Law, or to give only to women workers special menstrual leave with pay. Also the words "social status" in this article should be interpreted to mean only such status in the life of society as *oyabun* [boss] or *kobun* [henchman], but not a status provided in the Constitution or in law on reasonable grounds. For example, "social status" in the Constitution should be interpreted so as not to include the following: in respect to public officials who are recognized in the Constitution, protection in the execution of their official duties under the Criminal Code,[6] but also punishment for corrupt practices,[7] and the impermissibility [of the application to them] of [liability for injury arising from] necessity [to avert a present danger]; [8] heavier penalties

---

6. Article 95 deals with crimes of obstruction of officials engaged in the performance of their official duties.

7. Chapter XXV of the Criminal Code deals with crimes of official corruption.

8. Justice Saitō's extremely terse phrase is unclear. The phrases supplied in brackets are based on Article 37 of the Criminal Code, which deals with the exemption from punishment of "an act unavoidably done to avert a present danger to the life, person, liberty, or property of oneself or any other person."

for repeated offenders and for those guilty of crimes [of negligence] in their professional capacities; remission of punishment in the case of relatives; or the status referred to in the provisions of Article 65 of the Criminal Code.[9]

Filial piety, which is morality between parent and child, is, after all, the means by which descendants revere their ancestors and, as expressed in the majority opinion, the great fountainhead of human ethics and a universal moral principle of mankind. To recognize the status of lineal ascendants in law in order to follow this morality for the sake of maintaining the order of the state and society definitely has a foundation in reason. It is therefore proper to interpret the status of lineal ascendant as not included in the term "social status" in the Constitution.

The purpose of the Criminal Code is to maintain the order of state and society, to preserve the rights of the people, and to punish those who infringe such order or rights in accordance with the circumstances of their crimes. Accordingly, the punishment of crimes is based on the social and moral responsibility of the criminal offender as subject of his responsibility relations and not on his treatment as the subject in "political, economic, or social relations" as prescribed in Article 14 of the Constitution. Justice Mano confuses the subject in relation to rights with the subject in responsibility relations, and he misconstrues the subject of a crime as the subject of a right to commit a crime. As a result, he contends that the punishment of crimes comes within the category of treatment in political relations under Article 14 of the Constitution. However, Article 14 of the Constitution proclaims that all of the people are equal under the law. This proclamation was stipulated following the provisions regarding the respect of individuals in Chapter 3, which deals with rights and duties of the people. Therefore, this article should be interpreted as the fundamental provision regarding the rights or status of the people, namely, that the people are to receive equal treatment as subjects in fundamental legal relations and are not to be treated discriminatorily without cause. There is absolutely nothing in the fundamental legal relations of citizens that would justify giving to citizens the right or

9. Paragraph 1 of Article 65 reads: "When a person collaborates in a criminal act in which the status of the criminal is an element, that person is an accomplice even though lacking such status."

status to impair the order of state and society or to violate the fundamental rights of others. Much less is there any reason for them to enjoy the constitutional right or status of receiving equal treatment with respect to their responsibility for behavior for which there is no right. As regards the punishment of crimes, the Constitution separately provides proper guarantees in Article 31 and the following. Such being the case, the Criminal Code in accordance with various types of designated status recognizes the formation of crimes and provides different penalties in accordance with their relative gravity. This is a question of legislative policy concerning the conditions under which the responsibility of the offender must be investigated; it cannot be a question of compliance with Article 14 of the Constitution. It is basically erroneous for this Court in the past to have come lightly to the view of the legality of claims of violation of Article 14 of the Constitution in criminal cases, and I think that this should be changed immediately.

However, the original judgment explains as follows:

The provision of Article 205, paragraph 2, of the Criminal Code, viewed in the light of its origin, fondly preserved under the name of a so-called beautiful custom a matter which derived from the idea of severe punishment for patricide, which was regarded as the equivalent of the murder of one's lord because it was considered to be treachery against a parent who, in respect to the child, was viewed as the family head or as a protector or as a figure of authority.

But, as I shall explain later, such an explanation is nothing but irresponsible loose talk with absolutely no historical foundation. To agree with a statement of this type, it would be necessary to have strict and clear evidence. The original judgment also explains that this provision "derived as it is from quite feudalistic, antidemocratic, and antilibertarian ideas, runs counter to the grand spirit of the Constitution, which stresses the legal equality of all human beings." It must be stated that to go this far is democratic infantilism, which cannot but be surprising, and a deplorable idea of civil liberties. Why is it feudalistic to respect in the Criminal Code the great fountainhead of human ethics and a universal principle of mankind? Why is it antidemocratic to impose a more severe punishment upon murder or injury resulting in death of lineal ascendants, which all people recognize as being immoral? Furthermore, does anybody have the right under the Constitution to take away the life of another? If, as Justice Mano insists, independence, which is the basis of the equality of all men, is accompanied by responsibility, and if democracy is, after all, based on the equality of basic human rights between individual and individual, then it must be said to be equal and democratic that a man, no matter who he might be, who has taken the life of another have his own life taken away. If we stand on such a view of democracy and go a step further and follow the logic of the original judgment, I wonder if we might not say that even the provisions of part of Article 199 or Article 205, paragraph 1, of the Criminal Code, which make a life sentence or a sentence of two or three years' penal servitude sufficient [punishment] for one, even though he has taken the life of another, because of his status as a defendant in a criminal case, "run counter to the great spirit of the Constitution which stresses the legal equality of all human beings" and are therefore null and void? Actually, in Anglo-American law an especially severe penalty for the murder of lineal ascendants is not sanctioned, because any person killing another is generally subject to the death penalty. Why does not the original judgment respect the life of the victim which, above all, is guaranteed constitutionally simply as that of a human being?

In addition, the original judgment holds "that the fact that the provisions concerning accusation and indictment against grandparents and parents were abolished points directly to this (the abolition of the provisions concerning the murder of ascendants)." However, the abolition of Articles 259 and 270 of the former Code of Criminal Procedure [10] was due to the influence of the power of those who mistakenly believed that the ideas of loyalty and filial piety in this country constituted a basis for extreme nationalism. Actually, it would not have caused any inconvenience if these articles had been retained as long as there was also Article 263 (Article 234 of the new Code) [11] and, although they [Articles 259 and 270] have been abolished, Article 248 of the Code of Criminal Procedure [12] (Article 279 of the former

10. These articles dealt with accusation and indictment of grandparents and parents.

11. Article 234 reads: "If there is no person to file a complaint, in respect to an offense subject to prosecution on complaint, a public prosecutor may, on the application of any person interested, designate a person who can file a complaint."

12. Article 248 reads: "If, after considering the character, age, and situation of the offender, the gravity of the offense, the circumstances under which the offense was committed, and the

Code) is still applicable. Therefore, those who blindly welcome such an unnecessary amendment, wagging their tails and flapping their ears as it were, have a feudalistic and slavish disposition.

Primarily, filial piety is the road descendants follow to respect ancestors. Looking only at our nation, our ancestors who lived before us numbered certainly over a billion, and the present descendants number only a little over eighty million. We should remember over and over again that every word or phrase we use, the very mouths and lips that form those words, and even you and I are the heritage of our ancestors. We must reject completely such ideas as those of the original judgment and of the minority opinions, which must be called conceited notions of ingratitude, lacking in understanding of this morality, and aimlessly chasing after innovations.

Next let me say a few words about the minority opinions. The Mano opinion cites as significant the motto to be found on the building of the Supreme Court of the United States and the Universal Declaration of Human Rights of the United Nations. But, alas, in America the laws of the various states are not necessarily identical, and accordingly, it is needless to say that in practice justice cannot be equal under such differing laws. In addition, it is a fact well known throughout the world that there are many racially discriminatory laws in the United States. For this very reason it is necessary that the four words which the writer of the opinion quotes as a motto be engraved on that white marble on the Supreme Court building; they may be a warning lesson for our Constitution but they are completely unworthy as a model. It goes without saying that the Universal Declaration of Human Rights is a declaration to the whole world and is, of course, greatly welcome to us who are internationally discriminated against at present [1950, two years before the end of the occupation] in political, economic, and social relations. But it is not proper to quote such an international declaration as an aid in the interpretation of a constitution or other laws of a specific country. Therefore, to cite these at the beginning of an opinion interpreting Article 14 of our Constitution is, if not deceiving people with a devil's mask, like selling dog's meat while displaying a lamb's head.

---

conditions subsequent to the commission of the offense, prosecution is deemed unnecessary, prosecution may not be instituted."

I have already touched on one or two of the arguments that follow, but, in short, I find it unbearable to read the rest of the opinion for it develops an academically prostituted theory that is a national disgrace—a theory based on self-centered egoism under the beautiful name of democracy.

The Hozumi opinion mainly criticizes the legislation concerning the legal penalties of Articles 199 and 200 of the Criminal Code. But under the former Criminal Code only the death penalty and life imprisonment were sanctioned for the crime of murder, just as is the case in the legislation of many foreign countries. Therefore even the "murder of one's own child" and especially infanticide, when committed to hide a family disgrace or because of difficulties in raising the child, was out of necessity treated as manslaughter, and even if the maximum reduction of the second grade was made, these crimes had to be subjected to heavy penal servitude (more than nine years but less than eleven years). So, in practice there was often nothing to do but to grant a special amnesty in such cases. In view of this experience, when the present Criminal Code was being enacted a draft amendment was made in order to handle these cases by making it possible to impose imprisonment of not less than five years. At the same time the original draft concerning the suspension of execution of sentence, which provided that only those sentenced to imprisonment of less than one year or penal servitude of less than six months (so-called short term imprisonment) were to be entitled to such suspension, was changed to read that those who are sentenced to penal servitude or imprisonment of less than two years are entitled to suspension of execution of sentence; and this was changed to imprisonment of less than three years, as in the present Code, so that it would be applicable [to suspension of execution]. Therefore, penal servitude for more than three years, as in Article 199 of the Criminal Code, was mainly designed to be applied to cases of infanticide, although the death penalty or life imprisonment was intended to apply to those who killed adults. Furthermore, the former Criminal Code contained in Book III, Chapter 1, section 13, exhaustive provisions for offenses against the persons of grandparents and parents; in particular, Article 362 reads: "Descendants who commit murder or manslaughter against their grandparents shall be sentenced to death." Thus, the only punishment for what was termed murder of ascendants was the death penalty. But the present Article 200 of the Criminal Code, mitigating the former article, has made it possible to impose penal servitude for life in these cases.

In addition, when the thirteenth section of the former Code was amended the terms "grandparent" and "parent" were abolished and a new term "lineal ascendant," which was originally a term used in civil law, was used; and at the same time, the provisions concerning more severe punishment for assault causing injury, false accusation, and slander against lineal ascendants were abolished and, in general, penalties prescribed by law for the offenses committed against lineal ascendants were all mitigated. (The case of murder of ascendants has already been discussed; death resulting from injury by assault or from other offenses used to be punished by the death sentence, which now is reduced to life sentence or servitude of more than three years.) Besides, the provisions of Article 365 of the former Criminal Code, which prohibited resort to the principles of special pardons and nonindictable offenses, were repealed and the new Code made it possible to take self-defense and, of course, extenuating circumstances into consideration. I would like to have you who wrote that opinion go ahead and explain to me, if you can, why the above amendments preserve the idea of severe punishment for patricide, what is left of the old framework, and what is unreasonable as legislation! The problem is rather whether or not the method of providing legal penalties under the present Code is proper. The legal penalties under the present Criminal Code mitigate the penalties sanctioned by the former Code and at the same time bring together under one article, dealing with one charge, all the penalties for crimes which, though committed in different ways, are the same offense. There is no other example in the world of a code in which the variety and scope of legal penalties are so wide and numerous. The penalties of every article in our Criminal Code do not, as scholars often mistakenly argue, set forth single evaluations of only one fact relevant to the conditions constituting a single crime; rather, it should be especially noted that, anticipating the existence of so-called repeated crimes, related crimes, inclusive crimes, and, of course, habitual crimes, comprehensive provisions were made so that all of these could be handled. Such a way of providing penalties cannot be considered as following in a strict sense the principle of legality [*nullum crimen sine lege, nulla poena sine lege*]. At the time that the old Criminal Code was revised the selection of legal penalties and the weighing of penalties to be imposed were not much different from what the old Criminal Code had provided; but as time passed, the penalties provided in the old Code were gradually forgotten, and at present there is a general tendency to use as a standard the lightest type and the shortest term of legal penalty. In calling a lenient sentence the mercy of the law, crying out for suspension of execution of sentence in every utterance, slandering the dead, and neglecting the victim, things have come to the point where fundamental human rights seem to exist only for the surviving offender in the courtroom.

In short, we must say that the opinion of the other disputant looks only at the letter of the present Criminal Code but shows no awareness of its historical background, and that it is based on the preconceived idea that, as under the old order, crimes against ascendants are dealt with only by severe penalties.

Lastly, the majority opinion concluded that this case should be sent back to the original court according to the main clause of Article 413 of the Code of Criminal Procedure. However, I am of the opinion that this case can be judged immediately according to the evidence examined in the original court and the records of the proceedings there; and I think that the decision should be made immediately by this Grand Bench according to the proviso of the same article for the sake of economy.

(TRANSLATED BY KURT STEINER)

Hanreishū, II, No. 3, 191 (Criminal)

EDITORIAL NOTE: The accused murdered his mother and younger
sister and threw their bodies into a well. The crime was caused by
a number of factors: the postwar shortage of food, the poverty of
the family, which forced the mother and sister to work desperately
to earn enough to live, and the accused's unwillingness to contribute
to the family's livelihood. The situation between the accused and
his mother and sister led to violent quarrels; and finally, after the
two women declared that they would provide no food as long as
the accused refused to earn his share of the family income, he
murdered them both.

The issue of parricide was not raised in this case. The grounds
for appeal to the Supreme Court are clearly brought out in the
decision.

Grand Bench decision, March 12, 1948: Dismissed.

REFERENCES

Constitution of Japan. ARTICLE 13. All of the people shall
be respected as individuals. Their right to life, liberty, and the
pursuit of happiness shall, to the extent that it does not interfere
with the public welfare, be the supreme consideration in legislation and other governmental affairs.

ARTICLE 31. No person shall be deprived of life or liberty, nor shall any other criminal penalty be imposed, except according to procedure established by law.

ARTICLE 36. The infliction of torture by any public officer and cruel punishments are absolutely forbidden.

FORMAL JUDGMENT

The appeal in the present case is dismissed.

REASONS. Point 1 of attorney Nishimura Masando's argument for appeal is as follows:

The original judgment is an illegal one which applied the law on the basis of an erroneous interpretation, to wit: it applied Articles 199 and 200 of the Criminal Code to the accused and handed down the death penalty. But this is in contravention of the Constitution because Article 36 of the new Constitution provides as follows: "The infliction of torture by any public officer and cruel punishments are absolutely forbidden." Because the death penalty is the cruelest of all punishments, the provisions regarding it in Articles 199 and 200 of the Criminal Code should properly be interpreted as having been abrogated by the new Constitution. Nevertheless, the original decision passed the sentence of death on the accused, applying to him the provisions in Articles 199 and 200 of the Criminal Code concerning the death penalty, which is absolutely prohibited by the new Constitution and automatically null and void. Therefore, we are convinced that it cannot avoid proper revocation as an illegal decision, which applied the law on the basis of an erroneous interpretation.

Life is precious. One human life is of more importance than the whole earth. The death penalty is certainly the grimmest of all punishments. It is the ultimate one and is indeed unavoidable. The reason is simply that it involves the eternal deprivation of life, the source of dignified human existence. Every modern country as a function of its general sovereign power must exercise the right of punishment. Therefore, they have made legal provisions recognizing or not recognizing the death penalty as a variety of punishment, the nature of the crimes for which it is to be inflicted, and the manner in which it is to be carried out. Thus, the criminal courts make judgments in concrete cases whether the death penalty or some other punishment will be inflicted on the accused.

A verdict of death that has been decided in the above manner must actually be carried out according to methods and procedures established by law. In view of these considerations, the institution of the death penalty always requires deep thought and consideration from the standpoint of both national criminal policy and humanity.

Nevertheless, if we review the history of punishment in each country, we can perceive that the death penalty and its utilization have—like everything else—changed, shifted, and developed in accordance with history and circumstance. Very recently in our own country we have had a striking illustration of such change in the termination of various types of death penalty by the abolition of the Peace Preservation Law, the National Defense and Security Law, the Army Penal Code, the Naval Penal Code, the Military Secrets Preservation Law, the Law concerning Special Rules for the Punishment of Wartime Crimes, and others.

Accordingly, what is the attitude of the new Constitution regarding the death penalty? Are the provisions of the Criminal Code that apply the death penalty invalid because of unconstitutionality, as one would expect from the assertion of the attorney?

First of all, Article 13 of the Constitution provides that all of the people shall be respected as individuals and that their right to life shall be a supreme consideration in legislation and other governmental affairs. However, at the same time in the same article, it must naturally be presumed that in cases in which the basic principle of the public welfare is violated even the right of the people to life can be legally limited or taken away. Then, again, in accordance with Article 31 of the Constitution, even though the life of the individual is precious, it is clear that a punishment that would deprive the individual of life can be inflicted under appropriate procedures established by law. That is to say, the Constitution [of Japan], like those in most civilized countries at the present time, must be interpreted to assume and approve the retention of the death penalty as a form of punishment. In other words, the threat of the death penalty itself may be a general preventive measure, the execution of the death penalty may be a means of cutting off at the root special social evils, and both may be used to protect society. Again, this [approval of the death penalty] must be interpreted as giving supremacy to the concept of humanity as a whole rather than to the concept of humanity as individuals; and continuation of the death penalty must ultimately be recognized as necessary for the public welfare.

The attorney claims that the provisions of the Criminal Code concerning the death penalty are unconstitutional because of the provision of Article 36 of the Constitution, which absolutely forbids cruel punishment. The death penalty, as we pointed out above, is both the ultimate and the grimmest of punishments; but the death penalty, as a punishment, is not generally regarded as being one of the cruel punishments referred to in the said article. Nevertheless, the death penalty, when the method of carrying it out is generally recognized as cruel from the humanitarian point of view of a particular period under certain circumstances, must then, like other punishments, be termed cruel. Therefore, if a law is enacted that calls for a cruel method such as those used in the past—burning at the stake, crucifixion, gibbeting, or boiling in a cauldron—then that law itself must be regarded as truly in contravention of Article 36 of the Constitution. As was pointed out above, the argument of the attorney that interprets the death penalty as a cruel punishment and holds the provisions of the Criminal Code regarding the death penalty to be unconstitutional is groundless.

Point 2 of the attorney's argument for appeal is as follows:

The original judgment is illegal because the trial procedure was not exhausted, to wit:

That the defendant may have been suffering from a mental disorder at the time of the crime is strikingly clear from the record as presented below:

1. Question (from the presiding judge): "As was said before, his mother and younger sister were suffering from a lack of food, and even though they complained bitterly about the accused's not working seriously to bring in rice, it would never occur to an ordinary person to kill them. Were there any other considerations?"

Answer (from the accused): "There was nothing else in particular." (From p. 177a of the record.)

Question (from the presiding judge): ". . . As for the cause, would it or would it not be considered usual for an accused to say that he decided to kill someone for those reasons?"

Answer: None recorded. (From p. 177b of the record.)

2. The prosecutor in his argument said of the accused, "There seems to be reason to doubt that any mental abnormality had appeared. . . ." (From p. 186 of the record.)

3. The attorney in his argument said of the accused, "There seems to be reason to feel that he was suffering from some kind of mental illness at the time." (From p. 187a of the record.)

Now, since the mental state of the accused at the time of the deed seems related to matters that should be investigated under the authority of the court, a situation in which there is clear doubt concerning the mental state of the accused, as in the present case, would seem to be one in which it is properly under the jurisdiction of the court either to entrust it [the examination] to expert opinion or for the court on its own to determine whether or not the accused was suffering from a mental disorder, to judge its extent, and to determine whether or not Article 39 of the Criminal Code is applicable. [This article provides that insane persons shall not be punished and that sentences shall be reduced for weak-minded persons.] Consequently, the fact that the court heedlessly sentenced the accused to death without resorting to such action is illegal on the grounds that the trial procedure was not exhausted and we believe that it cannot avoid revocation for this reason.

However, even a minute examination of the record will show that there was not sufficient ground for believing that the accused at the time of the criminal action in this case was suffering from a mental disorder. Therefore the original decision, which also found that the accused had no mental disorder, was not illegal on the grounds that the court proceedings were not exhausted, even though no resort was made to expert opinion or other examination of the accused's mental condition. The argument is groundless.

The third point of the argument for appeal is as follows:

The original judgment is illegal because it omitted a decision which must be shown in the verdict, to wit:

In the original trial the attorney said of the accused, "There seems to be reason to feel that he was suffering from some kind of mental illness at the time." (From p. 187a of the record.) Because he argued thus and asserted that as a matter of fact the existence of a mental disorder in the accused at the time of the criminal action constituted a legal reason preventing the formation of an offense in the present case, the original judgment in spite of the necessity for a decision in regard to the above argument did not make a decision in this matter. Consequently, we believe that it cannot avoid complete revocation because it is an illegal judgment which omitted a decision in respect to a point that had to be judged.

However, according to the protocol of the public trial in the first instance, the attorney in the original trial did nothing more than assert that there was fear that the accused may have had a mental disorder, and because that cannot be interpreted as an argument stating a reason as stipulated in Article 360, paragraph 2, of the Code of Criminal Procedure, even though the original judgment did not decide on that point, it is not an omission of a decision. The argument is groundless.

Accordingly, we decide as in the formal decision in accordance with Article 10, No. 1, of the Court Law,[1] and Article 446 of the [former] Code of Criminal Procedure.[2]

The above is the unanimous opinion of the Justices.

Further, the supplementary opinions regarding point 1 of the argument of appeal follow.

*   *   *

The opinion of Justices Shima Tamotsu, Fujita Hachirō, Iwamatsu Saburō, and Kawamura Matasuke.

The Constitution absolutely forbids cruel punishments. Accordingly, granting that the death penalty is naturally a cruel punishment, the Constitution provides no grounds in any of its other provisions for recognizing the maintenance of the death penalty. However, if one interprets Article 31 of the Constitution from the reverse side, the Constitution does not directly prohibit the death penalty as a cruel punishment because the death penalty can be inflicted as a punishment in accordance with the provisions of the law. However, the Constitution goes no further than to establish a provision such as the above, reflecting the people's feelings at the time that the Constitution was enacted; it should not be regarded as eternally approving the death penalty. The judgment of whether certain punishments are cruel is a question that should be decided according to the feelings of the people. However, because the feelings of the people cannot escape changing with the times, what at one time may be regarded as not being a cruel punishment may at a later period be judged the reverse.

Accordingly, as a nation's culture develops to a high degree, and as a peaceful society is realized on the basis of justice and order, and if a time is reached when it is not felt to be necessary for the public welfare to prevent crime by the menace of the death penalty, then both the death penalty and cruel punishments will certainly be eliminated because of the feelings of the people.

In such a situation the interpretation of Article 31 of the Constitution will probably be limited as a matter of course and the death penalty will be eliminated as a cruel punishment which

1. Article 10 of the Court Organization Law requires the Grand Bench to make decisions on issues of constitutionality.

2. *Former Code of Criminal Procedure.* ARTICLE 446. When an appeal against a judgment in the second instance is found groundless, it shall be dismissed by means of a judgment.

contravenes the Constitution. However, it cannot be said that we have already reached such a stage today. Consequently, we cannot accept the argument of the attorney which asserts that the original judgment is illegal for the reason that the death penalty is a cruel punishment prohibited by the Constitution.

*   *   *

The opinion of Justice Inouye Nobori.

I believe that the reasons for the decision in the present case as recorded above are generally acceptable, but I would like to enlarge somewhat on the legal basis.

Haphazardly and without reference to the wording of the law, one cannot state simply and positively in a word that the death penalty is or is not cruel. The use of the word "cruel" can vary greatly. For example, there are people who use it, as in the argument for appeal, thus: "Because the death penalty snatches away precious human life, is there anything crueler?" (For the time being, we shall call this usage in the wide sense.) But the following also can probably be said: "Isn't the word 'cruel' not usually used in such a sense? Because it is used especially in situations of massacre, mass slayings, or brutal mayhem, is it not used but seldom in respect to murder or bodily injury?" (For the time being, we shall call this usage in the narrow sense.) But this is not a clear enough statement of the problem.

The question before us is not put in this way; concretely, it is the question of whether the phrase "cruel punishment" in Article 36 of the Constitution may or may not be used to include the death penalty (both here and below "death penalty" refers to that punishment carried out by accepted methods of contemporary civilized countries). (Our question here is whether the text of the Criminal Code that provides for the death penalty is invalid because it contravenes Article 36 of the Constitution. In brief, the question is whether the said article [Article 36] can be interpreted as absolutely prohibiting the death penalty.) Thus, because this is a simple question of the interpretation of a law, the basis of the text of the law is a matter of importance. Because, as I have written above, I believe the word "cruel" can be used both broadly and narrowly, I think that it is unreasonable to settle this question only on the basis of the wording of Article 36 of the Constitution and that it is necessary to seek the basis of the text of the law in other provisions.

Accordingly, Article 13 of the Constitution provides, "All of the people shall be respected as individuals. Their right to *life,* liberty, and the pursuit of happiness shall, *to the extent that it does not interfere with the public welfare,* be the supreme consideration in legislation and other governmental affairs." and Article 31, "No person shall be deprived of *life* or liberty, nor shall any other criminal penalty be imposed, except according to procedure established by law." [Emphasis in original.]

Putting these two together and interpreting both, it must be recognized that the Constitution acknowledges the possibility that for the public welfare human life may be taken as a punishment, according to procedures established by law. When we examine Article 36 in contrast to this, it is reasonable to interpret "cruel punishment" therein as not including the death penalty, namely, that the said article does not mean that it absolutely does not permit the death penalty. (Thus, because the said article uses the word "cruel" in the narrow sense and because I think that this usage is common, I believe that the above interpretation is reasonable, even from the standpoint of the meaning of the word itself.)

The opposing view holds that Article 31 is limited by Article 36. However, if Article 31 is examined dispassionately, this view must be regarded as being nothing more than an unreasonable and farfetched interpretation. If Article 36 is taken to mean that the death penalty is absolutely impermissible, then it becomes absolutely impossible to take human life as a punishment, even though there may be formal procedures for doing so, and therefore it would not only be unnecessary to insert the word "life" in Article 31 but, on the contrary, it should not be so inserted. After all, to the extent that the word "life" appears in Article 31, the development of the interpretation set down above [of Articles 13 and 31], which is opposed to this idea [of impermissibility], is reasonable and is not an awkward interpretation of the meaning of the Constitution. In addition, no basis in the text of the law can be found for the interpretation that Article 36 includes an absolute prohibition of the death penalty.

The above is a formal, theoretical interpretation. Unfortunately, the conditions of our society and other factors at the present time make it impossible to think that provisions regarding the death penalty in the Criminal Code can rightly be immediately and completely declared invalid. I believe that the other justices have written enough on this point and on other substantial reasons.

Finally, in Justice Shima's supplementary opinion I surmise that he is perhaps controlled by a thought or feeling such as the following: "Whatever one may say, I agree with the statement that the death penalty is an unpleasant thing and that it will be well when the time comes, without a day's delay, when that sort of thing will not be necessary." I do not think I am second to anyone in regard to this feeling. However, it is obvious that the Constitution does not state that the death penalty is absolutely impermissible and, of course, does not direct its retention. Thus, when the time comes that the death penalty is no longer necessary or when the feelings of the entire people can no longer tolerate it, the National Diet will abolish the provision for the death penalty or, even though it may remain, judges will not select it. The true situation at the present time is that no one willingly hands down the death penalty.

(TRANSLATED BY J. M. MAKI)

Hanreishū, IX, No. 5, 924 (Criminal)

EDITORIAL NOTE: The accused was arrested in October, 1948, for complicity in illicit brewing. He was charged with permitting the principal offender—the person doing the actual brewing—to use his premises and with serving as a caretaker during the latter's absence. He was found guilty and sentenced to three months' hard labor.

He lost on appeal and then carried his case to the Supreme Court. The principal ground for his appeal was that the tax collector entered his premises and searched them without a warrant. The collector's report, based on evidence gathered during the entry and search, was the principal evidence in the trial. Because the accused was not arrested at the time of the entry and search, he argued that Articles 33 and 35 were violated, for they provide for arrest, entry, search, and seizure without warrant only when a crime is actually being committed.

Grand Bench decision, April 27, 1955: Dismissed.

REFERENCES

National Tax Violation Control Law. ARTICLE 3, paragraph 1. In regard to cases in which it is found that a violation relating to the national indirect tax is actually occurring or that such violation has already occurred and the tax collector is unable to obtain the authorization required under paragraph 1 or paragraph 2 [1] of the preceding article, he may take the action [entry, search, or seizure] provided for in paragraph 1 of the said article on the spot if it is necessary for the gathering of evidence and for quick action.

Constitution of Japan. ARTICLE 35.   1. The right of all persons to be secure in their homes, papers, and effects against entries, searches, and seizures shall not be impaired except upon warrant issued for adequate cause and particularly describing the place to be searched and things to be seized, or except as provided by Article 33.

2. Each search or seizure shall be made upon separate warrant issued by a competent judicial officer.

ARTICLE 33.   No person shall be apprehended except upon warrant issued by a competent judicial officer which specifies the offense with which the person is charged, unless he is apprehended, the offense being committed.

FORMAL JUDGMENT

The appeal in the present case is dismissed.

REASONS. Concerning the substance of attorney Kwŏn's appeal: Article 35 of the Constitution guarantees the right of the people to be secure in their homes, papers, and effects against entry, search, and seizure, except as provided by Article 33. It is clear that the legal intent of Article 35 is that in cases in which the guarantee of nonapprehension given in Article 33 does not exist, the right of the people to be secure against search, seizure, and so forth, likewise is not guaranteed.

Moreover, because Article 33 stipulates that, even though arrest be made without the warrant called for in that article, the guarantee of nonapprehension does not apply when a crime is actually being committed, it must be stated that the guarantee of Article 35 also does not extend to cases in which the crime is actually being committed. Therefore, at least in cases in which an offense is actually being committed, even though the law [National Tax Violation Control Law, Article 3] prescribes that searches, seizures, and so forth can be effected on the scene of the offense by

1. The said paragraphs require that in cases of entry, search, or seizure in the course of investigation of alleged violations the tax collector must obtain court authorization.

someone [e.g., a tax collector] other than a judicial police officer or without a warrant issued by a judicial police officer, the problem is only that of the propriety of the legislation itself, and there is no room for the question of a violation of Article 35 of the Constitution to arise. Consequently, we cannot accept the assertions [in the appeal], based on grounds differing from the above, that the provisions of Article 3, paragraph 1, of the National Tax Violation Control Law contravene Article 35 of the Constitution and on that premise that there has also been a violation of procedural law in the appeal judgment.

Concerning point 1 of the argument of attorneys Kwŏn and Ikenabe:[2] It was established in the original decision that the materials in dispute were the liquors, unrefined sake, and yeasts involved in the illicit brewing in question and the machines, utensils, and containers used in their manufacture and, moreover, that the said materials were in the possession of the principal offender in the present crime. Therefore, since the confiscation of the above materials was carried out in accordance with the stipulations of Article 60, paragraph 3, and Article 64, paragraph 2, of the Liquor Tax Law (prior to amendment under Law No. 43 of 1949), the original verdict cannot be regarded as illegal as the argument [for appeal] contends.

Concerning points 2 and 3: The original judgment in finding the accused guilty of the crime of complicity, also found as a fact of the crime of the principal offender his relation with the accused. But, because it did not make a finding in the form of a judgment

---

2. Summarized in this note are points 1–4, 6, and 7 of the argument of the attorneys: Point 1. Because the materials in question were in the possession of the principal offender, not the present accused, they could not be offered in evidence in the trial.

Point 2. This was a double argument: that it was improper to designate the principal offender without a trial and that it was improper to confiscate his possessions.

Point 3. The original judgment was improper in affirming complicity without establishing the principal offense.

Point 4. This was the contention that the verdict of guilty had been pronounced without sufficient evidence, especially on the question of whether the principal offender had received a government permit for brewing.

Point 6. This maintained that the trial procedure had not been exhausted because the principal offender had not been examined as to whether the defendant was actually responsible for caretaking, even though the latter had admitted it.

Point 7. This was to the effect that only the confession of the accused was used in establishing the crime and that the report in question dealt only with the principal offense.

Points 5, 8, and 9 are not summarized here for they are not needed to understand the opinions dealing with them.

of the crime of the principal offender, there was no need for proceedings or a judgment of that person as the argument [for appeal] contends. Also, the said person's right to trial was not violated by this act [the finding of fact in the original judgment].[3] Moreover, that the seizure in question was not illegal is as explained in the previous point. The argument is groundless.

Concerning points 4 and 6: The facts that are pointed out in the original decision can be judged on the basis of the cited evidence. The arguments here, because they do nothing more than criticize the finding of the facts and the choice of the evidence in the original decision, do not constitute legal reasons for appeal.

Concerning point 5: According to the record of the trial proceedings, the documents in question were submitted only with the intention of presenting a summary in court solely for reference to the circumstances of the crime and should not be regarded as presenting documentary and other evidence for the defense. Consequently, we cannot accept the argument that the original decision is illegal because the above documents were not presented as evidence in open court in the original trial.

Concerning point 7: According to the report in question compiled by an official of the Finance Ministry, it is possible to prove that the utensils, machinery, and so forth, used in the illicit brewing in this case were confiscated in the home of the accused. Because it is clear that the above document can be used as corroboration for the confession of the accused, the argument is groundless.

Concerning point 8: Because this argument asserts the illegality of the original decision on the premise of facts not admitted in the original decision, it is not acceptable.

Concerning point 9: That the weighing of the offense in the original trial cannot be regarded, as the argument maintains, as an infringement of "trial by an impartial tribunal" guaranteed by the Constitution is clear from a number of precedents of this

---

3. Neither the argument for appeal nor the decision is clear on this point. Apparently the argument (see points 2 and 3 above) was that the original judgment should be quashed because of its unconstitutional action both in denying the right to trial of the principal offender, who was not on trial in the present case, and affirming complicity without establishing the principal offense. The decision holds that since in the present trial the fact of the relationship between the accused and the principal offender was established, therefore, the issue of the trial of the principal offender was not germane.

Court. Consequently, this Court decides as in the formal judgment.

This decision is the unanimous opinion of all the Justices, except for the supplementary opinions of Justices Kuriyama Shigeru, Saitō Yūsuke, Kobayashi Shunzō, and Iriye Toshio, and the minority opinion of Justice Fujita Hachirō in regard to the substance of the argument for appeal of attorney Kwŏn.

* * *

The supplementary opinion of Justices Saitō Yūsuke and Kobayashi Shunzō in regard to the substance of attorney Kwŏn's argument for appeal follows.

Article 35 and the provision of Article 33 of the Constitution cited in Article 35, paragraph 1, relate to criminal procedure, not to administrative procedure. Provisions relating to administrative actions need only be regulated reasonably by legislation, in accordance with Articles 11 to 13 of the Constitution and, above all, the second part of Article 13. (As the Kuriyama opinion given below states, there naturally cannot be arbitrary regulation on the pretext of serving the public welfare.) Thus, Article 3 of the National Tax Violation Control Law is the legal provision relating to administrative procedures concerning indirect taxes (for details see the Iriye opinion below), and in the light of its content it cannot be held that it is lacking in respect for the second part of Article 13 of the Constitution and in contravention of the said article. Consequently, the argument that the provisions of the above control law contravene Article 35 of the Constitution, which deals with criminal procedure, and the assertion of a violation of procedural law, using the preceding as premise, cannot be accepted.

* * *

The supplementary opinion presented by Justice Iriye Toshio regarding the substance of attorney Kwŏn's argument for appeal follows.

In regard to the rejection of the appeal in the present case, I have reached the same conclusion as the majority opinion, but I cannot agree with their interpretation, given therein as the reason for the rejection of the substance of attorney Kwŏn's argument for appeal, of the phrase "as provided by Article 33" in Article 35, paragraph 1, of the Constitution. I hold the same view as that presented by Justices Saitō and Kobayashi in their supplementary opinion, that Article 35 of the Constitution and the provision of Article 33 referred to in the first paragraph of Article 35 deal solely with criminal procedures; and that Article 3 of the National Tax Violation Control Law is a provision for administrative action in respect to indirect taxes. I also cannot accept the assertion that the provisions in question in the above control law violate Article 35 of the Constitution, which deals with criminal procedures, and on that premise violate procedural laws.

I believe that the argument of the attorney given above should be rejected only in respect to the reasons given in the above views, and below I clarify the reasons and express my opinion on this point.

(1) That the provisions of Article 35, together with the various provisions of Article 33, concern criminal procedure and do not apply directly to administrative procedures, other than criminal ones, is understandable from the enactment of the new Constitution, the position in the Constitution of that article, and its relation to other constitutional provisions. However, this interpretation may be thought improper for two reasons: certain restrictions on fundamental human rights regarding person, home, papers, possessions, and so forth, may be necessary in administrative procedures, other than criminal, because of the requirements of the public welfare; or, there must be strict limitations only on criminal procedures and administrative procedures may be left freely to administrative authority.

The Constitution notes, however, the special character of the administrative process, namely, that administration is carried out to achieve complex public objectives and, accordingly, that it is desirable that the concrete content and procedures of the administrative process should be the most appropriate for the achievement of administrative objectives.[4] Therefore, it is right and

---

4. There is no specific provision in the Constitution that can be clearly regarded as the basis of Justice Iriye's argument here. However, it is reasonable to assume that Article 73, which outlines the numerous administrative functions of the cabinet, was the principal basis for his point.

proper to construe appropriate regulations relating to limitations necessary for administrative procedures that may affect fundamental human rights relating to person, residence, papers, possessions, and so forth, as not falling directly under the provisions of Articles 33 and 35 of the Constitution but as being entrusted to the legislative process within the limits of Articles 12, 13, and 31 of the Constitution. However, I construe this to mean that, of course, legislation should be in accordance with the provisions of the above Articles 12, 13, and 31 of the Constitution, and that any required limitation upon fundamental human rights in such cases should naturally be the minimum necessary for the public welfare and should be entrusted to legislative policy within the above limits.

(2) The procedure under Article 3 of the National Tax Violation Control Law is a special one for the investigation of cases of violations of indirect tax [laws] and is carried out according to Article 2 thereof; the investigation of violations of indirect tax [laws] carried out by tax collectors in accordance with the same law is a procedure of financial administration regarded as necessary to insure the collection of indirect taxes. These are not criminal procedures. The procedures of Article 3 of the same law that accompany the investigation used in the handling of such violations are also procedures of financial administration, not criminal procedures.

Criminal procedures in accordance with the said law in respect to cases of violation of indirect national tax regulations may be initiated only after indictment under Article 17 of that law. Some may, perhaps, consider "action by notification"[5] concerning indirect national taxes as in substance a criminal procedure. On that assumption they may maintain that investigation of violations of indirect national tax regulations—a procedure prior to

---

5. "Action by notification" (*tsūkoku shobun*) is defined on page 682, of the *Shin Hōritsugaku Jiten* ("New Dictionary of Jurisprudence"), Wagatsuma Sakae, ed. (Tokyo: Yuhikaku, 1958), as follows:

Administrative action which involves the issuing of a notification ordering delivery to a designated place of confiscated goods or the payment of appropriate sums in fines or monetary penalties in cases in which the competent tax office has established proof of violation in respect to indirect national taxes, customs, tonnage dues, the government monopolies, and so forth, by means of an investigation of said offenses. It is an administrative procedure involving determination of a penalty, but not founded on the procedure in criminal investigation. . . .

indictment—and the incidental procedures under Article 3 of the control law are also criminal procedures.

However, action by notification, as provided for by Article 14 of the said law, is notification concerning matters such as the delivery or payment at a specified place of appropriate fines or monetary penalties, confiscated goods, appropriate monetary assessments, and expenses arising from the delivery of documents and the transportation and storage of confiscated articles. These are only actions in financial administration that place a monetary obligation on violators of the indirect tax law in order to achieve the full collection of taxes. Also, the monetary obligations, it must be noted, are of a basically different character from fines in that they are not imposed against the will of the other party and in that, even if imposed, they are not considered a conviction. Again, action by notification, rather than being considered as either a punishment or a sanction, should preferably be conceived of as a special procedure in financial administration, a "friendly settlement" under which—if the state is to guarantee its right to collect taxes, especially the easily evaded indirect tax—the state and the individual (when the former is on the verge of punishing the latter) arrive, after having taken into account both the circumstances of the violation and the individual's examination of his own conscience, at a friendly agreement under which the latter is pardoned.

It is well also to note that this is the concept of *Vergleich* [in original] in German law, the source of the procedure. The legislative history of the Law for the Handling of Violators of the National Indirect Tax, which was the predecessor of the Tax Violation Control Law, can also be referred to in this matter. The earlier law was enacted in September, 1890, and went into effect on January 1, 1891. In the beginning, action by notification had a strong flavor of punishment, and perhaps it can be considered to have been equivalent to criminal procedure; but when the said law was completely revised under Law No. 67 of 1900 and during the Diet deliberation on it, it could be seen that action by notification had the essence of friendly settlement and was not a judicial matter. This can perhaps also be grasped from the reasons for the revision of the accompanying regulations.

Again, Article 18 of the law in question in this case provides that in cases resulting in a criminal indictment, articles confiscated or taken into custody under the above procedure are to be handed over to a public prosecutor; and it is stipulated that when they are so handed over, the articles in question must be handled by the public prosecutor as confiscated matter according to the provisions of the Code of Criminal Procedure. That this stipulation was especially so enacted can be taken as proof that the procedure prior to the indictment is an administrative, not a criminal, one. Also, simply because the stipulations of the said article exist does not mean that the articles are properly admissible as evidence in subsequent criminal procedures; it can properly be construed that the admissibility of evidence in criminal procedure must be decided on the basis of whether or not the procedure at the time the said articles were confiscated or taken into custody did not differ in substance from the requirements of Article 35 of the Constitution. Accordingly, because of this stipulation I believe that, conversely, Article 35 of the Constitution need not always and necessarily be applied to the procedure under discussion here.

Therefore, in view of what is described above, Article 35 of the Constitution does not apply to Article 3 of the National Tax Violation Control Law, and accordingly there is no room for the problem of the contravention of Article 35 to arise.

In the next place, considering the problem of the constitutionality of Article 3 of the National Tax Violation Control Law in relation to Articles 12, 13, and 31 of the Constitution, its [Article 3's] content furnishes no particular reason for deeming it unconstitutional.

After all, action by notification regarding indirect taxes as described above is, in essence, a procedure of financial administration, not a criminal procedure; but it has some resemblance to criminal procedure and some dissimilarity to general administrative procedure because of the notification regarding payment or delivery of the appropriate fine or monetary penalty or of objects involved in confiscation. Moreover, since it includes a serious limitation on fundamental human rights, both in the investigation relating to the handling of violations that precedes such penalties and in the permissibility of forcible entry, search, and seizure, it is natural that limitations at least as rigorous as those for criminal procedures be established by legislative measures. However, Article 3, paragraph 1, of the above control law provides for special handling of cases of indirect tax violations on the actual scene of the violation. These procedures are necessary for the gathering of evidence and for quick action when it has been discovered either that the violation is actually occurring or that it has actually occurred. Paragraph 2 of the same article provides by law for special cases in which speed is necessary for the gathering of evidence. Such situations, for example, are those in which there is an individual who can be assumed to have violated the law, or shows obvious indications of such violation, or is in possession of things obtained or provided through a violation of indirect tax laws. Only in this type of emergency situation can entry, search, and seizure be recognized and carried out without authorization from a judicial officer, as measures necessary for financial administration. At the same time, these measures do not contravene the guarantee of fundamental human rights required by Articles 12, 13, and 31 of the Constitution because strict regulations corresponding to those of criminal procedures have been established that eliminate clearly improper actions [see footnote 1, p. 166].

Because the report in question, compiled by Nakakita Nobuo, a Finance Ministry official, and one other, was compiled legally, there was nothing illegal in its submission as evidence. Therefore, the argument cannot be accepted.

(3) The majority opinion interprets the provision "except as provided by Article 33," in Article 35, paragraph 1, of the Constitution, and makes clear that when the guarantee of nonapprehension does not exist under Article 33, the right to immunity against search, seizure, and so forth under Article 35 also is not guaranteed. It also finds in respect to offenses actually being committed that "as provided under Article 33," which makes an exception from the guarantee of Article 35, means that it is sufficient that an offense is actually being committed and that apprehension is not required.[6] Using this premise it explains the relation

6. This is not an exact quotation of the majority opinion. However, the meaning is made clear in the remainder of Justice Iriye's opinion and in point 3 of Justice Fujita's opinion.

between Article 3 of the National Tax Violation Control Law and Article 35 of the Constitution. However, I oppose this interpretation of Article 35 and I interpret "as provided for by Article 33," as stated in Article 35 of the Constitution, to apply to cases of apprehension (1) in which the offense is actually being committed and (2) in which the offense is not actually being committed but the warrant called for in Article 33 has been issued and the apprehension carried out in accordance with it.

In my opinion, Article 35 of the Constitution provides for the inviolability of home, papers, and effects in criminal procedures; and, if due occasion arises for entry, search, or seizure thereof for adequate cause, a warrant which clearly designates the place to be searched and the things to be seized is required; and each such search or seizure must be carried out upon separate warrant issued by a competent judicial officer. This procedure is rigorously and carefully defined and care must be exercised in respect to the specification of the things to be seized and the place to be entered. However, the unique exceptions to this are the situations in which apprehension can be constitutionally carried out under the guarantee of Article 33. It is proper to interpret these [exceptions] as admitting entry, search, and seizure of homes, papers, and effects without the warrant as specified in Article 35. In all probability, Article 33, in cases of the apprehension of a person after an arrest that restrains the greatest and most fundamental freedom—that of person—has been carried out constitutionally, establishes the principle that, in regard to entry, search, and seizure of homes, papers, and effects within the necessary limits related to arrest, a [additional] warrant is not especially required. And, again, in case of constitutional apprehension under the guarantee of Article 33, even though the necessary search and seizure related to that apprehension are carried out without warrant as provided for in Article 35, the place and things to be searched for and seized can be specified [in the warrant required by Article 33]. Not until Article 33 and Article 35 are brought together and interpreted in this way can the constitutional intent of the guarantee of fundamental human rights, which is contained in the stipulations of these two articles, be fully realized. To interpret, as the majority opinion does, the situation dealt with in Article 33 as one that does not require [actual] apprehension must be regarded as an incomplete realization of the guarantee of fundamental human rights expressly set forth in Article 35.

*　　*　　*

The supplementary opinion of Justice Kuriyama Shigeru regarding the substance of attorney Kwŏn's argument follows.

Because I find it difficult to grasp the meaning of the majority opinion and because there is a minority opinion that holds that Article 3 of the National Tax Violation Control Law does not conform with Article 35 of the Constitution, I would like to make clear my own opinion in this case.

(1) I think it proper to construe the expression "as provided for by Article 33," in Article 35 of the Constitution, as including not only arrest while an offense is actually being committed and arrest under warrant, but urgent arrest as well. Consequently, the phrase "as provided for by Article 33," in Article 35 refers to cases in which it is permissible to collect on-the-spot evidence of a crime followed by arrest. However, if the situation is one in which an arrest can actually be made, an interpretation of this provision that would make it possible to gather evidence of an offense at the place where the offender is actually present—even though it does not result in an arrest—would, I believe, be not unreasonable because, compared to a case in which the collection of evidence is accompanied by arrest, it is not disadvantageous to the offender. For the above reason I believe that Article 3 of the National Tax Violation Control Law (hereafter referred to simply as the Control Law) is not in contravention of Article 35 of the Constitution in providing that in cases in which it has been discovered that a violation involving national indirect taxes is being carried out or has been completed, a tax collection official can conduct entry, search, or seizure in a place in which the violator is actually present, even without authorization from a judicial official. In this I arrive at the same conclusion as the majority opinion.

(2) Justice Iriye's opinion concerning the limitation of fundamental human rights with respect to person, home, papers, and effects that is required in effecting administrative procedures, because of the special nature of the administrative process, takes the

view that proper provision relating to them may be entrusted to the legislative process within the purview of Articles 12, 13, and 31 of the Constitution; this can be interpreted as reasonable.

However, because the Constitution of Japan proclaims and guarantees that fundamental human rights are eternal and inviolate rights, this guarantee [Article 35] cannot be lightly taken away by a legislative or other action based on the special character of the administrative process (Articles 11 and 98 of the Constitution). I would like to point out that it is completely at variance with the basic concept of fundamental human rights guaranteed by the Constitution of Japan to think that the fundamental rights and freedoms of the people concerning person, home, papers, and effects—rights that must be highly respected—can be properly regulated by the legislative process for the sake of administrative objectives, no matter what might have been the case under the Meiji Constitution. Article 13 of the Constitution, which is cited by some disputants, does recognize limitations on fundamental human rights and freedoms for the public welfare; but this article is based strictly on the guarantee of fundamental human rights, namely, its application. It does not recognize the revocation, the limitation, or the nonapplication of that guarantee or the willful limitation of rights and freedoms by legislative or other action for the sake of administrative objectives on the pretext of serving the public welfare.

Some disputants also state that necessity of financial administration comes under the heading of the public welfare, but the absolutist view, which treats the simple administrative objective of the necessity to collect taxes as the public welfare, does not conform with the ideal of the public welfare as stated in Articles 12 and 13 of the Constitution of Japan. Again, some disputants declare that while Article 35 of the Constitution does not apply to Article 3 of the Control Law, the latter does not contravene Article 31 of the Constitution. But the view that holds that Article 35 does not apply, although Article 31 does, cannot escape being regarded as self-contradictory because what is termed "procedure established by law" in Article 31 is the procedure on which stand the guarantees stipulated in all subsequent articles.

The punishment of tax violations has undergone a drastic change recently with the abolition of the so-called fine system and the adoption of the imprisonment system, as is well known. For example, in earlier days tax violations were sought out and dealt with in order to make good the losses to the national treasury, but with the revision of the penal provisions of the tax law in 1947 as the turning point, the special characteristics of tax violations that differentiated them from general penal offenses disappeared. Next, Articles 2 and 3 of the Control Law refer to "violations," not "crimes," and although following a term different from that in the Code of Criminal Procedure, if there is an indictment of the offender, the facts of his infringement do not differ from the facts of what constitutes a tax offense, and the evidence of such an infringement is the same as evidence for an offense (see Article 18 of the Control Law). Especially, even though the "authorization" of a judicial officer under Article 2 of the Control Law is called "authorization," in substance it is the "warrant" of Article 35 of the Constitution. Thus, if there are not reasonable grounds sufficient for suspecting that a specified crime has been committed, it is clear from the provisions of Article 35 of the Constitution that haphazard search and confiscation in investigation for purposes of [tax] collection cannot be recognized under such authorization. (If this is not the case, then Article 2 of the Control Law would be in contravention of Article 35 of the Constitution because the authorization would have to be recognized as being like a general warrant [i.e., one not "particularly describing the place to be searched and things to be seized"] and again such an authorization would have to be held unconstitutional.) Consequently, some disputants term the above "administrative procedures," but what are dealt with in Article 2 and equally in Article 3 of the Control Law are in reality criminal procedures and it is clear that Article 35 applies to them.

I believe that what I have described above applies also to those parts of the opinion of Justices Saitō and Kobayashi that are common to Justice Iriye's opinion.

* * *

The minority opinion of Justice Fujita Hachirō regarding the substance of the argument of attorney Kwŏn.

(1) That Article 35 of the Constitution, and the provisions of Article 33, and those subsequent thereto, are provisions for crimi-

nal procedure and are not directly applicable to administrative procedures is as in the opinion (part 1) of Justice Iriye.

(2) However, are the procedures of Article 3 of the National Tax Violation Control Law simply those of financial administration (as in part 2 of Justice Iriye's opinion) and entirely without any characteristics of criminal procedure?

The National Tax Violation Control Law is the successor of the Law for the Handling of National Indirect Tax Law Violators (Law No. 67 of 1900) and is a relic from [the days of] the old Constitution. At that time, the latter law was regarded as possessing [the character of] administrative action—as was summary decision in the case of violation of police regulations—but in reality it should have been regarded, up to a point, as being a punitive action falling under the administration of justice. There is no disputing the fact that the action by notification recognized in the National Tax Violation Control Law has the objective in financial administration of guaranteeing the collection of taxes, but this cannot be regarded as purely a matter of procedure in financial administration. It must be understood that tax authorities do possess characteristics associated with certain punitive procedures relating to violations of tax laws—but these differ in their intrinsic nature from the true judicial process because they do not possess the power of coercion.

Article 14 of the same law in respect to action by notification stipulates the following:

The head of the National Tax Administration Bureau or the head of a tax office . . . may issue notifications regarding the delivery of . . . goods involved in confiscation or the payment of the appropriate amount in the case of fines or monetary penalties on showing cause when he is convinced of the existence of an offense.

Except for the application of penal provisions fixed in the tax law and other laws, of course, such tax officials have no authority to force delivery of confiscated objects or to collect appropriate fines or monetary penalties; it is unreasonable to regard this as nothing more than the exercise of the power to collect taxes. In the same law the effectiveness of suspension of prescription of public proceedings by action by notification is established (Article 15); and additional proof that the above procedure is like criminal procedure is to be found in the fact that through action by notification such an official can exclude further litigation. Such an act resembles a judicial decision under Article 16, which states: "When a violator has carried out the terms of a notification he will not again be confronted with a suit in regard to the same matter." Accordingly, the procedure of investigation set forth in Articles 2 and 3 of the same law provides that a tax official by virtue of his authority can gather evidence to establish the existence of an infringement. This, in reality, does not differ from the action of criminal investigation carried out by a police officer or a judicial police officer in ordinary criminal procedure.

Thus, indeed, the same law (Article 18) recognizes that evidence that has been gathered by the above procedure is transformed into material evidence in a criminal procedure by stating "in case a charge of violation has been made." Even though for the time being the investigative procedure in the same Articles 2 and 3 cannot be called pure criminal procedure, there is no doubt that it involves actions that in large measure have the characteristics of criminal procedure.

I myself believe, as I stated at the outset, that Article 35 of the Constitution is a provision for criminal procedure and that it has no direct application to administrative procedure. However, as pointed out above, I am also confident that it is reasonable to conclude that the stipulations of Article 35 are intended to apply to the investigative procedures set forth in Articles 2 and 3 of the law in question, which possess many of the characteristics of criminal procedure.

(3) With regard to the interpretation of ". . . or except as provided by Article 33," in Article 35, paragraph 1, of the Constitution, I agree with Justice Iriye. That is, the phrase "as provided by Article 33," indicates a case of an arrest of an offender, either with warrant or without warrant, while a crime is actually being committed; but even in a case where a crime is actually being committed, it is not permissible to enter, search, or seize homes, papers, or effects, without a warrant, and without direct intent of arresting the offender. Only in a few exceptional cases closely related to the apprehension of an offender is it permissible to take forcible measures without a warrant; such is the intent. Under Article 220 of the new Code of Criminal Procedure, when a public prosecutor, an assistant public prosecutor, or a judicial

police officer arrests a suspect—whether or not the offense is actually being committed—he can seize, search, or inspect without a court warrant, but only at the spot of arrest. The former Code of Criminal Procedure provided that a public prosecutor or a judicial police officer "when haste is necessary at the scene of a crime," regardless of whether it was the spot of arrest, had the right to seize, search, or inspect (Articles 171 and 181); but this was revised as above in accordance with the intent of Articles 33 and 35 of the new Constitution.

To say, as the majority opinion does, that it is possible to carry out the above procedures without a warrant and regardless of whether there is an arrest, is to go back to the old Constitution and to ignore the intent of the new Constitution, which springs from the great principle of respect for human rights.

(4) As I have pointed out above in respect to the interpretation that the procedures of Articles 3 of the National Tax Violation Control Law possess the character of criminal procedures and that Article 35 of the Constitution is applicable thereto, I am forced to the conclusion that the provisions of the same Article 3 —granting a tax collector the authority to take the actions of inspection, search, and seizure without a warrant from a court and without relation to the apprehension of the offender, even supposing that the violation is actually being committed—are in contravention of Article 35 of the Constitution and invalid. (This law, as I have described above, is a heritage of the old Constitution and with the coming into effect of the new Constitution it should be revised quickly in accordance with the intent of Article 35.)

Thus, in the present case, the original decision, which held the defendant guilty, using as evidence the report prepared by the Finance Ministry official, Nakakita Nobuo, and one other, which was compiled by the said illegal procedure, is illegal; and on this point the argument for appeal must be considered as being justified.

(TRANSLATED BY IKEDA MASAAKI)

Hanreishū, IX, No. 2, 217 (Criminal)

EDITORIAL NOTE: In the general election of October 1, 1952, the seven original accused were working for the election of a candidate for the House of Representatives in the Fourth District of Nagano Prefecture. They were arrested, charged, and found guilty of a number of violations of the Public Offices Election Law. Their sentences ranged from four months' imprisonment with hard labor (with a three-year stay of execution) to a fine of ¥5,000, and in addition, their rights of suffrage and eligibility for election were suspended.

On appeal, the appellate court reduced all sentences. However, except for one accused, it upheld the suspension. The six remaining accused then appealed to the Supreme Court on the grounds of the unconstitutionality of the suspension of their rights.

Grand Bench decision, February 9, 1955: Dismissed.

REFERENCES

Public Office Election Law. ARTICLE 252. Persons who have committed any of the crimes mentioned in this chapter (excluding the crimes in Article 240 <Violation of Restrictions concerning Election Offices, Resting Places, etc.>, Article 242 <Failure to Report Establishment of Election Offices>, Article 244 <Violation of Various Restrictions concerning Election Campaigns,

Part 2> and Article 245 <Violation of Restrictions on Courtesy Calls after the Day of Election>) shall not have the right to vote or be eligible for election as provided for in this law for the following periods: five years from the day the judgment becomes finally binding in case the punishment is a fine (but in the case of those who receive a stay of execution of such punishment, the period shall be from the day the judgment becomes finally binding until liability for the execution of the said punishment ends); and for the period from the day the judgment becomes finally binding until the sentence has been served or until the sentence has been remitted (except in case of prescription of sentence), plus the succeeding five years thereafter in case the punishment is heavier than imprisonment without hard labor. The time to the end of the liability for the execution of punishment, after the judgment has become binding, is to be treated in the same manner.

With regard to a person who has been condemned to punishment for a crime mentioned in Article 221 (Bribery and Inducement with Interest), Article 222 (Group Bribery and Group Inducement with Interest), Article 223 (Bribery and Inducement with Interest directed against Candidates and Persons Elected), or Article 223 (2) (Illegal Utilization of Newspapers and Magazines) and who is punished again for a crime mentioned in Articles 221 to 223 (2), the term of five years in the preceding paragraph shall be extended to ten years.

The Court can, depending upon circumstances and simultaneously with the pronouncement of sentence, declare to a person specified in paragraph 1 that the provisions of that paragraph depriving him of the right to vote and the eligibility for election for the term of five years or during the term of stay of execution of sentence shall not apply, or that the said term shall be reduced, or declare to a person specified in the preceding paragraph that the term of ten years in the said paragraph shall be reduced.

Constitution of Japan. ARTICLE 14. All of the people are equal under the law and there shall be no discrimination in political, economic or social relations because of race, creed, sex, social status or family origin.

Peers and peerage shall not be recognized.

No privilege shall accompany any award of honor, decoration or any distinction, nor shall any such award be valid beyond the lifetime of the individual who now holds or hereafter may receive it.

ARTICLE 15. The people have the inalienable right to choose their public officials and to dismiss them.

All public officials are servants of the whole community and not of any group thereof.

Universal adult suffrage is guaranteed with regard to the election of public officials.

In all elections, secrecy of the ballot shall not be violated. A voter shall not be answerable, publicly or privately, for the choice he has made.

ARTICLE 44. The qualifications of members of both Houses and their electors shall be fixed by law. However, there shall be no discrimination because of race, creed, sex, social status, family origin, education, property or income.

ARTICLE 1. The Emperor shall be the symbol of the State and of the unity of the people, deriving his position from the will of the people with whom resides sovereign power.

Preamble. [See text in Appendix I.]

FORMAL JUDGMENT

The appeal in the present case is dismissed.

REASONS. Concerning point 1 of the argument for appeal by attorney Ikeda Katsu:

According to the provisions of the Public Office Election Law, there is discrimination, as maintained in the argument for appeal, between those who have been condemned to punishment for general criminal offenses and those who have been sentenced for so-called election crimes (crimes provided for in paragraphs 1 and 2 of Article 252 of the aforementioned law) with respect to treatment regarding suspension of their voting rights and eligibility for election. The argument for appeal asserts that the discriminatory treatment accorded by the said law to those punished for such crimes—who should be treated equally in respect to their exercise of vital, fundamental human rights, which are inseparably connected with the people's sovereignty—runs counter to the intent of Articles 14 and 44 of the Constitution, unlawfully takes away the people's right of suffrage, and violates fundamental human rights guaranteed by the Constitution. The argument accordingly maintains that the provisions of paragraphs 1 and 3 of Article 252 of the Public Office Election Law, which the appeal decision applied in this case, violate the Constitution.

However, since all the election crimes under Article 252 of the Public Office Election Law will impair the fairness of elections, and since those who have been found guilty of them should be disqualified to take part in elections for actually having impaired the fairness of elections, it is right and proper to exclude such individuals from participation in elections for a certain specified period. This is naturally based on reasons different from those for the suspension of voting rights and eligibility for election of persons found guilty of general crimes.

Therefore, even though the treatment of those sentenced for election crimes—namely, a suspension of voting rights and eligibility for election—is much more severe than in the case of those sentenced for general crimes, it cannot be stated, as the argument for appeal does, that this discriminatory treatment is unreasonable. (Above all, paragraph 3 of the said article paves the way in actual cases for mitigation of the verdict in accordance with the circumstances of the crime and other conditions: for example, paragraph 1, which provides for suspension, may not be applied; or the period of such suspension may be shortened. Therefore, it is not appropriate to sweepingly denounce the said article for providing much harsher treatment [for election-law violators] than that given to those sentenced for general crimes.)

Under a Constitution that proclaims the sovereignty of the people, the right of voting for public office is one of the people's most important privileges as the argument states, but for that reason alone the fairness of elections must be maintained all the more rigorously. Once anyone impairs such fairness and is found disqualified to take part in elections, it is right and proper to deprive him for a while of his right to exercise the suffrage and to be eligible for election in order to insure the fairness of elections and to call for serious reflection on his part. Consequently, such action cannot be deemed to be a wrongful deprivation of the right of suffrage.

In view of the foregoing, the assertion made in the argument for appeal that the provisions of the Public Office Election Law contravene the Constitution cannot be accepted.

Point 2 of the above argument, the assertion that the weighing of the offense is improper, does not constitute a reason for appeal under Article 405 of the Code of Criminal Procedure. Also, a close examination of the record does not provide grounds for applying Article 411 of the Code of Criminal Procedure to the present case.[1] Consequently, the Court decides as in the formal judgment, in accordance with Article 408 of the Code of Criminal Procedure.[2]

This opinion is the unanimous decision of the Justices, except for the opinions of Justices Inouye Nobori, Mano Tsuyoshi, Saitō Yūsuke, Iwamatsu Saburō, and Iriye Toshio in respect to the first point of the appeal.

*　　　*　　　*

The opinion of Justices Inouye Nobori, Mano Tsuyoshi, and Iwamatsu Saburō in respect to point 1 of the argument for appeal follows.

We do not presume to object to the position, represented by the majority opinion itself, that the stipulations of paragraph 1 and paragraph 3 of Article 252 of the Public Office Election Law do not run counter to the provisions of Articles 14 and 44 of the Constitution (see the decision regarding point 1 of the argument). However, the provisions of Article 252, paragraph 1, of the Public Office Election Law do nothing more than provide that, as a legal fact, persons who commit violations as specified in those provisions are to be punished in accordance with the said article and paragraph; and this produces the legal effect that such persons are not to enjoy, for the periods set forth in the said paragraph and article, the rights to vote and to be eligible for election as provided for in the Public Office Election Law. That is to say, the effect of the above suspension of the rights to vote and to be eligible for election follows automatically from the law itself through the existence of the constitutent element of the law pointed out above; it was not produced by means of a declaration in the decision to the effect that the said article and paragraph were to be applied in the verdict, which would set forth the above penalty.

However, since paragraph 3 of the article states:

1. See footnote 3, p. 46.
2. See footnote 4, p. 16.

the Court can, depending upon circumstances, and simultaneously with the pronouncement of sentence, declare to a person specified in paragraph 1 that the provisions of that paragraph depriving him of the right to vote and the eligibility for election for the term of five years or during the term of stay of execution of sentence shall not apply, or that the said term shall be reduced . . .

it may—if the above is read carelessly—perhaps be thought that a court, when pronouncing sentence, must always and without fail decide whether or not the provisions of Article 1 should be applied in the judgment. However, the legal meaning of the above is only that a legal effect that follows automatically and legally from the application of the provisions of paragraph 1 may be eliminated; it does not prescribe that a court must, first of all, in a judgment in which the above penalty is pronounced, decide whether the legal effect provided for in paragraph 1 has been produced through the application of the said paragraph. This may be easily understood not only from a comparison of the provisions of paragraphs 1 and 3, but also from the fact that in paragraph 3 after "shall not apply" comes the phrase "or that the said periods shall be reduced"; it is therefore made clear that it is possible to alter or shorten the stipulated period, the legal effect of which is produced automatically with the application of the provisions of paragraph 1. (In this situation, naturally, the above should not be construed in such a way that if initially in the decision the rights to vote and to be eligible for election are suspended for five years by applying the provisions of paragraph 1, then later the said period can be reduced by applying paragraph 3.)

Furthermore, the point under discussion is also made clear by the fact that paragraph 2 of the same article prescribes that, in accordance with the existence of the prescribed legal fact, the term of five years under paragraph 1 will naturally become ten years by virtue of law, without resort to a verdict through a judgment. In short, the provisions of Article 252, paragraph 1, of the Public Office Election Law do not mean that they [the provisions] must be applied in a judgment by the court in a case of violation of that law as stipulated in the said article and paragraph; and also, they are applicable only at the time of an election when it is to be decided whether the person punished has the right to vote or to be eligible for election.

Even supposing for the moment that the above provisions are

unconstitutional and null and void for the reasons stated in the
argument for appeal, it is completely wide of the mark in a case,
such as the present one, of a violation of the Public Office Election
Law to say in respect to the original decision, in which the said
article and paragraph are not actually applied, that it is in violation of law or ordinance, or to prate about the unconstitutionality
of the said article and paragraph. It is even more of a mistake to
idly raise this issue in respect to an administrative act that has held
that a person to whom the said article and paragraph have been
applied at the time of an election did not possess the rights to
vote or to be eligible for election.[3] It must be said that the argument in respect to this point does not conform with the lawful
reasons for appeal.

Moreover, the stipulations of paragraph 3 of the said article in
effect prescribe that in due consideration of the circumstances involved, mitigative action may be taken. This is so because, if a
court that pronounces sentence as provided for in paragraph 1
of the same article, in cases involving election law violations as
set forth in the same paragraph, does not resort to this action,
then the effect in law of the same paragraph in the same article
follows naturally. In actual fact, in the original judgment the
stipulations of the above paragraph 3 were applied to the accused
and a sentence was pronounced that reduced by two years the
period provided for in paragraph 1. If the aforementioned action
had not been taken under the provisions of paragraph 3, naturally,
in law, the accused would have lost the rights to vote and to be
eligible for election for five years from the date the judgment became binding, in accordance with the legal provisions of paragraph 1; but since the original judgment applied the provisions
of paragraph 3, they were exempted from two years of the term
of suspension, and thus the accused received a benefit and in no
way incurred injury. Consequently, the reason for appeal, maintaining that the provisions of paragraph 3 are unconstitutional

3. The argument presented up to this point in this opinion can be restated as follows: If a
person is convicted of an election law violation he will be given the appropriate sentence. However, the suspension of rights provided for in Article 252 of the Public Office Election Law,
though it can be regarded as a penalty, is not imposed on the violator of the law by the judge
when he hands down sentence. The suspension of rights automatically applies, unless the judge
takes the mitigative action provided for in the same article. Therefore, the denial of the right
to vote or to be eligible for election is a constitutional administrative act, based on law, which is
applied to the person concerned only at election time.

and that the original judgment in which the said provisions are applied is unlawful, is, in essence, equal to a demand for an alteration of the original verdict that would be inimical to the interests of the accused, and does not constitute legal grounds for an appeal.

Therefore, point 1 of the argument for appeal is not relevant to the legal grounds for appeal, and there is no need to render judgment whether such grounds exist.

*　　*　　*

The opinion of Justices Saitō Yūsuke and Iriye Toshio in respect to point 1 of the argument for appeal follows.

That the assertions made in the argument for appeal do not constitute a legal basis for appeal is as in the opinion of Justices Mano, Inouye, and Iwamatsu. Even supposing that they do constitute a reason for appeal, the drift of the argument is based on the assumption that the right to vote and eligibility for election are important fundamental rights related to the people's sovereignty and also are universal, eternal, and inherent human rights which, constitutionally, cannot be infringed, even by law.

It is true that in the preamble of the Constitution of Japan it is proclaimed that sovereign power resides in the people; and in paragraphs 1 and 3 of Article 15 it is provided that the people have the inalienable right to choose their public officials, and that "universal adult suffrage is guaranteed with regard to the election of public officials." Therefore, it can be said that the right to vote is an important fundamental right related to the people's sovereignty. However, eligibility for election, in a strict sense, is not a right but is a capacity for the enjoyment of a right; at the same time it is a qualification required of all who become public officials, the servants for the entire people. Moreover, the text of Article 44 of the Constitution provides that "the qualifications of members of both Houses and their electors shall be fixed by law." Thus under our Constitution the right to vote and eligibility for election to both Houses are left entirely to the provisions of the law, unlike the practice in foreign countries.

Therefore, it cannot be said that these two rights are universal, everlasting, and inherent human rights that cannot be infringed upon even by laws based on our Constitution. On the contrary, under the Constitution any law can provide for the right to vote, the eligibility for election, and the conditions of disqualification relating thereto, and so forth, freely and reasonably as the occasion demands, so long as it does not violate the limitation provided for in the provisions of Article 14, Article 15, paragraph 3, and Article 44 of the Constitution. Consequently, the foregoing assumption on which the motion for appeal is based cannot be accepted. In addition, with regard to the fact that the provisions of Article 252 of the Public Office Election Law (Suspension of the Right to Vote and Eligibility for Election of Persons Punished for Election Crimes) do not run counter to the provisions of Articles 14 and 44 of the Constitution, we agree with the majority opinion.

(TRANSLATED BY IKEDA MASAAKI)

Hanreishū, V, No. 9, 1684 (Criminal)

EDITORIAL NOTE: The accused was charged with the murder of the husband of his paramour. There was considerable evidence that pointed to his guilt, but the defense argued that the confession of the accused and its use against him violated the constitutional guarantee that confession made under "compulsion, torture or threat . . . not be admitted in evidence." This decision is of interest because of the light it sheds on certain police methods and because of the minority opinions, which reveal the thinking of some of the justices on the nature of evidence and on the function of the courts.

Grand Bench decision, August 1, 1951: Quashed and retrial ordered.

REFERENCES

Constitution of Japan. ARTICLE 38.   No person shall be compelled to testify against himself.
1. Confession made under compulsion, torture, or threat, or after prolonged arrest or detention, shall not be admitted in evidence.
Former Code of Criminal Procedure. ARTICLE 336.   Findings of fact shall be based on the evidence.
ARTICLE 337.   The judge shall be unfettered in deciding the probative value of evidence.

[Omitted are three references which have no direct bearing on the decision.]

FORMAL JUDGMENT

Judgment of the court of second instance set aside. Retrial ordered.

REASONS. Regarding item 1 in counsel's argument for appeal: As the appellant points out, the original judgment cites as evidence on which it bases its findings of fact the reports of the interrogations submitted severally by the judicial police and the prosecutor, both of which contain the accused's confession.

The accused had already, in the trial of first instance, challenged the reports of the interrogations tendered by the judicial police and the prosecutor, maintaining that the confession was the result of compulsion and torture. To quote from the district court transcript:

Question by Mr. Kurita (for the accused): "During the investigation by the police were you subjected to violence?"
Answer: "Yes. They questioned me every day. Sometimes it lasted until two in the morning. When I said, 'I don't know,' the police would hit and kick me. Often they would grab my hair and bang my head on the table. Once when I denied it because I really hadn't done it, one of them said, 'I'll take you to the gymnasium and beat you up!' They often gave me this rough treatment at night after the evening meal. Because of this severe questioning, I was completely worn out and thought, 'If a lie's what they want, I'll tell it and escape this torture.' And so I told Sergeant Tsuchiku that I had killed Joitsu, even though my confession was a lie. But since I had not done it, I couldn't give them a complete story. So I invented some parts and, for others, used what the police told me earlier for what I didn't know. They finally prepared a statement for me."
Question: "Was that the only bad treatment you received from the police?"
Answer: "Sometimes they wouldn't let me eat the food that my family sent in from the outside. When, because I hadn't done it, I said, 'I don't know,' they would say, 'You fat,

stubborn fool, why don't you be sensible and confess?' They kept this up day after day. This rough treatment I've described went on and on. It wore me out and I thought there's nothing for it but to let them put me on trial; then in court I'll tell the truth and be judged."

Question: "Wouldn't it have been better to tell the truth when you were examined later by the prosecutor?"

Answer: "He questioned me at the Takatomi police station and I was afraid that the police would punish me if I told a different story. So I said the same thing."

Question: "At the police station did you try to commit suicide?"

Answer: "Yes. Because I couldn't stand the treatment, I had made my false confession. I had brought disgrace upon the people of my village and on the fire brigade and could never return. On the way back from the lavatory I ran into the kitchen, grabbed a knife and tried to stick it in my throat. But the point was broken; a policeman took it away from me; and I couldn't do what I wanted to."

Question by counsel (Yamada): "How long did they question you every night?"

Answer: "When it went on late, until about 2:00 (presumably A.M.); when they finished early, until about 11:00 (presumably P.M.)."

The truth of the above claims of the accused was tested when, at its second session, the court of first instance on its own authority called as a witness, Tsuchiku, the person in charge of the judicial police at the time. At the request of counsel Officer Niwa was also called at the third session. (However, the judgment of first instance did not cite, as evidence, the police report on the accused.)

In the high court the accused also, in a similar fashion, challenged the reports of his interrogation tendered by the judicial police and the prosecutor.

Question directed at the accused by counsel (Daidōji) at the first session: "Between November 10 and 20 were you ever allowed to eat the lunches sent in by your family?"

Answer: "Yes. Four times."

Question: "Were you made to remain sitting Japanese-style [kneeling, knees together, with the weight of the body on the heels, uncomfortable even to the Japanese] for ten days in the night-duty officer's room?"

Answer: "Yes. I was made to sit formally for ten days."

Question: "You say you were beaten. Who beat you?"

Answer: "Sergeant Tsuchiku."

Question: "What did Officer Kawabe do?"

Answer: "He kept shouting at me most of the time."

Question: "And Officer Itō?"

Answer: "He kept pushing and poking me unmercifully."

Question: "And Officer Takagi?"

Answer: "He pulled my hair."

Question: "And Officer Tameoka?"

Answer: "He kept jerking the handcuffs left and right with my hands in them. This was too much for Officer Shimazu who loosened them for me. Officer Tameoka one morning— I forget the time and date—repeatedly banged my head hard on the table."

Question: "How long did the kind of treatment you have just described last?"

Answer: "For about ten days."

Question: "Were there times when the questioning began in the morning and continued on until 2:00 A.M. the following day?"

Answer: "Yes, there were."

Question: "Is it a fact that on the ninth day you tried to commit suicide or wished that you were dead?"

Answer: "Even though I had cooperated with them, the police humiliated me as I've said, and I felt so miserable that I thought I would be better dead. Not only that, but I wanted them to be haunted by my ghost."

Question: "Why didn't you tell the truth to the prosecutor when he questioned you?"

Answer: "The police who interrogated me ordered me to say the same to him as I had to them. So I said the same to the prosecutor as I had said to the police."

Question: "Was Sergeant Tsuchiku in the room at any stage while the prosecutor was taking your statement?"

Answer: "Yes."

Question directed at the accused by the presiding judge: "You say that your interrogation was attended with compulsion, threats, and torture. In the trial of first instance, however, Sergeant Tsuchiku absolutely denied this. What do you say to this?"

Answer: "If you doubt my word, please ask the people who were in the room with me. This will prove that I am telling the truth."

The high court on its own authority called as witnesses the following policemen all of whom had taken part in the interrogation of the accused: Abe Shizuo, Takagi Shinichi, Tameoka Isamu, Itō Genji, and Tsuchiku Ichirō. Yamazaki Keiichi and Shimado Kazumi (wife of the accused) were also called as witnesses at the request of counsel. These witnesses were all examined to test the truth of the accused's allegations. The interrogations of the witnesses disclose the following:

At the trial at first instance the witness Tsuchiku Ichirō had said, "At the interrogation of the accused we did not use compulsion, torture, etc.," but had confirmed that it "did happen that the accused at lunchtime tried to stab himself in the throat with a knife from the police station kitchen." On being asked by the presiding judge, "Wasn't it because he couldn't endure the unduly rigorous examination that he tried to commit suicide?" Tsuchiku had replied, "I don't think so." The judge had then asked, "Was it after that incident that the confession was made?" to which Tsuchiku had replied, "Yes, he confessed during the interrogation which took place that afternoon."

In the examination of witnesses in the high court, the witness Tameoka Isamu testified to the following effect: "During interrogation I neither dragged the accused by the handcuffs nor subjected him to any other type of torture or coercion." Finally, when asked by the presiding judge (high court), "Was the accused handcuffed while the witnesses were interrogating him?" Tameoka answered, "Yes, it was while he was wearing them."

The witness, Takagi Shinichi, testified, "During the interrogation of the accused I neither pulled his hair nor subjected him to any other type of torture or coercion." Finally, however, when Daidōji (for the accused) asked, "Was the accused interrogated by yourself, Itō Genji, Tameoka Isamu, Abe Shizuo, the four of you?" Takagi answered, "Two or three days before he confessed to the facts he was interrogated by the four of us."

The witness, Tsuchiku Ichirō, testified to the following effect: "I never began interrogating the accused after 10:00 P.M. and always handed over to him the food sent in by his family. I neither hit him nor subjected him to any other type of torture or coercion." When, however, the presiding judge (at the request of the accused) asked him, "Is it true that when the officer in charge of the police station interrogated him, the interrogation lasted until about 2:00 A.M.?" Tsuchiku answered, "Yes, it did." Similarly, when the presiding judge asked, "On that occasion did the officer in charge beat him?" Tsuchiku replied, "Yes."

In addition to the testimony of these people, who took part in the police interrogation, there is that of the witness Yamazaki Keiichi: "While I was being detained in connection with a fraud case, I was in the same cell with a certain Matsuyama. Matsuyama had sometime previously been held in the same police station as the accused. Matsuyama told me that he had been kept from sleeping by the police starting to interrogate the accused after ten o'clock at night."

The witness, Shimado Kazumi, testified: "While the accused was detained at the police station, I sent food in to him. There were times when it was returned to me uneaten."

Thus, the transcript contains the evidence of several witnesses that suggests that the testimony of the accused at the police station amounted to a confession under compulsion or torture. In particular, the very policemen who conducted the interrogation have directly admitted, as described above, that the interrogation was conducted while the accused was in handcuffs, that the interrogation lasted until 2:00 A.M., that four policemen interrogated the accused at one time, and that one policeman beat him. Naturally, the evaluation of this testimony and the decision whether the confession was given voluntarily at the police station and is admissible are matters that should be left to the unfettered discretion of the court of first instance, whose role is to decide questions of fact. Nevertheless, this discretion, though free, must naturally operate on the basis of reason; it cannot run contrary to the pattern of experience.

How, in fact, has the appeal judgment evaluated the above evidence of the policemen? In the present case, a careful perusal of the entire transcript does not reveal sufficient evidence to cast doubt on any of the testimony we have quoted. Thus, we are forced to the conclusion that if the court of first instance rejected as unworthy of belief the testimony of the very policemen who conducted the interrogation, then they exercised their judgment arbitrarily and unreasonably, and reached a conclusion contrary to the pattern of experience. If, on the other hand, they accepted as true the testimony that events took place in that way, but considered that there were additional circumstances which must be taken into account, then it was incumbent on them to examine the attendant circumstances adequately before admitting them as evidence. (For example, was the accused interrogated handcuffed, because, fearing that he was planning suicide, the police considered this an unavoidable precautionary measure? It is possible to infer from the transcript that he did plan suicide, but it does not however appear that handcuffs were used because of fear of that act.) There is, however, no indication that the court gave such attendant circumstances special study. If there are no circumstances meriting special consideration and if events actually took place in the manner described in the testimony of each of the quoted witnesses, then we must say that there are sufficient grounds for thinking that the statement made by the accused at the police station was given under compulsion and torture.

In short, we must conclude that in rejecting without convincing reasons the evidence of these witnesses, and in readily finding the facts constituting guilt on the basis of the accused's statements at the police station the high court was acting contrary to law, since it was acting either contrary to the pattern of experience (as described above) or on the basis of a failure to exhaust the fact-finding process. Moreover, in its decision the high court, by combining with other evidence the reports of the interrogation of the accused by the judicial police, finds that the facts constituting guilt existed. Hence, it cannot be said that this illegality on the part of the court clearly did not influence its decision. Accordingly, on this point, its decision must be set aside.

Therefore, without dealing with the other points raised by Mr. Daidōji Yoshio and the accused in the argument for appeal, we (by virtue of the powers vested in this Court by Articles 447 and 448 (2) [1] of the former Code of Criminal Procedure) render judgment as in the formal judgment above.

This is the unanimous opinion of this Court except for the minority opinions of Justices Sawada Takejirō, Inouye Nobori, Saitō Yūsuke, and Iwamatsu Saburō.

*   *   *

Justice Saitō delivered the following minority opinion with respect to item 1 in the argument for appeal.

It is true that, as the accused contends, the original judgment cited as evidence part of the testimony concerning the accused from the statements of the prosecutor and the judicial police. It is also true that there exists the testimony given by the accused in open court and that of the witnesses to which the accused refers. The rejection or evaluation of evidence, however, is something entrusted to the discretion of the high court; moreover, the latter is not in any way required by the relevant procedural statutes to give any reasons for rejecting or selecting evidence. It is beyond dispute that the original judgment, citing the testimony concerning the accused from the statements of the prosecutor and the judicial police, rejected the testimony of the accused and the witnesses tendered by counsel and reached the conclusion that the testimony of the accused in the depositions was not given under coercion, torture, intimidation, or in any way against his will. Thus, we can in no wise say that there was any illegality violating the pattern of experience to be detected in this conclusion. The contentions of the accused thus amount to a criticism of the way in which the court exercised its discretion; it is difficult to recognize this as legal grounds for appeal.

The majority opinion seizes upon one section of the testimony favorable to the accused and unreasonably argues that the pattern of experience is violated. One small part of the testimony of the witnesses quoted in the majority opinion permits the conclusion that the statement of the accused at the police station was a confession given under compulsion or torture. (On the other hand, there is absolutely no direct evidence that the testimony [of the

1. These articles correspond to Articles 411 and 413 in the new Code of Criminal Procedure. On Article 411 see footnote 3, p. 46 and on Article 413 see footnote 1, p. 92.

accused] in the statements of the police and, particularly, the prosecutor cited in the original decision was given under compulsion or torture.) At the same time, there is a greater volume of clear testimony that it was not given under compulsion or torture. Which of the two is the more reliable is not a question of the pattern of experience; it is something committed completely to the free choice of the high court. Nor is it required that the judgment give reasons for believing or disbelieving evidence. Thus, no question of illegality can arise from its failure to give such reasons. A fortiori the scope and limits of the inquiry are something to be left to the discretion of the court. Under the Code of Criminal Procedure mere "failure to exhaust the fact-finding process" can never constitute ground for appeal, in the absence of additional reasons. Not only that, but in the present case from the court of first instance onwards, many witnesses were examined on the question of torture and compulsion. To call this "a failure to exhaust the fact-finding process" is an irresponsible utterance completely at variance with the facts.

The majority in their joint opinion have conjured up the argument that the judgment is contrary to the pattern of experience and in violation of law because it fails to exhaust the fact-finding process; these are arguments that were never raised. It is completely impossible for me to agree.

*   *   *

The minority opinion of Justices Sawada Takejirō and Iwamatsu Saburō follows.

The majority opinion that there are proper grounds for appeal in this case amounts to a disagreement with the way the original court admitted and rejected evidence, a function that it performed lawfully within the scope of its discretion as the court on which is conferred the task of determining the facts. The majority opinion attacks that court's findings of fact. This cannot be regarded as one of the grounds for appeal recognized by law. On this point we are in complete agreement with the minority opinion of Justice Saitō. We wish, however, to elaborate somewhat on the reasons that he gives.

To begin with, this Court in its appellate capacity deals with questions of law, enquiring whether there are errors of law in judgments rendered by lower courts; this is what is termed the review of law. Hence, it is bound by the findings of fact lawfully made by the lower court whose role is, indeed, to find the facts. Findings of fact are to be made on the basis of the evidence (Former Code of Criminal Procedure, Article 336; New Code of Criminal Procedure, Article 317) and the evaluation of the cogency of the evidence (its credibility and probative value) is entrusted to the free discretion of the judges trying the case (Former Code, Article 337; New Code, Article 318). Naturally, under this "principle of free conviction"[2] the pattern of experience and the rules of logic are not completely excluded. It goes without saying that if facts are admitted from a certain piece of evidence in defiance of the pattern of experience or of the rules of logic, this can constitute ground for appeal to the Supreme Court in that the findings of fact are contrary to law. However, in order for a finding of fact to be contrary to the pattern of experience or to logic there must be a situation in which evidence that contains particulars that cannot exist under the pattern of experience was offered as material for the finding of fact; or there must be a situation in which the rules of logic and experience have been disregarded in the deduction of certain facts from the evidence, even though the evidence itself is reconcilable with the pattern of experience. Thus, provided a finding of fact by a trial court follows from the evidence cited in accordance with the pattern of experience and logic, one cannot—merely because there exists in the transcript a considerable amount of evidence that (it is admitted) the trial court did not accept and from which at first sight the contrary could properly be inferred—jump to the conclusion that the trial court's finding of fact was contrary to the pattern of experience.

The admissibility of evidence depends primarily on credibility. Thus, no matter how valid a piece of evidence may look on the surface, if the trial court does not believe it, then it has no probative value at all. The credibility of evidence is not determined solely by its content. For example, the credibility of oral testimony depends not only on what the witness says, but on his character, on his position, whether his interests are involved, on his

2. The term "principle of free conviction" means simply that judges are free to make their own evaluation of the evidence on the basis of inward conviction.

demeanor while testifying, and on the attendant circumstances. Moreover, it does not always follow that each one of these attendant circumstances separately and individually influences the credibility of oral testimony; normally the influence of all these attendant circumstances on credibility operates collectively and in unison. Again, when one compares and evaluates the credibility of a quantity of interrelated oral testimony the task becomes all the more intricate and complicated. To submit to logical analysis, one by one, these attendant circumstances likely to determine credibility and to evaluate individually the influence that each exerted on credibility would be well nigh impossible. This is particularly true in a court composed of a number of judges. If a court, heedless of this impossibility and taking the view that the thought processes of evaluation alone are universally capable of producing a conclusion by formal logic, when it is evaluating the credibility of evidence, attempts to force by the rules of logic a determination of each individual cause that has an influence on credibility, then it would be acting in defiance of the nature of things and its findings of fact would be likely to miss the mark. This is one of the reasons why the law has adopted the "principle of free conviction." This principle means, at the least, that a court in assessing the credibility of evidence need not consciously analyze and establish, one by one, the factors that are its premises, but may arrive at its conclusion in an overall intuitive fashion. To this extent, a court can be said to be freed from applying the rules of logic. Thus, it is sufficient for a collegiate court, when assessing the credibility of evidence, merely to give its conclusion of whether the evidence is to be believed or not; it is not necessary for it to confer and decide on the reasons for its belief or disbelief.

There are no reasons why any distinctions should be made between criminal and civil cases in this respect. Indeed, it could be said that there are grounds for affirming that it has far more significance in the former than in the latter. Article 191 (1) of the Code of Civil Procedure requires the court to give its "reasons" [for judgment]. Since this naturally means the reasons by which it arrived at its judgment, if taken completely literally, it might be interpreted to include the reasons underlying conclusions about the credibility of evidence, which by their nature form the basis for accepting something as evidence. However, as we have already explained, the "principle of free conviction" liberates a court from establishing such reasons. It is because of this principle that the precedents of the former Court of Cassation firmly maintain that a court need not state its reasons for disbelieving evidence. The Code of Criminal Procedure [Article 335], however, differs from the above provision of the Code of Civil Procedure; even in a judgment of guilty it is sufficient if the court sets forth only the facts constituting the crime, the reasons why the facts follow from the evidence, and the application of the law to the facts. The only exception is that where there are legal grounds barring the formation of the offense or where facts are alleged that are grounds for increasing, reducing, or remitting the penalty, the findings on such facts must be indicated.

Thus, no matter what contentions may have been made regarding the admissibility, credibility, or probative value of the evidence tendered, there is no legal requirement that the court show its findings one by one (Former Code of Criminal Procedure, Article 360; New Code, Article 335). Thus, in cases like the present one the court must, of course, follow up the allegation that the confession of the accused at the police station was given under compulsion or torture, but it is not required that the results of such inquiry be set forth. In other words, when it pronounces a judgment of guilty in circumstances like these, if it has decided that the confession was made under compulsion or torture, then it does not use the confession as material for its findings of fact. But if it has decided that this was not the case, its failure to state why it so decided does not bar its using the confession as material for finding facts. We shall not embark on any discussion of whether its failure to give the reason why it decided that there was no torture is a good or a bad thing; one cannot seize on this and try to argue from it that the court was acting contrary to law. On the contrary, if the court charged with deciding the facts (the appeal decision in fact examined the question adequately and accepted as evidence for its findings the confession that the court of first instance did not utilize) accepted the confession as evidence for its findings, then it is reasonable to infer that it considered that it was not made under compulsion or torture. For it is completely inconceivable that a court that has carried out such an examination will admit as evidence a confession that it considers was made under compulsion or torture. In this case, it is immaterial whether as a result of such examination sufficient evidence was presented to affirm that there was torture. If the evidence was not sufficient to convince the court, then the question of its probative value does not arise. Whether to believe a piece of evidence is a question of "free conviction"; as we have already explained in detail, the court is not required to give its reasons for believing or disbelieving evidence even when it finds the accused guilty. Thus, although, as the majority opinion maintains, there is evidence in the transcript that permits one to doubt whether the confession was voluntary, the majority view that the original judgment is contrary to law is untenable since one can infer from the text of the judgment that the court rejected that evidence *in toto*.

The majority opinion reads:

> How, in fact, has the appeal judgment evaluated the above evidence of the policemen? In the present case, a careful perusal of the whole transcript does not reveal sufficient evidence to cast doubt on any of the testimony we have quoted. Thus, we are forced to the conclusion that if the court of first instance rejected as unworthy of belief the testimony of the very policemen who conducted the interrogation, then they exercised their judgment arbitrarily and unreasonably, and reached a conclusion contrary to the pattern of experience.

In what respect is it contrary to the pattern of experience? This point is completely unclear; nor can we agree that the pattern of experience demands that, under the conditions described in the majority opinion, the testimony of the policemen called by counsel must be believed. Moreover, there is no evidence from which one can infer that torture was inflicted at the time the testimony in the statements that the original judgment accepted as evidence was given. Again, when we come to the allegation that the accused was beaten at the time he made his statement, the policemen who were examined as witnesses did not testify that they themselves beat him. As Justice Saitō remarks, there was some evidence that there was no torture; and if the appeal judgment accepted this and disbelieved the evidence cited by the majority opinion that there was, such a finding cannot be said to be contrary to the pattern of experience. It only means that the majority opinion, merely on the strength of the transcript, says that there was torture and sets aside the appeal judgment as being wrongful in its selection and evaluation of evidence, a matter entrusted exclusively to that court.

The majority appear to believe that the Supreme Court, as an appellate court, can decide only from the contents of the testimony that appears in the transcript the credibility of witnesses they have never seen examined. They would almost make it compulsory when giving a judgment of guilty to state the reasons for rejecting or accepting certain types of evidence. This is contrary to law, which has adopted the principle of free conviction, and would impose on the trial court an impossible task, which even the majority themselves could not perform. Thus, the majority would have the Supreme Court exceed its powers as a court that determines questions of law; in challenging the trial courts in the discharge of their exclusive right to accept and reject evidence they would interfere with the establishing of facts. We are completely unable to concur in this.

On this question we think that no distinction can be made between cases in which the problem is to apply ordinary legislation and cases in which it is to apply the Constitution. Furthermore, if the majority opinion's way of thinking should be accepted, then an improper result, the reverse of the present case, would be invited: where the trial court, recognizing that the confession of the accused had been given under compulsion or torture, had rejected it as having no probative value and had as a result found the accused not guilty on the ground that there was no proof of crime, the prosecutor would be able to appeal to the Supreme Court, alleging that there was considerable evidence inconsistent with compulsion and torture; and the Supreme Court would be able, merely on the basis of what was written in the transcript, to reject this finding of the lower court and to set aside their verdict of not guilty.

For this Court, for the reasons set forth in the majority opinion, to exceed its power as an appellate court and, contrary to the principles of procedural law, set aside the appeal decision, may mean that in many suits in the future the trial courts will be improperly restricted in deciding in accordance with the principle of free conviction whether to reject evidence and in making findings of fact; it may deprive them of their freedom in deciding the facts. Moreover, in the present case there was sufficient other evidence for a finding of guilt, even excluding the statements that became the problem. Thus, if the appeal judgment had not cited among the evidence the statement of the judicial police, no problem could have arisen. Again, if while citing it as evidence, it had stated that the evidence on which the majority opinion relies was untrustworthy in the light of the demeanor of the witnesses, then as an appellate court the Supreme Court could not have interfered. If the Supreme Court quashes the original verdict and orders a retrial, and the court of second instance proceeds to again take the above attitude, then the only result of the Supreme Court's action will be to delay the conclusion of the case.

It is sometimes said that if the Supreme Court adopts an attitude like ours, the provisions of the Constitution will become meaningless and this Court will become useless as a guardian of the Constitution. This is utterly ridiculous. Torture is contrary to the Constitution and officers engaged in investigations may not indulge in it. Should they do so they will be punished administratively and under the Criminal Code for the crime of criminal conduct by an official. Moreover, in all criminal trials there must be adequate examination by the courts of first and second instance as to whether there was torture, and if there was torture the testimony resulting from it cannot be admitted as evidence. Thus, the provision in the Constitution prohibiting torture, and the like, has not become a dead letter.

The Supreme Court, however, as an appellate court, is bound by the findings of the trial courts as to the presence or absence of facts (e.g., torture) in accordance with which they accept or reject evidence, provided that (as we have already explained) the trial courts in so doing have not acted in a manner contrary to law. Should a court decide that there had been torture but nevertheless accept as evidence the testimony to which it gave rise, then the Supreme Court would, of course, set aside that judgment. Similarly, if the procedure in the court were contrary to what the Constitution provides (e.g., if the trial were not conducted in open court) the Supreme Court again would set aside the judgment. In addition to this the important, nay, vital role of the Supreme Court, as the court that decides questions of law, is to examine with unfailing vigilance the constitutionality of the application of the law by the courts and of laws and orders enacted by the legislative and executive branches. It is absolutely nonsensical to talk of the Supreme Court's becoming useless or resorting to suicidal acts merely because it decides that in accordance with the basic premise of our procedural law, it is bound by the findings of facts made by the original verdict except when the law specially provides to the contrary. (The fact of whether or not one was tortured by the police is not a fact relating to judicial procedure.)

(TRANSLATED BY D. C. S. SISSONS)

Hanreishū, II, No. 14, 1853 (Criminal)

EDITORIAL NOTE: The facts of the case are clearly outlined in the
decision itself. This early decision is included because it deals with
the problem of slowness of justice, which has been a major and a
persistent one in the Japanese courts.

Grand Bench decision, December 22, 1948: Dismissed.

REFERENCES

Constitution of Japan. ARTICLE 37.   In all criminal cases the
accused shall enjoy the right to a speedy and public trial by an
impartial tribunal.

[Former] *Code of Criminal Procedure.* ARTICLE 411.   Except
as provided in the preceding article, where it is clear that the
court's acting contrary to legislation did not influence the decision
of the court, this shall not constitute grounds for appeal.

FORMAL JUDGMENT

Appeal dismissed. The thirty days during which the accused,
Nagashima, was in custody before judgment was given shall be
deducted from the sentence.

REASONS. Concerning the first point of the argument for appeal:
According to the file of the case, it appears that the three accused

were charged on December 24, 1947, before the Tokyo District Court with having plotted and committed the theft of ¥900 and some twenty sundry articles from members of the Allied occupation forces in the American barracks at Sōbudai (Kanagawa prefecture), at approximately 11:00 A.M. on January 14, 1947. The trial began on February 9, 1948, and the men were found guilty the same day. Appeals were lodged in the Tokyo High Court on the tenth and thirteenth of that month. The trial in the high court began on June 30, and on July 9 they were found guilty as in the district court. So much is clear from the file. Thus, about six and one-half months elapsed between the laying of the original charge and the handing down of the high court judgment. Within this period the actual trials were conducted comparatively smoothly. After the lower court judgment was given, however, it took about five months before the high court hearings commenced.

It may be presumed that this was caused by delay in preparing and transmitting the appeal documents, the result of the notorious shortage of staff in the courts, and the mass of criminal cases pending. Consequently, there has arisen the charge that the case was not tried expeditiously.

Whether the trial in the present case, however, involves a violation of Article 37, paragraph 1, of the Constitution, which guarantees a speedy trial, cannot be determined hastily without an investigation of all the circumstances. Let us assume for the sake of the argument that the trial in the present case was not speedy and that this was an infringement of the Constitution. What consequences would ensue? If the responsibility for the delay were attributable to the judges handling the case, they should, of course, be brought to book for neglecting their responsibility to administer justice and their other responsibilities. If, however, we were to set aside the high court's judgment, saying that since the trial was not speedy it was unlawful, there would be no alternative to a retrial. Thus, the progress of the case would be all the more impeded—a contradictory result working against the constitutional guarantee.

Even though the slow handling of the case by the courts was contrary to Article 37, paragraph 1, of the Constitution, we cannot interpret this as grounds for appeal, for it is clear that the delay did not affect the decision of the court. Thus, we cannot accept the contentions of the accused. (Other reasons for the judgment omitted.)

On this first item the Court is unanimous. . . . Accordingly, judgment is given as in the formal judgment under Article 446 of the [former] Code of Criminal Procedure.[1] In accordance with Article 21 of the Criminal Code the thirty days during which the accused, Nagashima, was in custody before judgment shall be deducted from the sentence.

(TRANSLATED BY D. C. S. SISSONS)

1. See footnote 2, p. 161.

Hanreishū, IX, No. 10, 1453 (Civil)

EDITORIAL NOTE: The decision in this case does not involve the interpretation of a specific constitutional provision. However, the concept of habeas corpus is so intimately related to individual liberty guaranteed under the Constitution that the decision is here presented. The facts of the case are adequately summarized in the decision itself. The earlier decision referred to was a very brief one involving an application for a writ of habeas corpus by convicted war criminals in Sugamo prison.

Grand Bench decision, September 28, 1955: Dismissed.

REFERENCES

Habeas Corpus Law.[1] ARTICLE 2. A person who is subjected to physical restraint other than by a lawful and proper procedure may apply for relief as provided in this law.

Such application may be made by any person on behalf of the person under restraint.

Habeas Corpus Rules. ARTICLE 4. An application under Article 2 of the Habeas Corpus Law may be made only where the re-

---

1. For a translation of this law as originally enacted see General Headquarters, Supreme Commander for the Allied Powers, *Political Reorientation of Japan September 1945 to September 1948. Report of Government Section, Supreme Commander for the Allied Powers* (2 vols.; Washington, D.C.: U.S. Government Printing Office, n.d.), pp. 1149–50.

straint, or the judgment or administrative decision relating to the restraint, is either patently without authority or patently and seriously violates a form or procedure established by law. Provided that such application may not be made where other suitable means are available for obtaining the objects of the writ, unless it is clear that the objects of the writ cannot be achieved by such other means within a reasonable period of time.

FORMAL JUDGMENT

Appeal dismissed. Appellant to pay the court fees of the appeal.

REASONS. This Court has already decided (*Hanreishū*, VIII, No. 4, 848 <Civil>) that an application for relief under the Habeas Corpus Law may be made only where freedom of person is restrained other than in accordance with a lawful and proper procedure and such restraint, or the judgment or administrative decision relating to such restraint, is patently without authority or patently and seriously violates a form or procedure established by law.

The facts of the detention of the applicant found by the lower court are briefly as follows:

On October 27, 1953, the applicant [a Chinese citizen] was charged before the Hachioji branch of the Tokyo District Court with violating the Foreign Exchange Law and the Foreign Trade Control Law and was remanded in custody. He was released on bail on March 26, 1954. At about 6:30 P.M. on November 8, 1954, at Yokohama prison, he was served with a deportation order issued by an immigration officer pursuant to Article 52 of the Immigration Control Order (Cabinet Order 319 of 1951, promulgated October 4, 1951, effective from November 1 of that year and remaining in force by virtue of Law 126 of 1952) and to paragraph 5 of the supplementary regulations (the number of this paragraph was changed from 21 to 5 by Law 126 of 1952). (The deportation order had originally been issued by an investigating officer of the Tokyo branch of the Immigration Department on September 5, 1951, pursuant to Article 17 of the Aliens Registration Law, after it had been discovered that he had entered Japan unlawfully, without the permission of the Supreme Commander for the Allied Powers. The execution of this deportation order

had, however, been subsequently suspended.) At 4:10 P.M. on
November 17, 1954, he was placed in confinement in the Yokohama Immigration Holding Center, of which the respondent is
the superintendent. He has been confined there continuously ever
since. The appellant contends that the Immigration Control
Order and the deportation order are contrary to the spirit of
Articles 33 and 34 of the Constitution and that, moreover, the
manner of his detention is contrary to Article 63 of the said
cabinet order. It is, however, clear from the facts that the restraint is neither (in the words of our previous judgment) "patently without authority" nor "a patent and serious violation of
a form or procedure established by law." Accordingly, the application should be dismissed without judging the issues that the
appellant raises. The appeal should, therefore, be dismissed under
Article 42 of the Habeas Corpus Rules as without grounds. Court
fees in connection with the appeal shall, in accordance with Article 46 of the Habeas Corpus Rules and Articles 95 and 89 of the
Code of Civil Procedure [2] be borne as decreed in the formal judgment (above).

This is the unanimous decision of this Court with the exception
of the minority opinions of Justices Kuriyama Shigeru, Kobayashi
Shunzō, Mano Tsuyoshi, Fujita Hachirō, and Ikeda Katsu.

*   *   *

The minority opinion of Justices Kuriyama and Kobayashi
follows.

We do not agree with the majority opinion that in this case we
should follow the precedent of this Court of April 26, 1954
(*Hanreishū*, VIII, No. 4, 848 <Civil>), and dismiss the application summarily as "clearly without grounds." We consider that
this Court must judge the issues raised in the application.

The precedent cited in the majority opinion dealt with an application for the release of war criminals on the ground that Article 11 of the Treaty of Peace with Japan and the law (Law No.
103 of 1952) that deals with the execution of sentences and with
pardons pursuant to that article of the peace treaty were unconstitutional. The constitutionality of Article 11 depends on whether
Japan's reasons for accepting the article were correct; and the

---

2. On Article 95, see footnote 1, p. 120; on Article 89, see footnote 7, p. 50.

problem raised relates only to those acts of government in respect to which a court should restrain itself from exercising its power of review of the constitutionality of legislation, that is to say, its power of judicial control. For this reason we think it was proper in that case for this Court to dismiss the application as "clearly without grounds" (Article 21, item 6, Habeas Corpus Rules).[3] The deportation of an alien for illegal entry into Japan is, however, a different problem and is one that may become the object of a legal judgment. Moreover, the crux of the applicant's case is his contention that the provisions of Articles 33 and 34 of the Constitution do not deal solely with criminal procedure and that the deportation order served on him by the immigration officer is accordingly contrary to the purport of Articles 33 and 34, and that, as a result, the superintendent of the Yokohama Immigration Holding Center has no authority to detain him since he is acting on the basis of an unconstitutional deportation order. If, as the applicant contends, the deportation order issued by the immigration officer is contrary to the spirit of Articles 33 and 34, then it is clear that there is no authority for holding him.

Whether there is such authority depends solely on how this Court, in the light of the facts relating to the confinement of the applicant in the present case, decides the question: "Do Articles 33 and 34 refer solely to criminal procedure?" Therefore, we do not consider, as does the majority opinion, that it "is . . . clear that the restraint in this case is neither (in the words of our previous judgment) 'patently without authority' nor 'a patent and serious violation of a form or procedure established by law.'" Accordingly, although we would agree to this Court's dismissing the appeal under Article 42 of the Habeas Corpus Rules[4] without hearing the parties, we consider that for the reasons we have stated, the application cannot be treated as "clearly without grounds" and that this Court must judge the issues raised in the application.

*   *   *

3. Article 21, paragraph 1, item 6, of the Habeas Corpus Rules provides that the Supreme Court may reject an application by a ruling "where the application is without grounds."

4. Article 42 of the Habeas Corpus Rules provides that the Supreme Court may dismiss the appeal without hearing the parties if, after considering the documents relating to the appeal, it is of the opinion that it is without grounds.

The opinion of Justice Mano Tsuyoshi follows.

The facts of the detention of the applicant are set forth in the judgment of the lower court and are not disputed by the parties. Thus, the facts of the case are perfectly clear and it is not a case involving difficulties in the findings about the taking of evidence. Thus, if on applying the law to the facts we find that the restraint is unlawful, we must restore to the applicant the freedom of person, which is now improperly denied him.

The majority opinion, however, states that it "is . . . clear that the restraint in this case is neither . . . patently without authority nor a patent and serious violation of a form or procedure established by law. Accordingly, the application in this case should be dismissed without judging the issues that the appellant raises." To me the meaning of this is extremely obscure. The majority opinion recognizes no need to judge the issues raised by the appellant. If, as a result of judging the issues raised by the appellant, it were found that the restraint was not unlawful, then the appeal, naturally, should be dismissed; but, conversely, if it were found to be unlawful, then it is equally imperative that the prisoner should be released. However, what the majority opinion seems to say is that without deciding whether the restraint is unlawful, it has dismissed the application on the ground that it is not patently unlawful. If this is their argument, it raises a serious problem. For the outcome of the judicial process to differ according to whether or not the illegality is patent would be destructive of one of the basic premises on which the administration of justice rests: that every judge knows the law and is bound by the law. Therefore, no matter how difficult the legal problem may be, or how troublesome the task, the judge must present a solution. A judge cannot be excused from making a decision on the ground that he does not know the law. Similarly, he cannot, merely by saying that the illegality is not patent, dismiss an appeal without deciding whether there is or is not illegality.

A judge's finding of whether the established facts reveal a breach of the law is closely related to the level of his ability. There will be cases where a brilliant judge can readily decide that the illegality is patent, but where a lesser judge cannot. Thus, if we are permitted to reject an appeal on the ground that there is no patent illegality, we connive at the anomalous situation in which a second-rate judge dismisses an application because he is second-rate. If it becomes the practice to dismiss difficult legal problems because the illegalities are not patent, then the judicial system will be shaken to its very foundations.

For my part, I cannot concur in the majority opinion which, without deciding whether the clear facts, which are not disputed by the parties, amount to unlawful restraint, has dismissed the appeal on the ground that there is no patent illegality. I consider that in the present case it is imperative to decide whether the restraint is unlawful (see my opinion, *Hanreishū*, VIII, No. 4, 852 ff. <Civil>).

*   *   *

The minority opinion of Justices Fujita Hachirō and Ikeda Katsu follows.

The majority opinion accepts the fact that the applicant is held by virtue of a deportation order issued under Article 52 of the Immigration Control Order and paragraph 5 of the supplementary regulations. However, it does not answer the applicant's (the appellant's) contentions that "the said Immigration Control Order and the deportation order contravene Articles 33 and 34 of the Constitution and that the procedure whereby he has been restrained violates Article 63 of the Immigration Control Order." Without in any way judging the substance of his contention that his confinement is unconstitutional and illegal, it dismisses his application on the ground that it is clear that his confinement "is neither patently without authority nor a patent and serious violation of a form or procedure established by law."

Article 2 of the Habeas Corpus Law reads: "A person who is subjected to physical restraint other than by a lawful and proper procedure may apply for relief as provided in this law." According to this article, a person when subjected "to physical restraint other than by lawful and proper procedure" may apply for relief as provided in the law. When there is such an application the court investigates whether the restraint has been imposed as a result of a lawful and proper procedure, and if it was not—in other words, if it resulted from other than lawful and proper procedure—then the court must immediately grant the relief provided for in this law. The requirements for a writ of habeas corpus as set forth in the Habeas Corpus Law have been stated in full above. The competent court cannot, on the ground that it is not patent to it whether the restraint accords with lawful and proper procedure, refuse to grant the relief that the law provides. Not only does this follow naturally from the basic principle behind the enactment of the Habeas Corpus Law, but it is clearly so provided in the Habeas Corpus Law itself.

Article 4 of the Habeas Corpus Rules, however, provides that an "application under Article 2 of the Habeas Corpus Law may be made only where the restraint or the judgment or administrative decision relating to the restraint is either patently without authority or patently and seriously violates a procedure or form established by law." We should, however, note that Article 4, as its title, "Requirements for an Application," indicates, refers to the "requirements that make an application formally correct"; it does not relate to requirements that provide an application with grounds for acceptability. Article 23 of the Habeas Corpus Law delegates to the Supreme Court the task of making the necessary rules relating to applications, examination, and trial. This Court, pursuant to this power, has made such rules dealing with "Requirements for an Application." In doing so, it has merely adopted regulatory measures to confine applications within fixed bounds in order to prevent the courts from being plagued with irresponsible and groundless applications. The word "patent" in the Rules refers to the application. It means that if on reading the contentions in the application it is not patent that the restraint is unlawful and improper, then the application cannot be accepted. Putting it another way, it means that, if the arguments in the application are incoherent or completely *non sequitur* or if, even admitting the interpretation of facts and law contained therein, it is patent that the imprisonment is not unlawful and improper, then the court may dismiss the application without trying the issues contained therein. (That this provision relates to the summary dismissal of an application is clear from its title "Requirements for an Application." It means that if the requirements are not fulfilled, the application should, in accordance with Article 21 (1) of Habeas Corpus Rules, be dismissed by a ruling as incompetent.)

Since the rule relates to the dismissal of applications [without trial] we should, when deciding whether the requirements have been fulfilled, be as liberal as possible. Otherwise, by dismissing cases unheard, the objects of habeas corpus will be defeated. If the application itself satisfies this requirement of "patency" and if the arguments it contains are prima facie logical, then it cannot be dismissed as not satisfying the requirements of the law. If this provision is to be interpreted, as it has been in the majority opinion, to relate to the issues so that a court can refuse to grant the writ of habeas corpus unless the test of "patency" is satisfied, it would be an improper limitation on Article 2, Habeas Corpus Law, and therefore, because of the object of that law and its relation to the Constitution, Article 4 of the Habeas Corpus Rules must be held valid.

When we examine the application in the present case the grounds on which the applicant attacks the legality of his imprisonment are substantially those recited in the judgment of the lower court under the heading, "Facts," paragraphs 2 (*a*), (*b*), and (*c*). For example, the contention dealt with in 2 (*a*) is, briefly, that whereas Articles 33 and 34 of the Constitution require that, except when an offense is in process of being committed, no one shall be subjected to any imprisonment, detention, or other physical restraint except upon a warrant issued by a competent judicial officer (or, at the very least, one that has been issued with the participation of a judicial officer), the applicant in this case was, nevertheless, detained by virtue of a deportation order issued by an administrative officer, a subordinate of the minister of justice, not a judicial officer.

Thus, the restraint in this case is in contravention of the above constitutional provision. Since it is a clear fact that the restraint in this case was imposed without the participation of a judicial officer, then, leaving aside for the moment the correctness or incorrectness of the applicant's interpretation of the law, his contention itself is prima facie logical. Thus, it is impossible to hold that the application is not in conformity with the law on the ground that it does not satisfy the requirement of "patency" set forth in the same article. That is to say, the application in the present case is provided with "the requirement for an application" set forth in the same article. Accordingly, its substance must be examined and the correctness of the applicant's contention must be judged.

We consider that the majority opinion failed to observe that "patent" in Article 4 of the Habeas Corpus Rules relates to "requirements for an application" and that, misinterpreting the meaning of "patent," they were mistaken in not trying the issues raised in the application and in uncritically reaffirming the lower court's decision, which rejected the application as being without grounds.

(TRANSLATED BY D. C. S. SISSONS)

Hanreishū, IV, No. 9, 1805 (Criminal)

EDITORIAL NOTE: The accused was found guilty in the district court of violations of the election law and was fined. The prosecutor appealed, demanding a heavier penalty, whereupon the high court sentenced the accused to three months' imprisonment. The accused then appealed to the Supreme Court on two grounds: (1) that the sentence was excessive in view of precedents, and (2) that he had been placed in double jeopardy, which is prohibited under Article 39 of the Constitution.

The second point raised the interesting legal problem of a conflict between the concept of double jeopardy of the new Constitution and of *ichijifusairi* under the former Code of Criminal Procedure. *Ichijifusairi* is defined in standard Japanese-English dictionaries as "double jeopardy." However, Japanese legal dictionaries use *non bis in idem* as the foreign-language equivalent of *ichijifusairi* and give the phrase *nijū no kiken,* a literal translation, for "double jeopardy." The standard English translations of the Constitution use the phrase "double jeopardy" in Article 39, but the original contains neither *ichijifusairi* nor *nijū no kiken* (see footnote 1 below).

Grand Bench decision, September 27, 1950: Dismissed.

REFERENCES

Code of Criminal Procedure. ARTICLE 351. Appeal may be lodged by a public prosecutor or the accused. [Paragraph 2 omitted because it is not relevant to this case.]

Constitution of Japan. ARTICLE 39. No person shall be held criminally liable for an act which was lawful at the time it was committed, or of which he has been acquitted, nor shall he be placed in double jeopardy.[1]

FORMAL JUDGMENT

Appeal dismissed.

REASONS. The grounds of appeal are as set forth separately in the "Reasons for Appeal," tendered by counsel, Mr. Kanemitsu. To deal with item 1: The principle of *ichijifusairi* is undoubtedly based on the fundamental concept that no person should more than once be exposed to the danger of standing trial to have his guilt determined for the same offense. It is proper to consider this danger in a particular case as a continuing single state extending from the beginning of the procedure until its end. Thus, the proceedings at first, second, and third instance of the same case are but parts of this continuous single jeopardy. It follows that in one case there is only a single danger no matter what the stage of the proceedings. This does not constitute "double jeopardy" or "twice jeopardy" [these phrases in English in the original]. Hence, an accused person is not put in twofold jeopardy if a prosecutor appeals against a judgment of guilty or of not guilty in a lower court, seeking a judgment of guilty or a heavier punishment. Thus, in the present case there is no violation of Article 39 of the Constitution and no one is twice charged with criminal liability. The appellant's contention, therefore, cannot be accepted.

As regards item 2: It is clear to us that the appellant has shown none of the grounds for appeal required by Article 405 of the Code of Criminal Procedure.[2] Nor, having read the whole transcript and considered the facts that the accused raises, are we able to conclude that a serious violation of justice will take place unless

1. An exact translation of the phrase here rendered, ". . . nor shall he be placed in double jeopardy," is: "nor shall he be more than once held criminally liable for the same offense."
2. See footnote 2, p. 77.

we use the powers vested in us and quash the decision. Hence, as the grounds for the appeal are insufficient, it cannot be sustained. Therefore, pursuant to Articles 414 and 396 of the Code of Criminal Procedure,[3] we give judgment as set forth in the formal judgment.

This is the unanimous opinion of the Court with the exception of Justices Hasegawa Taichirō, Sawada Takejirō, Kuriyama Shigeru, Saitō Yūsuke, and Fujita Hachirō.

* * *

The following is the supplementary opinion of Justice Hasegawa Taichirō, dealing with item 1 of the appellant's reasons for appeal.

The appellant bases his case on the fact that the Constitution of Japan has adopted Anglo-American legal concepts and that in the English translation of Article 39 the term, "double jeopardy," is used. He argues that this article has the same meaning as the relevant portion of the Fifth Amendment of the American Constitution, which reads ". . . nor shall any person be subject for the same offence to be twice put in jeopardy of life and limb." From this he argues that our Constitution has adopted the Anglo-American legal principle of "double jeopardy." He contends that the essence of the double jeopardy principle is that double jeopardy commences not merely when a final judgment is given,[4] but before, when a certain stage in proceedings earlier than judgment has been reached. In thus protecting the accused from being prosecuted more than once for the same deed to his disadvantage, it safeguards his position.

If we accept the contention that the second sentence of Article 39 of the Constitution[5] ("no person . . . shall more than once be held criminally liable for the same deed") means double jeopardy, then it must follow that the second part of the first sentence of the same article ("no person shall be held criminally liable for an act . . . of which he has been acquitted") is also naturally included in this principle. However, when we come to look at the

3. These articles refer only to minor procedural matters related to this decision.

4. A "final judgment" (alternatively, "irrevocable judgment" or "finalized judgment") is one that is at a stage where it cannot be set aside by any of the ordinary methods of appeal.

5. In the English translation Article 39 is a single sentence; in the original there are two, the second consisting of the passage in parentheses.

English translation it becomes apparent that the phrase "double jeopardy" is used only with respect to the second sentence of the article and is separated from the second part of the first sentence. If it had been intended to adopt the principle of double jeopardy in its original form, there would have been no need to make a distinction in the English translation between the second part of the first sentence of Article 39 and the second sentence of that article, and all that would have been necessary would have been to use words similar to those in the Fifth Amendment of the United States Constitution. In view of the fact that in making the English translation the distinction was made, it is impossible to say that this article and the Fifth Amendment have the same meaning. Thus, the appellant is too hasty in deciding on the basis of the English translation that Article 39 adopts the principle of double jeopardy in its original form. This safeguard of the position of the accused is sufficient if provided after final judgment. In the light of conditions in this country, it would be excessive to provide the safeguard in the form of double jeopardy where a judgment is not final or where an earlier stage in the proceedings has been reached. Thus, it is proper to conclude that when the Constitution was enacted the principle of double jeopardy was not adopted in its original form.

The appellant further relies on the fact that in enacting the new Code of Criminal Procedure, "Reopening of Procedure" was prohibited when disadvantageous to the accused, and Article 58 of the Criminal Code was repealed.[6] The purpose of these changes, the appellant argues, was to safeguard the position of the accused, and this accords with the intent of Article 39, which adopted the principle of double jeopardy. These changes, however, stem from the fact that Article 39 sets forth the principle of *ichijifusairi*, not that it adopts the principle of double jeopardy.

The appellant further notes that the new Code of Criminal Procedure gives great weight to the trial at first instance and provides that when at first instance a sentence of imprisonment is given, bail or the suspension of the execution of [a warrant of] detention is thereby revoked. It is argued that this confirms the authority of first instance judgments and that, as a corollary, it

6. Article 58 permitted a sentence to be altered when it was discovered after final judgment that the prisoner was not a first offender.

recognizes the principle that the accused is not to be subjected to the danger of the first instance judgment's being altered to his disadvantage. These provisions, however, were enacted solely to give effect to a particular policy in the field of penal law; they were not enacted because the principle of double jeopardy had been adopted. As explained above, Article 39 of the Constitution of Japan did not adopt the principle of double jeopardy in its original form. Thus, although criminal procedure permits appeals by a prosecutor to the disadvantage of an accused, this does not infringe any provision of the Constitution. I am unable to accept the arguments of the accused.

* * *

The following is the joint supplementary opinion of Justices Sawada Takejirō and Saitō Yūsuke dealing with item 1 of the appellant's reasons for appeal.

The term, *ichijifusairi*, in its primary and broad sense means that in ordinary judicial proceedings [7] once a matter has come before the courts it cannot be heard again, much less be decided again; it is not the same as a final judgment [8] with the effect of *res adjudicata*.[9] (In its narrow sense it means that in the same case no judgment can be made that differs as to the juridical relationships [10] decided by a previous final decision. Therefore, in civil procedure, after subsequent hearings have been held in the same case, a substantive judgment is given that fits the circumstances in both situations but has as its basis the same juridical relationships as in the previous final judgment; and in criminal procedure, especially under "acquittal," [11] a substantive judgment is given that reconfirms the previous final judgment. That is to say, in this sense there have been in fact both substantive hearing and judg-

7. "Ordinary" here refers to procedures in the Code of Criminal Procedure other than those in Articles 435 ff. and 454 ff. See footnote 12 below.
8. See footnote 4 above.
9. "A matter finally decided on its merits by a court of competent jurisdiction."
10. "Juridical relationships" is a direct translation of *hōritsu kankei*. It refers to those relationships in society that are governed by law and indicates areas in which law is effective in contradistinction to morality and religion, for example.
11. "Acquittal" is the standard English translation of *mensō*. However, *mensō* is defined in Article 337 of the Code of Criminal Procedure as acquittal which must be given if an irrevocable decision has been made; if the punishment has been abolished by legislation subsequent to the crime; if there has been an amnesty; and if the period of limitation of actions has expired. Only the first instance is referred to in this opinion. (Translator's note.)

ment; it does not mean that we do not carry out the procedures of hearing and judgment. To call this *ichijifusairi*, as is popularly done, is not only erroneous in fact, but is the source of mistaken theories and precedents.) Etymologically, *ichijifusairi* [literally, *ichiji* is "single matter" and *fusairi* "no reargument"] is an abbreviation of *dōitsu jiken fusaishinri* [literally, *dōitsu jiken* is "same case," *fusaishinri* "no retrial"]. Accordingly, the principle in its broad sense is a procedural concept whereby, so far as ordinary procedure is concerned, if the same case comes before the courts again, proceedings are discontinued and are not carried out. Naturally, it does not mean that a person shall not be held liable in substantive penal law. Extraordinary judicial procedures such as "Reopening of Procedure" and "Extraordinary Appeal to the Supreme Court" [Code of Criminal Procedure, Articles 435 ff., "Reopening of Procedure," and Articles 454 ff., "Extraordinary Appeal to the Supreme Court"] were especially established in order to defeat the principle [12] of *ichijifusairi* in its narrow sense; hence it goes without saying that we cannot apply the principle in its broad sense [in extraordinary procedure]. The "principle of double jeopardy" in the American Constitution would seem to correspond with *ichijifusairi* in its broad sense—in criminal procedure—in cases involving the death sentence or imprisonment.

However, Article 39 of our Constitution, as its wording indicates, merely says, "No person shall be held criminally liable. . . ." It is a provision relating to liability in substantive penal law. It does not, of course, include civil or administrative liability. It is not a provision directly establishing a principle relating to judicial procedure such as *ichijifusairi*. In particular, the second sentence of Article 39 goes no further than to establish a simple principle of substantive penal law that any child of three can understand: that no person shall be twice held criminally liable for the same offense. (There is no objection to translating this into English as "double jeopardy" in the sense of substantive penal law.) There is neither basis nor need for interpreting this pretentiously as something which "expands and strengthens the principle of *ichijifusairi*

12. The phrase, "to defeat the principle," here means to prevent it from operating against the interests of either the accused or the prosecutor, because Articles 435 ff. provide for reopening of procedure on behalf of the accused after a judgment has become irrevocable, and Articles 454 ff. provide for appeal by the prosecutor against an irrevocable judgment.

in criminal procedure and exalts it into a constitutional guarantee." Thus do we reach the conclusion that Article 39 means that a person shall neither by ex post facto legislation be made criminally liable for an act that was lawful at the time it was done, nor shall he, either by ordinary or extraordinary procedures, be held criminally liable for an act of which he has already been adjudged not guilty. (Thus, "Extraordinary Appeal to the Supreme Court" is permissible since because "the effect of the judgment in extraordinary appeal shall not extend to the accused," he is not charged with criminal liability.) Although it requires that no person can be twice punished for the same offense, it does not prevent his being charged with criminal responsibility to such degree as is right and proper as a result of an extraordinary procedure, even though a final judgment has already been given. Whether the extraordinary procedure is to his advantage or disadvantage is immaterial; nor does it prevent the punishment of an accomplice.

Thus, although it was proper in our new legislation to retain reopening of procedure where to the advantage of the accused, the repeal of the provisions that permitted reopening of procedure to his disadvantage [13] (except the provisions which permitted a judgment of "not guilty" to be changed to "guilty"—it was right that these should be repealed) and the repeal of Article 58 of the Criminal Code were completely contrary to reason. It was an obvious mistake, a very clear case of "going too far."

Under our new Code of Criminal Procedure the appeal system is, with respect to one case, a continuing procedure. This does not in any sense hold a person twice criminally responsible for one offense. Thus, the Code of Criminal Procedure in permitting appeals by the prosecutor does not in any way violate Article 39 of the Constitution.

* * *

13. The former (pre-occupation) Code of Criminal Procedure in Article 486 permitted reopening of procedure at the instance of a prosecutor (1) if, although a judgment of not guilty had been given, a judgment of guilty should have been given, (2) if the punishment inflicted had been too light, or (3) if a prosecution had been wrongly dismissed. The procedure was confined to cases in which either (1) the appropriate punishment was imprisonment of more than one year or death, (2) in a subsequent trial a court had come to a different conclusion about the evidence on which the original judgment relied, or (3) a judge or prosecutor involved in the case had been found guilty of improper conduct. (Translator's note.)

The following is the minority opinion of Justice Fujita Hachirō dealing with item 1 of the appellant's reasons for appeal.

In Article 39 of the Constitution it is provided that: "No person shall be held criminally liable for an act . . . of which he has been acquitted. Nor shall he more than once be held criminally liable for the same deed."

This clearly forbids a person's being subsequently found guilty once he has been adjudged not guilty of an act. It is also clear that it forbids, once he has been found guilty and punished, his being again punished for the act. The phrases, "once adjudged not guilty" or "once found guilty and punished," refer to situations in which innocence or guilt is definitely established by a final judgment. They should not be interpreted to include cases still in progress where although a judgment of guilt or innocence has been pronounced, it has not yet been confirmed. Thus, for a prosecutor to appeal against such a judgment and to seek the judgment of a higher court in no wise contravenes this article of the Constitution.

*   *   *

The following is the opinion of Justice Kuriyama Shigeru with respect to item 1 of the appellant's reasons for appeal.

The last sentence of Article 39 of the Constitution provides that no person shall be more than once held criminally liable for the same deed. It is too narrow an interpretation to say that this means merely that a person shall not be twice punished for an act of which he has been found guilty. Since the reinstitution of a prosecution, once it has been withdrawn (see Article 340 of the Code of Criminal Procedure), is also prevented by this safeguard, the last sentence of Article 39 should be interpreted as a safeguard against there being a second prosecution [in English in the original] for the same offense.

Even if the last clause of Article 39 is modeled on the common-law principle of double jeopardy (if it is modeled on this principle, it is not confined to the last clause but extends to the whole of the last sentence of Article 39), if in transplanting this to the Constitution of Japan it was transformed into *ichijifusairi*, its meaning as a constitutional safeguard becomes vague. I believe that, if this is interpreted as in the majority opinion, it becomes too narrow.

The starting point of our inquiry must be: "At what stage in

Japanese criminal procedure does the process of 'holding a person liable' (in the words of the aforementioned final clause) begin?" Since it accords with the fundamental spirit of the Constitution to interpret this right, equally with such rights as those contained in Articles 37 and 38, to the advantage of the accused, we should, as I have said above, interpret it as a guarantee against a second prosecution. Thus, we should consider the condition of being charged with criminal liability to begin when a court decides to hear the case. (It does not begin merely with the prosecution's laying the charge.) What the appellant's contention amounts to is that if the American principle of double jeopardy is applied in its original form, then it follows that once there is an appeal the case ceases to be a single, unbroken whole. In our criminal procedure, however, an appeal, from first instance at all events, is not considered an extraordinary remedy, but as a part of a continuing procedure, the situation of "being held liable" is single and continuous. Thus, for a prosecutor to appeal against a first instance judgment, even to the disadvantage of the accused, does not raise the problem of being "twice held liable."

I consider that, since the right claimed in the last clause of Article 39 of the Constitution is a right guaranteed to an accused person by whom—like the rights contained in Article 37 and 38, paragraph 1, of the Constitution—it can be waived, it is possible in such circumstances for there to be a reopening of procedure in which the accused is again held liable. When the reopening is advantageous to the accused, the legislators in the new law consider that he has waived his right, but they do not permit an application for reopening of procedure when it is disadvantageous to him. This is the natural consequence of the guarantee of Article 39 of the Constitution. Since under our new legislation appeal to the Supreme Court has become essentially an extraordinary method of relief, I consider that, like reopening of procedure, an appeal by the prosecutor to the Supreme Court to the disadvantage of the accused should not be recognized. This, however, has nothing to do with the interpretation of the last phrase of Article 39 and, therefore, does not necessarily raise constitutional issues.

For the above reasons the contentions of the appellant cannot be accepted.

(TRANSLATED BY D. C. S. SISSONS)

Hanreishū, VII, No. 13, 1523 (Civil)

EDITORIAL NOTE: The land reform was one of the most important economic changes sponsored by the occupation. Briefly, it more than doubled the number of owner-cultivators, involved the transfer of more than 5,000,000 acres of land, and resulted in the virtual elimination of landlords through the limitation of landholding to a maximum of approximately eight acres. The suit brought by the plaintiffs in the present case, as will be seen, was not so much an attempt to bring to naught the land reform program as it was to gain for the former landlords what they considered to be "just compensation." The plaintiffs lost in the court of first instance, the court of appeal, and the Supreme Court itself.

The opinions in the present case bring out clearly the tremendous significance—legal, political, and economic—of the land reform and, perhaps indirectly, at least indicate the impossibility of making a narrowly legal interpretation of the key phrase, "just compensation," in the present case.

Grand Bench decision, December 23, 1953: Dismissed.

REFERENCES

Constitution of Japan. ARTICLE 29, paragraph 3. Private property may be taken for public use upon just compensation therefor.
Owner-Farmer Establishment Special Measures Law. ARTICLE

6, paragraph 3. When there is a rental value for the land involved set under the Land Register Law, the price referred to in the previous paragraph shall be determined within the limits of amounts established as follows (but when, under the provisions of Article 6 (3), paragraph 1, of the Agricultural Land Adjustment Law, there is an amount set by the governor, it shall be that amount): for rice fields, forty times the appropriate rental value (but when, under the said article and paragraph, there is a rate established by a governor, it shall be that rate) and for dry fields, forty-eight times the appropriate rental value (but when, under the said article and paragraph, there is a rate established by a governor, it shall be that rate). When no rental value for the land in question is set under the Land Register Law, the price will be based on an amount determined by a city, town, or village agricultural land commission with the approval of the governor. However, when because of [other] special circumstances the amount for the land in question is determined by a city, town, or village agricultural land commission with the approval of the governor, the price will be based on the said amount.

FORMAL JUDGMENT

The appeal in the present case is dismissed. The cost of the proceedings is to be borne by the appellant.

REASONS. Concerning the first and third points in the arguments for appeal presented by attorneys Kamiya Takeo, Matsuura Shotarō, Mineda Chōnosuke, and Kobayashi Seiichi for the appellant, Tanaka Issaku: The government, when it set out to acquire agricultural land under Article 3 of the Owner-Farmer Establishment Special Measures Law (referred to below as the Owner Establishment Law), proceeded in accordance with the objectives [principally to establish owner-farmers] set forth in Article 1 of the law, and, of course, it naturally had to pay just compensation as provided for in Article 29, paragraph 3, of the Constitution. Nevertheless, under Article 6, paragraph 3, of the Owner Establishment Law, the price under the program for the acquisition of agricultural land could not be greater than forty times the rental value of rice fields or forty-eight times the rental value of dry fields (this maximum price is referred to below as "the

consideration for acquisition" or simply as "the consideration").
Accordingly, it is necessary to examine whether the consideration
provided for in the Owner Establishment Law coincides with what
is termed "just compensation" in Article 29, paragraph 3, of the
Constitution.

1. First, it is proper to interpret "just compensation" for property taken for public use as provided for in Article 29, paragraph 3, of the Constitution as being a proper sum reasonably
calculated on the basis of a value that can be considered as having
been determined by economic conditions existing at the time and
not as a sum that necessarily and always must conform completely
to a value so determined. Since, in the final analysis, the right of
property by its nature is to be defined by law in conformity with
the public welfare (Article 29, paragraph 2, of the Constitution),
in cases in which it is necessary to maintain or to advance the
public welfare, the right to utilize, to profit from, or to dispose
of said right of property may be limited. Moreover, in respect to
the value of said property rights there may also be special limitations, since it is also a fact that the establishment of such value is
not to be recognized as being on the basis of free exchange.

2. Accordingly, in examining the formulation of the consideration as determined by Article 6, paragraph 3, of the Owner Establishment Law, we find that its basis was already established by
Article 6 (2) of the Revised Agricultural Land Adjustment Law
at the time of the First Land Reform (see Law No. 64, December
28, 1945, and Agriculture and Forestry Ministry Notification
No. 14, January 26, 1946). The profit formula of the consideration was based on the value of the earnings of the owner-producer,
not on the value of the profits of the landlord; and it was designed
to maintain farm lands as productive areas and to support and
develop agricultural production and the stability of the position of
the producer. The above formula must also be regarded as proper
because it was in a law based on a national policy that had been
consistently carried out from the Agricultural Land Adjustment
Law (referred to below as the Agricultural Adjustment Law) to
the Owner Establishment Law (Law No. 43, October 12, 1946),
which was enacted during the so-called Second Land Reform.

According to the profit formula therein, the standard rate of
production for rice fields was to be calculated on the basis of an

actual yield of two *koku* [about ten bushels] of water-grown un-hulled rice per *tan* [approximately .25 acre] (the average for the five years from 1940 to 1944), and this was to be divided in the proportion of 1.143 *koku* to be delivered, and .857 *koku* to be retained [by the producer]. This was to be converted into a cash sum, at the end of 1945, of ¥150 per *koku* as the producer's price [for that delivered] and ¥75 per *koku* as the seller's price [for that retained for possible sale].

It is true that not only the items forming the basis for the cal-culation of compensation were reasonable, but that the figures themselves—namely, an income per *tan* of roughly ¥248.75, in-cluding the above cash sum of ¥234.36 plus an additional ¥14.39 [1]—must also be termed reasonable for the time (the previously mentioned First Land Reform). The price of rice mentioned above, which was used as the basis for calculation, was the of-ficial price (Article 3, paragraph 2, and Article 4, paragraph 2, of the Staple Food Management Law). In addition, because it must be recognized that special fixing of the rice price was an un-avoidable legal measure designed to stabilize the national economy and to guarantee the national food supply and that the price was adequate at the time, then for the most part this rice price is appropriate for the calculation of the consideration for acquisi-tion of farm land, and it cannot be said, as the argument contends, that it should not be used as a standard for deciding whether or not there was the just compensation provided for in the Con-stitution.

In addition, after deducting the cost of production per *tan* (¥212.37) [2] from the above cash income per *tan* (¥248.75), what remains (¥36.38) is exactly the net return per *tan* to the producer. Since as a cultivator he must take into account his profit, the following process of computation is not unreasonable: namely, to take 4 per cent of the production cost (¥8.50) as the profit and subtract it from the net profit (¥36.38) to arrive at the sum of ¥27.88, an amount adequate as a rental that could be earned through the possession of the land by the cultivator. When

1. The sum of ¥234.36 is arrived at by the following calculation: 1.143 *koku* times ¥150, plus .857 *koku* times ¥75. There is no explanation of the "additional ¥14.39." My own re-peated calculations of the sums given here and below yield different answers, but the differences are insignificant.

2. No explanation is given for this figure.

the capital necessary for the acquisition of this rental (¥27.88) is calculated at the rate of 3.68 per cent—the rate for government loans at the time—it comes to the rather considerable sum per *tan* of ¥757.60; this sum is the value on which the earnings of the cultivator of the farm land are based. When this value is divided by the then current standard rental value (¥19.01) per *tan* of average rice fields, the result is just under forty (39.85) and since the general and appropriate standard of forty times the rental value was set as the purchase price by the stipulations of Article 6, paragraph 3, of the Owner Establishment Law, the said sum [¥757.60] became the purchase price.

In regard to the consideration for the acquisition of dry fields, the earning value to the owner-cultivator of dry fields (¥446.98) is just under forty-eight times (47.90) the standard rental value of average dry fields (¥9.33). This earning value was calculated by taking 59 per cent of the earning value (¥757.60) to the owner-cultivator of rice fields, the proportion [59 per cent] being that between the selling price per *tan* of rice fields (¥727) and of dry fields (¥429) (according to the survey of March, 1943, of the Japan Hypothec Bank). This determination of the rate of forty-eight times the rental value is in accordance with the basis of calculation generally applied to rice fields.

Thus, in respect to both rice fields and dry fields, the items and the figures for the calculation of the consideration conform to a standard that is both objective and average. Because the aim was the acquisition of farm land in fulfillment of the conditions of Article 3 of the Owner Establishment Law in order to achieve the objective of the said law—namely, the wide and rapid creation of owner-farmers throughout our country—and thus to establish a position as owner-farmers for the great majority of cultivators, it is appropriate to interpret the situation as one not permitting, as a standard procedure, a price for each individual piece of farm land arrived at in the free market under ever-changing economic conditions.

Accordingly, it was proper that the Owner Establishment Law set, within the scope of Article 6, paragraph 3, a price for the farm land that had to be acquired under the land acquisition plan. The amount of compensation, at the very least, was sufficient within the standards established there, and it was an indication of the maximum limit beyond which it was impossible to go. Hence, it is impossible to argue, as the appellant does, that this price standard was only a tentative one, which allowed the establishment of a higher price after consideration of general economic conditions at the time of [subsequent] acquisition.

3. Furthermore, in addition to the aforementioned consideration for acquisition, the owners of farm land received compensation money based on a specific rate (¥220 per *tan* for rice fields and ¥130 per *tan* for dry fields) in proportion to the area of their land (Owner Establishment Law, Article 13, paragraphs 3 and 4). The method of calculating this compensation in respect to the amount that can be anticipated by the owner of the land as income from tenant rental of land not cultivated by himself is as follows: first, in respect to rice fields there is the standard tenant rental based on the above-mentioned yield of two *koku* per *tan* which, figured at the rate of 39 per cent for the standard tenant rental of ordinary rice fields, amounts to .78 *koku;* second, since tenant rentals had already been changed from payment in kind to payment in cash (Revised Agricultural Adjustment Law, Article 9 <2>), when the above quantity is converted into cash, at the rate of ¥55 per *koku* as the price to the landlord, it would amount to ¥42.90; finally, we arrive at the figure of ¥36.01 as the net earnings of the landlord after deducting the amount of ¥6.89 as the land charge for which the landlord was responsible (the sum resulting from the addition of the increase of the land tax of 1944 to the land charge per *tan* of ordinary rice land, as calculated by the Japan Hypothec Bank in March, 1943). The amount (¥978.53) obtained from reducing this to capital at the going rate on government bonds, as in the case of the previously discussed consideration for acquisition, is the landlord's profit value; and the difference (¥220.93) between this sum and the previously discussed earning value (¥757.60) to the owner-cultivator is the amount of compensation.

In respect to dry fields, the difference between the landlord's profit value (¥577.33) (which was calculated in the same proportion as that for rice fields, as in the case of the previously discussed consideration for acquisition) and the earning value to the owner-cultivator (¥446.98) amounts to ¥130.35 and is the compensation money for dry fields.

Thus, this must be considered reasonable indemnification through compensation from the standpoint of the landlord's profit value. Both the items and the figures of this calculation must be objective and average standards, like those used in determining the consideration for acquisition (see last section in 2. above). Thus, since in addition to the consideration for acquisition mentioned above, the landlord also received compensation that was reasonably calculated on the basis of his earnings as a landlord, there are no grounds for stating that the compensation for the owners of acquired farmland was unjust.

4. To go on, the consideration for acquisition provided for in Article 6, paragraph 3, of the Owner Establishment Law was based on Article 6 (2) of the Revised Agricultural Land Adjustment Law (see Notification 14, 1946, of the Agriculture and Forestry Ministry). It remained as it was in spite of later economic changes and was unaltered even when the acquisition order relating to the dry fields of the appellant was served on November 25, 1947. However, the argument of the appellant on this point is that a price that might be considered adequate as just compensation at one time could become insufficient at another time because of changes in the economic situation, and it is asserted that what is just compensation must be determined solely on the basis of economic conditions existing at the time of acquisition.

To examine this point:

(a) Farm land in general is naturally limited in its extent; and it differs from ordinary commodities because of difficulties in increasing the supply by production and in calculating its value. Since the value, from the standpoint of earning [capacity], is also basically limited by the area of land, there are not only limits to production itself, but although the price of general commodities may go up and the costs of production increase correspondingly, earnings will not necessarily be in proportion. Consequently, it cannot be said that value based on earnings parallels commodity prices. Value can also be considered according to its dependence on demand, especially in relation to the characteristics of the farm land. At times when value is established by national policy it is not possible for the said value to be set by free exchange. What remains in respect to this allegation is simply whether or not such an official or controlled price is strikingly inconsistent with possible earnings under existing economic conditions.

(*b*) To briefly examine the development of our national policy on the agricultural land system: the Agricultural Land Adjustment Law was enacted by April, 1938, and was designed to stabilize the positions of both the landowner and the cultivator and to maintain and develop farm production; it was also designed to achieve the adjustment of farm land (Article 1) and, accordingly, the establishment and maintenance of owner-cultivators (Articles 4, 6, and 7). The policy to that end was pursued even more vigorously as the danger of war approached and was finally given even greater emphasis after the war through the powerful influence of the Allied nations. It culminated in the enactment of the Owner Establishment Law.

It may be that such a far-reaching reform as the scheme for the acquisition of farm land under the Owner Establishment Law would not have been realized so rapidly had it not been for Allied orders, but it did lay along the path of development of our own national policy; and it must be regarded as unlike other institutions in which change could not have been considered without Allied orders.

In respect to this point, when we go back and examine the course of change brought about in the character of our farm land after the enactment of the Agricultural Land Adjustment Law we see the following: (1) fixed limitations were applied to the transfer and other disposition of specified owner-cultivated farm lands (Article 6 of the Agricultural Adjustment Law of April, 1938), but these limitations were later extended to farm land in general in Article 7 (1) of the Revised Emergency Order for the Control of Farm Lands, etc., of March, 1944, and Article 5 of the Revised Agricultural Adjustment Law of December, 1945; (2) restrictions were placed on the utilization of farm land for purposes other than cultivation (Articles 3 and 5 of the Emergency Order for the Control of Farm Lands of February, 1941) and were continued in the Revised Agricultural Adjustment Law (Article 6 of the law as revised in October, 1946); (3) tenant rents were fixed with the rate of September 18, 1939, as the base (Article 3 of the Order for the Control of Tenant Rents of December, 1939) and the intent of that fixing was continued in the Revised Agricultural Adjustment Law (Article 9 <3> of the law as revised in December, 1945); (4) the principle of payment in cash was next established (Article 9 <2> of the Revised Agricultural Land Adjustment Law of December, 1945); and (5) the price of farm land was controlled on a fixed standard (Article 3 of the Emergency Order for the Control of the Price of Farm Land of January, 1941) and this control was continued in the Revised Agricultural Land Adjustment Law (Article 6 <2> of the law as revised in December, 1945).

Thus, prior to the enactment of the Owner Establishment Law, restrictions had already been placed on the free disposition of farm land and its utilization for purposes other than cultivation, the tenant rent had been set at a specific amount to be paid in cash, and the price of farm land controlled on a fixed standard. Because of this, the landlord's right to own farm land had already been considerably limited in respect to the rights of utilization, earnings, and disposition. The control over land prices by law had already reached the point at which there was generally no area for the creation of a free market price.

Thus, the change in the character of the right of ownership of farm land was a legal measure that accompanied a consistent national policy aimed at the establishment of owner-farmers; in other words, it was substantially a right of ownership of farm land determined by law in conformity with the public welfare as stated in Article 29, paragraph 2, of the Constitution.

(c) When we regard the relation between this problem and the rise in commodity prices in the period after the establishment of the basis for the consideration set forth in Article 6, paragraph 3, of the Owner Establishment Law, we see that there were also many revisions in the price of rice, which is most intimately connected with farm land—that is, revisions were made in the price to the producer (¥150 per *koku*) and the seller's price (¥75 per *koku*) between the time that the consideration was established at the end of 1945 and November 25, 1947, when the acquisition order in the present case was served. However, those revisions in the price of rice were measures to cope with the striking increase in production costs that arose principally out of the sudden changes in economic conditions in the postwar period. This was natural under

the rice-pricing policy, which was based on income to the cultivator, who was also the producer. There was no reason why there
should be immediate and corresponding revisions in the price of
farm land in respect to the owners—the landlords who had no
direct connection at all with production itself.

Even though the price may be an official or controlled one fixed
by law, it would be properly established if it conformed to the
economic state or various other conditions of the people. But since
such an official or controlled price is established for the public
welfare, it need not necessarily and always coincide completely
with a price in conformity with earnings under the economic conditions of the times nor, still less, must it coincide with a price
that has been created in a free market. Therefore, it cannot be
said that the standard for the consideration is not just compensation because it does not correspond exactly to other commodity
prices determined in a free market at the time of the acquisition.

5. For the reasons stated above, it is reasonable to regard the
consideration for acquisition of Article 6, paragraph 3, of the
Owner Establishment Law as conforming with just compensation
under Article 29, paragraph 3, of the Constitution. The assertion
of the plaintiff that differs from this is based on a personal opinion
and cannot be accepted. Accordingly, the argument that the appeal decision was in violation of Article 29, paragraph 3, of the
Constitution is without foundation.

Concerning the second point of the argument: [3] The appeal decision held that the consideration for acquisition of Article 6,
paragraph 3, of the Owner Establishment Law did not violate
Article 29, paragraph 3, of the Constitution. Since its correctness
has already been explained in relation to points 1 and 3, this point,
which asserts that the trial procedure resulting in the appeal decision was incomplete and which is based on a premise different
from the one here presented, is without grounds.

Accordingly, the decision is as stated in the formal judgment,
in accordance with Articles 401, 95, and 89 of the Code of Civil
Procedure.[4]

This decision is the unanimous opinion of the Justices, except

3. The argument held that the court of appeal had not exhausted the trial procedure because
it had not held formal hearings on the method of calculation of the basis of the acquisition price.
4. See footnote 7, p. 50 on Articles 401 and 89 and footnote 1 on p. 120 on Article 95.

for the supplementary opinion of Justice Kuriyama Shigeru and the dissenting opinions of Justices Inouye Nobori, Iwamatsu Saburō, Mano Tsuyoshi, and Saitō Yūsuke.

*   *   *

The supplementary opinion of Justice Kuriyama Shigeru follows.

Regarding the "just compensation" of Article 29, paragraph 3, of the Constitution, there are minority opinions, but mine alone is supplementary.

Since the phrase "for public use" in Article 29, paragraph 3, is a guarantee that the right of private property will not be taken away for the benefit of private individuals, it must be interpreted, on the other hand, to mean that should the necessity for public use arise, the property can be expropriated against the will of the person possessing the right. (This provision should probably be interpreted to mean the same as the English text.) But the phrase "public use" in Article 29, paragraph 3, means, among other things, "for the benefit of the public," and it need not be interpreted as necessarily providing for certain public uses in the material sense.

Again, even though certain specific individuals in concrete cases become beneficiaries as the result of expropriation, there is nothing wrong if the general objective of such expropriation by the government is for public use. As in the case of the present law (the Owner-Farmer Establishment Special Measures Law, hereinafter termed the Owner Establishment Law) even though the farm land which was acquired by the government through forced sale for public use, as stated in Article 1 of the law, was sold to specific tenant farmers, there was no change in the basic character of the objective of expropriation.

The guarantee in the said paragraph is also not limited to public enterprises, which are the objects of the Land Expropriation Law. It is clear that since contractual rights and benefits are also a part of the right of private property, they too can be expropriated if it is necessary for public use. For example, in cases where the state converts certain types of enterprises to public ownership for public use, I believe that it is possible for it to buy up by legal force the holdings of private stockholders in those enterprises, uniformly and according to certain general standards. Whether uniform purchase according to a general standard is reasonable as a form of concrete expropriation should preferably be examined as a question of just compensation. Since, in any event, expropriation under Article 29, paragraph 3, of the Constitution is applicable to public enterprises, which come under the ordinary Land Expropriation Law, there is no reason why the applicability of the paragraph should be limited formally to cases to which that law applies.

As for the guarantee of Article 29, paragraph 3, of the Constitution, its primary principle is that the expropriation of private property cannot be carried out if it is not done for public use and its secondary principle is that just compensation should be paid in cases of expropriation. The objective of expropriation under this paragraph is public use; but the right to private property, which can be expropriated, is in substance one that can be determined in conformity with the public welfare as stated in Article 29, paragraph 2; and the just compensation clause of paragraph 3 provides for compensation for loss of the right of private property.

It is a commonly held idea in the free countries of the world at the present time, particularly after the first and second world wars, when capitalism has reached a high stage of development, that since the right of private property is regarded as capital and that those who possess it can control and direct the many who do not, the right of property carries with it the social responsibility to conform with the public welfare. That our own Constitution has emerged naturally from the same concept is clear when the provisions of Article 29 are matched with those of Articles 25 and 28. It goes without saying that the right of property herein described includes the contractual rights and benefits involved in the establishment and transfer of rights to real estate and the receipt and transfer of financial investments. For example, the Interest Restriction Law, the Ground and House Rental Control Order, the Agricultural Land Adjustment Law, the Agricultural Land Law, and the Commodity Price Control Order, which regulate such things as contracts for the lending of money, rentals for land and buildings, and the market price of agricultural land, are all based on the intent of Article 29, paragraph 2, of the Constitution.

According to the same paragraph, the rights of ownership and of free contract may always be regulated in accordance with the public welfare, for they are not rights based on the concept of the freedom of the will as they were thought to be in the eighteenth century and the beginning of the nineteenth. For example, the extent to which the substance of diverse property rights can be determined by law is to be measured not by the benefit to the possessor of those property rights, but by the public welfare. Consequently, even though the courts decide whether there has been just compensation when the law provides for it in order to make possible the expropriation of such a right of private property, it is clear that there must be a consideration of the social responsibility which resides in the expropriated property—not only a comparison of the public benefit, which made the expropriation necessary, with the benefit to the individual who suffered it. Accordingly, even if we make a similar assessment of value when the right of private property may not have been expropriated for just compensation on a socially reasonable basis, it is clear that this assessment of value cannot necessarily be only an economic assessment of the loss [to the owner] of the expropriated property, but must be accompanied with an assessment of its social value.

Because expropriation is not a free transaction between the government and the rightful owner, but a forced purchase for public use against the rightful owner's will, there is no reason why the expropriatee should be compensated for the profit that he could anticipate in a free transaction. In other words, since expropriation is not designed to enrich the expropriatee, the minority opinion's argument—which places greater weight on the right of private property than on the assessment of social value, and which is based on the principle of free transaction in which compensation would be either a market price that the expropriatee would consider just or an assessment of value that would correspond to the objective value of the individual right of property—must be termed an interpretation not in conformity with the intent of Article 29, paragraphs 2 and 3, of the Constitution.

From the above point of view I shall examine the compensation provided in the Owner Establishment Law. At the time of the enactment of that law, the landlord's right of ownership of farm land, because of the Agricultural Adjustment Law, had already been placed under a number of restrictions: a limitation on disposition, a limitation on changes in utilization, a limitation on land confiscation, and the conversion of rental to a cash basis. In other words, the substance of the right of ownership of farm land had been deprived of its characteristic right of feudal control by Article 29, paragraph 2, of the Constitution and was treated as having an inherent social responsibility, which could be made gainful by individual cultivation. Thus, in the case of noncultivating landlords it [right of farm land ownership] had become a right of private ownership from which a controlled cash tenant rental could be obtained. As a result, the Owner Establishment Law, designed to create landed farmers by expropriating the tenant lands of absentee landlords and a specified area of the tenant lands of the resident landlords, positively did not violate in any way the intent of Article 29, granting that compensation be made for the loss of those ownership rights from which earnings could be gained from cash tenant rentals controlled by the Agricultural Adjustment Law.

Since the controlled amount stipulated in Article 6 (2) of the Agricultural Adjustment Law was not originally established as the amount for forced purchase—against the will of the owner —of the farm land, Article 6, paragraph 3, of the Owner Establishment Law provides for compensation for the loss incurred by the landlord through the forced sale by payment of a consideration for farm land which is based on the value of the earnings of the owner cultivator. Thus the landlord was placed in a position in which he could earn through his own cultivation. This alone could be termed just compensation. Nevertheless, since the payment of compensation money, as provided for in Article 13, paragraphs 3 and 4 of the said law, was designed to supplement the above considerations in reference to such circumstances as the yield and location of the farm land, in my opinion it is reasonable that the two together must be treated as the just compensation called for in Article 29, paragraph 3, of the Constitution.

Next, persons dissatisfied with the amount of the consideration for farm land acquired under Article 3 of the Owner Establishment Law can demand an increase by bringing suit in accordance with Article 14 of the same law; but I believe that such action cannot be regarded as a suit for an increase of the just compensation as explained previously, but as one for an increase within the limits of the consideration for acquisition as stipulated by the same law. Because laws respecting specified rights of private property in accordance with Article 29, paragraph 2, of the Constitution must use the public welfare as the standard for measuring their substantial reasonableness—for example, in respect to such questions as whether there should be control of either exchange or price, or, if there is to be control, the extent to which it is proper in the national life—it is clear that the reasonableness of such controlled sums established by law, excepting certain special provisions (for example, Article 6, paragraph 3, of the Owner Establishment Law), lies outside judicial control. For all that, the right to receive redress in the courts has not been taken away to the slightest degree, even though under the present law the right of the expropriatee to sue for an increased amount is limited, as stated in the law.

*   *   *

The opinion of Justices Inouye and Iwamatsu follows.

We cannot agree with the majority opinion that purchase under the present law (the Owner-Farmer Establishment Special Measures Law throughout [this opinion]) corresponds to purchase under Article 29, paragraph 3, of the Constitution; that, further, the purchase price set under Article 6 of the present law is the maximum price; that, for the above reasons, a lawsuit involving the above is not permissible; and that it [the purchase] is constitutional. We should like to record first the grounds for our position.

Fundamentally, Article 29, paragraph 3, of the Constitution applies to cases in which individual plots of land are bought up on a narrowly limited basis for public enterprises such as railroad construction. It cannot be considered as dealing with a revolutionary situation such as the present one in which purchase under the law was designed to confiscate the agricultural land of landlords throughout the entire country and to present it to the tenant farmers. (The presentation to specific tenant farmers of land that was bought up is not employment of it for public use. From this point of view, that action does not strictly conform to Article 29, paragraph 3. "For public use" is a concept narrower than "for the public welfare.")

Furthermore, if there is purchase under Article 29, paragraph 3, of the Constitution, it is necessary to ascertain for each plot of land a concrete and fair market price in each individual case by means of an investigation and appraisal of the peculiar characteristics of each plot; uniform purchase according to general standards, which disregard individual peculiarities, as under the method of purchase provided for in the present law, is not permissible.

Moreover, if purchase in this case is to be termed purchase under Article 29, paragraph 3, of the Constitution, then, because the same paragraph must be regarded as establishing just compensation as a necessary condition, the person who is bought out, if he considers the purchase price not to be just, must possess the right of appeal in the courts for an increase that would result in a just price. It is not permissible to say that the maximum price is established by law and that the institution of a suit for a higher one is not sanctioned. Article 14 of the present law permits appeal for an increased price only within the limits of the legally established rate and it is generally understood that it does not recognize appeals for greater amounts. The majority opinion depends on that interpretation. (We also must recognize that there are reasonable grounds for such an interpretation, viewing the situation from the intent of the entire law, but for reasons recorded below we cannot agree with it.) Thus, if the person who is bought out presents an appeal for an amount above the legally stipulated price, the court does not judge whether such an excess portion is just or not; it simply turns such a plea away as not in accordance with the law. In regard to such an excess portion, the person who is bought out is always deprived of the right to a suit in court, which is one of the rights guaranteed in the Constitution. In this situation, the hearing of the court must go into a determination of whether the amount in question is just, because it must not simply turn the case away.

For the time being, in giving Article 29, paragraph 3, of the Constitution a wide interpretation, as the majority opinion does, in order to make the buying up provided for in the said article constitutional, at the very least the right of appeal to establish a just price should also be recognized; in addition, if a set period for access to the courts is established, it must be a reasonable one providing a sufficient margin of time.

If the theory of the Supreme Court regarding Article 29, paragraph 3, as stated in the majority opinion is accepted, and if purchase according to the price and method as set forth in the present law is accepted as constitutional, there is the danger that henceforth the way will be opened for repeated unreasonable purchases under such laws as the present one, based on legislation passed in the name of the aforementioned constitutional provisions. Consequently, the guarantee in paragraph 1 of the same article seems on the verge of great peril. We are gravely concerned about this.

Purchase under this law was a part of the land reform carried out under the orders of the commanding general during the occupation and was outside the scope of the Constitution (see the memorandum on land reform dated December 9, 1945). This is a fact well known to all and scarcely needs mentioning. Nevertheless, the landlords of the time resigned themselves to it as being both truly inevitable and irresistible, and submitted. Without this as a premise the purchase cannot be fully understood.

The government at the time obeyed the intent of the above order and pressed for the rapid realization of the purchase. It speedily drafted the present law, presented it to headquarters, and received approval. The Diet also passed the law because it had to in order to carry out orders. Headquarters granted approval after careful scrutiny of the bill. After the enactment of the law urgent orders were issued (memorandum concerning land reform, dated February 4, 1948) to carry out the purchase rapidly, in accordance with the procedures set forth in the law.

Initially, of course, detailed orders regarding such items as method and price were not received, but because the speedy execution of the purchase according to the above procedures was urgently ordered after the passage of the law, the purchase under the above law must be said to have been executed completely under orders. Consequently, the purchase under the present law was concluded before independence and derived its validity outside the Constitution and under the authority of the commander. Both issues relating to pending legislation and the purchase itself (the transfer of the rights of ownership) have gained their validity in the same way. Presumably the present law only permits litigation concerning the price because it is absolutely impermissible to contest the transfer of title.

There is a difference from ordinary voluntary transactions in deciding the permissibility of litigation concerning only amount of the price in cases in which the right of ownership was forcibly taken away without any reference whatever to the will of the one from whom purchase was made. In such cases it is possible to differentiate between the transfer of title and the determination of the price: the transfer of title becomes valid after the conclusion of the act of purchase; in litigation involving the price, only the amount can be regarded as unsettled. (In regard to this point, Justice Mano apparently holds the same opinion.)

However, today, after the establishment of peace, since the authority of the commander no longer exists, the courts cannot apply such authority to laws with an unconstitutional content. Thus, it is perfectly clear from the stipulations of Article 29 that a situation in which land was bought up from landlords and presented to tenant farmers without the payment of just compensation is not permissible. Thus, it must be held that the party from whom the purchase was made can litigate concerning the price until a just amount has been determined. On this point we would like to join in the interpretations of Justices Mano and Saitō concerning Articles 6 and 14 of the law. Our reasons for such an interpretation are generally the same as those set down by the same Justices. We entertain grave doubts whether a land reform that included the forcible seizure of land on a broad, general, and one-sided basis—as in the present law—and its presentation to other individuals, is permissible under a constitution that maintains strict respect for private property (the question of whether the reform is good or bad being separate).

Leaving that aside for the moment, we think that, within [the meaning of] purchase under Article 29, paragraph 3, of the Constitution, it is impermissible to legalize a highly dubious price such as in this law, to carry out a stipulated procedure that seems to provide some basis for an interpretation that it is absolutely not allowable to sue for a greater amount, and, moreover, to limit the period for bringing suit to a time so short as to be in reality well-nigh useless. We also think that in the future such laws must not be enacted in the name of the said Article 29. This is the reason we have written out our opinion at such great length.

*   *   *

The opinion of Justice Mano in the present case follows.

I believe that the judgments of first instance and of appeal should be quashed and the case sent back to the court of first instance.

Article 29, paragraph 3, prescribes as follows: "Private property may be taken for public use upon just compensation therefor." "Just compensation" herein designates a price corresponding to an objective worth to be found concretely and individually in the property in question.

The compensation prescribed in Article 6, which is established for cases in which farm land is to be purchased by the government in accordance with Article 3 of the Owner-Farmer Establishment Special Measures Law (referred to below as the Owner Establishment Law), is nothing more than an abstract one calculated on a special and average basis.

Thus, the consideration in Article 6 of the Owner Establishment Law, no matter how many words are devoted to it, in the end cannot be termed a price corresponding to an objective worth to be found concretely and individually in the farm land so purchased. Consequently, it must be said that it is not permissible to consider this to be "just compensation" as set forth in Article 29 of the Constitution.

Therefore, it is reasonable to conclude that persons dissatisfied with the amount of the consideration provided in Article 6 of the Owner Establishment Law can plead for a larger amount through litigation, as provided for in Article 14 of the same law.

The [argument given] above is the essence of my thinking.

The majority opinion holds that the consideration set forth in Article 6 of the Owner Establishment Law is the absolute maximum for the purchase of farm land and if there is dissatisfaction with the amount set by this limit, it is impossible to institute proceedings.

If Article 6 of the Owner Establishment Law possesses that significance, then it must be that this provision is both unconstitutional and invalid because it provides for the handing over of private property for public use without just compensation as described above.

Thus, I do not believe that Article 6 of the Owner Establishment Law provides for the maximum possible consideration for the purchase of farm land. Because the purchase of farm land under the Owner Establishment Law is a tremendous administrative undertaking, Article 6 of the law does nothing more than establish a regular standard for the convenience of the administrative agency in the execution of the task of determining the consideration for acquisition. That is, Article 6 establishes a maximum to be used in the reciprocal negotiations involved in establishing the consideration for acquisition. It is only a relative maximum limit on the consideration, which must be respected by the administrative agency.

Thus, terming it a relative maximum is, expressing it in another way, not terming it an absolute maximum. Then, Article 14 of the Owner Establishment Law provides that "those who are dissatisfied with the amount of the consideration" as determined by the standards discussed above "can request an increased amount by court action." Again, to put it in other words, in cases in which the amount of the purchase price as determined by the administrative agency and as bound by the standards of Article 6, does not amount to "just compensation" as provided for in the Constitution, the stipulation of Article 14 is a reasonable means for permitting dissatisfied persons to request, through the medium of court proceedings, an increased amount which would be just compensation. The reason is that if the method of determination of the consideration as set forth in Article 6 is absolute, then if an amount insufficient to be just compensation results, this article must be regarded as unconstitutional and invalid. If there is no relief, as provided in Article 14 in the form of a request for an increase in the amount to the level of just compensation, then the stipulations of Article 6 become unconstitutional and invalid, and consequently the execution of the program of farm land purchase would become extremely difficult, if not impossible.

The maximum reciprocal limit, according to Article 6, for a consideration in regard to the administrative agency, opens the way for an ultimate adjustment in the courts to achieve just compensation as stated in the Constitution. By means of such relief, Article 6 not only does not become unconstitutional and invalid, but the execution of the tremendous program of the purchase of farm land becomes relatively easy. At the same time, the fundamental rights of the people, as set forth in the Constitution, can also ultimately be extended and protected by the courts without being obstructed.

It is my view that the relationship between Articles 6 and 14 of the Owner Establishment Law can be understood if they are regarded as a harmonious and unified aspect of the entire structure of law, including the Constitution, by means of an interpretation of their significance as described above.

In the majority opinion Article 6 is regarded as having established an absolute maximum for the consideration for acquisition, and it is argued that if the administrative agency sets an amount that does not reach that maximum, parties dissatisfied with it can, by instituting court proceedings under Article 14, request an increase to the limit set in Article 6. As I pointed out above in relation to this issue, Article 6 is unconstitutional because it results in the presentation for public use of private property without the granting of just compensation as guaranteed by the Constitution. In order to prevent Article 6 from being treated as unconstitutional, I believe that it is necessary to interpret the significance of Articles 6 and 14 and their relationship as in my opinion described above.

The criticism of my view that holds that if it is permissible to request an increase in the price to the level of just compensation, then the execution of the farm land purchase program would become impossible, is based on a possibility that might be realized.

However, from the time that the transfer of title to the farm land on the basis of the consideration set in Article 6 has been decided upon, until the actual establishment of the owner-farmer through the acquisition of farm land, no hindrance of any kind should arise.

What would remain unsettled would be only a judgment concerning the request for an increase in the amount [of the consideration]. However, this is a question that would have to be settled in the courts; it is not one to be decided by an administrative agency. Consequently, there is no necessary reason why the administrative agency would be prevented from carrying out the program for the purchase of farm land because the above problem remained undecided and unsettled.

Thus, by permitting suit for an increased amount, the expenditures of the state for such payments might be increased; but the necessary increase in price to the level of just compensation is required by the Constitution, and there is not the slightest reason to entertain any quibbles about that issue. In essence, in such situations the problem of offering just compensation must be settled by means of the national budget, namely, through the assumption of the burden by the entire people. As is to be frequently observed in both legislation and actual administration, the attitude that the burden of sacrifice in the settlement of a situation must be assumed by only the few people who are involved in the matter is a fundamental error.

Again, in regard to the matter of a request for an increase in amount, since the one-month period for instituting a suit is stipulated in Article 14, at present the question is limited only to cases in which suits are still pending in the courts. If the majority opinion had permitted suits for an increase to the level of a consideration that for the land was equal to an objective one individually determined, that is, one conforming to just compensation, then there are those who fear that the result would be the creation of inequity between those who brought suit and those who accepted the consideration determined by the administrative agency and did not request an increase. Nevertheless, in any case, it is to be expected that there will be differences in treatment between those who fail to exercise their rights or remain unaware of them and those who assert their rights in court through their own efforts and at their own expense within the legal period, in so far as it is permissible to exercise those rights in law and in court. But this cannot be criticized as being unjust.

In short, I fear that by means of the standards established in Article 6 of the Owner Establishment Law, or similar ones, private property will be taken for public use for a value consideration less than its objective price on an individual basis. That is to say, any law that involves the disregard, the slighting, the defiance, or the evasion of the guarantee of just compensation in Article 29 of the Constitution should be viewed with grave concern both now and in the future. This goes beyond the minor issues of the present case and is a great problem of fundamental human rights connected with the roots of our economic structure.

In the present case, the judgments of first instance and appeal, which held that the stipulations of Article 6 of the Owner Establishment Law set the maximum limit on the consideration for acquisition of farm land and for that reason alone rejected the plaintiff's plea for an increased price, are illegal, and the argument for appeal is valid. Consequently, it is proper to annul them and to return the case to the court of first instance for retrial.

*   *   *

The dissenting opinion of Justice Saitō follows.

It is my understanding that the stipulations of Article 6, paragraph 3, of the Owner-Farmer Establishment Special Measures Law do nothing more than set a tentative standard for the purchase of farm land; that in cases having special circumstances, mentioned in the provisions of the same paragraph of the same law, those special circumstances should be consulted; and that in addition, when payment of compensation is made under Article 13, paragraph 3, of the same law and, upon careful consideration, it falls short of being just compensation, it is possible to institute court proceedings for an increased amount according to Article 14 of the same law. Accordingly, I believe that points 1 and 2 of the argument for appeal are reasonable.

In the final analysis, "just compensation" of Article 29, paragraph 3, of the Constitution means compensation for the objective economic value of the private property so taken. Therefore, in cases in which there is a free market value for that property, it is proper that such value be determined by the market price at the time that the property is taken. However, since transactions in farm land were controlled under existing law and this meant that a free market price could not exist legally, the appropriate economic value for the farm land to be purchased had to be determined by the standard of what was called the earning value to the owner-cultivator. From this point of view, the value mentioned in Article 6, paragraph 3, of the aforesaid law must be termed just according to the tentative standard for purchase.

However, the value in the said law, as is explained in detail in the majority opinion, did not take into the slightest account such items as the actual yield of the farm land in question at the time of purchase or any other special circumstances. (According to Article 3, No. 1 and Article 2, No. 2 of the Regulations for the Enforcement of the Owner Establishment Law, such things as the water supply of the land in question, the quality of the transportation, the conditions of utilization, and the ordinary yield are set forth as items that might be listed in a request for approval of special circumstances. In addition, in the case of tenant farms there are other items, such as the amount and reduction or remission of tenant rentals; and also, in Article 13, paragraph 4, it is stipulated that conditions such as "the yield and the location of the farm land in question should be considered.") Only the calculation of the value—directly in the case of rice land, and indirectly in the case of dry fields—on the basis of a producer's price at the end of 1945 of ¥150 per *koku,* on the assumption that there was a uniform national yield of two *koku* per *tan* on the basis of the national average yield for the five-year period from 1940 to 1944 of unhulled rice per *tan,* is provided for. Consequently, it is very obvious that it cannot be said, as the majority opinion does, that the value is "a proper sum reasonably calculated on the basis of a value that can be considered as having been determined by economic conditions existing at the time," if one considers the value of land having a yield of more than two *koku* at the time of acquisition, which was not at the end of 1945.

Hence, the majority opinion in this explanation contradicts itself and cannot escape the fate of natural collapse and elimination. (As one might expect, Article 2 of the Regulations for the Enforcement of the Agricultural Land Law, as the standard for rental value as of July 30, 1950, raises the price at the rate of about seven times more, calculated by multiplying by 280 for rice land and 336 for dry fields.) I absolutely cannot agree with the majority opinion.

Above all else, it can be perceived that Article 6, paragraph 3, of the Owner Establishment Law is not binding, not only from the provisions of that article and paragraph, but also from the fact that the same law has the stipulations provided by Article 13, paragraphs 3 to 5. If Article 6, paragraph 3, had binding force, then the compensation provided for in Article 13, paragraph 3, must be termed wrongful payment with no basis in law. Consequently, the provisions of Article 14 of the law must be broadly interpreted, as stated in the beginning.

(TRANSLATED BY J. M. MAKI)

XVII: THE MEANING OF "MINIMUM STANDARDS OF WHOLESOME AND CULTURED LIVING" IN ARTICLE 25

Hanreishū, II, No. 10, 1235 (Criminal)

EDITORIAL NOTE: The case involved in this decision was a simple one. As will be seen from a reading of the text, the accused was arrested, tried, convicted, and sentenced to four months in prison for purchasing and transporting a small quantity of rice in violation of the law controlling staple foods.

Grand Bench decision, September 29, 1948: Dismissed.

REFERENCES

Constitution of Japan. ARTICLE 25. All people shall have the right to maintain the minimum standards of wholesome and cultured living.

In all spheres of life, the State shall use its endeavors for the promotion and extension of social welfare and security, and of public health.

Staple Food Management Law. ARTICLE 1. The present law, in order to guarantee staple foods for the people and to stabilize the national economy, has as its aims the control of foodstuffs, the regulation of price, supply and demand, and the control of rationing.

FORMAL JUDGMENT

The appeal in the present case is dismissed. In respect to the defendant, ninety days of the period of detention for trial shall be included in the regular penalty.

REASONS. The substance of the appeal of the defendant is as contained in the document of appeal attached separately.

Article 25, paragraph 1, of the Constitution provides as follows: "All people shall have the right to maintain the minimum standards of wholesome and cultured living." However, it has neither a meaning nor a content that permits the hasty conclusion set forth in the plea, as follows: "It is impossible to preserve life or maintain health on the current food ration. . . . The purchase and transportation of food in short supply are the exercise by the people of what is termed the right to livelihood."

In the first place, in the history of mankind, political thought at the time constitutionalism developed held that the individual will should be respected as much as possible and that the state should be prevented as much as possible from interfering excessively with the freedom of the individual will. That is to say, the thought was: that government is best which governs least. Accordingly, in the constitutions promulgated in various countries, guarantees of fundamental human rights and individual freedoms were provided to some extent. Thus, the people's economic activity caused a system of free competition to flourish briskly under laissez-faire and achieved a striking development. But as a result the gap between the rich and the poor was striking, a small number of wealthy and a great number of poor were produced, and contemporary social injustice was created.

Such actual social conditions made the nation, on the other hand, acutely aware of the necessity of putting into operation certain positive policies, and here it became necessary for the modern state as an institution to attempt to participate in a new and positive way. This is called social services and social legislation. Thus, when Article 25, paragraph 2, of the Constitution states, "In all spheres of life, the State shall use its endeavors for the promotion and extension of social welfare and security, and of public health," it is a declaration concerning one duty of the nation—to endeavor to strengthen and extend the social services, which are the positive actions of government accompanying the changes in social life described above. Paragraph 1 of the same article is a declaration of the responsibility of the nation, as a similar positive action of government, to manage state affairs so that all of the people can maintain the minimum standards of wholesome and cultured living. That must, in the main, be carried out by the enactment and enforcement of social legislation, but the maintenance and elevation of such a standard of living must be regarded as a function of the state. That is to say, the nation must assume that responsibility broadly toward all the people; this is a governmental function. But the state does not bear such an obligation concretely and materially toward the people as individuals.

In other words, this provision does not directly bestow on the people as individuals such a concrete and material right in respect to the nation. As social services and social legislation are established and broadened, the concrete and material right to livelihood of the people as individuals will be established and perfected.

Nevertheless, when the appellant argues that because his right to livelihood was actually guaranteed directly and materially by the above provision of the Constitution, and because his purchase and transportation of staple food in short supply were the exercise of his right to livelihood, then the stipulations of the Staple Food Management Law, which make such conduct illegal, are unconstitutional, his argument is based on a mistaken interpretation of the said article and is unacceptable.

The Staple Food Management Law, in order to guarantee staple foods for the people and to stabilize the national economy, has as its aims the control of foodstuffs, the regulation of price, supply and demand, and the control of rationing. It also establishes the procedures, methods, machinery, and organizations necessary for the achievement of those aims.

In a situation in which the national economy experiences a serious shortage of the important staple foods, no matter what the cause, it should be clear to anyone that if no measures of control are taken and if the acquisition of such foods is left to free competition and a free market, then maldistribution or the disappearance from the market of such basic foods would occur because of buying up, hoarding, or the holding back of goods in the expectation of a better price; this would accordingly invite a striking rise in prices and then a great majority of the people would experience a serious shortage of such staple foods. The Staple Food Management Law was established in 1942, during the war, as a result of the war-induced shortage of basic foods; but since this shortage has continued as much as ever in the present period because of the postwar conditions, it cannot be said that the necessity for continuing the said law has disappeared. In regard to this point too, the intention of the said law is to stabilize as much as possible the conditions of life for the welfare of the entire people, and it is truly legislation in accordance with the intent of Article 25 of the Constitution. Thus, it is clear that the argument that treats the present law as unconstitutional and invalid is in error in respect to this point also.

Next, even though it is termed only a violation of the Staple Food Management Law, the substantial content of this crime is extremely complex. In cases in which the circumstances of such a crime may be regarded sympathetically, the public prosecutor may treat it as a misdemeanor not requiring an indictment or dispense with a public action. Even in the courts there may be commutation of punishment, or a stay of execution of sentence, or—when special circumstances exist—a remission of punishment or a finding that the action did not constitute a crime. On the other hand, if it is found that the crime has been a vicious one, severe punishment can be inflicted. These [situations] all require the examination of the facts and must appropriately be left to discretionary judgment in each individual case.

The above is the opinion of Chief Justice Tsukazaki Naoyoshi, and Justices Hasegawa Taichirō, Shimoyama Seiichi, Mano Tsuyoshi, Otani Katsushige, Shima Tamotsu, Fujita Hachirō, Iwamatsu Saburō, and Kawamura Matasuke.

*   *   *

The opinion of Justice Sawada Takejirō follows.

Among the fundamental human rights proclaimed and guaranteed in the constitutions of modern countries are two types diametrically opposed in respect to their relation to the power of the state. The substance of the one type of right can be realized only through the restraint of state power; by contrast, the substance of the other type can be realized only through the exercise of state power. Few words are needed to point out that the fundamental human rights and freedoms regarding life and person belong to the former. Likewise, it scarcely need be said that this type of right has long been proclaimed and guaranteed in the constitutions of various countries.

However, because in modern countries that have affirmed capitalism it is impossible not to have people who cannot fully perfect their lives if the constitution guarantees only those fundamental human rights involving freedoms that are not to be interfered with by the power of the state, we can now observe in constitutions promulgated in the twentieth century stipulations that proclaim and guarantee for the first time the right of the people to existence or to the maintenance of life. The stipulations of Article 25, paragraph 1, of the Constitution of Japan belong to this type; and it goes without saying that the content of these rights differs from the content of fundamental human rights or freedoms realized through the restraint of interference by state power, and that they relate to benefits to the life of the people realized through the exercise of state power. Thus, paragraph 2 of the same article provides: "In all spheres of life, the State shall use its endeavors for the promotion and extension of social welfare and security, and of public health." When it is considered that the state [here] proclaims its basic program for fully equipped welfare services and guarantees to the people that appropriate services will be established so that they can enjoy the above benefits in their daily lives, then it must be said that the rights referred to in Article 25, paragraph 1, of the Constitution do not bestow any benefits other than ones that the people can enjoy in their daily lives by means of various social services such as those relating to public health, education, and recreation or those designed for social welfare, such as public insurance systems, old-age pensions, vocational training centers, homes for the aged, orphan asylums, and protective centers, all of which the state provides. It must also be said that not all actions regarded by individuals as necessary for their livelihood are free [under this article] in respect to state power, which is said [by some] to be unable to punish, prohibit, or restrict [such actions] by law or order. Accordingly, the provisions of the said paragraph do not prohibit the state from enacting laws and orders—to the extent necessary for the public welfare and for the effectuation of the provisions of the Constitution of Japan—designed to punish, restrict, or prohibit even acts that are regarded by the individual as essential for the preservation of life.

Thus laws and orders promulgated by the state, since they can provide for the punishment, prohibition, or restriction of acts that are necessary to sustain individual life, cannot be said to be invalid on the ground that they contravene the paragraph in question. Accordingly, the arguments of the appeal that acts involving the purchase and transportation of food to supplement the staple food ration, which is insufficient to maintain life, constitute the exercise of a right bestowed on the people by the stipulations of Article 25, paragraph 1, of the Constitution, and that the provisions of the Staple Food Management Law that penalize the exercise of such a right are in violation of the said article and paragraph, are invalid and cannot be accepted.

Furthermore, our postwar food supply is not sufficient to satisfy the needs of all the people by means of domestic production alone, and it is an obvious fact that the possibility of our freely importing from abroad the amount of the deficiency is virtually nonexistent under present conditions. Under such national conditions, if the purchase and transfer of food are left without restriction to the free will of the people, then inevitably the poor and those who do not produce food would be unable to maintain a minimum standard of living. Consequently, the fact that the state makes provisions so that all the people can enjoy a minimum standard of living by means of a distribution of food as equal as possible to rich and poor alike, results from its respect for and maintenance of the rights of the people guaranteed by Article 25, paragraph 1, of the Constitution of Japan and, simultaneously, from the fulfillment of the obligation of the state set forth in paragraph 2 of the same article.

Although it existed before the Constitution of Japan came into effect, the Staple Food Management Law was enacted with the aim of controlling food as one method of carrying out the above provision. This is clear from Article 1 of the said law, which provides: "The present law, in order to guarantee staple foods for the people and to stabilize the national economy, has as its aims the control of foodstuffs. . . ."

As a method of achieving that aim, the present law and the attached regulations do not leave the delivery, import, export, transfer through trade, transportation, processing, and so forth, of food to the free will of the producer, consumer, or other private interests but, as a matter of principle, reserve such activity to the machinery of the state or to only those who have received permission or license from the state and prohibit the people from dealing as they please in food; thus, the establishment of provisions for the punishment of those violating such regulations is proper.

Consequently, the said law and the accompanying regulations are necessary both for the enforcement of the provisions of the Constitution of Japan and also for the public welfare. Furthermore, they also conform to the provisions of Article 25 of the Constitution of Japan; and because the said law violates no other provisions, it is not invalid. Therefore the original trial is not illegal for applying an invalid statute in the original judgment when sentencing the defendant to imprisonment at hard labor as provided for in the penal provisions of the Staple Food Management Law. The argument for appeal is groundless.

* * *

The opinion of Justice Inouye Nobori follows.

What the argument for appeal states is in essence that in our country at the present time it is impossible for the people to obtain the nourishment necessary to sustain their activities from the food that is distributed to them, and that consequently they may even die because of malnutrition. Therefore, those who do not have the means to produce food must somehow or other turn to others for it in order to sustain life. At the same time, because the Staple Food Management Law and the accompanying statutes close the avenue for the acquisition of food from others by prohibiting the purchase, transportation, and so forth of foodstuffs, the conclusion is reached that they violate the Constitution, which guarantees the people's inviolable right to life.

In the argument there are references to Article 25 of the Constitution and phrases such as, "It is impossible to maintain health and to sustain life on only the present ration." The right as stipulated in the above Article 25 is considered to be a so-called right to a benefit, but it cannot be considered a right to demand either a sufficient ration or some other positive act of assistance from the state; this can be understood from a reading of the argument. It is completely meaningless to claim the above right of demand in a criminal appeal asserting the invalidity and unconstitutionality of a prohibition regulation in respect to the infliction of punishment on the accused because he violated the prohibition contained in item 7, Article 23, of the Enforcement Regulations of the Staple Food Management Law. Furthermore, in the argument use is made of words such as, "the exercise" of the right to livelihood in Article 25; but whether this wording means the right to life as that is usually understood or a civil liberty, it probably means free activity for the purpose of maintaining life. (If it were believed and asserted that Article 25 in addition to the guarantee of the inviolability of such things as life and freedom also produced some kind of right for the people to carry out direct action, such as the purchase and transportation of food, then this article would be almost meaningless. Article 25 is not a provision concerning direct action by each individual person as claimed above, and perhaps no one would claim that such a special right flows from the said article.)

In essence, the terms, "Article 25 of the Constitution" and "the exercise of the right to livelihood" in the argument are used by the accused, who is no lawyer, and he believes that paragraph 1 of the said article is a provision guaranteeing the inviolability of life and liberty, but regardless of these technical terms, the true meaning of the argument can be perceived in the gist of what is printed at its outset. At any rate, to treat the argument as meaningful, I think that we can understand its substance if we view it as above and if we make a general reading of the whole argument. Consequently, I think that the first part of the text of the reasons for the judgment in the present case is not too essential as an answer to the argument, and there are points with which I am not completely in agreement. Since the latter part of the text does answer the argument, I think that there are some points that should be covered a little more thoroughly and others that are insufficiently developed, and I would like to try to supplement these points below.

The present rate of food production in our country is certainly insufficient to provide nourishment for all the people, and there are also certain restrictions on the importation of food from abroad. Under present conditions in which it is impossible to do what one would like, if everything were left to free trade without any restrictions on food, the producers and the wealthy, if we visualize the worst possible conditions, would probably hold back their supplies for better prices or hoard; and groups of speculators would hoard for the purpose of speculation. The above admits of no doubt in view of past experience. As a result, food would rapidly find its way only into the hands of those who possess special means or facilities for its acquisition, and without the present system of control the majority of the people, it is not difficult to anticipate, would rapidly fall into extreme want.

In view of the above, there may be some who would insist that to entrust the problem to the free market would improve the movement of food supplies and would on the contrary improve the state of such supplies. It might be possible to say that this would occur if the supply were sufficient to meet the demand or if there were a surplus, but in a situation in which there is an absolute shortage, even if the movement of supplies would improve somewhat under a free market, there would be a striking increase in price resulting from such things as the hoarding and holding back for a better price mentioned above. We must note the present situation of the general working class that is without property (workers and those with lower incomes constitute the great majority of the people) and unable to do much with its present income. Under such conditions there is sufficient reason to expect widespread disturbances resulting from the food shortage. Thus, even taking into account the fact that the importation of food is permitted under present conditions, it is absolutely not to be expected that enough can be brought in to permit the whole amount to be left to free trade.

Therefore, the objective of the law under dispute is to provide for the wide and equitable distribution of food to the people, without distinction between rich and poor, by turning as much as possible over to the government, excepting only the amount reserved for the producer. Consequently, the objective of the present statute, far from being unconstitutional, is in accord with the spirit of the Constitution. Naturally, even though the objective may be good, it will not do, of course, to have the procedure at fault. I believe that it is necessary to recognize the prohibition in question as being necessary for the achievement of the objective of control. (See below.) (I cannot here pursue a detailed economic discussion, but I believe that the above constitutes the policy and the viewpoint of the executive branch and of the legislative branch, which enacted the Staple Food Management Law. Because there are reasons that can be considered sufficient as outlined above, it is absolutely impossible for the Court completely to deny this.)

As I have shown above, the substance of the law is not bad, it is only that various difficulties have arisen because the present food ration is not sufficient to provide the necessary nutrition. But that is probably a problem of government administration. The supply of supplementary foods seems to be improving somewhat because of the strengthening of controls and the increase in the official price. If the supply of supplementary foods becomes sufficient, then nutrition will be adequate even if staple foods remain in somewhat short supply. In addition, if the transportation, and so forth, of the allotted food to be distributed is carried out well, there will probably be no reason not to expect a certain improvement. Again, if violations of the law in question diminish as a result of the people's self-discipline, the so-called black market will disappear and as a result the amount beyond what is to be delivered will increase, and if the greater portion of food is directed into the proper channels, then the state of the food supply will take a considerable turn for the better.

Thus, if the absolute amount of food is still insufficient, even with the entire supply from both domestic production and permissible imports, then there is nothing to do but to await the day of revival with self-discipline and diligence and to endure the shortage equally through the control of all the people. A situation in which only the wealthy are well fed and warmly clothed although all the rest are on the verge of starvation cannot be tolerated. And again, even if, happily, the absolute amount turns out to be barely sufficient to feed all of the people, then violations of this law will disappear and there will be reason to feel that the insufficiency of food for each individual will be relieved by the fact that the entire amount of staple foods will flow into the proper channels.

No one will disagree that there are various difficulties arising from the strict control of the purchase of food because the amount of the ration is insufficient, but this law is an absolutely necessary one. It is a regulation for the public welfare. If it were not for this, it is reasonable to assume that far worse conditions would exist than is the case. (See above.) On the other hand, I do not deny the necessity for control, and perhaps the present law is too strict and may need to be made less severe, but we have been taught by past experience that the objectives of such control cannot in reality be achieved by moderate means. Laws concerning the control of food were at the beginning more moderate, but it was impossible to achieve true control and it is well known that inevitably enforcement had to become more and more severe. Thus, the severity of the present law is unavoidable. However, because it is impossible for the people to obtain the necessary nutrition from only the present ration, it must be recognized that a certain amount of care should be exercised in the application of the law. This law may be duly or unduly strict, but it applies only to the principal staple foods and it does not absolutely forbid the purchase, transportation, and the like, thereof. These actions are allowable with legal permission. In the past this system of permission has probably not been employed too much, but that is a problem of practical application. The law itself establishes a moderate procedure.

In addition, the system of the public prosecutor's use of a stay of prosecution is also recognized, as is the stay of execution of sentence. There may be cases in which the principle of justification for an illegal act may be considered, but careful consideration must be given to its application in concrete cases. Among items that have come before us (the Supreme Court), this is the only case that can be recognized as having arisen out of necessity to provide food for one's self or family, and there hasn't been a single other case in which such evidence has been presented.

There is no bad reason for inflicting punishment on a person who acts as a so-called vicious black-marketeer only for his own special profit and violates controls that are recognized as necessary from the standpoint of all the people. In regard to the application of the law there is nothing to do but to rely on the good sense of the executive and judicial branches. In respect to the unconstitutionality of the law itself, it is difficult to agree with an argument that asserts that it is generally inapplicable. (The point is, of course, different, but similar situations involving crimes such as robbery can probably be thought of. It cannot be said that there are no cases of persons who are without property and to whom employment is not given and who cannot earn a living unless they resort to theft, but there is perhaps no one who would assert that penal laws that impose punishment for such crimes of theft are unconstitutional.)

* * *

The opinion of Justice Kuriyama Shigeru follows.

Under the Constitution of Japan the examination of the constitutionality of statutes lies in the courts, as is true in the United States. This is done when necessary in the handling of cases; it is not a system under which judgment is made as to whether, in abstract, a certain law is contrary to the Constitution. Thus, it must be that the principle of constitutional review is limited to the examination of the unconstitutionality of provisions directly related to a case. However, the unconstitutionality of provisions directly related to a case does not always and necessarily mean that the entire body of the law has been made unconstitutional. For example, even though the appellant erroneously argues the unconstitutionality of an entire law, if the Court does not stop within the limits necessary for the disposition of the case and makes a decision that deals with other sections of the law not related to the case, its decision will become such abstract criticism of the law.

The majority decision after rendering its interpretation of Article 25, judged the Staple Food Management Law by going into another problem; thus it stated: "The Staple Food Management Law, in order to guarantee staple foods for the people and to stabilize the national economy, has as its aims the control of foodstuffs, the regulation of price, supply and demand, and the control of rationing. . . ." It concluded by saying: ". . . the intention of the said law is to stabilize as much as possible the conditions of life for the welfare of the entire people, and it is truly legislation in accordance with the intent of Article 25 of the Constitution."

However, if we look at the present case, we find that the accused appealed in respect to the punishment inflicted in the original judgment, as may be seen in its reasons: "The acts of the accused in this action fall under the provisions of Articles 9 and 31 of the Staple Food Management Law, Article 11, No. 5, of the Enforcement Order for the said law, and Article 23, No. 7, of the Enforcement Regulations of the said law." As the accused says in his argument for appeal, the above provisions were applied to his "purchase of about two pecks of unpolished rice and about half a peck of polished rice and his transportation thereof without a license." Accordingly, the present Court, in its adjudication of the appeal in this case, should judge the argument concerning the unconstitutionality of the application of the above provisions. Indeed, in view of the results, all seems well, for the majority opinion declares, "The Staple Food Management Law must be termed truly to be legislation in accordance with the intent of Article 25 of the Constitution."

But if, on the other hand, following similar reasoning, we conclude that it [the application of the provisions] is not in accordance with the intent of Article 25 of the Constitution, then for what purpose must we conclude that the entire body of the Staple Food Management Law is not in accordance with the said intent? (Except for the penal provisions of the law, only Article 9 is related to the present case; the stipulations relating to price adjustment and the control of distribution are not.) We only make judgments of the provisions concerned in cases of unconstitutionality; in cases of constitutionality we cannot make judgments concerning the whole. The above method of judgment [in the majority opinion] goes beyond the limit of the Court's powers of constitutional review and converts the Court in effect to a third house, which makes decisions in the same way that both Houses of the National Diet must make them.

Decisions relating to legislation that go above or beyond the disposition of cases that have developed within the limits of the powers of the Court are not legal decisions relating to the provisions applicable to the case and end as value judgments of the law itself. The National Diet establishes a policy for the extension and improvement of the public welfare (both social policy and economic policy are parts of this) and it legislates in order to transform policy into reality. A value judgment of the policy, namely, this legislation, is in itself a political criticism, and it is clear that the courts have no authoritative criteria for making such value judgments.

Relief in respect to policy can only be achieved through an appropriate and proper change in policy itself, by which the National Diet reflects public opinion, or through adequate action in its application by the executive branch, which is responsible for its execution. That the courts can discover no relief in law in respect to policy follows from their very nature. When we examine the decision of the majority in respect to the Staple Food Management Law we see that it argues the necessity for control of foodstuffs after describing the content and the aims of the said law; in the long run this creates the illusion that the Court is assuming the role of those who explain the reasons for legislation when a bill is presented in the National Diet. Thus, the illusion created is that the Court can decide matters of policy in the same way that the legislative branch can. In respect to this point I present the following for reference from the decision handed down by the Supreme Court of the United States in 1934 concerning a case of a violation of the Commodity Control Law of the State of New York (*Nebbia* v. *the State of New York,* 291 U.S. 502):

"Whether the free operation of the normal laws of competition is a wise and wholesome rule for trade and commerce is an economic question which this court need not consider or determine." [citation omitted] And it is equally clear that if the legislative policy be to curb unrestrained and harmful competition by measures not arbitrary or discriminatory it does not lie with the courts to determine that the rule is unwise. With the wisdom of the policy adopted, with the adequacy or practicability of the law enacted to forward it, the courts are both incompetent and unauthorized to deal. The course of decision in this court exhibits a firm adherence to these principles. Times without number we have said that the legislature is primarily the judge of the necessity of such an enactment, that every possible presumption is in favor of its validity, and that though the court may hold views inconsistent with the wisdom of the law, it may not be annulled unless palpably in excess of legislative power.[1]

Let us examine the present case on the basis of the premise of the right of constitutional review of legislation which has just been described.

1. This quotation comes from Headnote 12 in the U.S. Supreme Court decision cited. The Japanese translation is a faithful rendering of the original, except for the fact that the first sentence (in quotation marks here) was given as a part of the decision whereas it was actually a citation from an earlier one.

Even the majority opinion holds that the provisions of Article 25 do "not directly bestow on the people as individuals such a concrete and material right in respect to the nation." In my humble opinion, Article 25 of the Constitution is the standard and criterion given to the legislative branch with respect to social legislation. For example, Article 1 of the Labor Standards Law reads as follows:

Labor conditions must be sufficient for the fulfillment of the requirements of a life worthy of a worker. Because the standards for labor conditions established in this law are minimal, those people concerned with labor relations must strive to improve labor conditions and, of course, must not reduce the level of labor conditions using these standards as the reason.

Article 13 of the same law is as follows: "Labor contracts which stipulate conditions that do not reach the level of the standards established in this law shall be invalid in respect to those items." Examination of these stipulations makes clear where the guide lines of Article 25 of the Constitution are. What is similar to the provisions of the Labor Standards Law is truly what conforms to the guide lines of Article 25 of the Constitution. It is designed to achieve the public welfare. Laws that limit the economic activity of individuals through the management of foodstuffs, the control of commodity prices, and the prohibition of monopoly are controlled by Article 29, paragraph 2, Article 31, and others of the Constitution; they are not controlled by Article 25, which is designed to protect and aid by means of social legislation.

If the present case is adjudged in consideration of the above points, the following conclusion must be reached: if, as the wording shows, the substance of the argument for appeal is regarded as an attack on the Staple Food Management Law for being in contravention of Article 25 of the Constitution, then the argument, as an attack on the food policy, is completely wide of the mark and does not constitute a legal reason for appeal because the said article has no direct relation to the present case.

* * *

The opinion of Justice Saitō Yūsuke follows.

The provisions of Article 25, paragraph 1, of the Constitution provide that the people shall enjoy a type of what are termed rights to receive benefits—a type of fundamental human right having as its substance the receipt of certain positive benefits from the state; they do not provide for fundamental human rights of the character of civil liberties, which negatively are to be neither interfered with nor suppressed by the state. That is to say, the intent of the said paragraph and article is that the state should guarantee the livelihood of all those people who cannot earn a living by their own efforts; and it must be interpreted as providing that such people have the fundamental right to request the protection of the state in the maintenance of minimum standards of wholesome and cultured living. In the final analysis, the Constitution recognizes the right of all the people to enjoy the fundamental rights and freedoms; it guarantees that the right of the people to life, liberty, and the pursuit of happiness, to the extent that it does not interfere with the public welfare, shall not be subjected to interference or oppression.

Accordingly, in respect to the essence of those freedoms, it must from the very nature of things be possible for those who possess the spiritual and physical ability and means to maintain their own lives and liberties and to pursue happiness, without interfering with the public welfare, to enjoy life—that is, to enjoy the maximum standards of wholesome and cultured living. However, those who do not possess the psychological or material ability or means cannot enjoy even the minimum standards of cultured and wholesome living and are thus guaranteed only the empty name of human rights of the character of civil liberties, unaccompanied by any concrete benefits. Therefore the Constitution sets forth the provisions of Article 25, paragraph 1, in addition to other provisions concerning fundamental human rights and freedoms and proclaims, "All the people shall have the right to maintain the minimum standards of wholesome and cultured living." It is proper to interpret this to guarantee that the state shall offer the positive benefits of such living and protection to those persons who cannot enjoy such living through their own efforts.

Thus, in regard to this matter paragraph 2 of the same article provides, "In all spheres of life, the State shall use its endeavors for the promotion and extension of social welfare and security, and of public health." This provides the reverse of paragraph 1—namely, that the state has the responsibility to exert its efforts for the strengthening and broadening of social policy in respect to health, happiness, and tranquillity in daily life so that all of the people can enjoy at least the minimum standards of wholesome and cultured living.

Thus, the right to livelihood in Article 25, paragraph 1, of the Constitution is a fundamental right which enables the people to enjoy a proper living, but it is not a civil liberty, which protects the activities of life from interference or oppression by the state. In addition, it cannot be recognized as a right that enables the whole people, unconditionally and as a matter of course, to demand of the state the protection of livelihood that they themselves regard as necessary. This right is a fundamental one, which enables the people who cannot survive through their own proper efforts—that is to say, people who cannot live in accordance with the required conditions specified in law or other legislation—to request of the state the proper safeguards to livelihood, in accordance with procedures established by law.

As a result, it must be said that those arguments are in error that interpret the above constitutional provision: to have the intent of recognizing, as a matter of course and unconditionally, that the government has the legal responsibility to provide food necessary for the maintenance of health and the sustenance of life to each and every individual person; to recognize the right of each individual, as a matter of course, to purchase and transport freely the food required to make up the deficiency; and to state that any law which holds such actions illegal is invalid because unconstitutional. The Staple Food Management Law was in force before the promulgation of the new Constitution. Because it is clearly provided in Article 1 of the said law that it was enacted in order to carry out the control of the rationing, the regulation of price, supply and demand, and the management of food in order to guarantee food for the people and to stabilize the national economy, it is perfectly obvious that the aim of its enactment was for the public welfare—that is, to stabilize and guarantee the entire economic life, as well as food, for the whole people.

Thus, first, in Article 2 of the said law, as an urgent measure for achieving that objective, the scope of the food to be controlled by the government is limited to the so-called principal foodstuffs, which are defined by cabinet order as wheat, rice, and others. Then, under the provisions of Article 3 of the said law, as the basic plan for the management of the designated principal foodstuffs, the government carries out forced purchases (so-called delivery or import) from producers or others at a price set after inspection and transfers the purchases to food management groups (food-rationing public corporations) or others at a set price or without compensation, by sale, transfer, loan, or other action. Finally it carries out delivery or loan or transfer to the general consumer or others through central or local rationing bodies (food-rationing public corporations) or other groups on the basis of a food-rationing plan determined by the government or regional administrators (in accordance with an enforcement plan determined by the agriculture and forestry minister based on a fundamental plan of food rationing formulated by the director-general of the Economic Stabilization Board). In addition, Articles 9 and 10 of the said law provide that the government by executive order at times when it is regarded as being especially necessary, in order to carry out the control of food in accordance with the above stipulations of the law, can issue the necessary orders for the rationing, processing, manufacture, transfer, movement, price or other matters specified and defined in the above law of the principal foodstuffs. It is further specified that the government can limit or prohibit the freedom of action of individuals in such matters. It is further provided in Article 31 of the said law that violators of the control orders can be punished; in supplementary orders the necessary rules for the execution of the above are also set forth. Nevertheless, the objective of the enactment of the said statute was to stabilize and safeguard the public welfare—the economic livelihood of the entire people, including the food supply—and, as a principal means to that end, to force the delivery from the producers of surplus foodstuffs which remained after they had taken what they could retain, and to distribute as much as possible to the general consumer.

Consequently, because the so-called producers—those among the people who possess the means of production—are not to suffer direct injury to their livelihood or their lives through this statute, and because the general consumers—those who do not possess the means of production—are, rather, to have their lives and livelihood protected by this law, this law, under the conditions regarding food and other economic problems both at the time the law was enacted and since the promulgation of the Constitution under similar urgent conditions, neither unduly denies nor restricts the lives or the livelihood of the people which are guaranteed [protection] under the Constitution; rather, the reverse is true. Thus, it cannot be said that this law is in contravention of the provisions of Article 25 of the Constitution regarding the right to benefits in daily life. Furthermore, the said law, in respect to the rationing, transfer, movement, price, and other matters specified in the said law, and in order to maintain the public welfare, can both restrict and prohibit individual freedom of action; but it also recognizes exceptions to the above, and it further recognizes methods by which those of the people who cannot reasonably support themselves can request on suitable occasions protection of their livelihood by means of license or approval of a special ration, and so forth. Because of the above it cannot be said, from this point of view, that it is in violation of the provisions of Article 25 of the Constitution.

Again, even though the amount of the food ration that each individual receives is insufficient to maintain health or to sustain life—because of the shortage of food, or maldistribution, or because of deficiencies or defects in the machinery or method of rationing—this is a question of what can or cannot be done in actual fact, regardless of legality; or it is a question of skill in the application of the law [in such a situation]. It is impossible, for those reasons, to declare directly that the law in question is invalid because it is unconstitutional.

Furthermore, there is the question of careful consideration of a concrete case in which there may be punishment of conduct which necessarily had to be carried out in order to maintain the livelihood of one's self or family under urgent conditions such as those described above. However, on the assumption that there is an appropriate penal provision, this is a question of whether there are grounds for what is called justification of an illegal act that exclude the applicability of the law in question in individual concrete cases; it is not a question of whether, in general, certain penal provisions in themselves are or are not constitutional. Thus in the present case, because there is neither the assertion nor proof that the situation was one of truly unavoidable urgency or that there were grounds for the justification of an illegal act, and because there was only the assertion that the transportation in this case was carried out heedlessly without a license—because a license could not be obtained from the regional director—in order to supplement the food shortage in the family, therefore, even from the point of view that there may have been justification of an illegal act, the argument absolutely cannot be accepted.

*   *   *

In accordance with the reasons given above, the appeal in the present case is dismissed on the basis of Article 446 of the Code of Criminal Procedure.[2] Furthermore, in accordance with Article 21 of the Criminal Code, ninety days of the defendant's period of detention for trial in the present case shall be included in the regular penalty.

Accordingly, we decide in accordance with the formal judgment.

(TRANSLATED BY J. M. MAKI)

2. See footnote 2, p. 161.

Hanreishū, IV, No. 11, 2257 (Criminal)

EDITORIAL NOTE: Late in November, 1946, the workers in a
metal factory in Suita city near Osaka went on strike after some
days of fruitless negotiation with management. They resorted to
"production control," popular as a strike technique for several years
following the end of the war, under which the workers took over
management of the plant and continued its operation.

In December of the same year the strikers sold a quantity of steel
plate belonging to the company in order to provide cash for wages
and other operating expenses. For this the leaders of the strike were
arrested, tried, and convicted to six months' imprisonment for theft
of company property. They lost on appeal and carried their case
to the Supreme Court.

Grand Bench decision, November 15, 1950: Dismissed.

REFERENCES

Constitution of Japan. ARTICLE 12.   The freedoms and rights
guaranteed to the people by this Constitution shall be maintained
by the constant endeavor of the people, who shall refrain from
any abuse of these freedoms and rights and shall always be responsible for utilizing them for the public welfare.

ARTICLE 28.   The right of workers to organize and to bargain
and act collectively is guaranteed.

ARTICLE 29.   The right to own or to hold property is inviolable. Property rights shall be defined by law, in conformity with the public welfare.

Private property may be taken for public use upon just compensation therefor.

Labor Relations Adjustment Law. ARTICLE 7.   Strike activity as used in this law is activity, such as strikes, slowdowns, lockouts, and other activity, carried out by those involved in labor relations with the aim of achieving or opposing demands, and refers to anything that prevents the normal operation of business.

Labor Union Law (prior to amendment by *Law No. 174 of 1949*).

ARTICLE 1.   This law has as its objectives, through the protection and development of the right of collective bargaining and the guarantee of the right of organization, a contribution to economic prosperity and an improvement in the position of labor.

The provisions of Article 35 of the Criminal Code will be applied to proper acts which are carried out with the aim of achieving the objectives of the preceding paragraph by activities such as collective bargaining by laborers.

Criminal Code. ARTICLE 35.   An act done in accordance with law or ordinance or a justifiable act done in the course of due business is not punishable.

Criminal Code. ARTICLE 235.   A person who steals the property of another commits the crime of larceny and shall be punished with imprisonment at forced labor for not more than 10 years.

FORMAL JUDGMENT

The appeal in the present case is dismissed.

REASONS.   Regarding the first point in the argument for appeal of attorneys Kamimura Susumu and Makino Yoshio: The argument states that the original judgment errs in its understanding of the nature of production control, denies that production control is one method of exercising the right to strike, and is contrary to law in that it limits the methods of using the right to strike. While thus criticizing the judgment it also maintains that production control is included in the phrase "and other" activity in Article 7 of the Labor Relations Adjustment Law. It also asserts that there can be no limitation imposed on the exercise of production control by laborers as a method of striking. However, the above legal clause does nothing more than offer definitions of strike activity and tells nothing of the legality or the propriety of strike activity or any other kind of activity that might accompany it. Thus, even though production control may be included in the "other" activity it is impossible to reach the hasty conclusion from that alone that there is a freedom to exercise it. In respect to the limits of the legality of concrete strike activity, it is necessary to arrive at a decision from a different angle. Leaving aside for the moment the question of whether the explanation of the original verdict in respect to the concept of production control is valid, the final judgment that the conduct of the accused in the present case is illegal is proper, as will be described below. The argument here is groundless.

Regarding the second point of the argument: The argument, on the ground that the Constitution recognizes the right of laborers to strike, asserts that earlier concepts of civil and private law must be abandoned, and from this point of view it asserts that it is neither illegal nor improper for laborers by means of the strike to oppress the will of the capitalist who is the employer or to realize their demands by that means. However, the Constitution while guaranteeing the laborer the right to organize and to bargain and act collectively, also guarantees to all the people fundamental human rights such as the right to equality, civil liberties, and the right to property. These various fundamental rights are not to be completely set aside before the unlimited exercise of the right of workers to strike, and also, the latter does not possess an absolute supremacy over the former.

Of course, it is desirable to have harmony between these various general fundamental human rights and the rights of labor; not to disrupt this harmony is a limitation on the propriety of the right to strike. Where must this point of harmony be sought? It is determined by an over-all examination of the spirit of the system of law. Of course, the liberties of the employer and his property rights are also not absolutely unlimited and it is natural that they be restricted to a certain extent for the benefit of labor's right of collective action and so forth. But, to the degree that was pointed out in the original decision, it must be recognized that to oppress the free will of the employer and to obstruct his control over his property are not permissible. Such action gives undue weight to the right of labor to strike, improperly infringes on the rights of the employer, and disrupts the harmony required by law. The argument is groundless.

Concerning the third point in the argument: The argument asserts, on the ground that production control does not differ in nature from a strike, that it is strike action divested of illegality in the same manner that a strike is. However, our present legal system is built on the foundation of the system of private property and both the profits and the losses of an enterprise are traceable to the capitalist. Accordingly, the administration of an enterprise and the supervision and direction of the manufacturing processes reside in the authority of the capitalist or his representative, who is responsible for administration.

Even though, as the argument contends, the laborer stands alongside the entrepreneur as a working partner, the laborer, for that reason, does not naturally possess the rights of employment and of earnings from the enterprise and does not have authority in respect to the right of operation. Thus, it is not permissible for the laborer to employ methods of striking that shake the foundations of the private property of the entrepreneur. To be sure, the strike also produces an infringement on the right of property, but that is only the nonfulfillment of the obligation of the labor force to perform. Thus, in the so-called production control in this case, the management of the enterprise was carried out by those who did not possess the right to it, to the exclusion of the wishes of those who did. For this reason, even though both the strike and production control are similar in that they violate private property, there is no reason to disregard their differences. If in the former there is no illegality, there is no reason why it should be the same in regard to the latter. Accordingly, the argument cannot be accepted.

Concerning the fourth point: The argument, seizing on the point in the original judgment that production control is justifiable when the employer limits production, asserts that there is freedom to carry out production control as a method of strike action in any situation whatsoever. However, because the original judgment also recognizes that the production control in the present case is not one in which the employer limits production, whether or not production control is recognized as justifiable in such a situation is not related to the present case. That the conduct of the defendants in the present case was improper is as has been pointed out in relation to other arguments. The argument is groundless.

Concerning the fifth point: The argument attacks the original judgment, which held that the steel plates in the present case were not completely removed from the possession of the company [during the strike], that the conduct of the accused in wilfully removing them from the factory constituted the taking of the possessions of the company, and that they could not escape criminal responsibility for theft. The argument further states that under production control the possession of ownership rights resides in labor and that, because the company had nothing more than indirect possession, in the abstract, there cannot be the taking of possessions, i.e., theft. It also claims that the accused did not intend either to take the possessions away illegally or to appropriate them.

However, the workers' taking over the factory, its installations, materials, and so forth, at the outset of the so-called production control constituted illegal possession and, in regard to the steel plates in question, there was illegal seizure of possessions under the control of the company at the time. However, the original decision held that there was an actual deed of appropriation when the plates were removed from the factory. When this is considered in the light of the evidence, the acts of the accused when they took the plates out of the factory without the permission of the company and put them under their own control with the objective of disposing of them in order to provide money for salaries for the workers during the strike, constituted the taking of company property with a full consciousness of the illegality of the act. The original decision was proper in holding that this was the crime of theft.

The original decision, although holding that in production control the labor organization seizes the factory, equipment, materials, and everything else and places them under its control, and recognizing that in the present case the accused had already begun production control, held that, on the other hand, the steel plates in question "had not been completely removed from the possession of the company." Even though it is said that from the time the production control began the labor organization had placed under its own control the factory, the equipment, the materials, and everything else, it must be understood, in respect to the individual materials, that because they were still on company premises that they were also still in the possession of the company. Thus, there are no grounds for the argument that the original decision was contrary to law.

Concerning the gist of the argument for appeal of attorney Kamimura Susumu: The argument (points 2 and 3) asserts that production control is proper strike action and that each individual activity under proper strike action, within the limits necessary for the achievement of the objectives of a strike, comes under the provisions of Article 35 of the Criminal Code as provided for in Article 1, paragraph 2, of the Labor Union Law, and thus is not to be considered illegal. However, Article 1, paragraph 2, of the Labor Union Law does not provide that Article 35 of the Criminal Code must be unconditionally applied to collective bargaining and other activities of labor unions; it goes no further than to recognize its applicability to proper activities carried out to achieve the objectives set forth in the Labor Union Law (see Grand Bench decision of the Supreme Court, May 18, 1949).

The legality of certain strike activities in each strike must be determined by relating, on the one hand, the objectives of the strike and the individual activities that constitute the procedures of the strike, and on the other, the entire structure of the existing legal system. Thus, the argument is groundless in holding that production control and the individual activities involved in it are all rightful acts. (That the actions of the accused in question here are not to be recognized as rightful is as has already been pointed out in regard to the argument of appeal of attorneys Kamimura and Makino.)

The judgment of the other points in this argument is as has been described in respect to the argument for appeal of attorneys Kamimura and Makino.

Concerning the first point of the argument of attorney Takagi Umon: That the argument cannot be accepted is in accordance with the explanation given in respect to the fifth point of the argument of attorneys Kamimura and Makino.

Concerning the second point: The original verdict pointed out in its first section that the defendants had taken out the steel plates in order to obtain "money for the payment of salaries of union members and other operating expenses" and for "the restoration of electrical installations"; in its second section it asserted that each of the accused had wilfully taken the plates from the plant "in order to provide for the payment of wages for union members during the strike." Because the verdict does not hold, as the argument states, that the plates were taken out "in order to provide for the expenses of the strike," there is not, therefore, any internal inconsistency as the argument also states. The argument attacks the original verdict for having held certain things which it did not hold, and is groundless.

Concerning the third point: The original decision held that the principal element in production control is the labor union, but because it also held that the accused were those responsible for the actual deeds of taking and transporting the steel plates in dispute, then it naturally follows that the accused themselves must be held responsible for their acts, without reference to whether other union members should also be held responsible for the act. Accordingly there is nothing contrary to law in the original verdict as the argument contends.

Concerning the fourth point: That this argument is groundless is as explained in regard to points two and those following it in the arguments of attorney Kamimura and Makino.

Concerning points 1, 2, and 3 in the arguments for appeal of attorneys Morinaga Eisaburō and Fuse Tatsuji: That these arguments cannot be accepted is as explained in regard to points 2 to 5 of the argument of attorneys Kamimura and Makino.

Concerning point 4: The original decision did not find that the steel plates in question were idle material, and it also did not hold that their sale was illegal because it was in violation of the previous management policy of the company. The original decision, without touching on the above facts, held that the method of strike under discussion was illegal, that, accordingly, the conduct of the accused was not legal strike action, and that it constituted the crime of theft. That the original verdict was proper is as explained in regard to points 2 to 5 in the arguments of attorneys Kamimura and Makino. For this reason the argument is groundless.

Concerning point 1 (*a*) of the argument of attorney Osawa

Shigeru: The argument, seizing on a phrase in the text of the original judgment, attacks the judgment as having as its constituent element the principle of the social assistance policy of the totalitarian state, which denies the principle of the sovereignty of the people, and as being an irresponsible utterance, forgetful of the great constitutional principle that the rights of organization, of collective bargaining, and of the strike are fundamental human rights, eternal, inviolate, and natural. However, in respect to the significance of the right to organize, to bargain collectively, and to strike, what the original judgment pointed out is, in essence, the same as what the present Court has held (Grand Bench decision, May 18, 1949)—namely, that the rights to organize, to bargain collectively, and so forth, are fundamental human rights of the laborer. No evidence can be seen of a denial of the principle of popular sovereignty. Accordingly, in the original judgment there are no points in contravention of the Constitution or of the Labor Union Law, as the argument contends, and the argument is groundless.

Concerning points 1 (b) and (c): That neither point can be accepted is as explained above in regard to points 2 and those following it in the argument of attorneys Kamimura and Makino.

Concerning point 2 (a): It is difficult to accept this argument for the same reasons as were explained in regard to point 5 of the argument of attorneys Kamimura and Makino.

Concerning point 2 (b): The argument attacks the original judgment for being both deficient and inconsistent in reasoning because it held on the one hand that production control deprives the consumer of freedom of will or subjects his will to extreme oppression and is thus illegal, although on the other hand it recognizes production control in the case of limitation of production by the employer, which involves an even greater deprivation and oppression of the will of the consumer. However, because the original judgment held that the production control in the present case was not carried out like production control by the employer, whether or not the latter is legal is not related to the present case. Because the original decision in holding that the action of the accused constituted the crime of theft was, in the final analysis, proper, is as described above, and the argument cannot be accepted.

Concerning the argument for appeal of attorney Aoyanagi

Morio: That points 1 to 5 of the argument cannot be accepted is clear from the explanation given in respect to points 2 to 4 of the argument of attorneys Kamimura and Makino.

Point 6 of the argument claims that since the transfer of control over the materials, and so forth in the plant, at the time the labor union began production control, was illegal, then, if it is recognized that there was at that time intent to appropriate the steel plates in question, the crime of theft was immediately produced, but that if the intent to appropriate was produced only at the time that the plates were removed from the premises, then the crime was that of embezzlement. However, because there was illegal possession, even from the time that the accused took possession of the steel plates at the initiation of the production control, then later when they were appropriated it was the crime of theft, not that of embezzlement. Thus, the fact that this was the crime of theft came into existence for the first time when the steel plates were removed, is as explained in reference to the fifth point of the argument of attorneys Kamimura and Makino. The argument is completely groundless.

*   *   *

For the reasons given above, decision is rendered as in the formal judgment in accordance with Article 446 of the former Code of Criminal Procedure.[1]

This decision is the unanimous opinion of the Justices.

(TRANSLATED BY J. M. MAKI)

1. See footnote 2, p. 161.

XIX: "NO-POLITICAL-ACTIVITY" CLAUSE IN AN EMPLOYMENT CONTRACT AND THE FREEDOM OF ASSOCIATION

Hanreishū, VI, No. 2, 258 (Civil)

EDITORIAL NOTE: The plaintiff was employed as the chief sewing teacher of the Tokachi Girls' Commercial School in Hokkaido on May 8, 1948. The employment contract, good for fourteen years, in addition to the usual items concerning salary and living accommodations, stipulated that the plaintiff would not be dismissed because she was a Communist, a fact recognized by the school, and that she would not engage in political activity on the school grounds.

On November 27, 1948, the plaintiff was dismissed on the charges that in violation of the contract she had sold communist propaganda to a student on the school grounds and that she had provided lodging in the girls' dormitory for a man who was apparently a Communist party member and for others who had quit their jobs at the school.

The plaintiff sued for nullification of the cancellation of the contract, but lost in both the court of first instance and the court of appeal. Her appeal to the Supreme Court was based mainly on alleged violation of fundamental human rights.

Decision of the Second Petty Bench, February 22, 1952: Dismissed.

REFERENCES

Constitution of Japan. ARTICLE 19.   Freedom of thought and conscience shall not be violated.

[Omitted here is Article 20, not touched on in the decision and apparently cited as a reference only because the appeal listed freedom of religion as one of the freedoms allegedly violated.]

ARTICLE 21.   Freedom of assembly and association as well as speech, press and all other forms of expression are guaranteed.

No censorship shall be maintained, nor shall the secrecy of any means of communication be violated.

FORMAL JUDGMENT

The appeal in this case is dismissed. The cost of the appeal is to be borne by the appellant.

REASONS. Concerning the first point of the appeal: That the fundamental human rights guaranteed by the Constitution are not absolute and can be limited by obligations freely contracted under special public or private law, has been made abundantly clear by a decision of this Court (see Grand Bench decision, April 4, 1951, *Hanreishū*, V, No. 5, 215 <Civil>). The above principle applies equally to cases in which a person is employed on the condition that he not engage in political activity within a prescribed area. Since the appellant voluntarily entered into employment at the respondent school on condition that she refrain from political activity within the school grounds, the said special agreement is valid and cannot be declared void because it is contrary to public order and good morals as viewed by the Constitution and the Civil Code. Consequently, this argument for appeal is groundless.

Concerning the second point: The publisher of a book entitled *The Problem of Love* by Nuyama Hiroshi (both facts established in the original decision) was the Japan Young Communist League, as the argument for appeal states; consequently, the original decision was in error when it designated the "Publications Bureau of the Japan Communist League" as the publisher. Nevertheless, this was only a clerical error in the decision concerning the name of the publisher and did nothing to impair the essential nature of the publication in question. Thus, because the original decision established legally, on the basis of evidence, that this book contained communist propaganda, it is impossible to detect any illegality in the original decision arising out of insufficient grounds. Hence, this argument for appeal is groundless.

Concerning point 3: That the appellant, a member of the Communist party, subsequent to her employment in the school sought buyers among the girl students of the said school for *The Problem of Love*, which was written by a Communist and contained Communist party propaganda, and, moreover, sold it, was established in the original decision. It is also clear from the text of the original verdict that the conduct of the appellant, as described above, was judged to be in violation of the stipulation "not to engage in political activity within the school grounds," which was a condition of the employment contract entered into when the said school employed the appellant. It is evident that the above conduct of the appellant fell under the heading of political activity within the school grounds as stated in the said contract. Thus, it cannot be regarded as cultural activity as the argument for appeal contends. The decision of the original verdict is proper; there is no illegality in it as the argument for appeal contends; and the said argument is groundless.

Therefore, the decision in this case, as stated in the formal judgment, is the unanimous opinion of the Justices and has been made in accordance with Article 401 of the Code of Civil Procedure [1] and, in respect to the responsibility for the costs of the proceedings, with Articles 95 and 89 of the same Code.

(TRANSLATED BY IKEDA MASAAKI)

---

1. See footnote 7, p. 50; also footnote 1, p. 120.

XX: SLANDEROUS STATEMENTS IN A UNION NEWSPAPER AND THE FREEDOMS OF EXPRESSION AND ASSOCIATION

Hanreishū, V, No. 5, 214 (Civil)

EDITORIAL NOTE: The three petitioners were employees of the Tokyo Electric Express Railway Company and members of both the union of company workers and the Japanese Communist party. One was the head of a party cell in the union and the others were editors of two different newspapers published by the cell. In late October, 1949, each paper published and distributed to company employees stories alleging corruption in the relations between company directors and union supervisors in the assignment of workers, mistreatment of young and women workers, union malpractices, and excessive drinking among union and company officials. The company took the view that the stories were slanderous attacks on company policy and personnel and constituted a hindrance to efficient operations. It thereupon dismissed the three petitioners in February, 1950, in accordance with its disciplinary regulations.

The three then petitioned for reinstatement, but their petition was rejected in both the court of first instance and the appellate court. Their attorneys appealed to the Supreme Court on the grounds that their freedom of expression as well as their constitutional rights of organization and collective bargaining had been violated.

Grand Bench decision, April 4, 1951: Dismissed.

REFERENCES

Constitution of Japan. ARTICLE 12.   The freedoms and rights guaranteed to the people by this Constitution shall be maintained by the constant endeavor of the people, who shall refrain from any abuse of these freedoms and rights and shall always be responsible for utilizing them for the public welfare.

ARTICLE 21.   Freedom of assembly and association as well as speech, press and all other forms of expression are guaranteed.

No censorship shall be maintained, nor shall the secrecy of any means of communication be violated.

Code of Civil Procedure. ARTICLE 419-3.   Regarding *Kokoku* appeal under the preceding Article and the procedure therefor, the provisions concerning *Jokoku* appeal and the procedure for the *Jokoku* appeal instance as mentioned in Article 409-2 paragraph 1 shall, insofar as they are not contradictory with the nature thereof, apply *mutatis mutandis* in addition to the provisions of Article 418, paragraph 2.

FORMAL JUDGMENT

The special appeal to the Supreme Court in this case is dismissed. The cost of the appeal shall be borne by the appellants.

REASONS. Regarding points 1 and 2 of the reasons for appeal of attorneys Aoyanagi Morio and Osawa Shigeru: The summing up of the original decision held that the actions of the appellants (who were employees of the company that is the other party in this case) in publishing articles in the two Communist cell organs and distributing them to the employees of the said company, constituted conduct that undermined confidence in the company and hindered the management of its operations because the appellants took rumors to the effect that the company was following improper and unfair policies in the reassignment of personnel and disseminated them to the employees of the said company as if they were facts, even though the said rumors were baseless. It further concluded that this conduct fell under the appropriate sections of the disciplinary regulations of the company and that it could be reasonably dealt with by disciplinary discharge. That the above are set forth as the reasons why the said disciplinary discharge did not violate Article 21 of the Constitution is as stated in the argument of appeal.

The original decision in the first part of the summing-up states: "Article 21 of the Constitution, in respect to publication as in the present case, is no more than a guarantee against the imposition of executive restrictions." We cannot subscribe to that opinion for it may give rise to the mistaken view that publication may be freely restricted by legislative or other actions relating to state affairs but not executive in nature.

However, we find both proper and sustainable the latter part of the summing-up, which states:

The act of publication carried out under Article 21 naturally cannot be interpreted as having been guaranteed without any attendant responsibilities. Accordingly, persons who engage in such acts of publication must inevitably find themselves in a position in which they are responsible under both criminal and civil law for such acts.

After all, it is clear from the provisions of Articles 12 and 13 of the Constitution that the freedoms of speech, press, and all other forms of expression, as provided for in Article 21, cannot run counter to the public welfare and, in addition, that limitations on such freedoms by obligations freely contracted under special public or private law are unavoidable.

Therefore, the original judgment is correct when it states:

When the conduct of the appellants, who were employees of the company in this case, came under the disciplinary regulations of the said company, then a situation arose that naturally and necessarily had to be dealt with by the said company in accordance with the above regulations and it is impossible to construe Article 21 of the Constitution as having any effect on the validity of the above disciplinary regulations.

The argument of the appellants is therefore groundless.

Concerning points 3 and 4: Moreover, because the conduct of the appellants, as established in the original decision, involved the publication of baseless rumors concerning the company by a Communist party cell organ and the dissemination [of those rumors] to the employees of the company, not only is it clear that it constituted conduct not related to the right of workers to organize and to act collectively as set forth in Article 28 of the Constitution, but because we can agree completely with the decision on this point we find it difficult to accept the argument of the appellants.

Concerning point 5: [1] Because the reasons for special appeal to the Supreme Court must not only deal with [a question of] constitutional propriety and because the reason for such appeal must be recorded in the statement of reasons itself, the present argument, which merely cites from the statement of reasons for appeal in the first instance, is not in accord with law and cannot be accepted.

The Court renders decision as stated in the formal judgment according to Articles 95 and 89 of the Code of Civil Procedure.[2]

(TRANSLATED BY IKEDA MASAAKI)

1. The opinion here refers only to the final point in the appeal argument, which merely stated that the attorneys for the appellants "in addition . . . introduce all the arguments stated in the reasons for appeal in the first instance."

2. See footnote 1, p. 120 on Article 95 and footnote 7, p. 50 on Article 89.

Hanreishū, IV, No. 6, 1049 (Criminal)

EDITORIAL NOTE: The accused was found guilty of operating a fee-charging employment agency in violation of the law quoted below. His appeal was dismissed in appellate court. His attorney then appealed to the Supreme Court on the ground that the law prohibiting such agencies violated the freedom of choice of occupation guaranteed by the Constitution.

Grand Bench decision, June 21, 1950: Dismissed.

REFERENCES

Employment Security Law. ARTICLE 2. Every person shall be able to choose his occupation freely to the extent that it does not interfere with the public welfare.

ARTICLE 32. No person shall operate a fee-charging employment agency. However, this prohibition shall not apply to fee-charging employment agencies whose purpose is to render services, upon approval by the minister of labor, in finding appropriate employment for those who are engaged in professions calling for special skills, such as art, music, and entertainment.

In the event that the minister of labor grants approval under the preceding paragraph, he shall examine in advance the financial condition and moral character of the applicant for such approval and at the same time refer the matter to the Central Employment Security Council.

Persons engaging in profit-making employment-exchange enterprises shall, before starting such enterprises, deposit a bond of an amount to be determined after consultation between the minister of labor and the Central Employment Agency, but not exceeding ¥50,000, which will be sufficient for the payment of claims as stipulated in paragraph 4.

Persons who suffer damage as a result of the violation of this law, or of the provisions of orders based on it, by persons mentioned in the previous paragraph, enjoy the right to receive compensation from the bond provided for in the previous paragraph.

Persons who receive licenses to operate employment agencies at cost or to operate profit-making employment agencies must pay a license fee of an amount to be determined by the minister of labor after consultation with the director of the Commodity Price Agency and with the advice of the Central Employment Security Council.

Persons who engage in employment-exchange enterprises, operated either at cost or for profit, cannot receive under any guise whatsoever any actual expenses or commission or compensation, except for the commission that has been established by the minister of labor after consultation with the director of the Commodity Price Agency and with the advice of the Central Employment Security Council.

The effective period for the license provided for in paragraph 1 shall be one year.

The necessary matters involved in the procedures for applications for licenses, as provided for in paragraph 1, and other matters involving fee-charging employment agencies shall be determined by administrative order.

ARTICLE 64. Persons to whom any of the items below may apply may be sentenced to a prison term of not more than one year or fined not more than ¥10,000.

1. Persons who violate the provisions of Article 32, paragraph 1, or persons who conduct fee-charging employment-exchange enterprises without obtaining the permission of the minister of labor, in violation of the provisions of the same paragraph. [Omitted

are items 2, 3, 4, and 5, which deal with violators of provisions of
the law not quoted above.]

Constitution of Japan. ARTICLE 13. All of the people shall be
respected as individuals. Their right to life, liberty, and the pursuit
of happiness shall, to the extent that it does not interfere with the
public welfare, be the supreme consideration in legislation and in
other governmental affairs.

ARTICLE 22. Every person shall have freedom to choose and
change his residence and to choose his occupation to the extent
that it does not interfere with the public welfare.

Freedom of all persons to move to a foreign country and to divest themselves of their nationality shall be inviolate.

FORMAL JUDGMENT

The appeal in this case is dismissed.

REASONS. Articles 13 and 22 of the Constitution both contain
the restrictive phrase, "to the extent that it does not interfere with
the public welfare." The original judgment, as the summary of the
argument demonstrates, held that Article 32 of the Employment
Security Law is necessary for the public welfare under the conditions that now exist in our nation and that it is reasonable to
hold that it violates neither of the articles of the Constitution mentioned above.

The Employment Security Law, being different from the wartime control laws and regulations, is not designed merely to achieve
the adjustment of supply and demand of labor in order to attain
a sufficient working force for industry, as the argument for appeal
maintains. Its major purpose is to provide everyone, according to
his ability and under proper conditions, with an opportunity for
suitable employment, thereby promoting the stabilization of employment as a whole.

There have been many cases in the usual fee-charging employment agencies wherein contracts unfavorable to the workers were
entered into merely for the sake of profit, without regard for the
interests or the abilities of the workers or the achievement or
maintenance of the proper working conditions; or they were
entered into to gain compensation from any contract whatsoever

without regard to its conditions or anything else, or, to go still further, to be of service to capitalists possessed of the ability to pay large sums in compensation. It is an obvious fact that gross evils arose from the above situation. The Employment Security Law seeks to remove these evils in the cause of the public welfare and to provide every person with suitable occupation according to his capacity, thus stabilizing employment as a whole.

To that end the law prohibited the fee-charging employment agency, which in the past carried with it many abuses, and established a free and fair employment service operating as a public agency; it is in no way in conflict with any provision of the Constitution. Therefore, the argument for appeal is groundless.

Thus, the decision is made as stated in the formal judgment and in accordance with Article 408 of the Code of Criminal Procedure.[1]

The above is the unanimous opinion of the Justices.

(TRANSLATED BY IKEDA MASAAKI)

---

1. See footnote 4, p. 16.

Hanreishū, IX, No. 1, 89 (Criminal)

EDITORIAL NOTE: The accused was found guilty of operating a public bathhouse without a license from January to March, 1952, and fined ¥5,000. He lost on appeal to the high court and then appealed to the Supreme Court on the ground that the prefectural ordinance controlling the licensing of public bathhouses and the national law on which it was based were unconstitutional because they restricted freedom of choice of occupation. He also claimed that since the ordinance was unconstitutional on that ground, it violated the provision of Article 94 of the Constitution, which permits organs of local government to exercise certain powers "within the limits of the law."

Grand Bench decision, January 26, 1955: Dismissed.

REFERENCES

Constitution of Japan. ARTICLE 22. Every person shall have freedom to choose and change his residence and to choose his occupation to the extent that it does not interfere with the public welfare.

Freedom of all persons to move to a foreign country and to divest themselves of their nationality shall be inviolate.

ARTICLE 94. Local public entities shall have the right to manage their property, affairs, and administration and to enact their own regulations within law.

Public Bathhouse Law (As amended by *Law No. 187 of 1950*). ARTICLE 2. Any person who intends to operate a public bathhouse as a business must secure a license from the governor concerned after the payment of a fee to be determined by cabinet order.

The governor concerned, in cases wherein he deems that the site for the establishment of a public bathhouse or the structure or the accommodations thereof are improper from the standpoint of public sanitation or deems that the site for the establishment thereof is not properly located, may not grant the license provided for in the preceding paragraph. However, in such cases the governor concerned shall issue a notice of the denial of license, stating his reasons in writing.

With regard to the standards for the distribution of the sites for establishment mentioned in the preceding paragraph, the interested *to, dō, fu* [1] or prefecture shall establish them separately by ordinance.

Ordinance Providing for the Standards Under Articles 2 and 3 of the Public Bathhouse Law (*Fukuoka Prefectural Ordinance No. 54*, promulgated September 1, 1950, as amended in part by *Fukuoka Prefectural Ordinance No. 31 of May 31, 1952*). ARTICLE 1. In accordance with the provisions of Articles 2 and 3 of the Public Bathhouse Law, measures to be taken with respect to distribution of sites for the establishment, sanitation, and public morals of public bathhouses shall be as provided for in the present ordinance, excepting those that may be especially provided for by other laws and ordinances.

ARTICLE 2. In order to provide advice and suggestions as requested by the governor relative to the implementation of the present ordinance, a Fukuoka Public Bathhouse Establishment Council (hereinafter referred to as the "Council") shall be established.

Necessary matters concerning the Council shall be determined separately by the governor.

ARTICLE 3. The standard distance for the distribution of the

---

1. *To* is Tokyo Metropolis; *fu* (sometimes translated "urban prefecture") are the cities of Osaka and Kyoto; *dō* is Hokkaido.

sites for the establishment of public bathhouses shall be not less than 250 meters from already licensed public bathhouses in urban areas and 300 meters in rural areas.

The distance mentioned in the preceding paragraph shall be measured in a straight line and shall be the shortest distance between the public bath structures concerned.

ARTICLE 4. The standards for the construction and the accommodations of public bathhouses shall be as follows: [omitted here are the details, which involve separation of the sexes, dressing rooms, privacy, surveillance, and the like].

ARTICLE 5. The governor, in cases wherein he recognizes special circumstances such as topography, density of population, and so forth, may license enterprises without resorting to the standards provided for in the preceding two articles.

In granting licenses under the preceding paragraph, the governor shall consult the Council and seek its opinions.

FORMAL JUDGMENT

The appeal in the present case is dismissed.

REASONS. Concerning points 1 and 2 of counsel's argument for appeal: The argument for appeal asserts that the latter part of Article 2, paragraph 2, of the Public Bathhouse Law prescribes that, in cases wherein the site for the establishment of a public bathhouse is recognized as being not properly located, the governor concerned may not license the operation of such a bathhouse; and that Article 3 of the Fukuoka Prefectural Ordinance No. 54 of 1950 establishes the standards for ensuring the proper distribution, and so forth, of public bathhouses; but because such restrictions on the operation of public bathhouses do, in effect, limit unlawfully the freedom of choice of occupation, although the situation does not involve the violation of the public welfare, the provisions of both the Public Bathhouse Law and the Fukuoka Prefectural Ordinance contravene Article 22 of the Constitution.

Public baths, however, are welfare facilities of a highly public nature, indispensable to the daily life of the majority of the people. Moreover, in the event that their establishment be left to the will of the entrepreneur himself and necessary measures are not taken to preserve their proper distribution or to prevent maldistribution and excessive numbers, it is to be feared not only that such mal-distribution may cause inconvenience to many people who wish easy access to public baths daily but also that excessive numbers thereof may lead to futile competition and have an unfavorable economic effect on the enterprises, thereby giving rise to undesirable consequences such as a deterioration in the sanitary facilities of the bathhouses. It is, therefore, desirable in view of the nature of the public bathhouses as stated above and from the standpoint of both national hygiene and environmental sanitation, to prevent the above situation to the greatest extent possible. Accordingly, cases in which the sites for the establishment of public bathhouses are improperly located, thus leading to maldistribution or excessive numbers, run counter to the public welfare; and the establishment of provisions to the effect that licenses for the operation of public bathhouses, on the grounds set forth above, may not be granted is, therefore, not considered to be in conflict with Article 22 of the Constitution.

Moreover, the argument for appeal is based on the premise that the establishment of a stipulation to the effect that a license for the operation of a public bathhouse may not be granted on the grounds that its location is improper is unconstitutional, both because there is no violation of the public welfare and because it restricts the freedom of choice of occupation; and in addition the argument states that Article 3 of Fukuoka Prefectural Ordinance No. 54 of 1950 violates Article 22 of the Constitution. However, the above premise cannot be accepted, as has already been explained. Furthermore, since the provisions of the ordinance in question are based on Article 2, paragraph 3, of the Public Bathhouse Law, and establish the standards for the distribution of public bathhouses under paragraph 2 of the said article, it cannot be recognized that the provisions concerned violate the Constitution for the reasons stated in the argument. Consequently, this argument for appeal cannot be accepted.

Concerning point 2, second part: The argument for appeal also makes the following assertions: that notwithstanding the fact that the Public Bathhouse Law is based on the principle of the granting of licenses for the operation of public bathhouses, with the nongranting of licenses as the exception, Fukuoka Prefectural Ordinance No. 54 of 1950 is based on the principle of the nongranting of licenses, with granting of licenses as the exception; and that because the ordinance places an even greater restriction on the freedom of choice of occupation than the law does, it violates not only the spirit of the Constitution but also Article 94 of the Constitution, which provides that local public entities have the right to enact their own regulations "within law." However, the above ordinance is based on Article 2, paragraph 3, of the Public Bathhouse Law and establishes concrete standards for situations in which licenses for the operation of public bathhouses will not be granted, as provided for in paragraph 2 of the same article. Articles 3 and 4 of the above ordinance deal with such standards; and Article 5 establishes provisions for their relaxation, so that licenses can be granted without conforming to the standards of Articles 3 and 4.

Thus, the said ordinance concretely establishes detailed rules for cases of the nongranting of licenses as exceptions stated in the law, and does not substitute the principle of nongranting for the principle of granting. Therefore it cannot be recognized that there is an illegality in going beyond the scope of the law in the said ordinance as the argument for appeal maintains, and the argument cannot be accepted.

Concerning the gist of the appellant's own argument: Throughout the argument for appeal are points concerning unconstitutionality that cannot be accepted for the same reasons as have been handed down in respect to points 1 and 2 in counsel's argument as presented above. Other points in the argument involve only the assertion that in the original judgment there are violations of laws and ordinances or that there were no explanations of the circumstances; these do not constitute reasons for appeal as provided for in Article 401 of the Code of Civil Procedure.[2]

Hence, in accordance with Article 408 of the Code of Criminal Procedure[3] the Court hands down a unanimous decision as stated in the formal judgment.

(TRANSLATED BY IKEDA MASAAKI)

2. See footnote 7, p. 50.
3. See footnote 4, p. 16.

Hanreishū, XIII, No. 12, 3225 (Criminal)

EDITORIAL NOTE: This is the only Supreme Court decision dealing directly with the meaning of Article 9, the renunciation-of-war article, which is beyond question the most widely known and the most controversial article in the entire Constitution.

It should be noted that the Court confined itself rigorously to the issue of the constitutionality of the United States military bases in Japan. It touched not at all on the equally important question of the constitutionality of the Self-Defense Forces of Japan itself. The Okuno-Takahashi opinion points out that the issue was not pertinent in this case.

The so-called Sunakawa Incident occurred at the edge of Tachikawa air base, a major United States installation, on July 8, 1957, in the village of Sunakawa, in the metropolitan area of Tokyo, approximately twenty miles west of the center of the city. Japanese and American authorities had agreed earlier that a runway at the base should be extended. The Japanese government was responsible for carrying out the survey of the additional land required, which was under cultivation, and for its eventual acquisition from the owners. When the decision became known there was considerable local objection, and when the surveyors appeared on the above date they were opposed. A riot ensued and some of the rioters trespassed on the base. They did not damage American installations or attack American personnel. They were, however, arrested by the

Japanese police on the charge of illegal entry of an American base.

The seven accused, three workers, three students, and a railway employee, were tried in a division of the Tokyo District Court presided over by Judge Date Akio. On March 30, 1959, the court handed down a verdict of not guilty. In summary, the Date decision was as follows: The accused were not guilty because the Special Criminal Law under which they had been charged had been illegally enacted in the implementation of the Japan-United States Security Treaty of 1951, which was unconstitutional because it provided for the stationing of United States forces in Japan and the said forces constituted war potential, the maintenance of which was forbidden by Article 9. Therefore, to find the accused guilty would be in contravention of Article 31 which provides that no person shall suffer a criminal penalty "except according to procedure established by law." There was the additional point that the above law called for a penalty in excess of that for the identical crime of trespass listed in the Minor Offenses Law.

In view of the far-reaching legal, political, diplomatic, and strategic implications of the Date decision, the Tokyo Public Prosecutor's Office decided to carry its appeal directly to the Supreme Court, bypassing the Tokyo High Court. On April 3 the Court decided to accept the appeal, which was presented on June 3, 1959. It was widely believed in Tokyo that the Court's decision would be handed down by the end of the following September. That it took three months longer was an indication of the difficulty of the decision.

Although the Court was in unanimous agreement on the judgment itself, it should be noted that no fewer than ten justices differed in varying degrees over issues raised in the "Reasons" stated in the decision. Of special significance in the area of disagreement was the dispute over the nature of the right of constitutional review that the courts hold over treaties and other "acts of government." (See also the "Suzuki Decision," which follows this one.)

Grand Bench decision, December 16, 1959: Quashed and returned.

References

Constitution of Japan. Preamble. [See Appendix A.]

ARTICLE 9. Aspiring sincerely to an international peace based on justice and order, the Japanese people forever renounce war as a sovereign right of the nation and the threat or use of force as means of settling international disputes.

2. In order to accomplish the aim of the preceding paragraph, land, sea, and air forces, as well as other war potential, will never be maintained. The right of belligerency of the state will not be recognized.

ARTICLE 73, item 3.   The Cabinet, in addition to other general administrative functions, shall perform the following functions:

[. . .] (3) Conclude treaties. However, it shall obtain prior or, depending on circumstances, subsequent approval of the Diet.

ARTICLE 76, paragraph 3.   All judges shall be independent in the exercise of their conscience and shall be bound only by this Constitution and the laws.

ARTICLE 81.   The Supreme Court is the court of last resort with power to determine the constitutionality of any law, order, regulation, or official act.

ARTICLE 98.   This Constitution shall be the supreme law of the nation and no law, ordinance, imperial rescript or other act of government, or part thereof, contrary to the provisions hereof, shall have legal force or validity.

2. The treaties concluded by Japan and established laws of nations shall be faithfully observed.

Japan-United States Security Treaty.[1] Preamble. Japan has this day [September 8, 1951] signed a Treaty of Peace with the Allied Powers. On the coming into force of that Treaty, Japan will not have the effective means to exercise its inherent right of self-defense because it has been disarmed. There is danger to Japan in this situation because irresponsible militarism has not yet been driven from the world. Therefore, Japan desires a Security Treaty with the United States of America to come into force simultaneously with the Treaty of Peace between the United States of America and Japan. The Treaty of Peace recognizes that Japan as a sovereign nation has the right to enter into collective security arrangements, and further, the Charter of the United Nations recognizes that all nations possess an inherent right of individual and collective self-defense.

---

1. For the full text of this treaty see: United States of America, Department of State, *United States Treaties and Other International Agreements* (Washington, D.C.: Government Printing Office, 1952), III, Part 3, 3169–91.

In exercise of these rights, Japan desires, as a provisional arrangement for its defense, that the United States of America should maintain armed forces of its own in and about Japan so as to deter armed attack upon Japan. The United States of America, in the interest of peace and security, is presently willing to maintain certain of its armed forces in and about Japan, in the expectation, however, that Japan will itself increasingly assume responsibility for its own defense against direct and indirect aggression, always avoiding any armament which could be an offensive threat or serve other than to promote peace and security in accordance with the purposes and principles of the United Nations Charter.

Accordingly, the two countries have agreed as follows:

ARTICLE I. Japan grants, and the United States of America accepts the right, upon the coming into force of the Treaty of Peace and of this Treaty, to dispose United States land, air, and sea forces in and about Japan. Such forces may be utilized to contribute to the maintenance of the international peace and security in the Far East and to the security of Japan against armed attack from without, including assistance given at the express request of the Japanese Government to put down large-scale internal riots and disturbances in Japan, caused through instigation or intervention by an outside Power or Powers.

ARTICLE III. The conditions which shall govern the disposition of armed forces of the United States of America in and about Japan shall be determined by administrative agreements between the two Governments.

Charter of the United Nations. ARTICLE 51. Nothing in the present Charter shall impair the inherent right of individual or collective self-defense if an armed attack occurs against a Member of the United Nations, until the Security Council has taken the measures necessary to maintain international peace and security. [. . .]

Special Criminal Law Accompanying the Administrative Agreement Based on Article 3 of the Japan-United States Security Treaty. ARTICLE 2. A person who, without good reason, enters a place, entry into which is prohibited because it is an area or installation (as stipulated in Article 2, paragraph 1 of the Administrative Agreement) utilized by United States armed forces, or who does not withdraw from such place on request may be sentenced to not more than one year's imprisonment at hard labor or a fine or a minor fine not exceeding ¥2,000. . . .

[*Minor Offenses Law.* ARTICLE 1. A person who comes under any of the following items shall be punished with penal detention (maximum of thirty days) or minor fine; . . .

(32) A person who, without good reason, goes into a place where entrance is forbidden or a rice paddy or other cultivated field; . . .]

FORMAL JUDGMENT

The original judgment is quashed. The present case is returned to the Tokyo District Court.

REASONS. Concerning the appeal brief of Nomura Sadao, chief prosecutor, Tokyo District Prosecutor's Office: In essence, the original judgment holds that Article 2 of the Special Criminal Law Accompanying the Administrative Agreement Based on Article 3 of the Security Treaty between Japan and the United States of America is in contravention of Article 31 of the Constitution and is null and void. Its premise is that the retention [in Japan] of the military forces of the United States of America is impermissible and in contravention of the stipulation of Article 9, paragraph 2 (first part), of the Constitution, which states that war potential will not be maintained.

I. Initially, we render judgment concerning the meaning of the first part of Article 9, paragraph 2, of the Constitution. To begin with, Article 9, as a result of the defeat of our country and in accordance with the acceptance of the Potsdam Declaration, is a reconsideration of the militaristic conduct of the Japanese people, which resulted from our nation's errors in the past; it also expresses the people's resolve that "never again shall we be visited with the horrors of war through the action of government"; and it was enacted by the people, who "desire peace for all time." It is also a provision that, conjointly with the spirit of international cooperation set forth in the Preamble and Article 98, paragraph 2, embodies the pacifism which is the special characteristic of our Constitution. That is to say, it is proclaimed in Article 9, paragraph 1, that the Japanese people aspire "sincerely to an international peace based on justice and order," and also that they "forever renounce war as a sovereign right of the nation and the threat or use of force as means of settling international disputes"; and again in the second paragraph of the same article that, "In order to accomplish the aim of the preceding paragraph, land, sea, and air forces, as well as other war potential, will never be maintained. The right of belligerency of the state will not be recognized."

Thus, the said article renounces what is termed therein war and prohibits the maintenance of what is termed war potential; naturally, the above in no way denies the inherent right of self-defense, which our country possesses as a sovereign nation, and the pacifism of our Constitution has never provided for either defenselessness or nonresistance. As is clear also in the Preamble of the Constitution, "We, the Japanese people, . . . desire to occupy an honored place in an international society striving for the preservation of peace, and the banishment of tyranny and slavery, oppression, and intolerance for all time from the earth. We recognize that all peoples of the world have the right to live in peace, free from fear and want." Even so, it must be said that it is proper that our country, in the exercise of an inherent national function, be able to take the measures necessary for self-defense so that we can maintain our own peace and security and preserve our existence. That is to say, we, the Japanese people, under Article 9, paragraph 2, of the Constitution, do not maintain what is termed war potential in the same article, but we have determined to preserve our peace and security because the insufficiency of our nation's defensive strength produced thereby is not compensated for by trusting to what is termed in the Preamble of the Constitution "the justice and faith of the peace-loving peoples of the world." Now, that is certainly not, as the original judgment sets forth, limited to such military security measures as are handled by the Security Council and other organs of the United Nations. If there are to be guarantees of the security of our country in order to preserve its peace and security, it is natural that we be able to select, in order to achieve such aims, appropriate measures and methods regarded as suitable under existing international conditions. Article 9 of the Constitution in no way prohibits a request to another country for security guarantees for the maintenance of the peace and safety of our country.

Thus, in considering the legal meaning of Article 9, paragraph

2, as based on the intent of the said article set forth above, it is proper to interpret what is stipulated as the nonmaintenance of war potential in the same paragraph to mean that what is forever renounced, as set forth in the first paragraph of the said article, is the resort to what is called aggressive war through the maintenance by our country of what is termed war potential and the exercise of the rights of command and control over it. Accordingly, entirely apart from the question of whether or not paragraph 2 of the said article prohibits the maintenance of war potential for the purpose of self-defense, it must be understood that the war potential prohibited by the said provision is that over which our country can exercise the rights of command and control, that is, it stipulates the war potential of our own country and what is here termed war potential is not applicable to foreign military forces, even those which may be retained in our country.

II. Next there is the question whether or not the retention of the military forces of the United States of America is in contravention of the intent of Article 9, Article 98, paragraph 2, and the Preamble of the Constitution. However, in the judgment of this issue, because the above retention is based on the Japan-America Security Treaty, which is at issue in this case, then the said judgment must be made on the premise of whether or not the content of the said treaty is in contravention of the aforesaid constitutional provisions.

Nevertheless, the above security treaty was concluded on the same day as the Treaty of Peace with Japan (Treaty No. 5, April 28, 1952 [the effective date of the treaty, not the date of conclusion]) and is closely and indivisibly related to it. For example, Article 6 (*a*) of the Treaty of Peace states, "Nothing in this provision shall, however, prevent the stationing or retention of foreign armed forces in Japanese territory under or in consequence of any bilateral or multilateral agreements which have been or may be made between one or more of the Allied Powers, on the one hand, and Japan on the other," and recognizes the retention of foreign military forces in Japanese territory. The Security Treaty in the present case is a treaty that was concluded between Japan and America in respect to the retention of the armed forces of the United States of America, which are foreign armed forces as recognized under the above provision. The above provision of the Treaty of Peace was signed and approved by a majority of some forty individual nations of the sixty then participating in the United Nations.

Thus, the objective of the above Security Treaty, according to its preamble, was to recognize that our country at the time the Treaty of Peace became effective, in view of the fact that it did not have effective means of self-defense and because of the necessity to cope with irresponsible militarism, had the right, as a sovereign nation, to enter into collective security arrangements. Also, on the basis of the fact that the Charter of the United Nations recognizes that all nations possess the inherent right of individual and collective self-defense, it is clear that the security treaty also determines the necessary matters for the maintenance of the security and defense of our country, such as approval of the right of the United States of America to station its forces in and around our country to deter armed attack as a temporary measure for our defense. For this reason it must be stated that the content of the above Security Treaty has an extremely important relation to the security and peace of our country as a sovereign nation and, in turn, to the very foundation of our existence. Again, in respect to the conclusion [of the treaty], the cabinet at that time, on the basis of constitutional provisions and after protracted negotiations with the United States, executed it in due form as an important policy of our country. Subsequently, after having been given careful consideration in both the House of Representatives and the House of Councillors, including a discussion of whether or not it was in conformity with the Constitution, it received the consent of the National Diet as a lawful and proper instrument, as is well known.

Moreover, the Security Treaty in the present case must be regarded as having a highly political nature which, as was pointed out above, possesses an extremely important relation to the basis of the existence of our country as a sovereign nation. There are not a few points in which a legal decision as to the unconstitutionality of its content is simply the other side of the coin of the political or discretionary decision of the cabinet, which concluded the treaty, or of the National Diet, which gave its consent to it. Consequently, the legal decision as to unconstitutionality has a character which, as a matter of principle, is not adaptable to review by a judicial court, which has as its mission a purely judicial function; accordingly, it falls outside the right of judicial review by the courts, unless there is clearly obvious unconstitutionality or invalidity.[2] It is proper to interpret this primarily as a matter that must be entrusted to the decision of the cabinet, which possesses the power to conclude treaties, and of the National Diet, which has the power to approve them; and it ultimately must be left to the political review of the sovereign people. Thus, this matter is not concerned either with the unconstitutionality of the Security Treaty or with the actions of the government that are based on the treaty or with whether the case is one in which it [the treaty] has become a basic premise, as in the present case.

III. To continue, in examining what the stipulations of the Security Treaty and of the Administrative Agreement based on its Article 3 signify in regard to the retention of the armed forces of the United States of America, the above United States forces are, of course, foreign forces and are not war potential of our country itself. It is clear that the powers of command and control over them reside completely in the United States of America and that our country does not similarly possess those powers as it would in respect to its own armed forces. Also, these armed forces are so retained in accordance with the intent set forth in the Preamble of the Treaty, as described above, and as is shown in Article 1 of the Treaty: "Such forces may be utilized to contribute to the maintenance of the international peace and security in the Far East and the security of Japan against armed attack from without, including assistance given at the express request of the Japanese Government to put down large-scale internal riots and disturbances in Japan, caused through instigation or intervention by an outside Power or Powers." Its objectives lie only in the maintenance of peace and security in our country and in the Far East, including Japan, and in acting so that the horrors of war will not again be visited on us. That our country has sanc-

2. Because of the importance in this decision of the phrase rendered here and below as "clearly obvious unconstitutionality or invalidity," and in a different context "clearly and obviously unconstitutional and invalid," I should point out that the Japanese original is somewhat stronger than the English equivalent I have had to use. A literal rendering of the Japanese phrase would be "unconstitutionality and invalidity that are extremely obvious at a glance," but it would be awkward to use such a phrase as often as the text requires. The exact connotation of the original will be retained if "clearly obvious" is taken to mean "clearly obvious to an unmistakable degree."

tioned such retention of troops can be grasped from the fact that it is nothing more than a means of supplementing the insufficiency of our country's defensive strength while relying on the "justice and faith of the peace-loving peoples of the world."

If so, then such retention of United States armed forces must certainly be in accord with the intent of Article 9, Article 98, paragraph 2, and the Preamble of the Constitution, and it absolutely cannot be admitted that it is in violation of the said provisions or that it is clearly obvious that it is unconstitutional and invalid. Thus, this matter is not concerned with the issue of whether Article 9, paragraph 2, of the Constitution does not permit the maintenance of war potential for the purpose of self-defense.

(In addition, the Administrative Agreement was not specially approved by the National Diet, but the government after the completion of the signing on February 28, 1952, did present to the Foreign Affairs Committee of the House of Representatives, in early March, both the Administrative Agreement and the minutes taken at the time of its conclusion. Subsequently, the government also submitted to questioning by the above committee, the Legal Affairs Committee of the House of Representatives, and others. Thus, there is controversy over whether or not the Administrative Agreement itself should have received the consent of the National Diet, but the government declares that because the Security Treaty, which includes the basic stipulations for the Administrative Agreement, had received the consent of the National Diet, there was no necessity that there be special and separate National Diet consent to the Administrative Agreement. In the National Diet on March 25, 1952, a plenary session of the House of Councillors defeated a resolution to the effect that because the Administrative Agreement was a treaty under Article 73 of the Constitution it had to receive the approval of the Diet as set forth in the same article. Also, a plenary session of the House of Representatives on the twenty-sixth day of the same month of the same year, rejected a resolution to the effect that the Administrative Agreement went beyond the scope of regulations dealing with the disposition of American armed forces as authorized under Article 3 of the Security Treaty and that its content was such as to require the consent of the National Diet under Article 73 of the Constitution. Then, judging from the above facts, the Administrative Agreement, which stipulated the conditions regulating the disposition of American forces, must be recognized as being within the scope of the terms of Article 3 of the Security Treaty, which had already received the consent of the National Diet, and it cannot be admitted that it is unconstitutional and invalid simply because it had not expressly received the consent of the National Diet.)

Hence, the original judgment in finding that the retention of the armed forces of the United States of America is impermissible and in contravention of the first part of Article 9, paragraph 2, of the Constitution has departed from the proper sphere of the power of judicial review of the courts and has erred in its interpretation of the said provisions and of the Preamble of the Constitution. Accordingly, its holding that Article 2 of the Special Criminal Law, which is the premise of the present case, is unconstitutional and invalid is also improper; the argument for appeal in respect to this point ends by having reasonable grounds; and the original judgment cannot escape being quashed, even without judging other points of the argument for appeal.

Thus, the Court decides as in the formal decision in accordance with Article 410, paragraph 1, Article 405 (*a*), and Article 413 of the Code of Criminal Procedure.[3]

This decision is the unanimous decision of the Justices except for the supplementary opinions of Justices Tanaka Kōtarō, Shima Tamotsu, Fujita Hachirō, Iriye Toshio, Tarumi Katsumi, Kawamura Daisuke, and Ishizaka Shuichi and the opinions of Justices Otani Katsushige, Okuno Kenichi, and Takahashi Kiyoshi.

*   *   *

The supplementary opinion of Justice Tanaka Kōtarō follows.

I support both the formal judgment and the reasons for this decision, but I would like to supplement the reasons in the following two points.

I. I speak in regard to a point with which the reasons in the present judgment do not deal. Basically speaking, the legal problem in the present case has been extremely simple and clear. The case deals only with the entry of the defendants without good

3. See footnote 1, p. 92 on these three articles.

reason into an installation in which trespass was forbidden by the Special Criminal Law. It would be sufficient for the court of original instance only to apply Article 2 of the said law to the facts in the present case. However, the original decision judged Article 2 of the Special Criminal Law to be unconstitutional by relating the said Article 2 to the question of the constitutionality of the retention in Japan of the armed forces of the United States of America under the Japan-America Security Treaty and treating the retention as a violation of Article 9, paragraph 2, of the Constitution. Thus, the original judgment goes back to a problem not necessary for a solution of the present case, and uselessly complicates the discussion.

I believe, even assuming for the moment that the said retention is unconstitutional, that Article 2 of the Special Criminal Law itself has a *raison d'être* unrelated to that issue and is valid. In the final analysis, though there be dispute concerning the constitutionality of the retention and again assuming for the moment that it is unconstitutional in any event because the fact of such retention actually existed at the time, we can admit two matters as far as legislative policy is concerned: the fact had to be respected, and measures had to be taken for proper protection [of the American forces].

Generally, in cases where a certain fact exists, even though it may be illegal in itself, the existence of the technical legal principle which, at least in part, deals with legal relationships on the premise of the acceptance of such a fact, can be fully acknowledged in jurisprudence. Treating the future elimination of an illegal fact as a separate problem, respect for an existing fact and the preservation of the legal order are the foundations of law. It is thus that we can avoid confusion in the legal order and the improper consequences produced by the unrestricted extension of the effects of the illegality of certain facts. There are many such instances, but as the simplest example we can offer the case of a foreigner who, even though having entered the country illegally, must be secure in his life, liberty, and property as long as he remains therein. How much more is this true in the present case in regard to the retention of armed forces, which is neither unconstitutional nor illegal.

In the present case, if we consider the already existing fact that foreign troops are inside the country at the present time, there is a perfectly reasonable ground for Article 2 of the Special Criminal Law, which stems from this fact, even without reference to international custom and international courtesy. What the original verdict touches on, the commensuration of the statutory punishments in Article 1 (32) of the Minor Offenses Law and the crime of intrusion on a habitation [Criminal Code, Article 130] ends as a problem of legislative policy.

In essence, the question of the constitutionality of the retention of the United States armed forces on the basis of the Japan-United States Security Treaty is not of a character to be judged primarily on the premises of decisions taken in such cases as the above. There is absolutely no connection between this problem [of constitutionality] and the validity of Article 2 of the Special Criminal Law. The original judgment which, believing that there was such a connection, held that such retention is unconstitutional and that consequently Article 2 of the said law is unconstitutional and invalid, is improper. On this point alone the original judgment cannot escape being quashed.

II. The original judgment, on the basis of the erroneous logical process pointed out above in I., entered into various important questions such as Article 9 of the Constitution, self-defense, the Japan-United States Security Treaty, and pacifism—all relating to the constitutionality of the retention of the armed forces of the United States. For this reason it was unavoidable that the reasons for the present decision reveal the opinions of the present Court on those points. I set down below my own opinions in the sense that they supplement somewhat the reasons of the present decision in respect to the internationalism set forth in our Constitution.

The fact that as a general rule nations possess the right of self-defense for the sake of their survival is widely accepted. Self-defense is one of the most fundamental functions and duties of a nation. If so, then in order to achieve effectively the object of self-defense what means should be resorted to? A nation can consider such things as security guarantees by an international organization such as the United Nations or the conclusion of treaties with friendly countries for the purpose of guaranteeing security in addition to counting on the perfection of its own power of self-defense. The decision of the means to be selected and the degree of perfection and the structure of the power of self-defense must consider world conditions at the time and other circumstances; it is a purely political question which is left to the discretion of the government. What can be recognized legally is only the great principle that the state can or must devise the necessary and appropriate measures for self-defense as its obligation to the people.

Moreover, a country's self-defense is a moral responsibility in international society. Today the relationship of mutual solidarity among the various peoples has broadened and deepened to the point that a crisis for one people necessarily and directly affects other peoples. Accordingly, a country's self-defense is also something that cannot be considered individually, that is, only from its own standpoint. The fact that one country is protecting itself against aggression means that at the same time it is protecting other countries; also, a cooperative effort in the defense of other countries is a way of defending one's own country. In other words, today there no longer exists the concept of self-defense in the strict meaning of the term. The connection is simply this: self-defense is the defense of others; defense of others is self-defense. Accordingly, it must be recognized that though it be defense of one's own country or cooperation in the defense of other countries, each country bears a responsibility.

In general, as an internal national problem, each person defends the rights of himself and others against imminent and improper infringement; this is the so-called fight for rights and can be termed the demand for justice. This means the defense of the entire legal order; it is the same in international relations. The duty of defense does not arise expressly out of treaties; and it is of a nature that does not allow compulsion in its performance. However, it does arise from the natural world moral order—the concept of an international cooperative body which is the foundation of the mutual dependence and the relationship of solidarity existing among the various peoples. This can also be recognized in the spirit of international cooperation of the Preamble of our Constitution. Thus, the government's resort to certain measures in accordance with this spirit also lies within the scope of political discretionary action for which the government bears the responsibility.

The Security Treaty between the two countries of Japan and the United States, which has become a problem in the present case, can be understood only from the point of view just described. It cannot be stated that the intent of the present treaty is antagonistic to the pacifistic spirit of Article 9 of the Constitution. The spirit of the said article resides necessarily in the prohibition of aggressive war. It does not prohibit unavoidable resort to defensive measures in situations in which a state of war is produced by the fact of external aggression without relation to the intentions of our country, nor does it prohibit the taking of necessary and effective measures of preparation against such an affair.

The legality of a war arising from a so-called just cause, that is, one that by nature involves legitimate self-defense, in a situation in which the right of existence, the very life itself, of the country is threatened, has been generally recognized for many years. Because the aim of the Japan-United States Security Treaty arose out of the necessity for the defense of Japan so that there would be no aggression against our country because of the "power vacuum" and out of the necessity for the maintenance of peace and security in the Far East, which is indivisibly linked with the peace of the entire world, it cannot be said that there is a violation of the provisions of the said Article 9 even though United States forces are retained here as a result of this treaty. Accordingly, whether or not "retention" is included in the concept of "maintenance" of war potential of paragraph 2 of the said article—and we interpret it not to be included—is in substance an unrelated matter. If the logic of the original judgment be accepted, it is probable that even though American forces were not stationed in our country but were held on a stand-by basis in a foreign country, that would also become the "maintenance" of war potential and any treaty that would recognize that situation would likewise be held unconstitutional.

We must interpret Article 9 in its entirety, including paragraph 2, about which there is dispute over interpretation, through a discernment on the one hand of what is proclaimed in the Preamble regarding the idea of lasting peace and international cooperation and, on the other hand, of the current state of international society and the trends of the future. The method of teleological interpretation of what is based on reasonable intent, that is, neither adhering to the letter nor the original psychological intention of the legislator, is generally recognized as a common principle in the interpretation of all law. This must be particularly emphasized in the interpretation of the Constitution.

The spirit of pacifism in Article 9 of the Constitution is firmly coupled to the ideas of the Preamble of the Constitution. That spirit is the eternal renunciation of aggressive war and of the use of military power to settle international disputes. However, we must not erroneously interpret this to release our country automatically from the responsibility that it has toward the international community for the maintenance of peace and security. What is introspectively set forth in the Preamble of the Constitution cannot lead to a correct and uncontradictory interpretation of Article 9 unless we abandon the viewpoint of our country alone and adopt one in accord with eternal political morality, that is to say, unless we think in international terms.

If we take this view, the necessary power for self-defense that is possessed by the state, apart from its formal, legal status, must in actual fact acquire the character of a means of maintaining peace and security in the international community, which comprises various nations, while defending the state itself. In this present transitional period the threat of aggression has not been completely extinguished, and even granting the view that it is impossible to depend only on the power of the international community itself in respect to the maintenance of peace and security in that community, it is impossible to deny completely the above point. If this be so, then under present conditions it is impossible to liquidate entirely the "balance of power" of the past. However, if in the future the certainty of peace is greatly increased, then accordingly, the necessity for the balance of power will decrease and the reduction of arms will be gradually achieved. At the same time, in the present period of transition the power that each peace-loving nation must possess or utilize for self-defense will gradually assume an international character. Power with such a character will not be the same as the war potential that is prohibited under Article 9, paragraph 2, of the Constitution.

In essence, we must interpret the pacifism of the Constitution, not from the simple standpoint of a single nation, but from a point of view going beyond that, namely, from the dimension of world law in accord with the firm legal beliefs of all democratic, peace-loving countries. Both the attitude of paying absolutely no attention to the defense of one's own country and, of course, the attitude of having no interest in or enthusiasm for the defense of other countries—thinking only of one's self—are national ego-centrism "responsible to itself alone," as stated in the Preamble of the Constitution, and cannot be termed faithful to true pacifism.

We "aspire sincerely to an international peace," but that peace must be "based on justice and order" as is declared in the first part of Article 9 of the Constitution. Peace is the realization of justice and order, that is to say, it is indivisibly linked with the "rule of law." Efforts for true self-defense are a requirement for justice and at the same time are a responsibility toward international peace borne by all people.

For the above reasons, I believe that the statement of reasons in the present judgment is proper in that it recognizes that the original judgment, which held that the retention of the armed forces of the United States is in contravention of Article 9, paragraph 2, of the Constitution and impermissible, erred in its interpretation of the said article and of the Preamble of the Constitution.

* * *

The supplementary opinion of Justice Shima Tamotsu follows.

I am in accord with the majority opinion which interprets Article 9 as not denying the right of self-defense to our country and holds that the war potential referred to in paragraph 2 of the said article means war potential under the command and control of our country and not the war potential of foreign armed forces not in such a position.

Because of the above interpretation of the meaning of Article 9, paragraph 2, of the Constitution, by what means can the existence of our country be assured other than by the possession of war potential under our own command and control? (Accordingly, can we achieve self-defense by relying on foreign military forces not under our command and control?) In respect to this question, our Constitution does not stipulate anything directly, and we must interpret its intent to be that it is to be left to the discretionary decision of governmental groups.[4] Of course, because the fundamental spirit of our Constitution is pacifism and international cooperation, the governmental groups in making decisions on such matters must naturally remain as faithful as possible to that spirit. In this sense, the spirit of pacifism and of international cooperation must be interpreted to be the fundamental line for policy decisions by the governmental branch and the criterion for discretionary decisions. Accordingly, there is a definite limitation on the discretionary power of the governmental groups in respect to this point and it must be understood that any decision that clearly betrays the spirit of pacifism and international cooperation is impermissible. On the other hand, when it is recognized that a policy decision of the governmental branch has not gone beyond the limits of the power of discretion, the courts, which by their nature must not participate in politics, do not touch on the propriety of such a policy decision and must not discuss it.

What is in question in the present case is the decision by the nation's governmental groups to guarantee our country's existence through the retention of the armed forces of the United States of America following the conclusion of the Security Treaty and also whether that decision is clearly in violation of the spirit of pacifism and international cooperation and goes beyond the limits of discretionary power. From this standpoint the treaty was concluded on the basis of the view that it was necessary to take certain temporary measures for self-defense because our country had lost effective means with which to exercise the inherent right of self-defense and had renounced armaments though militarism had not yet been swept from the world. That the said treaty would go out of effect when it was recognized that effective means for the maintenance of security in the area around Japan had been created by United Nations forces is clear from its text. If we look at the problem thus, then it is clear that the governmental elements of

4. The key phrase "governmental groups," which I use here and below and render also as "political elements," is the translation of a Japanese phrase that could be defined broadly as "elements, groups, or sections in government or politics." As the argument below demonstrates, its specific meaning throughout the opinions given here is "the cabinet and the National Diet as branches of the government that are constitutionally responsible for the carrying out of certain governmental functions for which they are held politically accountable." Thus, the phrase connotes both governmental function and political responsibility.

our country arrived at that decision on the basis of their recognition of the fact that there is still danger of aggressive war in international society and in further consideration of the fact that the international situation is one in which the United Nations, as the organ for the maintenance of world peace and security, is still unable to carry out its ideal function. They decided that the most appropriate means for guaranteeing our country's existence was to conclude the Security Treaty and to allow the retention of American armed forces, complying to the greatest extent possible with the spirit of pacifism and of international cooperation in our Constitution. Thus, because it is impossible to decide that such an estimate of the world situation, which is the basis of the above decision, is clearly in error, it naturally follows that it is also impossible to decide whether the decision of the governmental groups who made that estimate on that basis clearly contravenes the spirit of pacifism and international cooperation and goes beyond the limits of discretionary authority.

Of course, in respect to this recognition of the world situation, it is not impossible that there be an estimate other than the one above; and it is also not absolutely impossible, on the basis of such a different political estimate, to argue that another way of maintaining our peace and security would be, on the contrary, through not permitting the stationing of any foreign troops whatsoever in our country. However, we cannot discern any basis for deciding which of these two mutually opposed views regarding the world situation is clearly erroneous. In the present world situation it is probably impossible for anyone to demonstrate beyond a shadow of doubt that it would be possible to maintain our peace and security without stationing any foreign troops in our country. The problem lies in determining which is the more effective and appropriate method of maintaining our country's peace and security under present world conditions while complying as much as possible with the spirit of pacifism and international cooperation: that of not allowing the stationing of any foreign troops at all in our country or that of permitting the stationing of American troops under the Security Treaty. Because we cannot discern any clue that could be used to decide whether either the former or the latter would be clearly inappropriate, we must say that it is impermissible for us to conclude that the decision made by our country's governmental groups to follow the latter course is one that goes beyond the limits of the power of discretion. Moreover, the decision on this point includes an extremely important political determination concerning our country's fate. The cabinet concluded the treaty under the prescribed procedures, obtained the consent of the National Diet, and also succeeded in obtaining the support of a great majority of the people in several elections. In view of this, it is proper that the above decision of the political elements be respected as a final decision taken within the limits of discretionary authority granted by the Constitution. It must also be understood that our Constitution does not provide that the courts, which must not by their nature participate in politics, may inquire into the propriety of such policy decisions or investigate them.

Because it cannot be said, for the above reasons, that our governmental groups' concluding the Security Treaty and permitting the stationing of American forces are unconstitutional, the original judgment, which held on the premise of unconstitutionality that the provisions of Article 2 of the Special Criminal Affairs Law are invalid, is improper and cannot escape being quashed.

*　　*　　*

The supplementary opinion of Justices Fujita Hachirō and Iriye Toshio follows.

We are in accord with the majority opinion, but we should like to make clear our reasons for agreement with it by means of the supplementary opinion below.

I. The Constitution of Japan established the separation of powers—legislative, executive, and judicial. The judicial power is exercised by all the courts (Article 76, paragraph 1). Also, the Court Organization Law stipulates that the courts shall decide all legal disputes (Article 3, paragraph 1). All civil, criminal, and administrative cases are regarded as falling under the jurisdiction of the judicial courts generally, without restriction as to particulars. Again, the Constitution grants to the courts the power to determine whether any law, order, regulation, or official act conforms to the Constitution (Article 81). As a result of these provisions all legislative and executive acts of state fall under the judicial power of the courts, including the right of constitutional review, to the extent that they involve legal disputes. This is what is termed judicial supremacy, the recognition of the supremacy of the judicial power over the legislative and executive; and it is treated as a special characteristic of the Constitution of Japan.

Nevertheless, there are also limits to the supremacy of judicial power. Under the concept of separation of powers in the Constitution, the basic principle is not only the separate establishment of the three powers, but also the mutual "check" and "balance" [Here and in the next paragraph the words in quotation marks appear in the original in parentheses.] among these three powers; and even though we refer to judicial supremacy, careful attention must be paid to the fact that the Constitution by no means recognizes the omnipotence of judicial authority. For example, acts of state which have a highly political content relating to the foundation of direct state power, even in cases involving legal disputes, accordingly lie outside the right of review of the courts, although there may be in law a possibility for a legal judgment of their validity or invalidity. It must be stated that such decisions must be left to the political elements, such as the government and the National Diet, that bear political responsibility toward the sovereign people and ultimately to the political decision of the people themselves. The limitations on this judicial power arise ultimately from the principle of the separation of powers; they must be interpreted to be limitations that are not expressly provided for, but inherent in the intrinsic nature of the constitutional judicial power because of such considerations as the high political content of acts of government, the character of the courts as judicial organs, and the procedural limitations necessarily accompanying justice.

Thus, in respect to the development and the theoretical basis of this matter and the scope of the acts involved, there must be certain variations, but for many years there have been precedents for them in the countries of Europe and America: *"acte de gouvernement"* in France, "act of state" or "matter of state" in Great Britain, or "political question" in the United States. In postwar West Germany *"Regierungsakt"* and *"Hoheitsakt"* have been approved in academic theory in relation to Article 19 of the Bonn Constitution. In our own country, as is well known, since the coming into effect of the Constitution of Japan, this has also come to be recognized by many scholars of public law as included in the concept of act of government.

II. In the present case the original judgment held that Article 2 "of the Special Criminal Law which accompanies the Administrative Agreement based on Article 3 of the Security Treaty between Japan and the United States of America" was unconstitutional and invalid, rejected the plea of the public prosecutor which argued its applicability, and handed down a verdict of not guilty in respect to the accused. But if we scrutinize the reasons set forth in the original judgment for holding invalid Article 2 of the Special Criminal Law, we find that the said article of the said law is a provision set up to preserve the legal benefits relating to peace and tranquillity inside the areas and installations of the armed forces of the United States of America retained in our country. Because our country's "permission for the retention of American forces comes under the maintenance of land, sea, and air forces, and other war potential which is prohibited by Article 9, paragraph 2 of the Constitution," and because "the American forces which are stationed in our country are not to be permitted under the Constitution," the result is that Article 2 of the Special Criminal Law, which was especially enacted in order to provide the legal benefits relating to peace and tranquillity inside the said installations and areas, is invalid because ultimately it conflicts with Article 31 of the Constitution. Thus, it is clear that the original judgment held Article 2 of the Special Criminal Law to be invalid on the premise that the act that permitted the retention of American forces in our country is in contravention of the Constitution. Hence, because the nucleus of the act that permitted the stationing of American armed forces in our country is the "Japan-United States Security Treaty" and because the stationing of American armed forces was carried out in fulfillment of the said treaty, then that a review in the present Court of the original judgment must initially take up the point whether or not the above Security Treaty in itself is in contravention of the Constitution, is as the majority opinion points out.

III. The Japan-United States Security Treaty and the Treaty of Peace with Japan (Treaty No. 5 of 1952) were signed on the same day, September 8, 1951. The former was based on the provisions of Article 6 (*a*) of the latter. It was concluded with the United

States of America as a security measure for our country after the Treaty of Peace went into effect; and it stands indivisibly related to the peace treaty. Thus, its security provisions arise from the fourth—"guarantee of security"—of the so-called seven principles of peace for Japan; how the security of our country could be guaranteed in the vacuum created by the lack of the power of self-defense following our renunciation of arms had already been a matter of diplomatic negotiation between the government of the United States of America and the Allied powers as an element of the treaty of peace that was bound to come. It is certainly not going too far to say that in substance the Security Treaty is a part of the Treaty of Peace.

The Treaty of Peace brought to an end the state of war between Japan and the Allies; it restored complete sovereignty to the Japanese nation; and it also enabled Japan, as an independent nation, to regain an honorable position in international society alongside the nations of the world. It goes without saying that it is also a treaty of great significance to the fate of our country. Thus, it must be stated that the treaty itself, as pointed out, is endowed with the greatest political character, bearing directly on the foundation of state power. Another matter that must be given special consideration in a study of the nature of this treaty is that our country was a defeated nation, at the time still under occupation, and the situation was not one in which a treaty of peace could be concluded on a footing of equality, as in the case of treaties between independent nations. Under the complex and ever-changing international situation it is probably superfluous to say that the diplomatic negotiations for such a treaty required careful political consideration. In this sense, it must be said that the Treaty of Peace and the Japan-United States Security Treaty, which is indivisibly related to it, possess an extremely high political content.

IV. We also believe that under the Constitution of Japan in respect to the limits on the judicial power that arise out of its own essential nature we must admit the concept of the so-called act of government. In regard to the limits that must be recognized in the concept of acts of government, at the very least because of the recognition of the concept itself, although there may be various types of problems, we must consider that such matters as the Japan-United States Security Treaty fall under this heading. Of course, it is natural if the government concludes such treaties and the National Diet gives its consent to them, that they may have the obligation under domestic law to review and judge the constitutionality of such matters on their own responsibility. In respect to such acts of state, the courts as a matter of principle must accept the decision of the governmental group; to put it in other words, we must arrive at the conclusion that such issues as the unconstitutionality of treaties of this kind lie outside the right of review of the courts. Thus, as in the present case, the validity of the Security Treaty cannot require a decision as the object of direct legal proceedings, and in respect to a decision on the validity of Article 2 of the Special Criminal Law, which is the applicable legal provision in the present case, even though there may be a case in which it is the basic premise, it equally lies outside the review of the courts for the same reason. As a result, there is nothing for a court to do save to recommend a hearing on the premise that the above treaty is constitutional and valid.

(We do not state that the Security Treaty lies outside the right of review of the courts simply because it is a treaty. We support neither the view that treaties are not the object of constitutional review because they stand alongside the Constitution or even because they may be the highest law of the land, supreme even over the Constitution, nor the view that because treaties all possess an international character they are not subject to the power of review of a single country. We believe that treaties also, as far as their validity in domestic law is concerned, are as a matter of principle subject to the review of the courts. But we also believe that treaties relating to so-called acts of government, such as the Security Treaty in the present case, which have the highest political content, lie outside both the power of review of the courts and the force of domestic law because they are acts of government.)

Furthermore, there is a final problem that must be considered. Even though acts of government lie outside the right of review of the courts as described above, whether actions that become problems fall in the category of acts of government must be decided, of course, by the courts. In addition, even in cases in which such actions are considered to fall in the category of acts of government, if they are nonexistent in actual substance or if, again, they are in clear violation of the provisions of the Constitution—

except for such cases in which the unconstitutionality is clearly obvious (this may be a situation that cannot be considered even a possibility)—the courts can declare such nonexistence or unconstitutionality. Even in such cases, there is no logical reason why the actions should be excluded from the review of the courts. We understand that while the majority opinion treated the Security Treaty in the present case as something which, as a matter of principle, does not involve the right of review of the courts, the fact that it held in the sense pointed out above that there was no unconstitutionality in the treaty was based on this thinking.

V. However, the original judgment, as set forth above, went beyond the limits of the right of review of the courts, went into the provisions of the Security Treaty in the present case, and held it unconstitutional; and further, it concluded that the stationing of American forces on the basis of the said treaty was unconstitutional and on that premise held also that Article 2 of the Special Criminal Law was invalid. The above was done on the basis of an erroneous interpretation regarding the limits of the right of review by the courts of acts of government and on this point the original judgment cannot escape being quashed.

(In regard to the approval of the Administrative Agreement: The fact that the "Administrative Agreement based on Article 3 of the Japan-United States Security Treaty" has the character of a treaty and requires the approval of the National Diet in accordance with the provisions of Article 73, paragraph 3, of the Constitution goes without saying. We believe that the Constitution actually requires that such approval be given in the National Diet after thorough discussion of the content of such an agreement either before or after the fact. <In the Senate of the United States at the time that the Security Treaty in the present case was approved consent was given after discussion of the content of the Administrative Agreement. This may be taken as a model.> However, in respect to the approval of this Administrative Agreement, the government declared that because the Security Treaty, which provides the basis for the Administrative Agreement, had already received the consent of the National Diet, there was no necessity to obtain separately the approval of the Administrative Agreement. As the majority opinion states, the National Diet in both the House of Councillors and the House of Representatives defeated resolutions which held that the Administrative Agreement had to receive the approval of the National Diet. What is particularly at issue in this case is a law relating to the areas and installations involved in the retention of the armed forces of the United States of America; but it cannot be said that the interpretation that holds, only in respect to this point, that the Administrative Agreement was comprehensively approved by the National Diet's approval of Article 3 of the Security Treaty, is necessarily improper. We consider that in respect to acts of the National Diet, such as Diet approval, the acceptance of the viewpoint of the government and the National Diet by the courts, as set forth above, is the rationale out of which flows the essence of the separation of powers.)

For the above reasons we are in accord with the majority opinion.

* * *

The supplementary opinion of Justice Tarumi Katsumi follows.

I. The points in dispute and the structure of the reasons for the present judgment.

The essence of the original judgment is as follows: The fact that our country has permitted the retention of American forces in accordance with the Japan-United States Security Treaty (its aspects dealing with matters of domestic law) means [that it has permitted] the maintenance of war potential, which is prohibited by Article 9, paragraph 2, of the Constitution. Therefore, the American forces cannot be permitted under the above provisions of the Constitution. This is nothing more than saying that the Constitution itself does not permit their existence. The above is the strongest and indeed only effective basis for holding that there is no reasonable cause for providing legal benefits relating to peace and tranquillity in the areas and installations of the American forces that afford them greater protection than that enjoyed by the people at large under the same kind of benefits. Namely, because Article 2 of the Special Criminal Law, for the purpose of protecting the American forces, provides for a heavier penalty than in the usual cases provided for in Article 1 (32) of the Minor Offenses Law, it gives special protection to the American forces without good cause and is invalid and in contravention of Article

31 of the Constitution, the gist of which is that "no person can suffer a criminal penalty except according to proper (Note by Justice Tarumi: Heed this word.) procedure." The facts of the conduct of the accused as set forth in the indictment are established by evidence, but there is no room for the application to them of the unconstitutional and invalid Article 2 of the Special Criminal Law. Their conduct does not constitute a crime, as a cause of action as set forth in the indictment.

Regarding this argument, the appeal brief holds:

Because there are a number of good reasons why Article 2 of the aforesaid Special Criminal Law must preserve broader than ordinary legal benefits relating to peace and tranquillity within the areas and installations of American forces, it is not in contravention of Article 31 of the Constitution (point 1). The Japan-United States Security Treaty which permits the retention of American forces is also not in contravention of Article 9, paragraph 2 (point 2). Moreover, the decision as to constitutionality, regarding the treaty properly speaking (its parts relating to domestic law) or regarding the actions of the government in respect to its conclusion or the actions of the Houses of the National Diet in approving it, is a matter that, under the Constitution, lies outside the limits of the right of constitutional review of the courts. The judgment of the original decision that the said treaty and the stationing of the American forces based on it are unconstitutional is improper because it errs in an interpretation of the Constitution and goes beyond the limits of the judicial power (point 3).

Thus, the principal problem to be adjudicated in the present case is whether Article 2 of the Special Criminal Law can be declared in contravention of Article 31 of the Constitution for the reasons set forth in the original decision.

First of all, what is the intent of Article 31 of the Constitution which is a major premise in this case? I believe that there are two opinions in our country on this question. The first is in general as follows: The intent of the said article is that no person shall suffer the imposition of any criminal penalty or disadvantageous trial, disposition, or action resembling criminal penalty, in criminal or civil matters or administrative affairs, except according to procedures established by law (procedural law) passed by the National Diet. Moreover, substantive law (criminal law, and the like) as the criterion for justice to which the courts must conform in the procedure for handing down criminal penalties cannot be clearly unreasonable or unjust, namely, cannot infringe upon the basic spirit of the Constitution—the respect for man, human rights, and the respect for freedom. In this sense, a provision for criminal punishment that is clearly unreasonable can violate Article 31 even though it does not directly infringe upon any other provisions of the Constitution. (The original judgment can be interpreted as following this opinion.)

The second opinion holds: Article 31 states only that criminal penalties and, in addition, disadvantageous actions which resemble them cannot be inflicted except according to procedural law passed by the National Diet; and it does not intend that substantive law (provisions concerning criminal penalties, and the like) need necessarily be clearly unreasonable and unjust in the meaning of the first opinion.

If the present decision held to the second opinion, it would be sufficient only if the following were stated and that would be the end of the matter: Article 31 of the Constitution does not include the meaning that provisions concerning criminal penalties in substantive law must not be clearly lacking in reasonable grounds. The original judgment held that Article 2 of the Special Criminal Law is lacking in reasonable grounds and for that reason the said article is held to be in contravention of Article 31 and invalid; this judgment is erroneous in its interpretation of Article 31, without any reference to legal reasons touching on its lack of reasonable grounds.

However, the present judgment does not set forth such an idea. But it can also be interpreted not to hold according to the doctrine of reasonable procedure put forth in the first opinion above. If we follow the second opinion, then we may go so far as to decide that the judgment is unnecessary in procedural law, nay, rather, one which should not be made (the courts must make their judgments in accordance with the law) and, from that point of view, it may be that there is room for an interpretation on the basis of the first opinion. However, according to my interpretation, it is premature to say that the present decision was made tacitly on the basis of the first opinion.

According to my interpretation, the present decision arrives at what is essentially the following conclusion: Treaties that possess a high political content with an extremely important relationship to the peace and security of our country, even to the very basis of its existence, differ from ordinary treaties. Their character is such that, as a matter of principle, it is not appropriate that the legal judgment of their possible unconstitutionality be made by review of the judicial courts, which have as their appointed task a purely judicial function. They fall outside the scope of the courts' right of judicial review (set forth in Article 81 of the Constitution) except when it is clearly obvious that they are unconstitutional and invalid. They must be handled primarily in accordance with the judgment of the cabinet, which possesses the right to conclude such treaties, and of the National Diet, which possesses the right of approval.

The Japan-United States Security Treaty, which is the basis for the retention of American forces—including the Air Force, which on July 8, 1957 [when the alleged crimes took place] was utilizing the land at Tachikawa Air Base in the town of Sunakawa—and the Administrative Agreement, based on Article 3 of the above treaty, must be interpreted to be treaties of high political content as described above; consequently, the judgment of the possible unconstitutionality of their content does not fall within the scope of the courts' right of review. (However, even in regard to such treaties, the courts possess the right of constitutional review in cases in which unconstitutionality and invalidity are clearly and obviously recognized, but the above treaty and Administrative Agreement absolutely cannot be recognized as being clearly and obviously in contravention of Article 9, paragraph 2, of the Constitution.)

The original judgment, in holding that the retention of American forces as provided for in the said treaty is in contravention of Article 9, paragraph 2, of the Constitution and impermissible, went beyond the scope of the right of review of the courts and erred in its interpretation of the said article and the Preamble of the Constitution; consequently, its holding that Article 2 of the Special Criminal Law in the present case is unconstitutional on the above premise is also improper. (Moreover, the above Administrative Agreement, viewed in relation to Article 2 of the said law, sets forth the conditions regulating the disposition of American forces on the basis of the above treaty and has some of the same characteristics as the above Japan-United States Security Treaty; but whether or not it is unconstitutional and invalid because it lacks the consent of the National Diet lies outside the right of review of the courts for the same reasons.)

According to the present decision, the judgment of the court of first instance, which held the above Security Treaty to be in contravention of Article 9, paragraph 2, of the Constitution for the reason that Article 2 of the Special Criminal Law violates Article 31 of the Constitution, both goes beyond the scope of the judicial power and is impermissible under the Constitution and in procedural law.

For that reason it must be said concerning the original decision, based on a judgment without competency, which held that Article 2 of the Special Criminal Law was lacking in reasonable grounds:

(*a*) from the standpoint of the first opinion set forth above: When it holds on the basis of a judgment without competency that Article 2 of the above special law is in contravention of Article 31 of the Constitution and is both illegal and unconstitutional (erring in its interpretation of the right of constitutional review set forth in Article 81 of the Constitution and erring in its method of interpretation of Article 2 of the Special Criminal Law), it does not necessarily follow that there must be a consideration of whether the interpretation of Article 9, paragraph 2, of the Constitution is substantially correct, and in respect to this last point, even though this be an appeal trial it cannot be reviewed.

(*b*) from the standpoint of the second opinion above: It cannot be stated that Article 2 of the special law contravenes Article 31 of the Constitution because it is without reasonable grounds, and therefore the conclusion of the original judgment that Article 2 of the said special law is in contravention of Article 31 of the Constitution because it is without reasonable grounds is one that may be beyond the competency of the courts. It is wrong in its interpretation of Article 31 of the Constitution and it is not necessary to enter into the question of its nature. Thus, for this reason alone the original judgment can be quashed.

The present decision does not make clear whether it holds the position of the first or second opinion, but no matter what the position, there is agreement that the original judgment cannot declare Article 2 of the above special law in contravention of Article 31 of the Constitution for the reasons that it set forth. It must be accepted that there is no opinion opposed to this conclusive reason.

The present judgment, while declaring that the courts do not possess the right of constitutional review in regard to the Japan-United States Security Treaty, did make a decision regarding whether or not it conformed with Article 9, paragraph 2, of the Constitution. For that purpose, it argued from the point that our country possesses the inherent right of self-defense and made clear the meaning of the above constitutional provision. It is clear that it made a substantial constitutional judgment to the effect that the Japan-United States Security Treaty, the conclusion of which was selected as the means for authorizing self-defense for the objective of peace by depending on foreign armed forces over which our country, as a party, could not wield the power of command and control, and the permission to station American forces in our country were not, at least, "clearly and obviously" in contravention of the above constitutional provision. Of course this judgment can be construed as having been an examination of whether the courts have the right of constitutional review even in respect to treaties of this character [not the question of the meaning of Article 9].

The verdict in this case indicates as a matter of precaution that even in regard to whether the Administrative Agreement, which is the basis of the Special Criminal Law, is unconstitutional and invalid because it did not formally receive the consent of the National Diet, the courts do not possess the right of constitutional review. Even though this may be a side issue, under our procedural law it will probably become a norm binding on the court after the case has been sent back.

II. The Right of Constitutional Review of the Courts.

The courts possess the power to determine the constitutionality of all laws, orders, regulations, and acts—including all treaties—as matters of domestic law (Article 81 of the Constitution). This is the principle. However, as a reflection of the concept of the separation of powers in our Constitution and of the character, the manner of utilization, and the effectiveness of the judicial power, certain acts of both Houses of the National Diet and of the government [cabinet] are regarded as not being appropriately subject to a determination of constitutionality by the courts, and because of this are excluded from the right of review of the courts. I am not completely familiar with what are termed "acts of government," or "acts of high authority not subject to review of the courts," or "political questions" in American and European constitutions, but in our country although it may be difficult to define the concept of "acts of government" or to list them exhaustively, there is the academic theory that there are some acts in both the National Diet and the government that should not be subjected to the right of constitutional review by the courts. The appeal brief in its third point clearly makes this assertion.

The present decision examined this point and held in respect to the Japan-United States Security Treaty as domestic law (and also the Administrative Agreement which is based on Article 3 of the said treaty) that it possesses a great importance for the security and peace of our country and for the very foundation of its existence, and that it is not appropriately subject to the courts' right of constitutional review. For this reason the fact that the review of the constitutionality of both treaties lies outside the scope of the authority of the courts, as set forth in Article 81 of the Constitution, reveals one limitation on the judicial power; it shows also that in law too, there are certain exceptions that are not subject to constitutional review by the courts. (In this decision what are generally called treaties are those that are publicly proclaimed to possess, either through their text or their intent, force as domestic law. Accordingly, these can be treated, as a matter of principle, as invalid when they are in contravention of the Constitution, just as in the case of general domestic law.) The courts cannot deny the validity in international law of these two treaties, but because, as has already been pointed out, the act of the government in concluding these two treaties and the act of consent of the National Diet are matters that lie beyond the scope of the judicial right of constitutional review, it follows that the right of constitutional review of those parts of the treaties dealing with domestic law that have arisen out of the said treaties also lies beyond the competence of the courts. I believe that the determination of the limits of the courts' right of constitutional review also lies within the authority of the courts.

However, in respect to the holding of the original verdict that "because the Japan-United States Security Treaty and the retention of American forces based on it violate Article 9, paragraph 2, of the Constitution, Article 2 of the Special Criminal Law violates Article 31 of the Constitution," the present judgment declares: that it is impermissible for the trial of first instance to have held that Article 2 of the said special law is in contravention of Article 31 of the Constitution on the basis of its decision—for which there is no authority—that the said treaty is unconstitutional; that treaties of a high political content, as pointed out above, are different from general treaties and general laws; that the judgment of the unconstitutionality of the content of such treaties lies outside the scope of the right of review of the courts, except in cases in which unconstitutionality and invalidity are clearly obvious; that such treaties must be left to the decision of the cabinet and the National Diet; that this is a case in which, as an exception, the courts also do not possess the right of constitutional review in respect to content as domestic law; that the above Security Treaty and the content of the Administrative Agreement are in agreement with the intent of Article 9, Article 98, paragraph 2, and the Preamble of the Constitution; and that it cannot be accepted that they are in violation of the said provisions and that their unconstitutionality and invalidity are clearly obvious.

In my opinion there is sufficient reason to hold that, if the high political content of these treaties, as pointed out above, is understood, then the provisions of the treaties must be respected and applied. This may be understood even without going into the problem of whether they conflict with Article 9, paragraph 2, of the Constitution, because in such situations the courts do not possess the right of constitutional review. Because logically only by an examination of the content of treaties can a judgment be produced that they are "unconstitutional and invalid" or that "the fact that they are unconstitutional and invalid is clearly obvious," the present decision seems to admit a substantive review for the purpose of a formal review (the review of the authority of the courts) of whether there is a substantive right of review of constitutionality. Even though the decision may be regarded as having been unnecessary in this case, it is justifiable.

(I believe that even in respect to laws with a highly political content, as is pointed out, it is worth going into such questions as: The courts must make a substantive review of constitutionality, but do they possess the authority to do so in cases such as this? Or, are not the courts, in these situations, restricted so that they do not have the authority to deny the applicability of laws having a highly political content or to hold them invalid for the reason of unconstitutionality, even when they may so consider them? Or, is the right of constitutional review of this nature?)

III. Article 2 of the Special Criminal Law and Article 31 of the Constitution.

It cannot be said that Article 2 of the Special Criminal Law is in contravention of Article 31 of the Constitution for the reasons set forth in the original judgment. The reason for that is the principal reason for this decision under procedural law. Even though the Court made the decision from the standpoint of the first opinion described above (the appropriate procedural opinion), I believe that there is no necessity to point out in this case, in the reasons for the decision, each individual reasonable ground contained in Article 2 of the special law. It is a task of the utmost difficulty to point out all the reasonable grounds regarding a single provision among the thousands of laws related to all the provisions of the Constitution and all other laws. The meaning of such a number of individual laws and of the whole corpus of law constituting their totality is something rich in implication and fluid in nature.

Now I would like to touch on one or two reasons that must be admitted in regard to Article 2 of the Special Criminal Law. First, criminal conduct in violation of the said law cannot occur unless it originates from the actual conditions arising from the use by American forces of areas or specially designated installations that have been permitted and are concretely established in Japan, or the vicinity thereof, on the basis of the Japan-United States Security Treaty and Article 3 of the Administrative Agreement. However, the retention of American forces in our country and their use of specified installations or areas are based on the above two treaties. At the same time, because the unconstitutionality of these treaties under our own Constitution cannot be held effective against the United States under international law, it is not without reason, regardless of the constitutionality or unconstitutionality of these treaties, that the peace and tranquillity of the installations and areas used by the American forces be given somewhat more protection than that afforded public and private, foreign and domestic installations and areas under Article 1 (32) of the Minor Offenses Law. (It is not that such protection is obligatory, but that it is permissible. This is a question of legislative policy.)

Second, in regard to the installations and areas to be protected under Article 2 of the Special Criminal Law: they are (a) based on treaty, (b) set up for the single important purpose of protecting the peace and security of our country, (c) foreign, and (d) used by armed forces. Because of these points they have an absolutely unique existence, differing from general foreign and domestic, public and private installations and areas in our country. Armed forces when emergency situations arise must carry out broad-scale organized activities, rapidly and at their discretion, free to the greatest extent possible from the interference of others. For this reason, even in peacetime, on the occasion of maneuvers or movements or other activities it is proper that the freedom of utilization of areas and installations by the armed forces and those attached to them (the freedom of use in the organized life of military personnel, civilian employees and their families) be guaranteed to a special degree. Unauthorized entry or bringing in of obstructions cannot be allowed. (Also there probably are occasions when military personnel in churches, homes, and movies in such areas must rush out on military business or assemble in open areas.) These matters too are related to the security of our country. There can also be dangerous objects in areas and installations utilized by armed forces and our police power does not fully extend over them.

Third, because they are military forces retained for the defense of our country, trouble should not arise out of mutual misunderstanding created by unauthorized entry into prohibited areas and installations used for defense, and there should be no bad effects on the friendly relations between the two countries. Consequently, or even as simple international courtesy, there are reasons why the American forces should be given the legal benefit of special protection. Article 92 of the Criminal Code provides criminal penalties for acts such as the damaging or removal of national flags or national symbols with the intent of insulting a foreign country; similar punishment is not provided for damage to our own national flag or national symbol (one can see similar examples in the legislation of foreign countries). Thus, in the same sense, legal protection in the form of legal benefits, as in the present case, can also be regarded as appropriate.

At any rate, even though we might assume that the Japan-United States Security Treaty and the Administrative Agreement are unconstitutional, our government has permitted the actual retention of American forces in the country, without rejecting the stationing of such forces for the reason of unconstitutionality, and thus American forces have good reason in international law—namely, the right—to remain. Viewing the problem thus, even if our government, making a distinction by simple agreement without any basis in treaty in favor of foreign armed forces retained here temporarily, passed legislation such as Article 2 of the Special Criminal Law, which would give them slightly greater protection, then could it not be said that this was reasonable and that such penal provisions were clearly not in violation of Article 31 of the Constitution?

* * *

The supplementary opinion of Justice Kawamura Daisuke follows.

I am in accord with the majority opinion, but since there may be a few matters that may be oversimplified in the reasons for the judgment concerning the Japan-United States Security Treaty, I shall set down a supplementary opinion concerning them.

I. In respect to the kind of arrangements that our country, which has renounced war and prohibited the maintenance of war potential under Article 9 of the Constitution, can make in order to maintain its security and existence, there is no special explicit statement in the Constitution; but to take appropriate measures of self-defense in order to maintain its own peace and security and to guarantee its survival is an inherent function of our country and is in accord with the spirit and the intent of the Constitution. This is stated in the majority opinion.

II. However, because the law does not predetermine a fundamental national policy to be followed in order to achieve the highest national objective of maintaining the peace and security of our country and guaranteeing its national survival, it is reasonable to interpret the matter as one that can be left to a discretionary decision of the political groups and will be based on suitable deliberation. That is to say, it can be surmised that in order to achieve the aforesaid national objective, the selection of national policy—that is, whether a security treaty should be concluded with another country or whether permanent neutrality should be established—can be determined by a discretionary decision that is reasonable and in accord with the achievement of national objectives. In respect to political decisions regarding such national policies, there exists no objective criterion to be used to determine if one policy is the absolute truth or if another policy contains no truth. Moreover, as can be seen in political practice, political value judgments in respect to the national policy in most cases possess a pluralistic character. Because this necessarily involves a conflict of values, it is proper to regard selection as something which, as a matter of principle, should be left to the discretionary or political decision of the political groups. Thus, it must be said that even though the question of correctness may arise in such decisions, the question of illegality does not necessarily follow.

However, in respect to the discretionary decision of the political groups concerning the type of treaty to be entered into, it is also reasonable to say that the treaty must be suitable for the achievement of the national objectives mentioned above and based on the standards of pacifism and international cooperation which are the fundamental principles of our Constitution. Therefore, the following interpretation is proper: the discretionary power of the political groups is to be respected, but there are specific limitations on that discretionary power; if measures are taken that are clearly in violation of the pacifism, the international cooperation, or any other provision of the Constitution through the transcending of those limits or the abuse of the discretionary power—as for example, a case in which there is a clear violation such as the approval of the stationing of armed forces for offensive purposes—then such measures become the object of a judgment of unconstitutionality in the courts.

III. Viewing the Security Treaty, which has become the basis for the retention of United States armed forces, from the above standpoint, the said treaty was concluded as a temporary measure until such time as adequate security measures would be established by the United Nations (paragraph 4 of the Preamble and Article 4). The following appears in the Preamble:

The Treaty of Peace recognizes that Japan as a sovereign nation has the right to enter into collective security arrangements, and, further, the Charter of the United Nations recognizes that all nations possess an inherent right of individual and collective self-defense.

In exercise of these rights, Japan desires, as a provisional arrangement for its defense, that the United States of America should maintain armed forces of its own in and about Japan so as to deter armed attack upon Japan.

The United States of America, in the interest of peace and security, is presently willing to maintain certain of its armed forces in and about Japan. . . .

Thus, it is declared that arrangements are entered into concerning the retention of armed forces for the defense of Japan and for the peace and security of the United States.

IV. In addition, in Article 1 of the said treaty it is stipulated, concerning objectives of the retention of United States forces, that they "may be utilized to contribute to the maintenance of the international peace and security in the Far East and to the security of Japan against armed attack from without, including assistance given at the express request of the Japanese Government to put down large-scale internal riots and disturbances in Japan, caused through instigation or intervention by an outside Power or Powers." The statement in the above objective, "to contribute to the maintenance of the international peace and security in the Far East," has given rise to the argument of unconstitutionality that holds that there is the danger that it might lead to involvement in a war not directly related to the defense of our country. However, whether such danger exists cannot be determined only by the content of the treaty; rather, this is a question that is governed by an appraisal and understanding of the situation in the Far East and the world. From another point of view, the peace of the Far East is intimately related to the maintenance of the peace and security of our country, and the retention of American forces in our country for the above purpose is something that would prevent aggression in the Far East before it occurs and would thus maintain peace and security there and thereby protect the peace and security of our country. Not only that, but there is no ground at all for holding that the appraisal and understanding of the political elements who are admitted to have concluded a treaty based on that view are illegal because they clearly erred in their understanding of the situation, as compared with the opposing view given above.

Also there is the opinion that the retention of American forces rings the countries of the Communist bloc with quasi-enemy nations and is in contravention of the spirit of pacifism and international cooperation of our Constitution. Naturally, speaking from the standpoint of the intent of our Constitution, there is no doubt but that it would be desirable to rely on the assistance of a United Nations force which would "include those peoples possibly opposed to us." Because it is clear that such a means of guaranteeing security is impossible under the present state of the United Nations, there exists no clear basis for a decision that there is another method—one that does not recognize the stationing of any foreign troops as compared with the one recognizing the retention of American forces under the Security Treaty—that would be the unique one for maintaining the existence of our country in true accord with pacifism and international cooperation.

In essence, the Security Treaty, as it expressly shows, was concluded to maintain our country's peace and security and to assure its existence. Also in respect to its content, no clear reason for unconstitutionality or illegality can be discerned in the discretionary decision of the political branch.

V. Next, because it has been thought that a problem of the violation of Article 98, paragraph 2, of the Constitution will be created under the principle of the supremacy of the Charter of the United Nations (Article 103 of the Charter) in the event of a conflict between the Charter and the Security Treaty, I would like to touch briefly on the relationship between the two.

According to the Security Treaty and the Treaty of Peace with Japan, both concluded on the same day, the Japanese nation assumed obligations based on the United Nations Charter (Article 5 $<a>$), and it is stipulated in Article 5 (c) that: "The Allied Powers for their part recognize that Japan as a sovereign nation possesses the inherent right of individual or collective self-defense referred to in Article 51 of the Charter of the United Nations and that Japan may voluntarily enter into collective security arrangements." Thus the Security Treaty can be recognized as one concluded by the Japanese nation in accordance with its desire to have

American forces maintained as a provisional measure for self-defense (paragraphs 3 and 4 of the Preamble), using its right to conclude security arrangements as recognized in the above Treaty of Peace. Subsequently both Japan and the United States affirmed that the military activities of the American forces must be carried out completely within limits not in violation of the Charter of the United Nations (Joint Declaration of the Prime Minister and the President, June 21, 1957, and the exchange of communications between the Foreign Minister and the United States Ambassador concerning the relationship between the Japan-United States Security Treaty and the Charter of the United Nations, dated September 17, 1957); namely, the military activities of the American forces based on the Security Treaty were interpreted as being permissible only in situations resulting from recommendations or resolutions of the organs of the United Nations and in situations in which it was recognized that the "inherent right of individual or collective self-defense" of Article 51 of the Charter of the United Nations was being exercised. In other words, the Security Treaty deviates from neither the Charter of the United Nations nor the Treaty of Peace and, on the contrary, it is proper to interpret it as being placed under the restriction that military activities can be carried out only within the framework established by these basic treaties.

Thus, it cannot be admitted that the Security Treaty or the retention of American forces is in conflict with the Charter of the United Nations or that it is in contravention of Article 98, paragraph 2, of the Constitution.

*   *   *

The supplementary opinion of Justice Ishizaka Shuichi follows.

I endorse the majority opinion, but set down the following supplementary opinion.

I. Because the majority opinion contains points difficult for me to fully understand concerning the relation between the right of self-defense and the security treaty between Japan and the United States in the present case, I add a few interpretations.

It is inconceivable that there can be any dispute over the fact that our country possesses the right to defend itself in order to prevent imminent and unjust violence to the end that it maintain its peace, security and existence, eliminate despotism, slavery, and intolerance, and occupy an honorable place in the society of nations. There is probably no one who would submit to a nation or group that does not aspire to international peace based on justice and order. It is proper that our country be able to exercise the right of self-defense in situations in which it must unavoidably be used in the face of imminent and unlawful violence. If such exercise were prohibited, the right of self-defense would become devoid of content and would come to naught. Because our country can exercise the right of self-defense the conclusion is that it also can take appropriate and effective measures suitable for the purpose.

Article 9 of the Constitution forever renounces war as a right of the nation and the use or threat of force as means of settling international disputes, and it also stipulates that in order to achieve the above aim, war potential will not be maintained. That absolutely cannot be interpreted to mean the complete prohibition of the maintenance of the means of defense, namely, the means to exercise the right of self-defense as stated above.

In the final analysis, war as a sovereign right of a nation and the threat or use of force as means of settling international disputes— all intended to decide matters through victory or defeat—can enable a nation to gain supremacy over a rival or cause the latter to submit, and are thus designed to lead ultimately to international dispute for the unilateral benefit of the [aggressor] nation. Article 9 of the Constitution must be interpreted as prohibiting the maintenance of war potential for such an end. Those matters differ completely in legal import from the exercise of the right of self-defense and methods of defense for that purpose, as already described above; a rigid distinction must be maintained between the two and they must not be admixed.

Occasionally, there are those who, putting forth the names of things resembling primitive or crude weapons as means of self-defense, argue that only the use of such implements by those who make them is permissible, as the occasion may demand; but in the light of the times it cannot be considered that such a method be counted among the means of national self-defense. Nevertheless, the legal possibility for the nation to organize and equip beforehand effective and suitable means for the exercise of the right of self-defense must exist.

Yet, the violence mentioned above differs vastly in aspect according to time and place; it is most difficult to imagine beforehand what it would be like. Consequently, it is probably also difficult to imagine beforehand the form of effective and appropriate means of defense. In my opinion, such questions as "Should or should not the nation have in actual existence efficient and appropriate means of defense against such disturbances?" or "If it does possess them, what should their form and scale be?" can best be decided by considering foreign and domestic situations and the transitions they go through.

(Of course, such form and scale must observe the limits, which are not or should not be violated. Such defensive actions must be understood to be those that must be taken until the disputes arising from violence are settled in accordance with the Charter of the United Nations.) Such matters are not to be touched on by decisions of the courts, which by their very nature are not to become involved in political affairs. They are all to be decided under the political responsibility of the government and the National Diet and do not lie within the legal area of review of the courts. This follows naturally from the fact that our Constitution is based on the separation of powers.

As I have pointed out above, our country on the basis of the constitutional possibility of possessing the means for defense, can conclude treaties with foreign countries in order to guarantee our country's security in the event that it does not possess the means to do so or that those means are insufficient; the government can also decide to receive military assistance for that purpose. After the National Diet has given its consent, such treaties cannot be held unconstitutional. Although my opinion differs somewhat from the supplementary opinions of Justices Shima and Kawamura (Daisuke) in regard to items 2 to 4 and the point of departure as well, because I believe that we eventually come together, I cite them also.

From this point of view, the Security Treaty between Japan and the United States in the present case cannot be held to be in contravention of the Constitution. Consequently, the original judgment, which held that stationing of American forces in our country on the basis of that treaty is constitutionally impermissible, cannot support its point.

II. In respect to whether or not the Supreme Court possesses the right of constitutional review of treaties, it certainly cannot be perceived that the majority opinion has clarified this issue. If one starts from the point that the word "treaty" does not appear in Article 81 of the Constitution, which establishes the right of constitutional review, and ends with a conclusion that denies the right of constitutional review to the Supreme Court on this matter, he will probably fall into a considerable error.

For example, if a treaty is concluded that conflicts with the Constitution in respect to the fundamental human rights of the people or the basic organization of our country, that is something that the Supreme Court should not view unconcernedly.

I endorse the opinion of Justices Okuno and Takahashi that the right of constitutional review of treaties resides in the Supreme Court and that the Security Treaty is not unconstitutional, and I support the opinion of Justice Otani on this point to the extent that it is not in contradiction with the opinion of the above Justices.

III. I refer now to an argument in the appeal that was omitted in the explanation of the majority opinion.

I concur with the first point in the supplementary opinion of Justice Tanaka and with the third point in the supplementary opinion of Justice Tarumi, but I add a few views.

The original judgment while holding on the one hand that the retention of the armed forces of the United States of America in our country is constitutionally impermissible, pointed out on the other hand, "To the extent that the Security Treaty and the Administrative Agreement continue in existence, it is proper that our country assume its obligation under international law to permit the retention of United States forces, to contribute the bases necessary for them, and to maintain peace and tranquillity in those installations." At the very least, from the standpoint of the United States of America, it has the right, granted by our country, to station its forces; and from the standpoint of our country, that must be recognized as a right to be respected. In my opinion, this is based on the view that even if a treaty is invalid in domestic law, it does not immediately lose its validity in international law.

From this point of view, at present the armed forces of the United States of America have the consent of our country and, because they are retained in our country under international law, the problem of unconstitutionality in our country is not at issue. At the least, until the fact of the above retention is legally dissolved under international law, it cannot be thought that the enforcement of criminal legislation designed to maintain peace and tranquillity in the installations for those armed forces involves any danger of an infringement of the spirit of the Constitution. Moreover, this affair differs completely in its legal benefits [for United States forces] from the crime of intrusion on a habitation in the Criminal Code or a violation of the Minor Offenses Law. For this reason, the kind of criminal legislation to be enacted is a question of legislative policy that falls under the political responsibility of the government and the National Diet. Regarding Article 2 of the Special Criminal Law in which these organs of government, in accordance with their political discretion, enacted penal provisions lighter than those in Article 130 of the Criminal Code, but heavier than those of Article 1 (32) of the Minor Offenses Law, it is difficult to see how the original judgment came to regard it as providing for an especially heavy penalty without reasonable cause. (According to the court record the installation used by the American forces was surrounded by a barbed-wire barricade and the area included barracks, residences, ammunition dumps, and runways. It must also be noted that the trespass in the present case took place in an area in the immediate vicinity of the extreme end of one of the runways and at several spots where someone had destroyed the said barricade.)

At any rate, the conclusion of the original judgment that Article 2 of the Special Criminal Law was directly in contravention of Article 31 of the Constitution must be declared to be extremely hasty.

* * *

The opinion of Justice Otani Katsushige follows:

I. I have the same opinion as that expressed in the "Formal Judgment" of the majority opinion, but in the "Reasons" I am opposed to the part that argues [in paraphrase]: Because the Japan-United States Security Treaty in the present case is of a highly political nature and has an extremely important relationship to our country's existence, the right of constitutional review does not extend to this treaty, unless it is clearly and obviously unconstitutional and invalid.

The essence of my judgment in this case is that Article 9 of the Constitution does not deny the inherent right of self-defense possessed by our country as a sovereign nation; and also—treating as a separate issue the problem of whether or not paragraph 2 of the same article prohibits the maintenance of war potential for the purpose of the exercise of the above right of self-defense—at least to the extent that foreign forces retained in our country are not under our power of command and control and are not stationed for a purpose prohibited in paragraph 1 of Article 9, it must be interpreted that such foreign war potential is not included in that provision. Thus, the American armed forces in our country under the Japan-United States Security Treaty are not retained with the aim of aggression or anything else prohibited by the above Article 9 of the Constitution. The fact that they are retained to contribute to the maintenance of peace in the Far East and to the security of our country is clearly reflected by the preamble of the Security Treaty and Article 1 of its text, Articles 5 (c) and 6 (a) of the Treaty of Peace with Japan, and Articles 51 and 52 of the Charter of the United Nations; and it must also be stated that they are not related to the war potential prohibited by Article 9, paragraph 2, of the Constitution. Nevertheless, it is also clear that the provision of Article 2 of the Special Criminal Law, which is designed to protect the security of the above American forces and which goes with the Administrative Agreement based on Article 3 of the Security Treaty, is also in no way in contravention of Article 31 of the Constitution.

For those reasons my opinion is that the original judgment is in contravention of law because of the erroneous interpretation of Article 9 of the Constitution, which is the premise of the said judgment; the appeal of the public prosecutor is well grounded; and the original judgment must be returned as the result of being quashed.

II. There are points on which I oppose the majority opinion; I record below the reasons why my opinion is opposed to that of the majority in respect to "treaties and the right of constitutional review."

Article 76, paragraph 3, of the Constitution says, "All judges

. . . shall be bound only by this Constitution and the laws" and Article 81 stipulates that the courts have "the power to determine the constitutionality of any law, order, regulation or official act," that is to say, the so-called right of constitutional review. Accordingly, do they possess the right of constitutional review of treaties? Initially, it is necessary to bear in mind two or three matters prerequisite to this problem.

The first of these is that treaties are contracts in international law between nation and nation, and, roughly speaking, they perhaps can be divided into two groups: those that possess binding force only on the nation, namely, are valid only in international law; and those that also have binding force on the people of a nation, namely, are valid in domestic law as well. Thus, legal disputes arising among nations concerning the interpretation of treaties or their international legal validity fall under the jurisdiction of the International Court of Justice (see Article 36, and so forth, of Regulations of the International Court of Justice, Treaty No. 2 of 1954). However, I believe that even the international law aspects of the validity of treaties in cases in which certain legal disputes arise over such aspects become the object of constitutional review by our courts.

Next, in respect to treaties possessing validity in domestic law, there are those that in themselves directly provide in whole or in part for [the achievement of] their purposes, and there are those in which the realization of their purposes is by means of the enactment of domestic laws. Thus, domestic laws in this situation naturally may be classified as "laws" in Articles 76, paragraph 3, and 81 of the Constitution and, accordingly, it goes without saying that they become the object of the right of constitutional review. It also must be stated that both treaties that are effectuated in themselves and those that are effectuated by domestic law are equally valid. After all, the reason for this is that the binding force of both on the people, that is, their legal validity, is completely identical—without the slightest difference.

The second prerequisite matter is the stipulation of Article 98 of the Constitution, which was as follows in Article 93 of the draft of the Constitution, "This Constitution and the laws and treaties made in pursuance hereof shall be the supreme law of the state and no public law or ordinance and no imperial rescript or other act of government, or part thereof, contrary to the provisions hereof, shall have legal force or validity." [5] The above principle was a suggestion of the headquarters of the army of occupation and was accepted by the government and presented to the committee on the revision of the Constitution; this is now common knowledge. It can be perceived that the above principle had the same intent as Article 6, paragraph 2, of the Constitution of the United States of America, which reads: "This Constitution, and the laws of the United States which shall be made in pursuance thereof, and all treaties made, or which shall be made, under the authority of the United States, shall be the supreme law of the land; and the judges in every State shall be bound thereby, anything in the Constitution or laws of any State to the contrary notwithstanding."

However, in a country like the United States in which there are a federal constitution and laws and treaties above the constitutions and laws of the respective states, the federal constitution and the laws and treaties enacted on the basis of it must be treated as the highest law in respect to the states; and it is appropriate that it be stipulated that the constitutions and laws of the states, which may be in violation of them in whole or in part, be treated as without validity, within those limits. But in a unified country such as ours it can be said as in the above draft that both laws and treaties really *are based on the Constitution.* There is no necessity to stipulate that these three things (Constitution, laws, and treaties) are to be regarded as the highest laws. (That is to say, leaving aside treaties for the moment, it is generally known that the Constitution is the highest law, that laws are enacted within the scope of the Constitution, and orders within the scope of law. When laws in conflict with the Constitution were passed, they were treated as not coming under the right of judicial review under the old Constitution; this continued during the fifty years of that Constitution.[6])

5. The draft of the proposed revision of the Constitution referred to here, from which this quotation is taken, may be found in *Political Reorientation of Japan: September 1945 to September 1948. Report of Government Section. Supreme Commander for the Allied Powers.* Appendix C: 9b, pp. 631–36.

6. What Justice Otani means here is not that unconstitutional laws were passed under the old Constitution, but that under that Constitution the courts did not have the power to review laws that might conflict with the Constitution.

The phrase "this Constitution . . . and the treaties made in pursuance hereof," was regarded as undesirable because it seemed to anticipate that unconstitutional treaties might be concluded, and so when the House of Representatives enacted the new Constitution the aforesaid draft was amended. Finally, as in the present Article 98, the early draft was split into two paragraphs and the first paragraph declared only that the Constitution is the supreme law of the nation and that no law, ordinance, imperial rescript, or other act of government, in whole or in part, contrary to the Constitution, is valid. Not only was the above reasonable, but the spirit so established emphasizes the supremacy of the Constitution and makes even stronger the obligation to uphold the Constitution in the succeeding Article 99 (see Article 76 of the old Constitution on this point [which provided for the continuation in force of existing legal enactments "as far as they do not conflict with the present Constitution" and did not provide for a duty to uphold the Constitution]).

Next, in paragraph 2 of Article 98 it is provided that treaties and established international laws shall be faithfully observed, but this explicit stipulation (there was none in the old Constitution) also must be interpreted to be a pledge to the world to respect such instruments in the future in view of the world criticism of our country for the violation of the Antiwar Pact [Pact of Paris], the Nine-Power Pact, and international law. Of course, this placing of treaties and laws in separate paragraphs must not be interpreted as providing that treaties in conflict with the Constitution, the fundamental law of the country, be recognized or that there is an obligation to uphold them. In brief, treaties—in exactly the same way as domestic law—after being concluded by the cabinet and approved by the National Diet, are then publicly proclaimed, and their binding force on the people arises from this public proclamation.

The third of the premises deals with the problem of priority of applicability in the event of a conflict between law and treaty. I believe that as a conclusion it is proper to interpret treaties as having priority. Moreover, because when treaties are concluded it is done with a knowledge of existing domestic law, the interpretation must be that in respect to the relationship between prior law and subsequent law, treaties which are subsequent law are to be regarded as having priority. Also, because when there is an amendment in domestic law subsequent to the conclusion of a treaty the domestic law can be enacted without reference to the wishes of the other party to the treaty, that treaties must have priority in such situations is, it is clear, a reflection of the principle of faithfulness [to the treaties].

III. I now enter into the principal argument of my opinion regarding the constitutional review of treaties.

Because in neither Article 76, paragraph 3, nor Article 81 of the Constitution does the word "treaty" appear, there is the view that there is no right of constitutional review of treaties. However, as explained above, there is absolutely no difference between treaties and laws in reference to the fact that their binding force on the nation and its people is produced by public proclamation and, as a result, it is proper that even though the word "treaty" does not appear in the above Article 76, paragraph 3, and Article 81 of the Constitution, it is naturally included in the word "laws," which appears in both those articles. (In regard to this matter, in Article 94 the word "regulations" appears but not in Article 81, and there is not the slightest doubt that regulations are the object of constitutional review.) In other words, it must be stated that treaties, at the same time that they have binding force on judges under Article 76, paragraph 3, in the same manner as domestic laws after promulgation, also become the object of the right of constitutional review in Article 81.

(There is the view that holds that Article 81 does not directly bestow the right of constitutional review but that such review is a natural and inherent function residing in the very nature of the courts, which are bound by the Constitution and the laws. According to this view, Article 81 is to be regarded as doing nothing more than to stipulate that the Supreme Court is the court of last resort in respect to the right of constitutional review.) Because our present courts are not constitutional but judicial courts, the force of a judgment of unconstitutionality must be construed as [arising from] a declaration that, properly speaking, in respect to the dispute concerned the applicability of the law or treaty, in whole or in part, be set aside or denied as unconstitutional; it must not be construed as a declaration that the treaty or law itself is invalid because it is unconstitutional. Thus, the scope of the power to make such decisions is limited to that which is included in the formal judgment, to the case itself, and to those involved in it. It does not possess what is termed general force. This must also be interpreted to mean that the cabinet and the National Diet have the political obligation to respect the decision of unconstitutionality by the courts and to take appropriate measures in accordance with the intent of the decision. If the power of constitutional review did not extend to treaties, then it would be possible to achieve by treaty constitutional revision or something with a similar aim without recourse to the procedure for constitutional revision which requires the direct approval of the people as provided for in Article 96 of the Constitution. Theoretically, to go that far could lead to an attack on the structure of the separation of powers or even to an alteration of those provisions pertaining to the guarantee of fundamental human rights. Would our Constitution really recognize this kind of a conclusion?

The latter part of the second reason of the majority decision reads as follows:

Moreover, the Security Treaty in the present case must be regarded as having a highly political nature which, as was pointed out above, possesses an extremely important relation to the basis of the existence of our country as a sovereign nation. There are not a few points in which a legal decision as to the unconstitutionality of its content is simply the other side of the coin of the political or discretionary decision of the cabinet, which concluded the treaty, or of the National Diet, which gave its consent to it. Consequently, the legal decision as to unconstitutionality has *a character which, as a matter of principle, is not adaptable to review by a judicial court, which has as its mission a purely judicial function; accordingly, it falls outside the right of judicial review by the courts, unless there is clearly obvious unconstitutionality or invalidity.* It is proper to interpret this primarily as a matter that must be entrusted to the decision of the cabinet, which possesses the power to conclude treaties, and of the National Diet, which has the power to approve them; and it ultimately must be left to the political review of the sovereign people.

Again, at the beginning of the third reason the opinion opens as follows:

To continue, in examining what the stipulations of the Security Treaty and of the Administrative Agreement based on its Article 3 signify in regard to the retention of the armed forces of the United States of America . . .

and after having handed down a constitutional judgment concerning the Security Treaty, it states in the middle part of the third reason,

If so, then such retention of United States armed forces must certainly be *in accord with the intent of Article 9, Article 98, paragraph 2, and the Preamble of the Constitution,* and it absolutely cannot be admitted that it is in violation of the said provisions or that *it is clearly obvious that it is unconstitutional and invalid.*

In the last part of the third reason it further holds:

Hence, the original judgment in finding that the retention of the armed forces of the United States of America is impermissible and in contravention of the first part of Article 9, paragraph 2, of the Constitution *has departed from the proper sphere of the power of judicial review of the courts* and has erred in its interpretation of the said provisions and of the Preamble of the Constitution. Accordingly, its holding that Article 2 of the Special Criminal Law, which is the premise of the present case, is unconstitutional and invalid is also improper . . . (the above italics are mine).

Summarizing the majority decision, it amounts to the following: that the Security Treaty possesses a highly political nature of great importance to the very existence of our country; that a decision as to the unconstitutionality of such a treaty, as a matter of principle, does not involve a decision of the judicial courts; and that, accordingly, the constitutional review of such a treaty, unless it is recognized as being "clearly and obviously unconstitutional or invalid," lies outside the scope of constitutional review of the courts.

The majority opinion, while holding as above, then hands down an interpretation concerning the essential nature of the Security Treaty and of the foreign armed forces in Japan on the basis of that treaty and then, after adding a fairly detailed constitutional interpretation, ends with the conclusion, ". . . such retention of United States armed forces must certainly be in accord with the intent of Article 9, Article 98, paragraph 2, and the Preamble of the Constitution, and it absolutely cannot be admitted that it is in violation of the said provisions or that it is clearly obvious that it is unconstitutional and invalid." Accordingly, it decides that the original judgment, which held that the retention of American armed forces based on the Security Treaty is in contravention of Article 9, paragraph 2, of the Constitution, is invalid because it "went beyond the scope of the right of judicial review of the courts."

IV. I find it extremely difficult to agree with the decision of the majority opinion as sketched above.

First of all, it goes without saying that not only among treaties but among laws as well many are of great importance to the existence of our country and consequently have a high political content. Would the majority opinion say that in the case of these [laws], as well as treaties, the exercise of the right of constitutional review is limited only to cases of clearly obvious unconstitutionality? If not, then it is clear that the logic is inconsistent. The reason is that treaties are concluded by the cabinet and approved by the National Diet; and the situation is exactly the same in the case of laws. In short, what the majority opinion has arrived at is an opinion that holds that the right of constitutional review does not touch important matters of state which are to be handled by the two powers, executive and legislative. It is clear that this is in extreme contradiction with the idea of the existence of a peaceful democratic nation under the rule of law instead of force, which our new Constitution points out, and with the idea of the mission of the courts, which have been entrusted by the Constitution to bring to realization the above rule of law. Thus, the right of constitutional review, which is the unique power of control that the judiciary has over the legislative and executive powers under the separation of powers in our Constitution, ends in the position of being completely unable to touch on important national affairs. (What is termed "clearly obvious unconstitutionality and invalidity" in the majority opinion is something which, by and large, does not exist. It exists only in name.) I believe that this threatens the very foundations of our system of the separation of powers.

I must also state that the majority opinion is deficient in reasons because it offers no reasons at all regarding the legal foundation for holding that the courts do not possess, as a matter of principle, the right of constitutional review of the Security Treaty in the present case. There is the theory—the act of government theory or the discretionary action theory—that there are among the acts of the cabinet or the National Diet, certain ones that the right of constitutional review does not reach. To reflect on the positions and the powers of the cabinet or the National Diet that flow from the system of the separation of powers: the acts of authority inherent in each of these organs or their inherent discretionary actions belong to the exclusive authority of each, and the other organs cannot infringe upon them; but when unconstitutionality exists in the content of the discretionary actions or the exercise of powers attached to that exclusive authority, then they become the objectives of the constitutional review of the courts. Not only is there no doubt that such a fact reflects the system of constitutional review, which is to bring into existence the rule of law as representing the supremacy of law over force, but it also must be said that it clearly reflects the text of Article 81 of the Constitution, which states that the courts have the "power to determine the constitutionality of *any law*, order, regulation, or *official act.*" [Italics added by Justice Otani.] (Moreover, it perhaps goes without saying that such documents as an instrument of surrender or a treaty of peace with an enemy country that has accepted unconditional surrender, from their very nature do not become objects of constitutional review.) Nevertheless, I absolutely cannot constitutionally endorse either the theory of acts of government or the theory of discretionary action.

Next, in regard to Article 81 of the Constitution in which the right of constitutional review is interpreted to be "the authority to determine constitutionality," that is, "the right to review constitutional propriety," the majority opinion in respect to the "review of constitutionality" of the treaty in the present case held that it was limited to "clearly obvious unconstitutionality and invalidity" and that it "lay outside the scope of judicial review of the courts" (my note: what is here termed judicial review is to be interpreted to mean constitutional review). Moreover, because it is said that the present treaty must be recognized as not "clearly and obviously unconstitutional and invalid" and that "it lies outside the scope of the right of constitutional review," I believe that the present case as far as constitutional review is concerned comes to an end there and, moreover, its constitutionality or unconstitutionality should not be judged. To put it in other words, because the majority states that except for "clearly and obviously unconstitutional and invalid" matters such judgments are "outside the scope of review," neither the constitutionality nor the unconstitutionality of any matter can be judged. If it is so judged, then the action is beyond the powers of the court and illegal. This fact is clear if one considers the rule that a decision of a higher court shall bind a lower court (see Article 4 of the Court Organization Law).[7]

Again, the phrase "clearly and obviously unconstitutional and invalid" has been taken to mean "unconstitutional and invalid as can immediately be understood by anyone." But can there ever be a defect that is unconstitutional and invalid as can be immediately understood by anyone in a treaty that has been concluded through the pooling of intellects over a long period and has been approved by the wisdom of the many? In short, the majority opinion can be considered as nothing more than a self-consoling excuse [for their position] regarding the right of constitutional review. Accordingly, the final position of the majority opinion is the same as saying that the right of constitutional review does not extend to treaties (or precisely, the Security Treaty in the present case).

On the other hand, there is the opinion that in the relation between treaties and the Constitution, treaties must, as far as possible, conform to the Constitution. This opinion also is based on the premise that there is the same complete power of constitutional review over treaties that there is in the case of laws, and differs fundamentally in point of view from the majority opinion in this case.

Next, the majority opinion in this case, although holding that the unconstitutionality is not clearly obvious, handed down a fairly detailed constitutional judgment in respect to matters "lying outside" the scope of constitutional review and then set forth as its conclusion the following: ". . . the retention of United States armed forces must certainly be in accord with the intent of Article 9, Article 98, paragraph 2, and the Preamble of the Constitution," and finally held that the original judgment was illegal because it went beyond the scope of the right of judicial review.

Now, this is the first case dealing with the question of treaties and the power of constitutional review that has arisen since the

7. The language of the original is clear and simple and is accurately rendered into English here, but the meaning in both languages is not clear. I believe that the meaning might be stated as follows: "The majority opinion on the issue of constitutional review means that, on the basis of the reasoning presented in this opinion at this point, no court can render any judgment of constitutionality because this Supreme Court decision is binding under law on all inferior courts."

institution of the Supreme Court. That the present treaty has undergone a thorough process of constitutional review—in the judgment as to its constitutionality and in the [majority's] argument
on the nature of the Security Treaty and of the forces stationed
in our country as set forth at the beginning of the third reason in
the majority opinion—is adequately demonstrated by the opinion
itself. This is especially clear from the fact that in the present case
no necessity at all is admitted in the law or in the trial that such an
important judgment must be made, because ". . . treaties (precisely, the Security Treaty in the present case) fall outside the
right of constitutional review, except for those clearly and obviously unconstitutional and invalid."

V. In my opinion the main reason why the new Constitution
has bestowed the right of constitutional review on the courts is
that "judges . . . shall be bound only by this Constitution and
the laws" (Article 76, paragraph 3). Thus, this recognizes the inherent function residing in the essential nature of the courts,
which forces them to interpret and to apply the law, and it must
be interpreted as bestowing that right. (In the United States, notwithstanding the fact that nothing is stipulated in the Constitution
regarding the right of constitutional review, the courts have
wielded that authority from first having independence to the present day.) Thus, I believe that what the Constitution intends in
respect to this right is that law be supreme over force; that a
society be achieved in which justice is attained by the rule of law;
and that the universal principle, as stated in the Preamble of the
Constitution, of "striving for the preservation of peace, and the
banishment of tyranny and slavery, oppression and intolerance
for all time from the earth," be achieved.

Thus, I also believe that rather than to rely on the handing
down of an occasional decision on unconstitutionality we should
depend on the hope of the subjective effect that results from the
prevention beforehand, through the very existence of the system
itself, of unconstitutional acts produced by force.

In regard to treaties possessing "a great importance to the existence of our nation and accordingly having a highly political content," the majority opinion holds that as a matter of principle the
right of constitutional review does not extend to them. In respect
to the relation between the Constitution and matters of impor-

tance to the nation, it must be said that the above position takes a light view of the Constitution and will soon lead to the thinking that force (authority) should be respected and law (the Constitution) be held lightly.

Formerly, in the old Constitution the responsibility for review was not legally well defined. However, the Privy Council existed as the principal advisory organ to the Emperor. Thus, the drafts of all treaties, important laws, and imperial ordinances had to undergo review as to their constitutionality in the said council, and even now it goes without saying that the council, in fact, had the duty of protecting the Constitution. Again, an example of the affirmation of the legal principle that the Constitution as the fundamental law of the nation was supreme over treaties is to be seen in Treaty No. 1 of 1929, "The Treaty Regarding the Renunciation of War" [Pact of Paris]. In Article 1 of this so-called antiwar treaty was the phrase, ". . . solemnly declare in the names of their respective peoples." That this treaty was ratified only after the reservation had been made that the phrase "in the names of their respective peoples" did not apply to our country is a clear fact of history. (The statement of reservation was as follows: "The Imperial Government . . . declares that it understands that the phrase 'in the names of their respective peoples' which appears in Article 1 of the Treaty does not apply to Japan in view of the provisions of the Imperial Constitution.") In respect to the function of constitutional review, is the new Constitution to be declared inferior to the Meiji Constitution?

Again, I think that a treaty like that establishing the Japan-Germany-Italy Tripartite Alliance, which was a motivating force for the outbreak of World War II and could be said to have had a high political content with an important relation to the existence of the nation, could be arranged in such a way that it could not be recognized as "clearly and obviously unconstitutional." But would the majority opinion accept its validity as a matter outside the scope of the right of constitutional review?

After all, the state of the world is ever changing, and if we consider also that the power of nations is also changing and shifting, then we must always keep clearly before us that the defense and protection of the Constitution, the fundamental law of the nation, must be firmly maintained. I believe that we must always pray for the sound health of the right of constitutional review, for the protection of fundamental human rights, and for the preservation of peace.

*   *   *

The opinion of Justices Okuno Kenichi and Takahashi Kiyoshi follows.

Article 9, paragraph 1, renounces war as a sovereign right of the nation and the threat or use of force as means of settling international disputes. Accordingly, it is proper to interpret the non-maintenance of war potential in paragraph 2 of the same article to be a prohibition of the maintenance of armed forces under the power of command and control of our country; it does not relate to foreign forces, which cannot be commanded or controlled by our country. Thus, because it is clear that the American armed forces retained in our country under the Security Treaty are not under the power of command and control of our country, it is also clear that they cannot be declared to be directly in contravention of Article 9, paragraph 2, of the Constitution. However, whether or not the retention of the above American armed forces is in violation of the spirit of Article 9, paragraph 2, of the Constitution or against the intent of the Preamble of the Constitution requires re-examination.

Because the retention of American armed forces in our country is based on the Security Treaty and is a part of its implementation, in determining the unconstitutionality of the retention of American armed forces, it is necessary first to determine, as a premise, whether the Security Treat is unconstitutional. Nevertheless, the majority opinion held in regard to the unconstitutionality of the Security Treaty that the courts did not possess the right of review. The import of that opinion is not whether the right of review of the courts does not extend to the unconstitutionality of treaties in general, or whether there is such a right of review of treaties, but that it does not exist in respect to the treaty in the present case because it is related to acts of government. But whatever the case, our view differs from that of the majority opinion.

In essence, treaties are contracts in international law between nation and nation, but at the same time there are cases in which treaties in themselves possess validity in domestic law, cases in which they possess no direct validity as domestic law, and cases in which they are implemented through the separate enactment of domestic law. We interpret the situation as follows: in cases in which treaties in themselves possess binding force over the people as domestic law, their validity as domestic law, as a matter of principle, stands in a position beneath the Constitution—the supreme law; these cases, like domestic law, become the object of the so-called constitutional review of the courts, which determines whether or not they conform with the Constitution as provided for in Article 81 of the Constitution. It is the same when treaties are judged as premises in suits. Also, it is natural that domestic laws for the purpose of implementing treaties come under constitutional review of the courts under the same article of the Constitution.

On the other hand, there are those who hold that because the word "treaty" does not appear in the above Article 81 the courts have no power of constitutional review over treaties. Even granting that the courts adjudge a treaty unconstitutional, that only denies the validity of the treaty as domestic law and does not deny its validity in international law (treating as separate issues whether the government would resort to the measure of renouncing the treaty or of amending it, or whether it would be held responsible under international law for the renunciation of the duty to implement the treaty), wherein it would still be valid; the courts under international law do not review or judge the validity of treaties themselves. It must be understood in this sense that the word "treaty" is not inserted in the above Article 81; this article is not to be understood to have the intent of denying to the courts the right of constitutional review of the validity of treaties in domestic law. Repeating the above, Article 81 of the Constitution stipulates the right of judicial review concerning all domestic law under the Constitution; and there cannot be any doubt but that the "regulations" of Article 94 not mentioned in Article 81 also properly become the objects of judicial review. Although treaties are not listed in the above Article 81, they also properly become the objects of judicial review in respect to their validity as domestic law. In this sense, it must be interpreted that treaties are included in the "laws" of Article 81. In the same way it must be interpreted that treaties are included as domestic law in "laws" of Article 76, paragraph 3, and Article 98, paragraph 1, of the Constitution.

Accordingly, there is no ground for declaring that because the word "treaty" does not appear in Article 98, paragraph 1, of the Constitution, treaties do not stand beneath the Constitution or that they do not become the object of constitutional review of the courts. We also believe that there are no grounds for saying that, because there is the obligation to respect treaties in Article 98 of the Constitution, even treaties that are in contravention of the Constitution are binding on the people and that the power of constitutional review of the courts does not extend to them. Also, if the power of constitutional review does not extend to treaties, then an extremely improper situation would arise in which the Constitution could easily be revised; or a situation would be produced that, by means of the conclusion of treaties either in contradiction of or running counter to the provisions of the Constitution, would in fact be similar to revision without having to resort to the procedures for constitutional revision.

Again, in regard to the limits of the right of judicial review, we certainly do not deny that there are certain areas, such as the so-called acts of government or political questions, into which the right of review does not extend. However, we cannot agree that only for the reason that the issue has a high political content or that it is one related to important national policy does it properly fall under this heading. In the long run, and fundamentally, acts such as the enactment of laws and the conclusion of treaties are, for the most part, matters with a high political content relating to important national policy; accordingly, because the right of constitutional review in respect to these requires, naturally, judgments of a high political content, when it is said that the right of constitutional review of the courts does not extend to such matters simply because they are declared to be problems of a high political content or to relate to important national policy, then the majority of important laws that become political problems cannot be touched by the constitutional review of the courts. Our Constitution provides expressly in Article 81 that the courts be given the right of constitutional review of all domestic laws and government actions. Consequently, we believe that not only is the above not in accord with the spirit of the Constitution, which has taken special care that there be no violation of the Constitution through actions of the National Diet and the government, but also that it provides no grounds for the judges to carry out their duty of protecting the Constitution laid on them by Articles 76 and 99 of the Constitution.

The majority opinion, in its two views—that the right of constitutional review of the courts does not extend to treaties and that there is no right of judicial review in respect to the Security Treaty in this case, which is regarded as falling under acts of government —may be considered to contain the greatest common measure of the issue. But it is logically inconsistent to declare that it is possible to judge what is "clearly and obviously" unconstitutional and at the same time hold that the Security Treaty in this case falls outside the scope of the right of judicial review of the courts. (Especially, it is extremely difficult to understand how those who from the beginning have held the view that there has been no right of judicial review of treaties can accept that reasoning.)

Nevertheless, we believe that to say that, since the Security Treaty has a highly political character because it has an extremely important relation to the basis of our national existence, review is limited to clear and obvious unconstitutionality, and furthermore to say that constitutional review in substance is not to be carried out, is not in accord with the intent of Articles 81, 76, and 99 of the Constitution as we have pointed out above. (Moreover, it must be recognized that the majority opinion, although declaring as its conclusion that the Security Treaty cannot be recognized as clearly and obviously unconstitutional, has by that process reviewed and decided that it is not unconstitutional.)

Not only is it possible for the judicial courts to review in purely legal terms the problem of whether the validity of the Security Treaty as domestic law is in contravention of Article 9 or other provisions of the Constitution, but we cannot discover any particular reason why the courts are prevented from reviewing and judging so-called acts of government.

In reviewing whether or not the Security Treaty is really in contravention of the spirit of Article 9 or the intent of the Preamble of the Constitution, we see that the said Article 9, paragraph 1, prohibits "war as a sovereign right of the nation and the threat or use of force as means of settling international disputes"; and its intent must be interpreted to be the same as that of the Antiwar Pact, which declared that the parties "condemn recourse to war for the solution of international controversies, and renounce it as an instrument of national policy." We also believe that it is in accord with Article 2, paragraph 4, of the Charter of the United Nations. Accordingly, Article 9, paragraph 1, of the Constitution does not in any way refer to a prohibition of or a limitation on our country's right of self-defense. We must understand that our country retains the "inherent right" recognized in every sovereign nation under international law as the "right of national self-defense." As is clear from the Preamble of the Constitution in the phrases ". . . we have determined to preserve our security and existence . . ." and "We recognize . . . the right to live in peace . . ." the Constitution recognizes our country's "right to existence." Nevertheless, if there is danger that our country would be exposed to armed attack from another country, it is natural that our country exercise the right of self-defense in order to protect its existence against such danger and that it be able to take measures in self-defense to prevent such armed attack; and it must be understood that the Constitution also does not prohibit this. After all, were our country to be exposed to armed attack and we unable to exercise the right of self-defense or to take defense measures—apart from waiting for our own destruction—it is clear that such a situation would be in contravention of the intent of the Constitution, which recognizes the right of existence. Thus, in such a situation to rely on the measures provided for in Articles 39 to 42 of the Charter of the United Nations for the preservation of our security and existence would be ideal. But because it is clear that under present conditions the above measures of the United Nations cannot be demonstrated to be either adequate or effective, then as a second-best policy, it is unavoidable that we conclude collective security agreements with specific countries and thus defend our peace and existence by means of the military assistance of such countries. Because it is said that the granting of permission to retain the armed forces of such countries on our territory is the only means of setting up defense measures based on our right of self-defense and our sovereignty, it is not in violation of the pacifism of the Preamble of the Constitution, and also it is not a matter included in the prohibition of Article 9, paragraph 2, of the Constitution.

Then also, the Security Treaty has been concluded between our country and America in accordance with the provisions of Article 5 (c) and Article 6 (a) of the Treaty of Peace. On the premise that there is danger of armed attack on Japan "because irresponsible militarism has not yet been driven from the world" (In regard to this evaluation of the international situation, which states that there may be such "danger," because it is a so-called political question it cannot be subject to review and judgment by the courts, and we believe that since the government and the National Diet already made such an evaluation in the preamble of the Security Treaty, it is a matter lying outside the control of the courts.), our country, utilizing "the right of individual and collective self-defense," which is approved by the Charter of the United Nations as being inherent in every nation, desires that United States armed forces be maintained in and about Japan in order to deter armed attack on our country and grants the right to the United States to station its forces in the above area; and the United States accepts the above. It was agreed that such armed forces "may be utilized to contribute to the . . . security of Japan against armed attack from without." It was also a collective security arrangement in which measures of self-defense were agreed upon, "if an armed attack occurs," on the basis of the "inherent right of individual and collective self-defense" of Article 51 of the Charter of the United Nations and under the restrictions of the United Nations Charter and the general control of the United Nations (see Joint Communiqué of June 21, 1957, and exchange of notes of September 14, 1957).

That is to say, the above treaty establishes measures for defense that are based on the right of self-defense inherent in every nation. Therefore it is difficult to call it a military alliance for the purpose of aggression. Accordingly, in terms of the above explanation it cannot be said that it is in contravention of either the spirit of Article 9 or the intent of the Preamble of the Constitution.

(Next, we add a word concerning the controversy arising from the fact that the Security Treaty provides that the American forces can be used to contribute to the maintenance of international peace and security in the Far East. The argument is that this is in contravention of the Preamble of the Constitution because there is the danger, arising from the fact that American forces may act for peace in the Far East, that our country may be involved in a war unrelated to our defense and that we may again be visited with the horrors of war. That the mobilization of American forces can be put into operation in accordance with the above provision of the Security Treaty only under the conditions set forth in Article 51 of the Charter of the United Nations or in accordance with a resolution or recommendation of an organ of the United Nations is recognized by both Japan and the United States in the exchange of notes mentioned above. Accordingly, in such a situation, it goes without saying that there must actually be an "occasion of armed attack" in the Far East. Thus, since there is a close and indivisible relation between the peace and security of the Far East and the peace and security of Japan, the occurrence of such an armed attack would simultaneously threaten the peace and security of Japan, and thus there is also produced the argument that such action of the American forces would constitute a guarantee of the peace and security of our country. Thus, the rightness or wrongness of the judgment that the peace and security of Japan are closely and indivisibly connected with the peace and security of the Far East is somehow related to a judgment of the international situation and of the military situation; this falls under the heading of the so-called political questions that should be decided by the government and the National Diet. We believe that because a judgment has already been made by the above organs and provisions established as described above, there is no room for the judicial courts to intervene and review the above judgment.)

As we have pointed out above, the Security Treaty cannot be termed in contravention of Article 9 or its spirit, or of the Preamble of the Constitution. (The Administrative Agreement did not receive special approval from the National Diet, but because it can be recognized as falling within the scope of the authorization of Article 3 of the Security Treaty which had already received the approval of the National Diet, it cannot be declared unconstitutional.) Accordingly, neither the above Security Treaty nor the retention of American forces based on the Administrative

Agreement can be called unconstitutional. Consequently, the fact that our country as the receiving country provides for the maintenance of the security of those military installations is natural. The enactment of the Special Criminal Law in the present case—designed to maintain the peace and tranquillity of the installations and areas of the American forces—and the prescription of punishments in respect to violations heavier than those provided in Article 1 (32) of the Minor Offenses Law are questions of legislative policy entrusted to the sphere of discretion of the legislative branch and, of course, cannot be termed in contravention of Article 31 of the Constitution.

Also, there is a difference of legal benefits because of the creation of a difference in legal penalties in the two cases, but it naturally cannot be said that because of this there is a violation of either Article 13 or Article 14 of the Constitution on account of unreasonable discriminatory treatment.

Moreover, the original judgment erred in its interpretation of the Constitution; the appeal in this case is reasonable; and the original judgment cannot escape being quashed.

We, of course, are in agreement with the formal judgment in the majority opinion, but we do differ on the reasons, as we show above. (Furthermore, whether Article 9 also means that our country is prohibited from maintaining its own war potential for self-defense not only cannot be recognized as being directly in dispute in the appeal brief but cannot be recognized as being necessary for a determination of the present case. Therefore, we do not make a judgment on that point here and now.)

(TRANSLATED BY J. M. MAKI)

Hanreishū, VI, No. 9, 783 (Civil)

EDITORIAL NOTE: Prior to the Sunakawa Decision the Suzuki Decision was the only one that touched on the problem of Article 9. In July, 1950, shortly after the outbreak of the conflict in Korea, the occupation authorized the Japanese government to establish a "National Police Reserve," designed to maintain domestic security and armed only with light weapons, but capable of definition as either "armed forces" or "war potential." Shortly after the occupation ended in the spring of 1952, Mr. Suzuki Mōsaburō, secretary-general of the Social Democratic party, petitioned the Supreme Court to declare the police reserve unconstitutional on the ground that its existence was in violation of the war potential clause of Article 9. The Court did not decide the issue.

Grand Bench decision, October 8, 1952: Dismissed.

REFERENCES

Constitution of Japan. ARTICLE 81. The Supreme Court is the court of last resort with power to determine the constitutionality of any law, order, regulation or official act.

FORMAL JUDGMENT

Suit dismissed; cost of the proceedings to be borne by the plaintiff.

THE FACTS. The substance of the claim made on behalf of the plaintiff is that all acts done by the defendant [the State] since April 1, 1951, in connection with the establishment and maintenance of the National Police Reserve (the administrative acts including, of course, all laws, ordinances, and regulations concerning the establishment and maintenance of the reserve force in addition to all acts in private law; items enumerated in the separate schedule being only examples) should be declared null and void and that cost of the proceedings should be borne by the defendant. The grounds on which he seeks such a judgment are as set forth in his appended petition and in his preliminary plea of July 16, 1952.

Counsel for the defense sought a judgment in the terms actually adopted in our formal judgment (above); his grounds are as set forth in his appended written reply.

REASONS. The plaintiff contends that the Supreme Court, although possessing the character of a judicial court, has an additional character whereby it exercises a special power, outside the judicial power and not belonging to either executive or legislative power, that enables it—both as a court of original jurisdiction and as a court of last resort—to determine in the abstract without adjudging any concrete legal dispute, the constitutionality of laws, ordinances, and regulations and of official acts.

When one examines the institutions of foreign countries in this regard, it is true that, in addition to countries where the judicial courts can exercise the right to determine questions of constitutionality, there are other countries where they cannot exercise this power, but where, instead, special organs are established for this purpose. The latter are empowered, irrespective of whether there exists a concrete legal dispute, to issue comprehensive and abstract declarations that laws, orders, and the like are unconstitutional, and to set them aside and invalidate them.

However, what is conferred on our courts under the system now in force is the right to exercise the judicial power, and for this power to be invoked a concrete legal dispute is necessary. Our courts do not possess the power, in the absence of such a concrete legal dispute, to hand down abstract decisions covering the future and relating to doubtful disputes concerning the interpretation of the Constitution and other laws, orders, and the like. In other

words, the Supreme Court has power to examine the constitutionality of laws, orders, and the like, but this power may be exercised
only within the limits of the judicial power. In this respect the
Supreme Court is no different from the lower courts (see Article
76, paragraph 1, of the Constitution). The plaintiff bases his case
on Article 81 of the Constitution, but this merely provides that
the Supreme Court is the court of last resort in cases involving
the Constitution. Accordingly, one cannot argue from it that the
Supreme Court has a power peculiar to itself to try constitutionality in an abstract sense or that it has exclusive jurisdiction, both
original and final, in such matters.

The plaintiff's point about the special qualifications required
of Supreme Court judges can be recognized as referring particularly to Article 41, paragraph 1, of the Court Organization Law;
this can, however, be sufficiently explained as stemming from the
fact that the Supreme Court bears the grave responsibility of judging important constitutional cases as the court of last resort.[1]

If, as the plaintiff argues, the Supreme Court has the power to
issue abstract declarations nullifying laws, orders, and the like,
then, since anyone could bring before the Court suits claiming unconstitutionality, the validity of laws, orders, and the like, would
be frequently assailed and there would be danger of the Court's
assuming the appearance of an organ superior to all other powers
in the land, thereby running counter to the basic principle of
democratic government: that the three powers are independent,
equal, and immune from each other's interference.

In short, under the system prevailing in our country, a judgment may be sought in the courts only when there exists a concrete legal dispute between specific parties. The argument that
the courts have power to determine in the abstract the constitutionality of laws, orders, and the like, in the absence of a concrete
case, has no foundation in the Constitution itself or in any statute.
It is clear from the arguments of the plaintiff that the present case
does not involve such a concrete legal dispute. Therefore, the
present suit does not conform with law. Neither the Supreme
Court nor any lower court has the power to hear such a suit.
Therefore, the suit cannot be transferred to a lower court.

1. The plaintiff's argument was that because of the high qualifications required of Supreme
Court justices, they were qualified to issue abstract pronouncements on constitutional issues.

For the above reasons this suit must be dismissed as not in conformity with law. The cost of the proceedings shall be borne as set forth above in the formal judgment in accordance with Article 89 of the Code of Civil Procedure.

This decision is unanimous.

(TRANSLATED BY D. C. S. SISSONS)

XXV: THE POWER OF THE CABINET
TO DISSOLVE THE HOUSE OF
REPRESENTATIVES

EDITORIAL NOTE: In view of the fact that the Constitution of Japan deals in great detail with many problems of government and governmental relations, it is striking indeed that it mentions only most casually the extremely important political problem of the circumstances under and the manner in which the House of Representatives can be dissolved. The citations of the relevant articles in Justice Mano's opinion reveal clearly the ambiguities involved.

On August 28, 1952, Prime Minister Yoshida brought about the dissolution of the House of Representatives by means of an imperial rescript which read simply, "In accordance with Article 7 of the Constitution of Japan, I [the Emperor] dissolve the House of Representatives." A member of the opposition party appealed to the Supreme Court to declare the dissolution null and void, not only on the grounds that the Constitution did not permit dissolution as it was carried out but that there were certain minor irregularities in the form of presenting advice and approval to the Emperor.

This decision is virtually identical with the Suzuki Decision. However, Justice Mano's opinion is interesting as a statement of judicial opinion on the highly political issue of dissolution.

Grand Bench decision, April 15, 1953: Suit dismissed.

REFERENCES

Constitution of Japan. ARTICLE 81. The Supreme Court is the court of last resort with power to determine the constitutionality of any law, order, regulation or official act.

Formal Judgment

The present suit is dismissed. The cost of the proceedings is to be borne by the plaintiff.

REASONS. If we point out the facts within the limits necessary for a judgment of this case, it is clear from the claim itself that this case is presented to the Grand Bench of the Supreme Court on the assumption that the present Court, in addition to being a judicial court, also possesses the character of a unique constitutional court which must adjudge the constitutionality of any law, order, or official act, both as a court of first instance and as a court of last resort.

However, under our present legal system, only purely judicial courts have been set up; and what is termed the right of constitutional review can be exercised by the courts, either higher or lower, without distinction and within the limits necessary for judgment in relation to concrete legal disputes between the parties concerned. That is to say, Article 81 of the Constitution cannot be interpreted as stipulating that this Court possesses simultaneously the character of a constitutional court of final resort and of a court of first instance that alone has the inherent right of constitutional review. The reason why this interpretation must be maintained is as has been shown in an earlier decision [the Suzuki Decision] and it is impossible to support the argument of the plaintiff, which springs from a point of view opposed to the above.

Thus, the present complaint, on the assumption that there exists a constitutional court—an idea not recognized under the present legal system—treats the present Court as being such a constitutional court and, moreover, ends as having been instituted as a case that must be considered as falling under [the jurisdiction of] such a court. However, in the present Court, which is recognized as being only a judicial court under the present legal system, the complaint must be rejected as not being in conformity with law.

Accordingly, judgment is rendered as in the formal judgment in accordance with Articles 202 [1] and 89 [2] of the Code of Civil Procedure.

---

1. This article reads: "An illegal suit any defect of which being unable to be rectified may be dismissed by a judgment without resorting to oral argument."
2. See footnote 7, p. 50.

This decision is the unanimous opinion of the Justices, except for the supplementary opinion of Justice Mano Tsuyoshi.

*   *   *

The supplementary opinion of Justice Mano Tsuyoshi follows.

Because, as a judge, I bear the responsibility of respecting and upholding the Constitution and because the question of the dissolution of the House of Representatives possesses a great value and significance in relation to both the present and future of Japanese politics, I would like to set forth here a view that I have held for some years. To be perfectly frank, I think that dissolution as in the present case is in contravention of the Constitution. The reasons thereof are as set forth in general below.

The Constitution uses the word "dissolution" of the House of Representatives only in Articles 7 and 69. The past disputes over the question of dissolution have centered mainly on these issues: Does the Constitution recognize a broad right of the cabinet to dissolve the House of Representatives in accordance with Article 7? Or is the cabinet's right of dissolution narrow, limited only to the situation in Article 69? To set forth my own opinion at the outset, I believe both (1) that in the case set forth in Article 69 the cabinet can dissolve the House of Representatives, and (2) that the Diet can also be dissolved by a resolution of dissolution passed by the House of Representatives on its own.

I. Article 69 of the Constitution provides as follows: "If the House of Representatives passes a nonconfidence resolution, or rejects a confidence resolution, the Cabinet shall resign en masse, unless the House of Representatives is dissolved within ten (10) days." When the first part of this provision applies, the cabinet has the responsibility of selecting either dissolution of the House of Representatives or resignation en masse and, accordingly, there can be neither doubt nor dispute that, interpreting only one side of this, the cabinet on such an occasion can dissolve the House of Representatives. However, the reason is not that the right of dissolution is acknowledged naturally to be in the cabinet under the principle of the separation of powers, because the right of dissolution is not, of course, a characteristic that necessarily attaches to executive power as it is understood under the separation of powers. Thus, the right of dissolution runs counter to the principle of the separation of powers, but the fact that it is recognized under the principle of checks and balances of state power, as will be described later, must, above all, be kept in mind. Therefore, in respect to dissolution in this situation [Article 69] it is necessary to completely separate the consideration of the legal problem of the constitutional power of dissolution from the political problem of the propriety of dissolution under actual political circumstances.

If dissolution is in conformity with the law, it does not become a problem for the courts, but in situations in which it is not politically appropriate, it goes without saying that a political responsibility toward the people is assumed. That is to say, in the general election following dissolution the sovereign people will fully criticize the action and will hand down the correct judgment by casting their independent votes.

II. Next, Article 7 provides, "The Emperor, with the advice and approval of the Cabinet, shall perform the following acts in matters of state on behalf of the people," and item three following is, "Dissolution of the House of Representatives." With this provision as the basis, many people arrive at the interpretation that the cabinet possesses broadly and generally the power to dissolve the House of Representatives, in other words, that the cabinet, regardless of the political propriety involved, can legally and constitutionally dissolve the House of Representatives at any time, freely and completely at its own pleasure. Thus, they interpret dissolution as being in conformity with the law and the Constitution. (Below I term these the "Article 7 group.")

The thinking of the Article 7 group, I believe, is in the long run erroneous. Article 1 of the Constitution establishes the principle that the sovereignty of the Japanese nation resides in the Japanese people and that the Emperor is the symbol of the nation and of the unity of the people. Article 3 provides, "The advice and approval of the Cabinet shall be required for all acts of the Emperor in matters of state, and the Cabinet shall be responsible therefor"; and Article 4, paragraph 1, stipulates, "The Emperor shall perform only such acts in matters of state as are provided for in this Constitution and he shall not have powers related to government." Therefore, the fact that in matters of state "the advice and approval of the Cabinet shall be required" is a condition already firmly established for Article 4; thus, "with the advice and approval of the Cabinet" in Article 7 is merely a repetition, as a matter of precaution, of something that might well be left unsaid. In a sense, it is completely superfluous.

Not only that, but there is not the slightest doubt insofar as constitutional interpretation is concerned that "the advice and approval of the Cabinet" is necessary in respect to the acts in matters of state provided for in Article 7. Also the phrase "on behalf of the people" in Article 7 is nothing more than a means of making even clearer for the sake of precaution the idea of popular sovereignty as already proclaimed in Article 1. This, too, is completely superfluous. Even if this were not in Article 7, it would produce no essential difference in the meaning of the said article. Thus if, as in the art of flower arrangement, one cuts away that which is superfluous, what is left is the pure form of Article 7, namely, "The Emperor shall perform the following acts in matters of state."

"The Emperor shall perform only such acts in matters of state" in Article 4 is taken over into Article 7, which lists the acts in matters of state that the Emperor can perform. Thus, Article 7 does no more than limit the types of acts of state that the Emperor performs. Accordingly, that this Article 7 does not provide that the cabinet can dissolve the House of Representatives is perfectly clear from the wording itself. The Article 7 group asserts that because the Emperor, in accordance with item three of Article 7, carries out "the dissolution of the House of Representatives . . . with the advice and approval of the Cabinet," the cabinet, which gives its advice and approval to the Emperor, substantially possesses the power to dissolve the House of Representatives. However, this is mere adherence to verbal trivialities in the text of Article 7 and is an arbitrary view, taking into account neither the broad principles nor other stipulations of the Constitution.

In general, as I have said before, the phrase, "with the advice and approval of the Cabinet" in Article 7, is completely superfluous. The Article 7 group deals too much with superfluities and it tries to lead us to accept the idea that the cabinet has the power to dissolve the Diet, but I believe that both the attitude and the method are fundamentally in error. There is no doubt that in Article 3 the advice and approval of the cabinet are necessary for all the Emperor's acts in matters of state, and from Article 4 it is clear that the Emperor possesses no powers related to government and that he carries out only such acts in matters of state as are provided for in the Constitution. Accordingly, it is also clear that government, namely, the functions related to the ruling of the country, belongs to organs of the state other than the Emperor.

Because government is both concrete and substantial in the politics of the state and because it is concerned with many things relating to the advantage and disadvantage of the people, directly and indirectly, it must be shared among the organs of the state other than the Emperor that bear the responsibility for it according to the two great constitutional principles of the separation of powers and checks and balances. On the other hand, because acts in matters of state are purely formal and ceremonial and do not exert any substantial influence on the interests of the people, they are entrusted to the Emperor, who is the symbol of the Japanese people: such is the spirit of Article 4.

According to item three of Article 7, the Emperor does not carry out the substantial act of government of dissolving the House of Representatives, but only the formal and ceremonial procedures relating to dissolution. Moreover, even in regard to the Emperor's execution of this act of state, "the advice and approval of the Cabinet shall be required," as provided in Article 3. It is clear that the advice and approval of the cabinet concern the acts of state carried out by the Emperor and not government, which is not related to the functions of the Emperor. Again, the responsibility borne by the cabinet as provided in Article 3 is to give its advice and approval to the acts of state carried out by the Emperor.

Responsibility concerning government, which is the essence of acts of state, must be borne by the several organs of the state that carry out government in accordance with the principles of the separation of powers and checks and balances. Consequently, the claim of the Article 7 group that either the Emperor or the cabinet possesses the right in government to dissolve the House of Representatives because the cabinet gives its advice and approval to the Emperor in matters of state or because it is responsible therefor, is an argument completely without foundation and one that puts the cart before the horse. If, as the Article 7 group does, it is said that the power to decide matters of government, which consists of concrete acts in matters of state, belongs to the authority of the cabinet because under Article 7 it gives advice and approval, then it is possible to arrive at the improper interpretation that the enactment of constitutional amendments and laws, which is the substance of what is involved in the promulgation of constitutional amendments and laws as set forth in Article 7, item 1, also belongs to the authority of the cabinet. It can be said that from this single point alone it is clear that the Article 7 group is in error. Moreover, that all organs of the state possess rights regarding the substance of government is a circumstance that can be understood from a general examination of the entire body of the Constitution.

Our Constitution stands on the foundation of the two great principles of the separation of powers and checks and balances. The constitution of any country under a constitutional system excludes dictatorial or absolute government in which the power of state is held by a single person or a single minority group and it also prevents the undue concentration or monopolization of power. Also, in order to protect the freedom of the people and fundamental human rights, it provides not only that the power to govern is divided but also that organs are established to wield that divided power as individual and independent arms of the state. Therefore, the usual powers of government, in accordance with the intrinsic nature of the governmental process, are divided into the three classes of legislative, judicial, and executive power—the power of legislation being in the legislative branch, the judicial power in the courts, and the executive power in the executive branch. Thus is power distributed. In our country this is generally called the separation of powers.

At the same time, the system of checks and balances has been adopted. This is a regulatory device designed to maintain equality of power among each of the above branches and to restrain them all as organs of the state. This is done because otherwise it might be difficult to achieve the smooth operation of government or because the evil of a jealous regard for independence would develop if only a separation of powers based on the intrinsic nature of the governmental process were followed. For example, the courts are given the right of constitutional review of both administrative actions of the executive branch and of the enactment of legislation, which belongs essentially to the legislative branch; and, on the other hand, the right of impeachment is given to the legislative branch in respect to judges, who belong to the judicial power, and in general the appointment of judges is under the authority of the cabinet. The Constitution stands on the foundation of the mixture and the coordination of the two great principles of the separation of powers and checks and balances. Therefore, regardless of whether it is because of the separation of powers or because of checks and balances, the authority given to one organ of the state under the Constitution is limited to the sphere in which it can act and, accordingly, this constitutes its positive limit in regard to action. The positive limit on the activity of a single organ of the state, in other words, is at the same time a negative limit beyond which the other organs of state cannot act. Those other organs are not permitted to go wilfully beyond this limit and to infringe on other areas. Accordingly, that the powers of the organs of the state thus divided constitutionally are mutually independent and cannot interfere with each other is a basic principle of the Constitution.

If it were possible for the power of government belonging to one organ of the state to interfere at pleasure with that of other organs of the state, it might happen that the power of the other two might be unduly or excessively concentrated on that of a single organ and the result might be a situation in which the greatest objectives of the Constitution—the rejection of dictatorial or absolutist government by the separation of powers and checks and balances, and the protection of the people's freedoms and human rights—would be trampled into the ground without a trace.

Here I should like to return and examine Article 7 briefly. "The dissolution of the Diet," speaking from the point of view of the intrinsic nature of the power of government, clearly does not belong to the executive power. There may be those in the Article 7 group who hold the rather simple thought that since the right to dissolve the House of Representatives is neither legislative nor judicial, it must then be executive. However, this is a mistaken argument arising from a true misunderstanding of the separation of powers.

The separation of powers, as I have explained above, is a structure in which the state power is divided equally into legislative, judicial, and executive parts, each according to its basic nature; at the same time, each independent organ of the state exercises the power that has been so divided. Simply to say that the state is divided into three parts is meaningless. The point of prime importance is that the power thus divided is exercised independently by each independent organ without interference from the others. The reason is that no matter how power is divided into thirds, or even into fourths or fifths, if the same organ can enjoy the combined use of the parts then it can be said, without injustice, that the division is completely meaningless. Because the basic premise is that within the scope of the power that has been divided into three parts there be no interference in the jurisdiction of the others, it is only natural that each of the organs wielding that divided power be mutually independent of the others, that it enjoy an autonomous existence, and that its basic constituents not be destroyed by the other organs. For example, the National Diet is given the power to designate the prime minister (Article 67), but from the standpoint of the principle of the separation of powers, the Diet cannot force the resignation en masse of the cabinet or the discharge of the prime minister. Similarly, from the standpoint of the principle of the separation of powers, the cabinet cannot dissolve the House of Representatives.

Next, let us view the problem from the principle of checks and balances. Is there a constitutional basis for the opinion that the cabinet possesses the right to dissolve the House of Representatives? This issue is the most vital one in the present problem and is the most important key point.

Constitutionally, the executive power is vested in the cabinet (Article 65). To put it another way, in terms of the principle of the separation of powers, the cabinet was given the right to exercise the executive power. The powers that are given to the cabinet, in addition to those of an essentially administrative nature, in accordance with the principle of checks and balances, are set forth in outline in Article 73, excepting those that are especially set forth in Article 6, paragraph 2, Article 69, Article 80, and so forth. Namely, Article 73 provides, "The Cabinet, in addition to other general administrative functions, shall perform the following functions: . . .." In items 1 to 5 that follow are listed functions that belong to the administrative power, whether or not specially designated; but since under the old Constitution administrative functions were treated as belonging to the sovereign powers of the Emperor, they were, as a matter of precaution, made clearly a part of the authority of the cabinet. Now, item 6 lists "the enactment of Cabinet orders" and item 7 reads, "Decide on general amnesty, special amnesty, commutation of punishment, reprieve and restoration of rights." It can be thought that the enactment of cabinet orders belongs, strictly speaking, to the legislative power and that general amnesty, special amnesty, and so forth belong to the judicial power; but under the principle of checks and balances these are especially delegated to the authority of the cabinet.

However, the "dissolution of the House of Representatives," which possesses great political and social significance, is not entrusted to the authority of the cabinet in Article 73. In Article 69 it is provided only that there are some situations in which the cabinet can dissolve the House of Representatives. Consequently, speaking from the viewpoint of the principle of checks and balances, we must conclude that the dissolution of the House of Representatives is not granted to the authority of the cabinet except for the situation set forth in Article 69. If, as with the Article 7 group, the interpretation is that the right of dissolution belongs to the cabinet simply on the basis of the phrase "dissolution of the House of Representatives," in item 3, Article 7, which lists the acts of state of the Emperor, then there is reason for the similar interpretation, on the basis of Article 7, item 6, which reads "Attestation of general and special amnesty, commutation of punishment, reprieve and restoration of rights," that these powers, too, belong to the cabinet. Then is it really necessary that the powers delineated in Article 73, item 7, which reads, "Decide on general amnesty, special amnesty, commutation of punishment, reprieve, and restoration of rights," be expressly entrusted to the authority of the cabinet? On the contrary, since Article 7, item 6, is not sufficient to establish the authority of the cabinet, without reference to Article 73, item 7, then proof that the dissolution of the House of Representatives is not entrusted to the power of the cabinet is that only Article 7, item 3, refers to it and Article 73 has no provision concerning it. Viewed thus, it must be said that it is impossible to adduce this power of the cabinet from Article 7, item 3. When the old Constitution was in force the true principle of the separation of powers was not recognized and the Emperor could dissolve the Imperial Diet at any time (Article 7), but the way of thinking that holds that because of the above situation the cabinet now has the power to dissolve the House of Representatives, must be completely swept away under the new Constitution.

Widening the point of view even more, I would like to consider the actual state of checks and balances of authority from [the viewpoint of] the entire Constitution. That the area of executive power in every modern nation has widened and strengthened with each passing year is a phenomenon common to every civilized country. In our country, too, it is likewise true, and the greater part of the power to rule touching directly on the daily life of the people, lies, in general, in the executive. This very executive power exists as a gigantic Leviathan [in original] in the structure of the modern nation.

The actual amount of power given to the executive under our Constitution is in itself an extensive and powerful thing. The prime minister, who is the head of the cabinet, can appoint the ministers of state and remove them at will (Article 68). Consequently, the cabinet is a collegiate body, but in reality it is under the absolute control of the prime minister, who possesses the power of life and death over his ministers. At least they can be easily placed under such absolute control. And again, the designation and appointment of justices of the Supreme Court and the judges of the lower courts belong to the powers of the cabinet (Articles 6, 79, and 80). In regard to such appointments, and so forth, the consent of the National Diet, the House of Representatives, the House of Councillors, or any other body is not required. (In the United States the judges of the federal courts are appointed by the president, but the consent of the Senate is required.) In addition, if, as the Article 7 group does, the cabinet is recognized as possessing the power to dissolve the House of Representatives, the prime minister, who is the head of the cabinet, then stands in a position to exercise an exceedingly great power of control over the legislative branch by wielding the power of dissolution of the House of Representatives.

Basically, the National Diet is a collegiate body of the representatives of the sovereign people and is naturally the highest organ
of state power (Article 41). On the other hand, the prime minister
is designated by resolution of the National Diet (Article 67) and
in the exercise of the executive power the cabinet is collectively
responsible to the Diet (Article 66). Thus, what is termed "the
exercise of the executive power" is only the exercise of that which
is inherent in the executive power in accordance with the principle
of the separation of powers; and, it goes without saying, this includes the exercise of the powers presented to the executive branch
under the principle of checks and balances. That is to say, the
cabinet, in the exercise of all the powers that have been allocated
to it constitutionally, must bear a responsibility to the National
Diet. In other words, the National Diet is the director and the
cabinet is the directed. It is clear from this relationship that the
National Diet is the master and the cabinet is the subordinate.
The National Diet is in a position of superiority and the cabinet
is in a position of inferiority.

However, if, as the Article 7 group does, it is maintained that
the cabinet can under law, with complete freedom and at any
time, dissolve the House of Representatives, a cabinet that has
been called to account can dissolve the House of Representatives
as it is carrying out its own responsibility, and the result will be
an improper evasion of legal responsibility by the cabinet because
of its obliteration of that responsibility. This, it must be said, is
an extreme reversal of the positions of master and subordinate. It
must be regarded as just as peculiar as a debtor's possessing the
right to behead his creditor. Under a system of representative
democracy as in our Constitution, the National Diet is a collegiate
body of representatives of the sovereign people. If the House of
Representatives, the principal constituent element of the National
Diet, can be legally dissolved by the cabinet, which is under its
direction, completely arbitrarily, wilfully, at any time, without
warning, and by surprise—in spite of the fact that the Diet is
clearly proclaimed the highest organ of state power in the text
of the Constitution and in spite of the fact that it is in a position
to carry out its responsibility as the director of the cabinet—then
the foundation of representative democratic government will
totter and the existence of the House of Representatives will flicker

like a lamp in an unceasing wind. Under these circumstances in which the cabinet can wield, as it were, a sword with the power of life and death, where are the independence and the authority of the National Diet? With this will not the separation of powers, checks and balances, democratic government, the roots of the Constitution all end in complete confusion and chaos?

We do not have to go far to find an example of what evil may come from this; it is a matter of only a little more than a decade in the past. Allow me to draw on numerous examples of Hitler's tyrannical dissolution of the Reichstag; I do not think it will be necessary to go to the trouble of producing additional proof. Tyrannical government will always appear if the legislature is weak. The legislature will become weaker and weaker if tyrannical government is put into practice. Democratic government will develop if the legislature is strong. The very strength of the legislature is a bulwark against the appearance of tyrannical government. Furthermore, elections under democratic government are based on the premise of equality of opportunity: they operate on the principle that all will compete for votes on a footing of equality and on the basis of fair play. Nevertheless, it is clear that surprise dissolution will give the government party an unfair advantage over the opposition party. An election carried out under the conditions of such a handicap would be unfair and would make it impossible for the will of the people to be expressed correctly. True democratic government cannot be achieved by elections that do not accurately express the will of the people, for such elections will make it impossible for democracy to develop fruitfully.

Again, if we adopt the conclusion of the Article 7 group, it necessarily follows that, as I said before, the prime minister under the Constitution can wield excessively strong power and influence over the executive branch and over the judicial and legislative branches as well. Thus, it is clearer than a vision of fire that the excessive powers given a single concrete personality, namely, a prime minister can easily be concentrated and as a result can lead readily to dictatorial or tyrannical government. It is well to reflect on this. Calmly and dispassionately. Do not our people who were plunged into the depths of destruction and who received a terrible baptism of fire during World War II fear and detest the revival of dictatorial or tyrannical government more than anything else? I do not hesitate to declare solemnly that any interpretation of the Constitution (which has emerged from the experience, the environment, and the conditions described above) that will permit the easy revival of dictatorial or tyrannical government and is without any firm foundation in positive law, as pointed out above, is the opinion of a nearsighted group that cannot truly comprehend the basic principles of the establishment of a democratic constitution. Mr. Ozaki Yukio, possessed of a wealth of experience and great learning, has declared clearly and candidly (see the *Yomiuri Shimbun*, January 3, 1949) that "if a clever person comes on the scene, we shall rapidly see the reappearance of the Hojo and Ashikaga periods" [3] if things are conducted on the understanding that Article 7 of the Constitution provides for dissolution. These are wise words. I believe that this is wisdom coming from a discernment of the true nature of things.

To sum up what I have described above my thoughts are as follows:

(1) The Emperor can carry out only formal acts in matters of state and does not possess the power to execute substantial acts of government such as the dissolution of the House of Representatives (Article 4). (2) The cabinet under the principle of the separation of powers cannot dissolve the House of Representatives. (3) The cabinet under the principle of checks and balances can dissolve the House of Representatives, but only in the situations provided for in Article 69. (4) Our National Diet is a collective body of representatives of the sovereign people under a system of representative democratic government and is the highest organ of state power (Article 41); and for this reason it is natural that the cabinet cannot dissolve the House of Representatives. (5) The cabinet in its exercise of the executive power is responsible to the National Diet (Article 66); conversely then, from this point too, it stands to reason that the cabinet cannot dissolve the House of Representatives.

Furthermore, among the Article 7 group there are some who claim that because there may also be situations in which a cabinet that commands majority support in the House of Representatives

3. The late Ozaki Yukio (1859–1954) was a member of the old Imperial Diet and the National Diet from 1890 to 1952. He is revered as a courageous fighter for democratic freedoms. The two historical periods he referred to were characterized by great political confusion.

cannot carry out its work, it can then under Article 7 dissolve
the House of Representatives; but speaking for myself, in such a
situation, as I shall describe later, it is better for a resolution of
dissolution of the House of Representatives to be passed in the
National Diet. Thus, on the other hand, the recognition of the
right of the cabinet to dissolve the House of Representatives must
be termed a perversion of logic. There are also those in the Article
7 group who claim that the cabinet can dissolve the House of
Representatives in situations in which the necessity has arisen to
confirm by means of a general election whether the House of Representatives truly represents the opinion of the people. But this
is a completely political argument regarding the propriety of
dissolution and has not a particle of value as a legal argument.

In addition, among the Article 7 group, there are scholars who
put forth the English parliamentary cabinet system as an argument. That argument runs as follows: Our Constitution chose [as
a model] the English parliamentary cabinet system (major premise); under the English parliamentary cabinet system the cabinet
can dissolve the House of Commons at any time (minor premise);
therefore, under our Constitution the cabinet can dissolve the
House of Representatives at any time (conclusion). But this is
nothing more than a formal syllogism.

Is it not impossible to discover anywhere in the Constitution
any basis for the major premise? Nowhere in the Constitution is
it stated that the English parliamentary cabinet system was chosen
[as a model]. Strictly speaking, only the provisions of Article 69
set forth anything that resembles the limited system of dissolution
that is recognized under the European continental system of parliamentary cabinets. Under these provisions, the House of Representatives by passing a nonconfidence motion or rejecting a confidence motion can force a resignation en masse of the cabinet,
and at the same time the cabinet, as a countermeasure, can resort
to the defensive strategy of causing the dissolution of the House
of Representatives. Article 69 was provided as a means for maintaining the [system of] checks and balances between the House of
Representatives and the cabinet by this device.

It is in error to go beyond the express provisions of Article 69
and to jump to the hasty conclusion that it directly, generally,
summarily, and completely adopted the principle of the English

parliamentary cabinet system; to make free use of the syllogism from the basis of that major premise; and to conclude that the cabinet possesses the general right of dissolution. The Constitution provides nothing that can be regarded as the foundation for such a major premise. England is a monarchy in which the Parliament is selected by the people and the cabinet by the monarch. But under the Constitution of Japan a system of democratic government was chosen and an organization established under which the National Diet is chosen by the people and the head of the cabinet by the National Diet. In England the monarch dissolves Parliament, but our Emperor possesses no power to carry out acts of government. Confusing the differences of the two basic systems is no method for producing a legal principle for true dissolution.

Dissolution of the House of Representatives or the House of Commons, as seen from world history, is something that has developed under a monarchical system; and today, after all, it amounts to no more than a heritage of the monarchical system. In countries in which the monarchical system has disappeared it is something that cannot be recognized at all or only with limitations. Today, to say that the principle of the English form of the parliamentary cabinet system has been adopted and to use it to explain everything is in itself fundamentally unreasonable. Again, in England, through an old tradition there has been much practice and consciousness of popular politics, but these are lacking in our country. Consequently, from the standpoint of actual practice, as was pointed out earlier, to recognize the broad right of dissolution in our country is extremely dangerous and fraught with mischief. Ultimately, the dissolution of the House of Representatives by the cabinet as recognized under the principle of checks and balances must be limited only to the situations under Article 69; this is proper.

III. Next, the act of dissolution of the House of Representatives by the cabinet that is recognized under the principle of checks and balances is limited to Article 69; however I also believe that to think that because of this reason dissolution of the House of Representatives is limited only to the situations in Article 69 is to be too narrow and misses the main point. The opinion that holds that dissolution cannot be recognized because there is no clear statement permitting it in the text of the Constitution is also too narrow-minded and cannot be termed correct. To take another example, the only places where the Constitution uses the phrase "resign en masse" are Articles 69 and 70, but probably no one will contest the fact that it is generally recognized that the cabinet on its own decision can resign en masse at any time.

In legal terms, the resignation en masse of the cabinet can be said to be carried out according to a unique right inherent in the cabinet itself. In the same manner, the National Diet by its own decision can pass a resolution to dissolve the House of Representatives at any time.[4] That is to say, the National Diet can dissolve the House of Representatives in accordance with a unique right inherent in itself. Even more, the National Diet because it is the highest organ of state power has no reason to accept any restraint from any other organ in respect to its independent passage of a resolution of dissolution of the House of Representatives. The National Diet, which is the representative of the people, on occasions when it believes it necessary to appeal to popular opinion, can pass its own resolution of dissolution of the House of Representatives and is naturally responsible to the people therefor. Because only the House of Representatives is dissolved [under the Constitution], there is the tentative doubt whether only a resolution of the House of Representatives is desirable.

At the time when the dissolution debate was actually being noisily carried out in the National Diet, the substance of the advice reported to the speakers of both Houses as a result of the study made in the Rules Committees of both Houses of the National Diet was that dissolution should not be carried out at the will of the cabinet, and that it was desirable when a resolution regarding the dissolution of the House of Representatives was approved that it be carried out as an act of state in accordance with Article 7.

If the House of Representatives is to decide on dissolution, the House of Councillors should probably pass a similar resolution—the appropriateness of this can probably be pragmatically grasped. However, from the legal point of view, because the House of Representatives is only one constituent element of the National Diet, and because a determination of the will of the National Diet

4. Note that there is no specific constitutional basis for the argument that Justice Mano presents here.

should consist of a decision by both the House of Representatives and the House of Councillors, it is proper to construe the dissolution of the House of Representatives as also requiring a resolution of the National Diet. Thus, on occasions when there is such a resolution of dissolution or dissolution in accordance with Article 69, then the act of the Emperor in matters of state, as set forth in Article 7, item 3, can be formally carried out. (Moreover, dissolution, leaving aside the problem of political propriety, is not a matter on which the courts must render judgment; but if a suit is brought involving the determination of legality or illegality, then it becomes a matter that the courts must judge in accordance with the appropriate legal procedures. I shall not here go into this point in detail.)

Finally, in regard to the present case, the dissolution carried out by the cabinet in this case is in contravention of the Constitution and is invalid because, as was set forth earlier, it was done in the absence of a resolution of dissolution by the National Diet and because it does not come under the situations set forth in Article 69. However, there is nothing to do but to dismiss the claim of the plaintiff in the present suit because the plea is illegal as a proceeding in court for the reasons set forth in the majority opinion and as recognized by the majority opinion.

(TRANSLATED BY J. M. MAKI)

Hanreishū, VII, No. 1, 12 (Civil)

EDITORIAL NOTE: During a session of the Aomori Prefectural
Assembly on March 13, 1952, a member, Yonaiyama Giichirō, on
being heckled from the Liberal party benches said, "I am not addressing the gentlemen of the Liberal party; I am addressing the
Governor. Unlike them, I did not become an assemblyman to enrich myself. I'm no jobber or huckster. I'm putting my best efforts
into studying the problems of the prefecture." On the same day he
expressed contrition and asked that his words be expunged. Nevertheless, as a result of this incident he was expelled from the Assembly on March 15 by a majority resolution.

He thereupon instituted proceedings in the courts to have his
expulsion set aside. Simultaneously, he sought an injunction sus-
pending the implementation of the resolution, pending judgment in
this suit. The Aomori District Court granted such an injunction
on April 28. On May 4 the prime minister, purporting to act under
Article 10, paragraph 2, of the Administrative Litigation Procedure
Law issued an objection to the injunction. The district court, however, holding that the prime minister's objection was not in conformity with the requirements of the law, on May 27 gave a
ruling refusing to upset its injunction. The Aomori Assembly appealed to the Supreme Court under Article 419 (2) of the Code of
Civil Procedure.[1] Although the decision does not bear directly on

1. *Code of Civil Procedure*, ARTICLE 419–2. Regarding a ruling or an order against which
an objection is not allowed to be made, *Kokoku* appeal may be specially filed with the Supreme

a constitutional point, the separate opinions do raise important constitutional issues.

Grand Bench decision, January 16, 1953: Dismissed.

REFERENCES

Administrative Litigation Procedure Law. ARTICLE 10, paragraph 2. A court can order, on petition or on its own authority, the suspension of the execution of an act by means of a ruling if it recognizes urgent necessity in order to prevent irreparable damage arising out of the execution of an act when a suit has been brought under Article 2 [which provides for suits requesting cancellation or modification of administrative actions]. However, this does not apply if there is danger that the suspension of execution will have a serious effect on the public welfare and if the Prime Minister has expressed an objection.

FORMAL JUDGMENT

Appeal dismissed; cost of the appeal to be borne by the appellant.

REASONS. The "Reasons for Appeal" prepared by counsel for the appellant (Mr. Hasegawa and Mr. Kimura) is among the annexed documents.

It is proper to interpret an objection by the prime minister under Administrative Litigation Procedure Law, Article 10, paragraph 2, as a matter that can be raised only before a court has issued an injunction under the same article. Article 10, paragraph 2, provides that the court "can order, on petition or on its own authority, the suspension of the execution of an act by means of a ruling. . . . However, this does not apply . . . if the Prime Minister has expressed an objection." This means that a court must not grant an injunction when the prime minister has expressed an objection. It cannot be interpreted to include cases where the objection is expressed after the injunction has been granted.

It is clear from the transcript that the court granted the injunction on March 15, 1952 [This is an error. The date should be April 28.], and that the prime minister's objection was issued later, on May 16. The objection, therefore, was not in conformity with law.

Court only when the said decision contains misinterpretation of the Constitution or any other constitutional inconsistency.

It naturally follows that this appeal, which relies on such an objection, is also not in conformity with law. Moreover, among the rulings of the lower court, which are the subject of the present appeal, the ruling granting the injunction is in no way illegal; and the ruling refusing to suspend the injunction rejected the prime minister's objection, thereby upholding the previous injunction. These lead to the same result as our decision in this case.

For the above reasons we cannot hear the appeal. As set forth in the formal judgment, the appeal is dismissed; the court fees of the appeal are to be borne by the appellant.

This is the unanimous opinion of this Court apart from the individual opinions of Justices Tanaka Kōtarō, Kuriyama Shigeru, Mano Tsuyoshi, Saitō Yūsuke, and Kobayashi Shuzō.

* * *

The minority opinion of Justice Tanaka Kōtarō follows.

The majority opinion, after this Court on its own authority examined the issue, dismissed the appeal on the ground that an objection by the prime minister under Administrative Litigation Procedure Law, Article 10, paragraph 2, must be made before a court has issued an injunction under the same article. A more basic problem, however, underlies the application for an injunction against expulsion. The problem is simply: "Can a court grant an injunction against the expulsion of a local assemblyman?" This question must arise in connection with the principal suit (the application for the abrogation of the expulsion of a prefectural assemblyman). The majority's interpretation of the provision of the law relating to such an injunction is based on the premise that a court undoubtedly can grant an injunction in the present case.

In this case, the prime minister gave the following reasons for his objection:

A resolution disciplining an assemblyman is different from an act of an ordinary administrative agency and is fully recognized by the Local Autonomy Law as an autonomous function the object of which is to maintain discipline within the assembly. Hence, the execution of a disciplinary resolution does not depend on the ultimate decision of a court; if it is halted by a court's ruling the result will be that the autonomous operation of local assemblies will be seriously and improperly obstructed and there will be the danger that eventually the central spirit of local autonomy will suffer damage.

I also consider that the expulsion in the present case should be entrusted to the decision of the assembly itself as a question of internal discipline, outside the realm of interference by the judicial power. In this regard I consider that the prime minister's objection does not go far enough since it recognizes some interference by court decisions [in areas other than internal discipline].

Of course, the judicial power is not completely unrelated to questions of the internal relations of assemblies. Certain aspects of the relation with the judicial power are provided for in the Local Autonomy Law. The judicial power is also concerned with the internal affairs of assemblies when they involve such principles as equality before the law as provided in the Constitution. But the assembly should be the final arbiter of the questions: "Has there been a breach of Articles 132 [dignified language], 133 [insults] or others of the Local Autonomy Law or of assembly bylaws? Should the offender be disciplined and, if so, how and to what extent (by admonition, apology, suspension, or expulsion—and if by suspension, how long)?"

The logical basis of this conclusion must be sought in the pluralistic nature of the legal system. Legal phenomena are omnipresent in human society; they are not necessarily confined to that part of society known as the state. International society has its own law and there exist various organizations within the national society, for example, nonprofit-making foundations, companies, schools, social organizations, sports clubs, and the like, each of which has its own particular legal system. The legal system is pluralistic just as society is pluralistic. Among these special legal systems there are some that have a connection with the legal system of the state, that is, the general legal system; and there are some that do not. The extent of this connection is a matter of legislative policy to be determined by the state from the standpoint of the public welfare. It follows that the degree to which the general legal system will permeate the internal legal relationships of, say, the Diet, local assemblies, and government and private schools and, consequently, the degree to which the judicial power can intervene will not be the same in each case. In short, it is definitely not contrary to reason to recognize that in the case of the Diet and local assemblies, there is an area within which these bodies should make their own decisions with complete autonomy and where the intervention of the judicial power is not sanctioned. Questions of disciplinary action such as in the present case must undoubtedly be considered to be within this area.

Of course, there are occasions, depending on the nature of the organization, where the law does not entrust expulsion to an organization on the basis of majority decision. Take, for example, the expulsion of a member from an unlimited partnership. This is dealt with in Article 86 of the Commercial Code. There, a decision by a majority of the partners is not sufficient; they must also seek a decision from the courts. (It is the same when revoking the rights of a partner to act for or to represent the firm.) In such a situation, in view of the special relationships in an unlimited partnership, it is recognized that the courts, acting on behalf of the general legal system, may participate in the internal affairs of the partnership in matters relating to expulsion and that a simple decision of the partners is insufficient. If, however, in cases of disciplinary action in local assemblies or the Diet, the people concerned could contest in the courts the propriety of each punishment inflicted and the facts on which it is based, then the courts would become the final arbiter in questions of expulsion of assemblymen and the situation would be no different from that respecting unlimited partnerships. (Legal relationships within companies are as a whole within the ambit of the general legal system. Hence, even where a partner can be expelled only by agreement of the other parties—as was the case before the law was amended in 1938—it is recognized that there can be a suit in the courts to have the expulsion declared invalid.)

In short, in matters concerning discipline within a local assembly, the fact that the assembly itself is the final arbiter is the same as the situation in the Diet. Even though the majority acts arbitrarily, punishing where the facts are doubtful or treating minor offenses with undue severity, the affair ultimately amounts to a problem of their discretionary power to determine the facts, and, consequently, whether they are acting wrongly is only a question of politics, not of law.

In this connection there is the view that there is a distinction of kind between expulsion on the one hand and admonition, apology, and suspension for a specified period on the other, and that only the latter are to be considered as internal discipline. This view, however, has absolutely no logical basis. Underlying it are perhaps such considerations as: to deprive an assemblyman of his status is the extreme penalty; or, the status of assemblyman is conferred by election. But these cannot be regarded as a basis [for such a view]. One could, of course, enact legislation to give effect to the theory that a person popularly elected to a legislative body cannot be expelled by a resolution of that body. (This theory would be equally applicable to the Diet and local assemblies.) Furthermore, if the expulsion of a university student, like his temporary suspension or a reprimand, is considered internal discipline, then there is absolutely no reason why a distinction should be made between the expulsion of an assemblyman and other forms of discipline.

Next, it is necessary for us carefully to consider whether expulsion can be included among the acts of administrative agencies within the meaning of the Administrative Litigation Procedure Law. An assembly is not an executive, but a deliberative organ. If an assembly were to perform administrative acts, it would be doing things that pertain to the power of the executive organ— the governor. The object of an administrative act is the individual citizen. It is impossible to imagine a situation in which a local assembly stands in the position of an administrative agency toward a citizen. A resolution of a local assembly has no effect on outsiders, hence, one cannot call it an administrative act. Furthermore, both scholars and judicial precedents have generally recognized that an assembly cannot be called an administrative agency. The same logic must apply in the case of a disciplinary resolution ordering expulsion.

One can also infer from such phrases in Article 10, paragraph 2, as "irreparable damage arising out of the execution of an act," "urgent necessity," and "danger that the suspension of execution will have a serious effect on the public welfare," that the Administrative Litigation Procedure Law does not intend "administrative acts" to include such things as expulsion, which derive from the internal discipline of an assembly. Such phrases cannot be regarded as fitting snugly with expulsions or injunctions arising therefrom. This law, in these provisions, cannot be thought of as contemplating cases of expulsion. The decision appealed against (Aomori District Court, Civil Division, May 27, 1952) states that

Article 10 "clearly recognizes injunctions against disciplinary actions toward assemblymen"; this is unreasonable. It has as its only reason the point that Article 10 "provides no special exceptions." It gives no logical interpretation of the provision.

The earlier decision regarding the injunction (April 28, 1952) speaks of "the complete cessation of the parliamentary activities of the petitioner who held the position of chairman of the opposition members' finance and budget committee at a time when much important legislation was pending," and regards this as "irreparable damage." Such circumstances, however, frequently attend expulsions. If we were to call this "irreparable damage," injunctions against expulsion would have to be granted in almost all cases. Moreover, in such cases the damage should be suffered by the individual who is the object of the administrative act (i.e., the expelled person). Here, however, this is not the case: the damage is suffered by the whole assembly or by the prefecture itself. Thus, it is apparent that the district court has from the outset been mistaken in extending the Administrative Litigation Procedure Law to cases of expulsion from assemblies.

In short, the courts are responsible for affecting the "rule of law" in the state and in other organizations, but there is a distinct limit to the matters with which they can be concerned. This varies with the nature of the group. First, the state naturally cannot challenge the correctness of a discretionary act of an administrative agency. Secondly, it cannot intervene—even where a legal condition exists and it is not merely a question of propriety—if the task of deciding whether the requirements of the law have been fulfilled is entrusted entirely to the independent decision of the group concerned. The present case is of the latter type. The legal system with which the courts are concerned is confined only to general matters; it does not extend to special matters. If the courts were able to intervene in questions arising in every special legal system, then every type of dispute in society would be brought before them and we should, on the one hand, be embroiled in the evils of the omnipotence of the courts, while, on the other, there would be no guarantee against the danger of the courts' coming to a standstill. The courts must not trespass beyond the proper limits of their authority.

This case arose as a problem concerning the boundaries between the judiciary and the executive; in fact, however, there is a more fundamental question: the interrelationship of two legal systems. The majority opinion on this very important issue—leaving aside the question of whether it is correct or not—does nothing more than hand down an interpretation of a procedural section of the Administrative Litigation Procedure Law from the premise that in a case of expulsion the judicial power applies as a matter of course. The premise, however, is mistaken; that the courts have no jurisdiction in such a case is incontestable.

Hence, there are grounds for the appeal. The rulings of the Aomori District Court (Civil Division, April 28 and May 27, 1952) should both, accordingly, be set aside as contrary to law.

* * *

The dissenting opinion of Justice Kuriyama Shigeru follows. Inasmuch as the assembly of a local public entity [2] is like each House of the Diet, a deliberative organ, its essential mission is to deliberate. Hence, it has the duty to proceed smoothly with its deliberations, and at the same time it has an inherent power [phrase in English in original] to establish such internal rules as may be necessary for discharging this duty. Even in the absence of any express provisions, to determine assembly rules, to establish internal discipline as a part of those rules, and to discipline members who have broken those established internal rules are clearly functions inherent in deliberative organs. But since there are punitive provisions, even though they concern internal discipline, they must be set forth in explicit statements. For this reason there is provided, in the case of the Houses of the Diet, Article 58 of the Constitution and, in the case of assemblies, Article 134 of the

2. The phrase, "local public entities," is an awkward English translation of a Japanese technical term, *chihō kōkyō dantai*, in which *chihō* is "local," *kōkyō* is "public," and *dantai* is "entity," although it might also have been translated "body" or "unit," which are closer to the original. However, all English translations of the Constitution use the phrase "local public entities."

It must also be pointed out that the concept is a complex one. According to the Local Autonomy Law, "ordinary local public entities" include the Tokyo Metropolis, the island of Hokkaido, the "urban prefectures" of Kyoto and Osaka, the forty-two prefectures, and all cities, towns, and villages; "special local public entities" include special wards (only in Tokyo Metropolis), associations of ordinary entities, and financial districts for the purposes of holding and managing property and buildings. Thus, the concept includes formal units of local government on a number of levels and of different types, and what might be termed "public corporations" with no powers of government in the strict sense.

Local Autonomy Law.[3] Disciplinary action is an inherent power residing in the deliberative organ; its nature is the same whether it be taken as a result of a resolution of both Houses of the Diet or of a local assembly. It goes without saying that Article 93 of the Constitution, which provides that assemblies shall be established as the deliberative organs of local public entities, presumes the existence of the inherent power to make internal rules for internal discipline. The inherent power with respect to internal discipline is based on the principle that one can manage one's own house by one's self and means that the deliberative organ maintains the independence of its deliberative activities against outside interference. (There is no essential difference between Diet and assembly in this respect.) Since the imposition of discipline for these ends is part of the actual operation of the assembly, a disciplinary resolution is final, though it involves expulsion; it is not the kind of matter in which the intervention of other organs should be permitted.

Under the system now in force the judicial power with respect to local public entities resides in the national courts (Local Autonomy Law, Article 14), and, as exceptions, there are express provisions, such as Article 176 of the Local Autonomy Law, to recognize intervention with respect to assembly resolutions by other organs where both an assembly and an executive organ have been established. Similarly, there are situations such as those covered by Articles 118 and 127 of the same law in which judicial examination of complaints against assembly resolutions is permissible. In all these cases it is specially provided that "proceedings can be instituted against the assembly in the courts." But a resolution of an assembly imposing discipline is different in nature from discipline carried out by an appointing authority, namely, an act done by an administrative organ (see Articles 3 and 55, National Public Service Law). It is not, in the words of Administrative Litigation Procedure Law, Article 1, "the act of an administrative agency"; it is an exercise of the inherent power of internal discipline possessed by a legislative organ for the purpose of regulating its deliberations. Hence, the exceptional appeals to the courts provided for in the various articles of the Local Autonomy Law referred

3. The articles referred to deal with the power of the Diet and of local assemblies to handle internal disciplinary matters.

to above are not recognized. A disciplinary resolution of an assembly, if it should be wrong, is to be rectified by the will of the residents, who are supreme in local government, either by the re-election of an expelled member or the dissolution of the assembly (Local Autonomy Law, Articles 136 [right of an expelled member to be seated if re-elected] and 13 [right of citizens to demand dissolution]). Thus, there is no alternative but to conclude that even though the Local Autonomy Law contains no express provision to this effect, it would be improper intervention in the activities of a local public entity if a court were to examine an assembly resolution expelling a member. Furthermore, as I have explained above, the expulsion in the present case is not "an act of an administrative agency" as required by the Administrative Litigation Procedure Law, Article 1; hence, the objection by the prime minister made pursuant to the proviso in Article 10, paragraph 2, of that law must also, I consider, be unlawful.

If it should be argued that, since the Constitution (Article 58) provides for disciplinary punishment in the case of the Diet but remains silent as regards disciplinary punishment in assemblies, the latter comes within the purview of the courts, then this shows a misunderstanding of the nature of disciplinary punishment as described above. Moreover, in the case of local public entities, the Local Autonomy Law is a charter enacted on the authority of Article 92 of the Constitution, and the powers of local public entities are established within the framework of that charter. (There is separation of powers here in that, although the courts are national courts, they also exercise the judicial power of local public entities.) Hence, the status of assemblies vis-a-vis the courts in regard to Article 135 of the Local Autonomy Law is no different from that of the Diet in regard to Article 58 of the Constitution.

Next, the opinion that treats expulsion as an exception and recognizes judicial scrutiny of it is [actually] only dealing with a question of legislation. (I think that questions of legislation in the operation of democratic government are in no way limited to the assemblies of local public entities.) For example, whether there is to be short-term suspension or expulsion (and, since expulsion does not disqualify a person [from standing for re-election], he may be re-elected) is a question of the degree to which either is adequate for the maintenance of internal discipline; and, so long as expulsion is retained as a means of disciplinary punishment, if there is to be a nullification of expulsion, there is no reason why access to the courts should be recognized only for it, thus differentiating it from other kinds of disciplinary punishment. Disciplinary dismissal of a public official by the appointing authority within the same branch of government results in disqualification [for government employment] for a period of two years (Article 38, National Public Service Law). Because this certainly is a question related to the system of civil law, it is an act of an administrative agency that might well bear ultimate examination by the courts. In contrast to this, questions relating to internal discipline imposed by national or local deliberative organs to insure the smooth progress of their proceedings are of such a nature that they should, in the interest of the preservation of their independence, be handled internally without exception, even where expulsion is involved.

For the above reasons the lower court should not have granted the injunction sought by Yonaiyama Giichirō on March 24, 1952, against his expulsion from the Aomori Assembly, but should have dismissed it together with the principal suit (the suit seeking the setting aside of the expulsion) as unlawful. Hence, there are grounds for the present appeal. The lower court's decisions, which are the subject of the appeal, should be set aside.

*   *   *

The opinion of Justice Mano Tsuyoshi follows.

I would dismiss the appeal, the court fees for the appeal to be borne by the appellant. Administrative Litigation Procedure Law, Article 10, paragraph 1, provides that if an action is brought for the quashing or modification of an illegal act of an administrative agency or if other proceedings are instituted concerning rights in public law surrounding such an act, the execution of the administrative act shall not thereby be suspended. Article 10, paragraph 2, provides that if such an action is brought: "A court can order, on petition or on its own authority, the suspension of the execution of an act by means of a ruling, if it recognizes urgent necessity in order to prevent irreparable damage arising out of the execution of an act. . . ." It is further provided in the same article and paragraph that: ". . . this does not apply if there is danger that the suspension of execution will have a serious effect on the public welfare and if the Prime Minister has expressed an objection."

However, in my opinion, since this provision stipulates that no injunction can be granted "if the Prime Minister has expressed an objection," it must be declared contrary to the constitutional principle of the separation of powers and invalid. Where a right has been infringed by an illegal act of an administrative agency and a legal dispute has arisen, the persons concerned must be able to bring an action in the courts to have the illegal act set aside or modified so that they may obtain redress. There is no doubt that this comes within the judicial power which the Constitution places in the hands of the courts. It is also clear that when such a suit is brought, whether to grant an injunction under the main provision of Article 10, paragraph 2, is a judicial action pertaining to the judicial power. The proviso to the same article, however, prohibits recourse to this judicial action, which would order suspension of the act complained of when the prime minister has expressed an objection. This is contrary to the separation of powers principle since it is the invasion of the judicial field by the prime minister, an administrative functionary, and is interference with the judicial determination whether or not to order the suspension of the act complained of.

The constitution of a country that enjoys constitutional government makes a horizontal separation of governmental powers and provides a system in which these separated powers are allocated to vertical, mutually independent organs of government, each of which is thereby enabled to exercise its respective governmental power. The object of the Constitution in so doing is to abolish autocracy whereby an individual or a small minority wields the power of the state, to prevent improper monopolization or concentration of power, and to protect the freedom and fundamental human rights of the people. These are the fundamental principles which make up the core of constitutional government. In dividing the characteristic governmental powers into the three functions—legislative, judicial, and executive—a separation of powers [this phrase in the original] is effected in which the legislative power belongs to the legislature, the judicial power to the courts, and the executive power to the executive. In our country it has been customary to call this principle, *sankenbunritsu:* [*sanken* means "three powers"]; *bun* [separate] means a horizontal separation of powers; and *ritsu* [stand] is to be interpreted as indicating that the separation is regarded as vertical with each independent organ carrying out its own function. The phrase *bunritsu* [stand separate] is indeed rich in implication and deep in significance.

The makers of the United States Constitution, however, approaching the matter realistically, felt that if the division of powers were effected merely on the basis of a theoretical division according to the nature of the governmental processes, the harmonious conduct of national affairs would not ensue. Therefore, when they decided on the separation of powers, they adopted a special system of checks and balances [this phrase in the original] to ensure equality of power between each organ of government and to enable each to restrain the others. Our new Japanese Constitution is also based on these two great interrelated principles, "checks and balances" and "separation of powers." Essentially, laws pertain to the legislative power; yet the power to examine the constitutionality of laws is allotted to the courts. Again, essentially, impeachment pertains to the judicial power; yet it is allotted to the Diet. These are notable examples of checks and balances.

The powers bestowed on one organ of government pursuant to the principle of the separation of powers delineate the bounds within which that organ may operate, and accordingly this constitutes the positive limit of the operations of such an organ. In other words, this positive limit on the operation of one such organ constitutes the bounds that other organs cannot wilfully trespass; therefore, this is a negative limit on the operation of the other organs. Under a constitutional system the powers allocated to each arm of government by the constitution are mutually independent. It follows that it is a basic principle that there can be no reciprocal interference. If a governmental power allocated to one organ of government could be invaded at will by another organ of government, then it would be easy for one organ improperly and excessively to engross two or more different powers, resulting in autocracy, and for the separation of powers to become meaningless. This would be the first step toward the ultimate obliteration of the principal object of the Constitution: to abolish autocracy and to protect the freedom of the people.

By this logic, it is the same when, under the principle of checks and balances, a power has been allocated to one of the organs of government. That is to say, each power so allotted is exclusive to the organ on which it is bestowed, and the others, even in matters where they would have the power according to the principle of separation of powers, cannot interfere. [Note omitted.]

Now let us look at the case before us. When a person whose rights are infringed by an illegal administrative act (not improper [exercise of] discretionary powers) seeks relief by bringing an action in the courts to have the act set aside or modified, the hearing of such a case by the courts is, by its very nature, an action pertaining to the judicial power. In such a case to suspend temporarily, by means of an injunction pending judgment, the legal effect of an administrative act considered unlawful, is no more than a judicial action inherent in the judicial power. You cannot say that because it is an administrative suit the courts are performing an act on behalf of the executive; this is as clear as day. Article 76 of the Constitution says that in the realm of judicial power: "All judges shall be independent in the exercise of their conscience and shall be bound only by this Constitution and the laws." It goes without saying that when the legislators by enacting laws provide the norms that the judge requires for performing his duties, the judge, as one who interprets and applies the law, must follow those laws. The proviso in Article 10, paragraph 2, forbids the granting of an injunction "if the Prime Minister has expressed an objection." It therefore would appear that an injunction cannot be given because of this. One cannot, however, accept that the law is omnipotent and can provide anything except that men be women and vice versa. The laws that are enacted as norms for the judges in performing their duties should be general and abstract in content; the judges pursue their judicial tasks by applying these to individual, concrete cases. On the other hand, when the content of the law is not abstract and provides that it is permissible for the prime minister to intrude his objection in a concrete case that is being disposed of judicially by a court, then as soon as there has been such an objection, the judicial proceeding is no more, but is transformed into an administrative act. In other words, the court, through intervention by the executive, is forbidden to deal with the matter judicially by granting the injunction, and the result is that the executive assumes control over the judicial disposal by a court of a concrete case. To put it bluntly, if, when a court is trying to dispose of a matter judicially, the prime minister issues an objection and the court then has to bow to the objection, where is the independence of judicial power? Is this not a jumble of the administrative and judicial powers? I cannot remember having seen or heard of a piece of legislation as ill-informed and as short-sighted as this. When the separation of powers, one of the great principles of the Constitution, is benighted and on the verge of being cast into confusion, it needs no genius to tell us that there is the danger that autocracy, totalitarianism, and Caesarism [this word in original] will rear their ugly heads. For this reason I consider that this provision concerning objections by the prime minister is unconstitutional and void.

It may be argued that this provision permitting the prime minister, as head of the executive department, to issue an objection was enacted because there are occasions when to order the suspension of the execution of an administrative act would have a grave effect on the functioning of executive power. I fully understand this. Nevertheless, to permit an objection to be made in a specific suit is contrary to the principle of the separation of powers and is, therefore, quite unacceptable. If it is thought that it would not be sufficient were the clause to read only, "if there is danger that the suspension of execution will have a serious effect on the public welfare," then would it not be satisfactory to provide a suitable, general, abstract limitation? Again, how can it be right in a case like the present one—a suit concerning the expulsion of a single member of a single assembly in a single locality—to permit an objection to a judicial disposition by the courts of an administrative act, which is outside the bounds of the prime minister's administrative direction and supervision? Surely, doesn't this give a strong impression that someone is trying to use a guillotine to behead a chicken?

Finally, there may be people who consider that this power of the prime minister to express an objection is necessary and proper for a harmonious adjustment between the judicial and executive powers in administrative suits. This is a "checks and balances" idea and is plausible at first sight. Checks and balances, however, should be provided in the Constitution, the highest law of the state. The Constitution may provide checks and balances as it sees fit. Where, however, it is sought to embody this concept of checks and balances in ordinary legislation, such legislation must not be permitted to infringe the principle of the separation of powers and other provisions of the Constitution.

To sum up, since the prime minister's objection in the present case is unlawful, the appeal which is based on the premise that such an objection is valid is entirely groundless and should be dismissed.

In the case before us, several of my colleagues have put forward the view that a person expelled from the assembly of a local public entity (hereafter referred to as "the assembly") cannot challenge his expulsion before the courts. This is a question of considerable importance concerning administrative litigation under the new Constitution and is absolutely fundamental in the case before us. I, therefore, believe it my duty to state my views on this problem. I consider to be correct the implied premise of the majority opinion that the person expelled may take the matter to the courts.

Unless one has the self-confidence, the logical prowess, and the courage not only to believe in natural law or neonatural law (which derives from that medieval concept of ecclesiastical supremacy which declares that man-made law is inferior to divine law) but also to affirm unequivocally that "any provision of the Constitution which is contrary to natural law is void," then it is obvious that all legal problems that arise in this now independent country must be traced back to the Japanese Constitution and examined as springing from there. History shows that for mankind to achieve nationhood under law and the constitutional state were the prizes won after a thousand years of joint efforts and striving toward self-realization. Mankind won laws that provided general norms in order to eliminate specific autocratic abuses; then it won constitutions, which are the basic laws of government, in order to eliminate whatever autocracy continued under those laws. Thus, the contemporary state subsists on a legal system based on positive law (including enacted law, case law, and customary law); it is a device whereby the people may enjoy stable lives under the rule of positive law. When this legal system based on positive law is shattered or when attempts are made to shatter it, i.e., when rights are unlawfully infringed or attempts are made to infringe them, it is the courts whose task it is to give relief. Where relief is given only by judgments of the courts in all legal disputes between citizens and between citizens and state, then the rule of might (*macht*) [word in original] by force and private justice are prohibited, and law (*recht*) [word in original], which preserves and improves the legal system, reigns like the sun majestically over all. It is indeed this that can be called the rampart—the ultimate guarantee of the rule of the law. Judicial power, which is vested in the courts as provided in the Constitution, means precisely the power to adjudge legal disputes. It follows that since this power to adjudge legal disputes is vested in the courts, it is not vested in the legislature or the executive.

Article 76, paragraph 2, of the Constitution reads, "No extraordinary tribunal shall be established nor shall any organ or agency of the Executive be given final judicial power." Article 32 of the Constitution provides that "No person shall be denied the right of access to the courts." Such is the form of our constitutional system in which the judicial power is firmly established by means of the separation of powers. To put it another way, the power to adjudge legal disputes is vested in the courts by the Constitution and the people are empowered by the Constitution to go to the courts to seek the adjudication of legal disputes. The Constitution does not allow such resort to the courts to be restrained unduly, even by laws. Justice Tanaka, Justice Kuriyama, and Justice Kobayashi base their argument on the premise that recourse cannot be had to the courts except where the Local Autonomy Law expressly permits (Articles 118, 127, 176). This same premise was the view adopted by the administrative courts (essentially not judicial courts but mere administrative agencies) in administrative suits in the days of the old Constitution. This, however, cannot possibly be accepted under the new Constitution, recognizing as it does the principle of the separation of powers. Once there is a legal dispute, under the Constitution (as we have explained above) there must be the right of resort to the courts. Not only are specific statutory provisions permitting this not required, but the imposition of any restraint by law on such resort to the courts is prohibited by the Constitution. In my opinion the argument of the three Justices is not based on the Constitution and is topsy-turvy.

Justice Tanaka disposes of the matter very simply by saying that "even though the majority acts arbitrarily, punishing where the facts are doubtful," disciplinary punishment in an assembly is "only a question of politics, not of law." This, however, is a wild argument resulting from inadequate knowledge and makes no attempt to get to the truth of the matter. The Constitution provides that "Regulations concerning the organization and operations of local public entities shall be fixed by law . . ." (Article 92). "Local public entities shall have the right to . . . enact their own regulations within law" (Article 94). Pursuant to these articles of the Constitution the Local Autonomy Law provides that "A local public entity shall be a juristic person" (Article 2, paragraph 1); an ordinary local public entity may not deal with judicial matters (Article 2, paragraph 4, item 1). An ordinary local public entity may enact any bylaw on matters covered by Article 2, paragraph 2, provided that such bylaw does not contravene laws or orders (Article 14, paragraph 1). "The assembly of an ordinary local public entity may, by resolution, impose disciplinary punishment on any assemblyman who has contravened this law or the rules of the assembly. The rules of the assembly shall specify what conduct is punishable" (Article 134). The types of punishment provided are: admonition or apology in open session, suspension for a limited period, and expulsion (Article 135). Thus, an essential prerequisite for the punishment of a member by the assembly is that he should have acted contrary to the Local Autonomy Law or an assembly rule. In other words, the assembly cannot punish a member arbitrarily, as it pleases: it can punish only where the specific conduct of the member is covered by a predetermined definite general rule. It may punish only pursuant to the law. Therefore, it obviously follows that where this is not pursuant to the law, the question of illegality arises.

If disciplinary punishment were merely discretionary it would be a matter within the confines of autonomous local government and certainly the question of illegality would not arise. Where the punishment, however, is not in accordance with what the law lays down, it becomes not only a "political question," but a legal question: it is illegal. For example, the punishment is clearly illegal in cases like the following: (1) where the wrong man is punished; (2) where there exist no grounds for punishment; (3) where a person, expressing himself within the bounds of free speech guaranteed by the Constitution, is punished for opposing proposals in which the majority concur; (4) when the assembly rule of procedure on which the punishment is based is itself invalid as contravening the Constitution or a law or order. Hence, the view that the question of illegality cannot arise in the case of disciplinary punishment is a dogmatic judgment, stemming from inadequate knowledge.

Justice Tanaka also states that the expulsion in the present case "should be entrusted to the decision of the assembly itself as a question of internal discipline, outside the realm of interference by the judicial power." He does, however, say that the judicial power may intervene in internal affairs of assemblies if there is a breach of the Constitution.

The judicial power, however, applies to all legal disputes. Hence it applies as a matter of course to an illegal expulsion. Thus, there is no cause to talk of "interference by the judicial power." This is why the Local Autonomy Law goes so far as to provide that local public entities may not "deal with judicial matters" (Article 2, paragraph 4, item 1). Justice Tanaka fails to disclose any reason why the judicial power, although extending to unconstitutional expulsion, does not extend to unlawful expulsion. In recognizing this discrimination his argument has no basis, either in the Constitution or in other positive law. It is a completely barren argument.

He says that the logical basis of this conclusion must be sought in "the pluralistic nature of the legal system." He notes that there "exist various organizations within the national society, for example, nonprofit-making foundations, companies, schools, social organizations, sports clubs, and the like, each of which has its own particular legal system." It, of course, goes without saying that any type of organization within the national community, if it is independent, has the power to maintain its internal discipline independently and autonomously in accordance with the legal system that prevails in that organization. That type of legal system, under the name of "articles of association," "special agreement," "constitution," "rules," or "bylaws," determines the objectives, the organization, the method of operation, and so forth, of the organization, which operates in conformity with such requirements. Nevertheless, should a legal dispute arise between the society and a member or between members, and should it remain unsolved despite attempts to settle it independently as befits an autonomous organization, we must always in the last resort be able to bring it before the courts and receive judgment (Constitution, Article 76, paragraph 1, and Article 32). Although the legal system is pluralistic, nevertheless, insofar as a legal system obtains throughout the whole country, all legal disputes, unless the Constitution expressly provides otherwise, must finally be subject to determination by the courts. If a member of an organization, aggrieved at an act done by the organization that was illegal (not merely unsatisfactory), were not able in the last resort to seek relief in the courts because of the special legal system obtaining in the organization— if all that was left to him was to set his teeth and cry himself to sleep—then there would be chaotic diversity throughout the country and this would inevitably produce insecurity and discontent among the people. Thus, it is as plain as a pikestaff that a unified, harmonious legal system throughout the nation could not operate and that the essentials of the constitutional state under law would be lost. My argument is that the legal system in the country must, in the final analysis, be unified and that it is only through the protection afforded by this unity that the legal system and the rule of law in a country can be completely fulfilled. No matter how vigorously the empty theory of the pluralism of the legal system is pressed, it needs no genius to tell us that there is no logical basis for the view that an illegal expulsion cannot be brought before the courts.

Justice Tanaka says, "An assembly is not an executive, but a deliberative organ. If an assembly were to perform administrative acts, it would be doing things that pertain to the power of the executive organ—the governor." An assembly makes bylaws and rules of procedure. But just as in the case of the Supreme Court, which becomes a legislature when it makes court rules, you cannot say that this makes the assembly a legislature *strictu sensu* within the meaning of the Constitution. The assembly, when it does so, is always acting as an administrative authority performing autonomous local administration. When an assembly as a deliberative body adopts a mere resolution embodying its views about an internal matter, this should not be considered as an administrative act vis-a-vis outsiders. However, since by virtue of Local Autonomy Law, Article 134, a resolution punishing a member has immediate effect as regards that member, it is an administrative act by an administrative agency. Accordingly, a member unlawfully punished undoubtedly may challenge this unlawful administrative act in the courts.

*   *   *

The supplementary opinion of Justice Saito Yūsuke follows.

In the "Reasons for Special Appeal," lodged [by the Aomori Assembly] on June 1, 1952, it is contended that, although the two rulings in the original decision are such that no appeal may be made against them by virtue of Article 10, paragraph 5, of the Administrative Litigation Procedure Law, which bars dissatisfaction as a ground for an injunction, an appeal for their setting aside can be made under Article 419 (2) of the Code of Civil Procedure since they are unconstitutional—subverting the principles underlying the separation of powers, infringing Articles 65 and 76 of the Constitution, and judging matters that ought not to be judged.

The first ruling of the Aomori District Court was, however, given on April 28, 1952. Therefore, it is clear that the special appeal against this ruling (see Summary of Grounds for Appeal, paragraph 2, and Grounds for Appeal, No. 5) was lodged after the expiration of the rigid time limit [five days] provided in Article 419 (2) of the Code of Civil Procedure and is therefore incompetent. (I oppose the view that the time limit is not rigid.)

The second ruling of the same court merely says that the prime minister's objection was not valid since it did not give any reasons and, hence, it could in no way affect the injunction already granted. To avoid any doubts it ruled that the injunction already granted be not set aside. The ruling in no way dealt with the constitutionality of any law, order, regulation, or official act. Thus, it is abundantly clear that this special appeal against the ruling, although purporting to deal with constitutionality (see Summary of Grounds of Appeal, paragraph 1, and Ground of Appeal, No. 4), is in fact merely an attack on the ruling for its finding whether the prime minister's objection, made under Administrative Litigation Procedure Law, Article 10, paragraph 2, satisfies Article 10, paragraph 3 [which requires a clear statement of reasons for the objection]. The appeal, it is perfectly clear, does not conform to the requirements for appeal under Article 419 (2) of the Code of Civil Procedure and is incompetent.

A judgment is nothing but a conclusion of a syllogism in which abstract law is the major premise and concrete facts comprise the minor premise. Hence, special appeal seeking the examination of constitutionality should naturally be permitted only in cases containing a conclusion, that is, a judgment regarding constitutionality in the original ruling. If, in the absence of such a conclusion in the original ruling, we should go to extremes and, imagining or creating the fiction that such a conclusion was implicit in the ruling, base our argument on the farfetched contention of unconstitutionality by one of the parties, then this would not only be to mistake the nature of a judicial decision, but would also violate the express provisions of Article 419 (2) of the Code of Civil Procedure, deviate from the primary mission of the Supreme Court, and call forth a multitude of pointless suits—straws that together would break the camel's back. This cannot be countenanced for an instant; it would be the idiocy of one who deliberately courts ruin.

The special appeal should accordingly be dismissed as incompetent.

*　　*　　*

The supplementary opinion of Justice Kobayashi Shunzō follows.

As regards the contention of the appellant concerning the prime minister's objection, I agree with the "Reasons" (above) in which it is held incompetent. However, I differ on the later point where it is said that the ruling granting the injunction in this case is not unlawful. I shall, therefore, give my reasons.

1. The essence of the democratic state is self-government; what we call government in the state is only the phenomenon of self-government. The system that this government gives rise to consists of tiers of lower-level, self-governing systems. These lower-level, self-governing systems ultimately constitute the structure of state power and are links in it. Again, in the same way as the Diet is the center of politics, which is the source of the strength

of state power, the assemblies of the local public entities (which are the lower-level systems) are also the centers of local politics and constitute the source of power in local self-government. However, since the local public entities are the self-governing systems that are links of state power, it goes without saying that theirs is a relative independence and that they manifest their functions within this limitation. Moreover, the concept of self-government embraces autonomy and independence, by which is meant that the organization conducts its internal operations in accordance with its own will and competence without any restriction from outside. Just as the Diet, the source of the strength of state power, has a high degree of autonomy and independence, the assemblies, the sources of power in local government, naturally, within their own limits of relative independence, have autonomy and independence. Only when we think along these lines can we expect to understand the structure and development of democratic government. The above can also be recognized from the organization and operations of local public entities, which are guaranteed by the Constitution and the Local Autonomy Law; from the inherent administrative power which they possess as an independent function; and from the legislative power, which is guaranteed within the limits of the law.

2. Since such is the character of the assemblies of local public entities, their proceedings and their resolutions (a term I use here and below as including their rulings) naturally are carried out autonomously and independently; this principle must be respected. However, approaching the problem from the standpoint that their independence is relative, it goes without saying that this can be restricted by laws and orders. Moreover, when we consider the relationship between the autonomy and independence of an assembly's proceedings and resolutions and the objects of those resolutions, it becomes apparent that the objects of resolutions include all functions permitted to local self-government and are of two kinds, viz., matters pertaining to the administrative and legislative processes, the scope of which is determined by laws and orders, and matters that pertain essentially to the political process and that the assembly can autonomously and independently proceed with up to and including the point at which resolution is made. Actions of the latter type are a part of the political process

that the assembly itself conducts by means of the principle of majority decision and are of such a nature that they can be finally settled by the authority of the assembly itself. It follows that matters in this category are not by nature fitted to be the subject of the judicial power. Hence, where it is desired that there should be resort to the courts, the law makes special provisions to that effect, even though the matter by nature falls within such a category: for example, suits contesting a decision made by an assembly concerning an election in the assembly (Local Autonomy Law, Article 118, paragraph 1, item 5) or the qualifications of a member (Article 127, paragraph 1, item 4), suits in which the head of a local public entity, after having caused a resolution to be reconsidered or an election to be repeated, still seeks the setting aside [on the ground it is still *ultra vires* or illegal] or the modification of the resolution or election for specified reasons (Article 176, paragraph 5). In other words, matters determined by an assembly primarily by the political process are not as a general rule the object of the judicial power. There are, however, exceptions in which suits are permitted, and these are expressly provided by the law. A case like the present, however, dealing with disciplinary punishment, definitely pertains to the political process and such questions as whether expulsion, suspension, or apology and admonition are appropriate, are by their nature not suitable objects for the judicial power; moreover, the law contains no provision permitting suits in such cases. To put it another way, matters relating to disciplinary punishment are dealt with and settled by the assembly through the political process, autonomously and independently by the majority principle. Whether it is lawful or unlawful is to be settled by the assembly itself by means of its own internal functions. From the standpoint of administrative law one could say that this is something within the discretion of the assembly; this is merely saying that since the matter is of such a character, such would be the result if it were to be classified. However, although matters relating to disciplinary punishment are of the nature that I have described, if the ruling imposing punishment is unconstitutional, the proper interpretation is that a person objecting thereto should be allowed to sue: for example, where the resolution imposing punishment contravenes the principle of equality under the law (Constitution, Article 14). Although, as I have explained above, assemblies are independent and autonomous—for they exist under the Constitution—as links of state power, this does not mean that they are free to violate the Constitution.

3. When considering the question from the standpoint of Article 3 of the Court Organization Law, which speaks of "all legal disputes" [that are to be decided by the courts], it is proper to interpret this as not including matters such as those relating to disciplinary punishment. One of the conditions that must be satisfied before we can speak of a dispute within the above meaning is that it must be something capable of being settled through the interpretation and application of the law by the courts. As regards matters of disciplinary punishment, the degree of difference between the penalties of expulsion, suspension, apology, and admonition which an assembly determines by its own power, as part of the political process, is certainly not a matter appropriate for a court (a third party outside the framework of local government) to settle by interpretation and application of the law. Moreover, even though a court did act, there would remain the difficult problem of whether it could reach a decision that would, in fact, take root and receive the acceptance of the local inhabitants.

Those who hold a view contrary to mine on this question probably base their argument on the excesses of majorities. Even though there may be occasions when the propriety of decisions imposing disciplinary punishment may become the object of criticism by society [the decision on] rightness or wrongness is inevitable under true democratic government, which adheres to the current principle of majority decision. If the courts were to invade such fields, they would be in danger of being embroiled in politics. Where, however, a decision by an assembly imposing such punishment contravenes the Constitution, even though we speak in terms of the nature of the dispute, the matter is one that the courts may handle and settle, nay, rather, it is one with which the courts, in the discharge of their basic function, must deal.

4. For these reasons, matters like the present case, which relate to disciplinary punishment, are not the proper object of the judicial power. Accordingly, it is not a case where an injunction should be granted. When an injunction has been issued and, under Article 10, paragraph 5, of the Administrative Litigation Procedure Law, no appeal may be made against such an injunction,

there remains only the procedure of a special appeal to the Supreme Court, but only where there are the grounds provided for in Article 419 (2) of the Code of Civil Procedure. However, in the present case the Aomori Prefectural Assembly in its Summary of Grounds for Appeal, paragraph 2, seeks the setting aside of the injunction. The appeal, however, was lodged later than the time limit of five days after the injunction was issued (Article 419 <2>, paragraph 2, Code of Civil Procedure). Hence, it cannot be said that this is a valid special appeal. Therefore, irrespective of the other reasons I have adduced, it must also be said that this case cannot be appealed against because it is one against which an objection is not allowable.

As regards the complaint in the present special appeal concerning the lower court's failure to set aside the injunction despite the prime minister's objection, I arrive at the ruling in this case set forth in the formal judgment, for, as stated at the beginning of the "Reasons" for the ruling, the prime minister's objection was already incompetent because the prime minister had not made it within the time permitted.

(TRANSLATED BY D. C. S. SISSONS)

APPENDIX I:
THE CONSTITUTION OF JAPAN

From The Constitution of Japan and Criminal Statutes. *Compiled by the Ministry of Justice, Tokyo, 1958. (Because this can be considered an official translation, spelling, punctuation, and so forth are exactly as they are in the original.)*

We, the Japanese people, acting through our duly elected representatives in the National Diet, determined that we shall secure for ourselves and our posterity the fruits of peaceful cooperation with all nations and the blessings of liberty throughout this land, and resolved that never again shall we be visited with the horrors of war through the action of government, do proclaim that sovereign power resides with the people and do firmly establish this Constitution. Government is a sacred trust of the people, the authority for which is derived from the people, the powers of which are exercised by the representatives of the people, and the benefits of which are enjoyed by the people. This is a universal principle of mankind upon which this Constitution is founded. We reject and revoke all constitutions, laws, ordinances, and rescripts in conflict herewith.

We, the Japanese people, desire peace for all time and are deeply conscious of the high ideals controlling human relationship, and we have determined to preserve our security and existence, trusting in the justice and faith of the peace-loving peoples of the world. We desire to occupy an honored place in an international society striving for the preservation of peace, and the banishment of tyranny and slavery, oppression and intolerance for all time from the earth. We recognize that all peoples of the world have the right to live in peace, free from fear and want.

We believe that no nation is responsible to itself alone, but that laws

411

of political morality are universal; and that obedience to such laws is incumbent upon all nations who would sustain their own sovereignty and justify their sovereign relationship with other nations.

We, the Japanese people, pledge our national honor to accomplish these high ideals and purposes with all our resources.

CHAPTER I. THE EMPEROR

ARTICLE 1.   The Emperor shall be the symbol of the State and of the unity of the people, deriving his position from the will of the people with whom resides sovereign power.

ARTICLE 2.   The Imperial Throne shall be dynastic and succeeded to in accordance with the Imperial House Law passed by the Diet.

ARTICLE 3.   The advice and approval of the Cabinet shall be required for all acts of the Emperor in matters of state, and the Cabinet shall be responsible therefor.

ARTICLE 4.   The Emperor shall perform only such acts in matters of state as are provided for in this Constitution and he shall not have powers related to government.

2. The Emperor may delegate the performance of his acts in matters of state as may be provided by law.

ARTICLE 5.   When, in accordance with the Imperial House Law, a Regency is established, the Regent shall perform his acts in matters of state in the Emperor's name. In this case, paragraph one of the preceding article will be applicable.

ARTICLE 6.   The Emperor shall appoint the Prime Minister as designated by the Diet.

2. The Emperor shall appoint the Chief Judge of the Supreme Court as designated by the Cabinet.

ARTICLE 7.   The Emperor, with the advice and approval of the Cabinet, shall perform the following acts in matters of state on behalf of the people:

(1) Promulgation of amendments of the constitution, laws, cabinet orders and treaties;

(2) Convocation of the Diet;

(3) Dissolution of the House of Representatives;

(4) Proclamation of general election of members of the Diet;

(5) Attestation of the appointment and dismissal of Ministers of State and other officials as provided for by law, and of full powers and credentials of Ambassadors and Ministers;

(6) Attestation of general and special amnesty, commutation of punishment, reprieve, and restoration of rights;

(7) Awarding of honors;

(8) Attestation of instruments of ratification and other diplomatic documents as provided for by law;

(9) Receiving foreign ambassadors and ministers;

(10) Performance of ceremonial functions.

ARTICLE 8.   No property can be given to, or received by, the Imperial House, nor can any gifts be made therefrom, without the authorization of the Diet.

CHAPTER II. RENUNCIATION OF WAR

ARTICLE 9.   Aspiring sincerely to an international peace based on justice and order, the Japanese people forever renounce war as a sovereign right of the nation and the threat or use of force as a means of settling international disputes.

2. In order to accomplish the aim of the preceding paragraph, land, sea, and air forces, as well as other war potential, will never be maintained. The right of belligerency of the state will not be recognized.

CHAPTER III. RIGHTS AND DUTIES OF THE PEOPLE

ARTICLE 10.   The conditions necessary for being a Japanese national shall be determined by law.

ARTICLE 11.   The people shall not be prevented from enjoying any of the fundamental human rights. These fundamental human rights guaranteed to the people by this Constitution shall be conferred upon the people of this and future generations as eternal and inviolate rights.

ARTICLE 12.   The freedoms and rights guaranteed to the people by this Constitution shall be maintained by the constant endeavor of the people, who shall refrain from any abuse of these freedoms and rights and shall always be responsible for utilizing them for the public welfare.

ARTICLE 13.   All of the people shall be respected as individuals. Their right to life, liberty, and the pursuit of happiness shall, to the extent that it does not interfere with the public welfare, be the supreme consideration in legislation and in other governmental affairs.

ARTICLE 14.   All of the people are equal under the law and there shall be no discrimination in political, economic or social relations because of race, creed, sex, social status or family origin.

2. Peers and peerage shall not be recognized.

3. No privilege shall accompany any award of honor, decoration or any distinction, nor shall any such award be valid beyond the lifetime of the individual who now holds or hereafter may receive it.

ARTICLE 15.   The people have the inalienable right to choose their public officials and to dismiss them.

2. All public officials are servants of the whole community and not of any group thereof.

3. Universal adult suffrage is guaranteed with regard to the election of public officials.

4. In all elections, secrecy of the ballot shall not be violated. A voter shall not be answerable, publicly or privately, for the choice he has made.

ARTICLE 16.   Every person shall have the right of peaceful petition for the redress of damage, for the removal of public officials, for the enactment, repeal or amendment of laws, ordinances or regulations and for other matters, nor shall any person be in any way discriminated against for sponsoring such a petition.

ARTICLE 17.   Every person may sue for redress as provided by law from the State or a public entity, in case he has suffered damage through illegal act of any public official.

ARTICLE 18.   No person shall be held in bondage of any kind. Involuntary servitude, except as punishment for crime, is prohibited.

ARTICLE 19.   Freedom of thought and conscience shall not be violated.

ARTICLE 20.   Freedom of religion is guaranteed to all. No religious organization shall receive any privileges from the State nor exercise any political authority.

2. No person shall be compelled to take part in any religious acts, celebration, rite or practice.

3. The State and its organs shall refrain from religious education or any other religious activity.

ARTICLE 21.   Freedom of assembly and association as well as speech, press and all other forms of expression are guaranteed.

2. No censorship shall be maintained, nor shall the secrecy of any means of communication be violated.

ARTICLE 22.   Every person shall have freedom to choose and change his residence and to choose his occupation to the extent that it does not interfere with the public welfare.

2. Freedom of all persons to move to a foreign country and to divest themselves of their nationality shall be inviolate.

ARTICLE 23.   Academic freedom is guaranteed.

ARTICLE 24.   Marriage shall be based only on the mutual consent of both sexes and it shall be maintained through mutual cooperation with the equal rights of husband and wife as a basis.

2. With regard to choice of spouse, property rights, inheritance, choice of domicile, divorce and other matters pertaining to marriage and the

family, laws shall be enacted from the standpoint of individual dignity and the essential equality of the sexes.

ARTICLE 25. All people shall have the right to maintain the minimum standards of wholesome and cultured living.

2. In all spheres of life, the State shall use its endeavors for the promotion and extension of social welfare and security, and of public health.

ARTICLE 26. All people shall have the right to receive an equal education correspondent to their ability, as provided by law.

2. All people shall be obligated to have all boys and girls under their protection receive ordinary educations as provided for by law. Such compulsory education shall be free.

ARTICLE 27. All people shall have the right and the obligation to work.

2. Standards for wages, hours, rest and other working conditions shall be fixed by law.

3. Children shall not be exploited.

ARTICLE 28. The right of workers to organize and to bargain and act collectively is guaranteed.

ARTICLE 29. The right to own or to hold property is inviolable.

2. Property rights shall be defined by law, in conformity with the public welfare.

3. Private property may be taken for public use upon just compensation therefor.

ARTICLE 30. The people shall be liable to taxations as provided by law.

ARTICLE 31. No person shall be deprived of life or liberty, nor shall any other criminal penalty be imposed, except according to procedure established by law.

ARTICLE 32. No person shall be denied the right of access to the courts.

ARTICLE 33. No person shall be apprehended except upon warrant issued by a competent judicial officer which specifies the offense with which the person is charged, unless he is apprehended, the offense being committed.

ARTICLE 34. No person shall be arrested or detained without being at once informed of the charges against him or without the immediate privilege of counsel; nor shall he be detained without adequate cause; and upon demand of any person such cause must be immediately shown in open court in his presence and the presence of his counsel.

ARTICLE 35. The right of all persons to be secure in their homes, papers and effects against entries, searches and seizures shall not be impaired except upon warrant issued for adequate cause and particularly describing the place to be searched and things to be seized, or except as provided by Article 33.

2. Each search or seizure shall be made upon separate warrant issued by a competent judicial officer.

ARTICLE 36. The infliction of torture by any public officer and cruel punishments are absolutely forbidden.

ARTICLE 37. In all criminal cases the accused shall enjoy the right to a speedy and public trial by an impartial tribunal.

2. He shall be permitted full opportunity to examine all witnesses, and he shall have the right of compulsory process for obtaining witnesses on his behalf at public expense.

3. At all times the accused shall have the assistance of competent counsel who shall, if the accused is unable to secure the same by his own efforts, be assigned to his use by the State.

ARTICLE 38. No person shall be compelled to testify against himself.

2. Confession made under compulsion, torture or threat, or after prolonged arrest or detention shall not be admitted in evidence.

3. No person shall be convicted or punished in cases where the only proof against him is his own confession.

ARTICLE 39. No person shall be held criminally liable for an act which was lawful at the time it was committed, or of which he has been acquitted, nor shall he be placed in double jeopardy.

ARTICLE 40. Any person, in case he is acquitted after he has been arrested or detained, may sue the State for redress as provided by law.

CHAPTER IV. THE DIET

ARTICLE 41. The Diet shall be the highest organ of state power, and shall be the sole law-making organ of the State.

ARTICLE 42. The Diet shall consist of two Houses, namely the House of Representatives and the House of Councillors.

ARTICLE 43. Both Houses shall consist of elected members, representative of all the people.

2. The number of the members of each House shall be fixed by law.

ARTICLE 44. The qualifications of members of both Houses and their electors shall be fixed by law. However, there shall be no discrimination because of race, creed, sex, social status, family origin, education, property or income.

ARTICLE 45. The term of office of members of the House of Representatives shall be four years. However, the term shall be terminated before the full term is up in case the House of Representatives is dissolved.

ARTICLE 46. The term of office of members of the House of Councillors shall be six years, and election for half the members shall take place every three years.

ARTICLE 47. Electoral districts, method of voting and other matters pertaining to the method of election of members of both Houses shall be fixed by law.

ARTICLE 48. No person shall be permitted to be a member of both Houses simultaneously.

ARTICLE 49. Members of both Houses shall receive appropriate annual payment from the national treasury in accordance with law.

ARTICLE 50. Except in cases provided by law, members of both Houses shall be exempt from apprehension while the Diet is in session, and any members apprehended before the opening of the session shall be freed during the term of the session upon demand of the House.

ARTICLE 51. Members of both Houses shall not be held liable outside the House for speeches, debates or votes cast inside the House.

ARTICLE 52. An ordinary session of the Diet shall be convoked once per year.

ARTICLE 53. The Cabinet may determine to convoke extraordinary sessions of the Diet. When a quarter or more of the total members of either House makes the demand, the Cabinet must determine on such convocation.

ARTICLE 54. When the House of Representatives is dissolved, there must be a general election of members of the House of Representatives within forty (40) days from the date of dissolution, and the Diet must be convoked within thirty (30) days from the date of the election.

2. When the House of Representatives is dissolved, the House of Councillors is closed at the same time. However, the Cabinet may in time of national emergency convoke the House of Councillors in emergency session.

3. Measures taken at such session as mentioned in the proviso of the preceding paragraph shall be provisional and shall become null and void unless agreed to by the House of Representatives within a period of ten (10) days after the opening of the next session of the Diet.

ARTICLE 55. Each House shall judge disputes related to qualifications of its members. However, in order to deny a seat to any member, it is necessary to pass a resolution by a majority of two-thirds or more of the members present.

ARTICLE 56. Business cannot be transacted in either House unless one-third or more of total membership is present.

2. All matters shall be decided, in each House, by a majority of those present, except as elsewhere provided in the Constitution, and in case of a tie, the presiding officer shall decide the issue.

ARTICLE 57. Deliberation in each House shall be public. However, a secret meeting may be held where a majority of two-thirds or more of those members present passes a resolution therefor.

2. Each House shall keep a record of proceedings. This record shall be published and given general circulation, excepting such parts of proceedings of secret session as may be deemed to require secrecy.

3. Upon demand of one-fifth or more of the members present, votes of the members on any matter shall be recorded in the minutes.

ARTICLE 58. Each House shall select its own president and other officials.

2. Each House shall establish its rules pertaining to meetings, proceedings and internal discipline, and may punish members for disorderly conduct. However, in order to expel a member, a majority of two-thirds or more of those members present must pass a resolution thereon.

ARTICLE 59. A bill becomes a law on passage by both Houses, except as otherwise provided by the Constitution.

2. A bill which is passed by the House of Representatives, and upon which the House of Councillors makes a decision different from that of the House of Representatives, becomes a law when passed a second time by the House of Representatives by a majority of two-thirds or more of the members present.

3. The provision of the preceding paragraph does not preclude the House of Representatives from calling for the meeting of a joint committee of both Houses, provided for by law.

4. Failure by the House of Councillors to take final action within sixty (60) days after receipt of a bill passed by the House of Representatives, time in recess excepted, may be determined by the House of Representatives to constitute a rejection of the said bill by the House of Councillors.

ARTICLE 60. The Budget must first be submitted to the House of Representatives.

2. Upon consideration of the budget, when the House of Councillors makes a decision different from that of the House of Representatives, and when no agreement can be reached even through a joint committee of both Houses, provided for by law, or in the case of failure by the House of Councillors to take final action within thirty (30) days, the period of recess excluded, after the receipt of the budget passed by the House of Representatives, the decision of the House of Representatives shall be the decision of the Diet.

ARTICLE 61. The second paragraph of the preceding article applies also to the Diet approval required for the conclusion of treaties.

ARTICLE 62. Each House may conduct investigations in relation to government, and may demand the presence and testimony of witnesses, and the production of records.

ARTICLE 63. The Prime Minister and other Ministers of State may, at any time, appear in either House for the purpose of speaking on bills, regardless of whether they are members of the House or not. They must appear when their presence is required in order to give answers or explanations.

ARTICLE 64. The Diet shall set up an impeachment court from among the members of both Houses for the purpose of trying those judges against whom removal proceedings have been instituted.

2. Matters relating to impeachment shall be provided by law.

CHAPTER V. THE CABINET

ARTICLE 65. Executive power shall be vested in the Cabinet.

ARTICLE 66. The Cabinet shall consist of the Prime Minister, who shall be its head, and other Ministers of State, as provided for by law.

2. The Prime Minister and other Ministers of State must be civilians.

3. The Cabinet, in the exercise of executive power, shall be collectively responsible to the Diet.

ARTICLE 67. The Prime Minister shall be designated from among the members of the Diet by a resolution of the Diet. This designation shall precede all other business.

2. If the House of Representatives and the House of Councillors disagree and if no agreement can be reached even through a joint committee of both Houses, provided for by law, or the House of Councillors fails to make designation within ten (10) days, exclusive of the period of recess, after the House of Representatives has made designation, the decision of the House of Representatives shall be the decision of the Diet.

ARTICLE 68. The Prime Minister shall appoint the Ministers of State. However, a majority of their number must be chosen from among the members of the Diet.

2. The Prime Minister may remove the Ministers of State as he chooses.

ARTICLE 69. If the House of Representatives passes a nonconfidence resolution, or rejects a confidence resolution, the Cabinet shall resign en masse, unless the House of Representatives is dissolved with ten (10) days.

ARTICLE 70. When there is a vacancy in the post of Prime Minister, or upon the first convocation of the Diet after a general election of members of the House of Representatives, the Cabinet shall resign en masse.

ARTICLE 71. In the cases mentioned in the two preceding Articles, the

Cabinet shall continue its functions until the time when a new Prime Minister is appointed.

ARTICLE 72. The Prime Minister, representing the Cabinet, submits bills, reports on general national affairs and foreign relations to the Diet and exercises control and supervision over various administrative branches.

ARTICLE 73. The Cabinet, in addition to other general administrative functions, shall perform the following functions:

(1) Administer the law faithfully; conduct affairs of state;

(2) Manage foreign affairs;

(3) Conclude treaties. However, it shall obtain prior or, depending on circumstances, subsequent approval of the Diet;

(4) Administer the civil service, in accordance with standards established by law;

(5) Prepare the budget, and present it to the Diet;

(6) Enact cabinet orders in order to execute the provisions of this Constitution and of the law. However, it cannot include penal provisions in such cabinet orders unless authorized by such law.

(7) Decide on general amnesty, special amnesty, commutation of punishment, reprieve, and restoration of rights.

ARTICLE 74. All laws and cabinet orders shall be signed by the competent Minister of State and countersigned by the Prime Minister.

ARTICLE 75. The Ministers of State, during their tenure of office, shall not be subject to legal action without the consent of the Prime Minister. However, the right to take that action is not impaired hereby.

CHAPTER VI. JUDICIARY

ARTICLE 76. The whole judicial power is vested in a Supreme Court and in such inferior courts as are established by law.

2. No extraordinary tribunal shall be established, nor shall any organ or agency of the Executive be given final judicial power.

3. All judges shall be independent in the exercise of their conscience and shall be bound only by this Constitution and the laws.

ARTICLE 77. The Supreme Court is vested with the rule-making power under which it determines the rules of procedure and of practice, and of matters relating to attorneys, the internal discipline of the courts and the administration of judicial affairs.

2. Public procurators shall be subject to the rule-making power of the Supreme Court.

3. The Supreme Court may delegate the power to make rules for inferior courts to such courts.

ARTICLE 78. Judges shall not be removed except by public impeachment unless judicially declared mentally or physically incompetent to perform official duties. No disciplinary action against judges shall be administered by any executive organ or agency.

ARTICLE 79. The Supreme Court shall consist of a Chief Judge and such number of judges as may be determined by law; all such judges excepting the Chief Judge shall be appointed by the Cabinet.

2. The appointment of the judges of the Supreme Court shall be reviewed by the people at the first general election of members of the House of Representatives following their appointment, and shall be reviewed again at the first general election of members of the House of Representatives after a lapse of ten (10) years, and in the same manner thereafter.

3. In cases mentioned in the foregoing paragraph, when the majority of the voters favors the dismissal of a judge, he shall be dismissed.

4. Matters pertaining to review shall be prescribed by law.

5. The judges of the Supreme Court shall be retired upon the attainment of the age as fixed by law.

6. All such judges shall receive, at regular stated intervals, adequate compensation which shall not be decreased during their terms of office.

ARTICLE 80. The judges of the inferior courts shall be appointed by the Cabinet from a list of persons nominated by the Supreme Court. All such judges shall hold office for a term of ten (10) years with privilege of reappointment, provided that they shall be retired upon the attainment of the age as fixed by law.

2. The judges of the inferior courts shall receive, at regular stated intervals, adequate compensation which shall not be decreased during their terms of office.

ARTICLE 81. The Supreme Court is the court of last resort with power to determine the constitutionality of any law, order, regulation or official act.

ARTICLE 82. Trials shall be conducted and judgment declared publicly. Where a court unanimously determines publicity to be dangerous to public order or morals, a trial may be conducted privately, but trials of political offenses, offenses involving the press or cases wherein the rights of people as guaranteed in Chapter III of this Constitution are in question shall always be conducted publicly.

CHAPTER VII. FINANCE

ARTICLE 83. The power to administer national finances shall be exercised as the Diet shall determine.

ARTICLE 84. No new taxes shall be imposed or existing ones modified except by law or under such conditions as law may prescribe.

ARTICLE 85. No money shall be expended, nor shall the State obligate itself, except as authorized by the Diet.

ARTICLE 86. The Cabinet shall prepare and submit to the Diet for its consideration and decision a budget for each fiscal year.

ARTICLE 87. In order to provide for unforeseen deficiencies in the budget, a reserve fund may be authorized by the Diet to be expended upon the responsibility of the Cabinet.

2. The Cabinet must get subsequent approval of the Diet for all payments from the reserve fund.

ARTICLE 88. All property of the Imperial Household shall belong to the State. All expenses of the Imperial Household shall be appropriated by the Diet in the budget.

ARTICLE 89. No public money or other property shall be expended or appropriated for the use, benefit or maintenance of any religious institution or association, or for any charitable, educational or benevolent enterprises not under the control of public authority.

ARTICLE 90. Final accounts of the expenditures and revenues of the State shall be audited annually by a Board of Audit and submitted by the Cabinet to the Diet, together with the statement of audit, during the fiscal year immediately following the period covered.

2. The organization and competency of the Board of Audit shall be determined by law.

ARTICLE 91. At regular intervals and at least annually the Cabinet shall report to the Diet and the people on the state of national finances.

CHAPTER VIII. LOCAL SELF-GOVERNMENT

ARTICLE 92. Regulations concerning organization and operations of local public entities shall be fixed by law in accordance with the principle of local autonomy.

ARTICLE 93. The local public entities shall establish assemblies as their deliberative organs, in accordance with law.

2. The chief executive officers of all local public entities, the members of their assemblies, and such other local officials as may be determined by law shall be elected by direct popular vote within their several communities.

ARTICLE 94. Local public entities shall have the right to manage their property, affairs and administration and to enact their own regulations within law.

ARTICLE 95. A special law, applicable only to one local public entity, cannot be enacted by the Diet without the consent of the majority of the voters of the local public entity concerned, obtained in accordance with law.

CHAPTER IX. AMENDMENTS

ARTICLE 96. Amendments to this Constitution shall be initiated by the Diet, through a concurring vote of two-thirds or more of all the members of each House and shall thereupon be submitted to the people for ratification, which shall require the affirmative vote of a majority of all votes cast thereon, at a special referendum or at such election as the Diet shall specify.

2. Amendments when so ratified shall immediately be promulgated by the Emperor in the name of the people, as an integral part of this Constitution.

CHAPTER X. SUPREME LAW

ARTICLE 97. The fundamental human rights by this Constitution guaranteed to the people of Japan are fruits of the age-old struggle of man to be free; they have survived the many exacting tests for durability and are conferred upon this and future generations in trust, to be held for all time inviolate.

ARTICLE 98. This Constitution shall be the supreme law of the nation and no law, ordinance, imperial rescript or other act of government, or part thereof, contrary to the provisions hereof, shall have legal force or validity.

2. The treaties concluded by Japan and established laws of nations shall be faithfully observed.

ARTICLE 99. The Emperor or the Regent as well as Ministers of State, members of the Diet, judges, and all other public officials have the obligation to respect and uphold this Constitution.

CHAPTER XI. SUPPLEMENTARY PROVISIONS

ARTICLE 100. This Constitution shall be enforced as from the day when the period of six months will have elapsed counting from the day of its promulgation.

2. The enactment of laws necessary for the enforcement of this Constitution, the election of members of the House of Councillors and the

procedure for the convocation of the Diet and other preparatory procedures for the enforcement of this Constitution may be executed before the day prescribed in the preceding paragraph.

ARTICLE 101. If the House of Councillors is not constituted before the effective date of this Constitution, the House of Representatives shall function as the Diet until such time as the House of Councillors shall be constituted.

ARTICLE 102. The term of office for half the members of the House of Councillors serving in the first term under this Constitution shall be three years. Members falling under this category shall be determined in accordance with law.

ARTICLE 103. The Ministers of State, members of the House of Representatives, and judges in office on the effective date of this Constitution, and all other public officials, who occupy positions corresponding to such positions as are recognized by this Constitution shall not forfeit their positions automatically on account of the enforcement of this Constitution unless otherwise specified by law. When, however, successors are elected or appointed under the provisions of this Constitution, they shall forfeit their positions as a matter of course.

APPENDIX II:
BIOGRAPHICAL SKETCHES OF
JUSTICES OF THE SUPREME COURT
OF JAPAN

Note: Basic biographical data was graciously supplied by the Secretariat-General of the Supreme Court. Additional data has been obtained from Gendai Nihon Jinmeijiten ("Biographical Dictionary of Contemporary Japanese"). Readings of names are as given in the biographical data from the Secretariat-General. Names are given in the Japanese style: surname first, given name second.

I. JUSTICES ACTIVE AS OF JANUARY 1, 1959

CHIEF JUSTICE: *Tanaka Kōtarō.* Born October 25, 1890, in Saga Prefecture. May, 1915, graduated from the Faculty of Law, Tokyo Imperial University. September, 1917, assistant professor of commercial law at Tokyo Imperial University; March, 1923, professor, Tokyo Imperial University. April, 1931, degree of Doctor of Law. 1933–1939, lectured on jurisprudence; from 1937 to 1939 dean, Faculty of Law, Tokyo Imperial University. October, 1945, director of the School Education Bureau of the Ministry of Education. May, 1946, Minister of Education. January, 1947, resigned. June, 1946, made member of House of Peers by imperial appointment. May, 1947, elected to House of Councillors and appointed chairman of the House of Councillors Education Committee. June, 1947, registered as lawyer. August, 1948, professor emeritus at Tokyo University. January, 1949, member of Japan Science Council. March, 1950, resigned from the House of Councillors and appointed Chief Justice of the Supreme Court. Between 1950 and 1957 traveled extensively in the United States, India, Italy, Switzerland, France, Germany, Brazil, and other countries. Is a member of the Catholic Church. Has written a number of books on problems of commercial law, legal philosophy, and non-

425

academic subjects. In 1957 he published *Kyōsanshugi to Sekaikan* ("Communism and a View of the World"). Since World War II he has taken a consistently conservative and anticommunist political position, but he is generally accepted as being a true liberal. He fought to defend academic freedom during the period of militarism.

JUSTICES (LISTED IN ORDER OF SENIORITY OF APPOINTMENT):

Otani Katsushige (surname also rendered as "Kotani"). Born December 24, 1890, in Kyoto. July, 1914, graduated from the Faculty of Law, Hōsei University (Tokyo). December, 1916, passed lawyers' examination; March, 1917, member of the Osaka Bar Association. December, 1941, degree of Doctor of Law. April, 1946, president of the Osaka Bar Association. August, 1947, justice, Supreme Court.

Shima Tamotsu. Born August 25, 1891, in Tokyo. (*The Japan Biographical Encyclopedia and Who's Who* states that he was born into a Nakanishi family.) May, 1916, graduated in French law, Faculty of Law, Tokyo Imperial University. July, 1918, judge, Tokyo District Court and Tokyo Local Court. April, 1923, sent to Europe and the United States to study the jury system. December, 1924, appointed judicial secretary and public prosecutor. April, 1925, lecturer in Tōhoku Imperial University (Sendai). August, 1930, judge of the Tokyo Court of Appeal. November, 1931, president of the Court of Appeal. April, 1935, justice, Court of Cassation (*Daishinin*). July, 1938, president, Tokyo District Criminal Court. August, 1947, justice, Supreme Court. Initially concentrated on civil law, but later became an expert in criminal law.

Saitō Yūsuke. Born May 21, 1892, in Yamagata Prefecture. March, 1917, graduated in German law, Faculty of Law, Tokyo Imperial University. December, 1918, judge, Osaka District Court and Osaka Local Court. March, 1926, judge, Osaka Court of Appeal. May, 1933, judicial secretary and public prosecutor. May, 1935, prosecutor, Tokyo District Criminal Court. 1937, sent to the United States and Europe. December, 1937, president, Kōchi District Court. May, 1941, justice, Court of Cassation. February, 1946, chief prosecutor, Hiroshima Court of Appeal. July, 1946, chief prosecutor, Osaka Court of Appeal. August, 1947, justice, Supreme Court.

Fujita Hachirō. Born August 5, 1892. March, 1917, graduated in German law, Faculty of Law, Tokyo Imperial University. March, 1919, judge, Tokyo District Court and Tokyo Local Court; December, 1923, division head, Kyoto District Court. April, 1929, sent to Europe and the United States. August, 1930, judge, Tokyo District Court. October, 1930, judge, Tokyo Court of Appeal. July, 1937, justice, Court of Cassation. February, 1941, president, Osaka District Court; March, 1944, president, Sapporo Court of Appeal. February, 1946, president, Osaka Court of Appeal. August, 1947, justice, Supreme Court.

Kawamura Matasuke. Born January 1, 1894, in Yamaguchi City. July, 1919, graduated in political science, Faculty of Law, Tokyo Imperial University. May, 1922–December, 1924, research in the theory of the state in France, Germany, and England. December, 1924, professor at Tōhoku University (Sendai) in the theory of the state. August, 1932, professor of Kyushū University (Fukuoka) in constitutional law. December, 1934, published *Chokusetsu Minshu Seiji* ("Direct Democracy"). March, 1938–July, 1939, dean, Faculty of Law and Literature, Kyushū Imperial University. October, 1945, member, Constitutional Problem Investigation Committee. June, 1946, published *Kempō Kaisei no Shomondai* ("Problems of Constitutional Revision"). July, 1947, member of Japan Science Council. August, 1947, justice, Supreme Court. May, 1948, published *Shin Kempō to Minshushugi* ("The New Constitution and Democracy"). August, 1948, received degree of Doctor of Law. Was active in early student movement.

Iriye Toshio. Born January 10, 1901, in Tokyo. December, 1923, graduated in German law, Faculty of Law, Tokyo Imperial University. October, 1925, appointed local administrative official and assigned to Saitama Prefecture. March, 1928, part-time lecturer in administrative law at Takushoku University (Tokyo). May, 1934, part-time lecturer in constitutional and administrative law, Faculty of Agriculture, Tokyo Imperial University; September, 1934, appointed part-time lecturer in public law at Tokyo University of Science and Literature. April, 1939, chief of the Third Section of the Cabinet Bureau of Legislation. September, 1945, chief of First Section of the Bureau of Legislation. November, 1945, vice-director, Bureau of Legislation; March, 1946, director, Bureau of Legislation. May, 1946, named member of House of Peers by imperial appointment. April, 1948, part-time lecturer in public law at Keio University. July, 1948, director of Bureau of Legislation of the House of Representatives. January–March, 1951, tour of inspection in the United States. August, 1952, justice, Supreme Court. September–October, 1956, inspected European judicial systems and attended first international conference of judges.

Ikeda Katsu. Born May 23, 1893. July, 1917, graduated in French law, Faculty of Law, Tokyo Imperial University. March, 1919, prosecutor, Tokyo District Court and Tokyo Local Court. July, 1926, judicial secretary. April, 1930, traveled to Europe and the United States and in June attended the tenth annual international conference on criminal law and prisons. March, 1935, prosecutor, Court of Cassation. January, 1940, prosecutor, Tokyo District Criminal Court. July, 1941, chief of the Criminal Bureau, Justice Ministry. April, 1945, chief prosecutor, Nagoya Court of Appeal. August, 1946, registered as an attorney with the Tokyo Bar Association. November, 1954, justice, Supreme Court.

Tarumi Katsumi. Born November 15, 1893. 1918, graduated in German law, Faculty of Law, Tokyo Imperial University. 1920, judge, Tokyo District Court and Tokyo Local Court. 1934, judge, Tokyo Court of Appeal. 1939, leader in the Judicial Research Institute. 1943, justice, Court of Cassation. 1945, president of the Tokyo District Criminal Court. 1946, president of the Miyagi Court of Appeal. 1947, president of the Sendai High Court. 1948, president of the Osaka High Court. 1951, president of the Tokyo High Court. 1955, justice, Supreme Court.

Kawamura Daisuke. Born June 2, 1893. 1919, graduated from Nihon University (Tokyo). February, 1922, registered as an attorney. May, 1949–November, 1951, instructor at the Judicial Research and Training Institute. November, 1956, justice, Supreme Court.

Shimoiizaka Masuo. Born January 29, 1894. March, 1918, graduated from the Faculty of Law, Tokyo Imperial University. January, 1921, judge, Yokohama District Court. July, 1922, judge, Tokyo District Court. July, 1932, judge, Tokyo Court of Appeal. October, 1939, traveled to China. April, 1941, president, Tottori District Court. March, 1943, president, Mito District Court. June, 1944, president, Niigata District Court. April, 1945, judge, Court of Cassation. September, 1947, president, Sapporo High Court. February, 1952, president, Nagoya High Court. June, 1955, president Osaka High Court. November, 1956, justice, Supreme Court.

Okuno Kenichi. Born November 18, 1898. March, 1923, graduated from the Faculty of Law, Tokyo Imperial University. July, 1925, judge, Tokyo District Court. January, 1931, judicial secretary. April, 1935, traveled to Europe and the United States. April, 1937, judge, Tokyo Court of Appeal. March, 1943, president, Sendai District Court. March, 1945, justice, Court of Cassation. August, 1945, director, Civil Affairs Bureau, Justice Ministry. February, 1948, Litigation Assistant to the Attorney General. October, 1948, director, Legislative Affairs Bureau, House of Councillors. January, 1951, travel to the United States. November, 1956, justice, Supreme Court.

Takahashi Kiyoshi. Born January 16, 1895. April, 1921, graduated from Faculty of Law, Tokyo Imperial University. September, 1922, registered as attorney and entered the Tokyo Bar Association. January, 1950–April, 1952, instructor, Judicial Research and Training Institute. January, 1957, justice, Supreme Court.

Takagi Tsuneshichi. Born March 15, 1893. July, 1916, graduated in English law from Waseda University (Tokyo). July, 1919, public prosecutor. April, 1921, public prosecutor, Nagoya District Court and Nagoya Local Court. June, 1923, registered as attorney. February, 1946, president, Shizuoka District Court. November, 1947, president, Yokohama District Court. April, 1949, president, Tokyo Domestic Court. February, 1952, president, Sapporo High Court. June, 1955, president, Hiroshima High Court. December, 1956, president, Nagoya High Court. June, 1958, justice, Supreme Court.

Ishizaka Shuichi. Born September 14, 1895. July, 1919, graduated from the Faculty of Law, Tokyo Imperial University. August, 1921, judge, Yokohama District Court and Yokohama Local Court. December, 1924, judge, Tokyo District Court and Tokyo Local Court. May, 1935, bureau director, Tokyo District Criminal Court. July, 1941, judge, Himeji Local Court. March, 1943, bureau director, Tokyo Court of Appeal. September, 1945, justice, Court of Cassation. November, 1947, judge, Tokyo High Court. October, 1948, president, Sendai High Court. September–November, 1950, observation of legal system in the United States. September, 1952, president, Hiroshima High Court. June, 1955, president, Nagoya High Court. December, 1956, president, Osaka High Court. June, 1958, justice, Supreme Court.

II. Past Justices of the Supreme Court

CHIEF JUSTICE: *Mibuchi Tadahiko.* Born March 3, 1880. July, 1904, graduated from the Faculty of Law, Kyoto Imperial University. November, 1907, judge, Tokyo District Court. April, 1923, justice, Court of Cassation. December, 1924, section chief, Tokyo Court of Appeal. 1926–1928, legal advisor, Mitsui Trust Company, Incorporated. April, 1911–March, 1942, lecturer, Keio University. August, 1947, chief justice, Supreme Court. March 2, 1950, retired on reaching age limit. Deceased, July 14, 1950.

JUSTICES:

Shōno Riichi. Born December 20, 1888. April, 1913, graduated from the Faculty of Law, Tokyo Imperial University. September, 1913, registered as attorney. April, 1946, president, Tokyo Bar Association. August, 1947, justice, Supreme Court. June, 1948, retired at own request. Deceased, December, 1956.

Tsukasaki Naoyoshi. Born May 10, 1881. 1908, graduated from the Faculty of Law, Kyoto Imperial University. 1909, began practice as attorney. 1925–1947, legal advisor, *Tokyo Nichinichi* (later *Mainichi*) newspaper. 1926–1927, research in Europe and the United States on the jury system and legal assistance for the needy. 1930, president, Tokyo Bar Association. March, 1947, president, Tokyo Bar Association. August,

1947, justice, Supreme Court. February 14, 1951, retired on reaching age limit. Deceased, March 26, 1957.

Hozumi Shigetō. Born April 11, 1883. July, 1908, graduated from the Faculty of Law, Tokyo Imperial University. September, 1908, part-time lecturer, Faculty of Law, Tokyo Imperial University. March, 1910, assistant professor, Faculty of Law, Tokyo Imperial University. 1912–1916, studied civil law and jurisprudence in Germany, France, and England. September, 1916, professor, Faculty of Law, Tokyo Imperial University. November, 1917, degree of Doctor of Law. Between 1930 and 1941 served three times as Dean, Faculty of Law, Tokyo Imperial University. July, 1937, imperial appointment to the Imperial Academy. February, 1944, professor emeritus, Tokyo Imperial University. February, 1949, justice, Supreme Court. Deceased, July, 1951.

Hasegawa Taichiro. Born December 1, 1881. September, 1911, graduated in law, Meiji University (Tokyo). March, 1915, became attorney. March, 1931–March, 1933, vice-president, First Tokyo Bar Association. April–August, 1947, president, First Tokyo Bar Association. August, 1947, justice, Supreme Court. November 30, 1951, retired on reaching age limit.

Sawada Takejirō. Born August 2, 1882. 1909, graduated from the Faculty of Law, Tokyo Imperial University. 1942, bureau director, Court of Administrative Litigation. April, 1945, arrested and imprisoned for expressing antiarmy, antiwar ideas. 1946, president, Court of Administrative Litigation. 1947, justice, Supreme Court. August 1, 1952, retired on reaching the age limit.

Shimoyama Seiichi. Born October 15, 1884, Okayama City. July, 1910, graduated in German law, Faculty of Law, Tokyo Imperial University. June, 1913, judge, Tokyo District Court and Tokyo Local Court. January, 1924, justice, Court of Cassation. September, 1934, president, Sapporo Court of Appeal. May, 1935, president, Hiroshima Court of Appeal. March, 1937, section director, Court of Cassation. February, 1939, president, Tokyo Court of Appeal. September, 1944, president, Court of Cassation. March, 1946, member, House of Peers. April, 1946, became attorney. August, 1947, justice, Supreme Court. October, 1954, retired on reaching age limit.

Inouye Nobori. Born April 10, 1885, Chiba Prefecture. March, 1913, graduated in German law, Faculty of Law, Tokyo Imperial University. February, 1917, judge. March, 1926, aide to Japanese delegation, international labor conferences in Geneva. December, 1927, judge, Tokyo Court of Appeal. March, 1933, justice, Court of Cassation; July, 1937, director, Research Section, Justice Ministry. August, 1947, justice, Supreme Court. April 9, 1955, retired on reaching age limit. Also lecturer at Keio, Meiji, and Senshū Universities, all in Tokyo.

Kuriyama Shigeru. Born October 10, 1886, in Fukui Prefecture. July, 1913, graduated in French law, Faculty of Law, Tokyo Imperial University; June, 1918, third secretary in Japanese embassy. February, 1919, aide to Japanese peace delegation at Versailles. October, 1921, member, Japanese delegation at Washington Conference. August, 1924, secretary in Japanese foreign service. December, 1927, first secretary in Japanese embassy. November, 1929, aide to Japanese delegation to London Naval Conference. January, 1932, Japanese representative at Lausanne reparations conference. May, 1933, director, Bureau of Treaties, Foreign Ministry; May, 1936, Envoy Extraordinary and Minister Plenipotentiary to Sweden, Norway, and Denmark. November, 1939, Ambassador Extraordinary and Plenipotentiary to Belgium. September, 1941, counsellor to the Ambassador Extraordinary and Plenipotentiary to French Indo-China. August, 1947, justice, Supreme Court. January 29, 1954, justice, International Court of Arbitration (The Hague). October 5, 1956, retired from Supreme Court on reaching age limit.

Iwamatsu Saburō. Born December 31, 1893 in Tokyo. July, 1917, graduated in German law, Faculty of Law, Tokyo Imperial University. March, 1919, judge, Tokyo District Court and Tokyo Local Court. April, 1928, sent to Europe and the United States. March, 1933, judge, Tokyo Court of Appeal. March, 1936, justice, Court of Cassation. July, 1939, leader, Judicial Research Institute. January, 1942, president, Hiroshima District Court. March, 1944, President, Osaka District Court. December, 1944, president, Tokyo District Civil Court. February, 1946, president, Fukuoka Court of Appeal. August, 1947, justice, Supreme Court. November, 1956, retired at own request. Expert in the law of compulsory execution and civil procedure.

Tanimura Tadaichirō. Born April 5, 1887. September, 1914, graduated in law, Chūō University (Tokyo). February, 1918, registered as attorney. March, 1938, elected president, Tokyo Bar Association. February, 1946, appointed vice-minister, Justice Ministry. June, 1947, resigned. April, 1951, justice, Supreme Court. November, 1956, retired at own request.

Motomura Zentarō. Born January 15, 1887. January, 1915, graduated in English law, Faculty of Law, Kyoto Imperial University. March, 1916, registered as attorney. May, 1951, chairman, Civil Liberties Committee, Japan Federation of Lawyers. January, 1952, justice, Supreme Court. January, 1957, retired on reaching age limit.

Kobayashi Shunzō. Born June 3, 1888, in Tokyo. July, 1914, graduated in German law, Faculty of Law, Tokyo Imperial University. 1914–1916, practiced as attorney. April, 1931–March, 1947, lecturer and later professor of civil law, Chūō University. 1932–1942, lecturer in civil law, Hōsei University (Tokyo). March, 1939, president, Second Tokyo Bar Association. December, 1947, president, Tokyo High Court (presiding over special sessions dealing with Anti-Monopoly Law and the Law of Popular Review of Supreme Court Justices). October, 1951, justice, Supreme Court. July–September, 1952 traveled to Europe and the United States. June, 1958, resigned from Supreme Court on reaching age limit.

Mano Tsuyoshi (given name frequently rendered "Takeshi"). Born June 9, 1888, Aichi Prefecture. July, 1914, graduated in German law, Faculty of Law, Tokyo Imperial University. July, 1914, registered as attorney in Tokyo. 1914–1916, graduate study, in law, Tokyo Imperial University. September, 1920, lecturer in civil law, Faculty of Agriculture, Tokyo Imperial University. April, 1940, first president, Second Tokyo Bar Association. August, 1947, justice, Supreme Court. June, 1958, retired on reaching age limit.

BIBLIOGRAPHY

This bibliography consists only of those works consulted in the course of the preparation of this study.

PUBLICATIONS OF THE SUPREME COURT OF JAPAN

Saikōsaibansho Hanreishū ("Collection of Supreme Court Precedents"). Compiled under the direction of the Committee on Supreme Court Precedents. Vol. I. Tokyo, 1947————. (Through Volume VII the *Hanreishū* carried the English subtitle, *Supreme Court Reports.*)

Saibansho Jihō ("Court Review"). Published by the General Secretariat of the Supreme Court on the first and fifteenth of each month. Tokyo.

Saikōsaibansho Kōtōsaibansho Hanrei Yōshi Shū ("Digest of Supreme Court and High Court Precedents"). Compiled by the General Secretariat. Tokyo, May, 1954.

Saikōsaibansho Kikō Kaikaku Mondai Kankei Shiryō ("Materials Relating to the Problem of the Reform of the Organization of the Supreme Court"). Compiled by the General Secretariat. 5 vols. Tokyo, June, 1957–April, 1958.

Saikōsaibansho Keiji Hanrei Yōshi Shū (*Jittaihō Hen*) ("Digest of Supreme Court Criminal Precedents. Substantive Law Section"). Compiled by the Shihō Kenshūjo (Legal Training and Research Institute). Tokyo, December, 1956.

Saikōsaibansho Keiji Hanrei Yōshi Shū (*Tetsuzukihō Hen*) ("Digest of Criminal Precedents. Procedural Law Section"). Compiled by the Shihō Kenshūjo. Tokyo, December, 1956.

Saikōsaibansho Keiji Hanrei Yōshi Shū. Tsuiroku ("Digest of Supreme Court Criminal Precedents. Supplement"). Compiled by the Shihō Kenshūjo. Tokyo, June, 1958.

Waga Kuni ni okeru Saibanshoseido no Enkaku ("Development of the Court System in Our Country"). Compiled by the General Secretariat. Tokyo, October, 1957.

The General Secretariat has also published the following translations under the general title: "Series of Prominent Judgments of the Supreme Court upon Questions of Constitutionality."

No. 1. *Judgment upon Case of Validity of Cabinet Order No. 325 of 1950.* Tokyo, 1954.

No. 2. *Judgment upon Case of Translation and Publication of* Lady Chatterley's Lover *and Article 175 of the Penal Code.* Tokyo, 1958.

No. 3. *Judgment upon Case of Bodily Injury Resulting in Death to Lineal Ascendant under Article 205-2 of the Penal Code.* Tokyo, 1959.

No. 4. *Judgment upon Case of the So-called "Sunakawa Case."* Tokyo, 1960.

TRANSLATIONS OF LAWS UNDER AUTHORIZATION OF THE MINISTRY OF JUSTICE

The Civil Code of Japan. (EHS Law Bulletin Series.) Tokyo: Eibun-Horei-Sha (The Publishing Institute of Japanese Law in English Version), 1959.

The Code of Civil Procedure. (EHS Law Bulletin Series.) Tokyo: Eibun-Horei-Sha, 1955.

The Constitution of Japan and Criminal Statutes. Tokyo: Ministry of Justice, 1958. (This is an invaluable collection including, in addition to the Constitution, nineteen translations of codes, laws, and regulations dealing with criminal affairs.)

Law of Procedure in Non-Contentious Matters and Law for Special Regulations Concerning Procedure of Administrative Litigations. Tokyo: Eibun-Horei-Sha, 1954.

REFERENCE WORKS AND DICTIONARIES

Dai Roppō Zensho ("The Great Compendium of the Six Codes"). (1958 ed.) Tokyo: Sanseidō.

Gendai Nihon Jinmeijiten ("Biographical Dictionary of Contemporary Japanese"). Tokyo: Heibonsha, 1955.

Genkō Nihon Hōki ("Complete Collection of Laws, Statutes, and Ordinances of Japan"). Compiled by the Judicial and Legislative Research Section of the Secretariat of the Minister of Justice. Tokyo: Ministry of Justice, n.d.

Gyōsei Kikō Zu. Shōwa 33 Nendo Han ("Administrative Organization Chart. 1958 edition"). Compiled by the Administrative Management Bureau of the Administrative Management Agency. Tokyo: Printing Bureau, Ministry of Finance.

Suekawa Hiroshi (ed.). *Hōgaku Jiten* ("Legal Dictionary"). Tokyo: Nihon Hyōron Shinsha, 1959.

Japan Statistical Yearbook. 1958. Compiled by the Bureau of Statistics, Office of the Prime Minister. Tokyo: Printing Bureau, Ministry of Finance, 1959.

Jujiro Ito. *A Japanese-English Dictionary of Legal Terms with Supplement.* Tokyo: Daigaku Shobo, 1953.

Kenkyusha's New Japanese-English Dictionary (1954 ed.). Tokyo: Kenkyusha. (I list this standard dictionary because I have followed as far as possible its translations of the titles of laws, government offices, and so forth in the interests of uniformity of nomenclature, a difficult problem in Japanese studies.)

Wagatsuma Sakae and Miyazawa Toshiyoshi (eds.). *Roppō Zensho* ("Compendium of the Six Codes"). (1960 ed.) Tokyo: Yūhikaku.

Wagatsuma Sakae (ed.). *Shin Hōritsugaku Jiten* ("New Dictionary of Jurisprudence"). Tokyo: Yuhikaku, 1958.

WORKS IN JAPANESE

Hanrei Kaiko. 1956 Nendo. Bessatsu: Hōritsu Jihō. ("Precedent Review. 1956. Supplement: Law Review"). Tokyo: Nihon Hyōron Shinsha, 1957.

Hanrei Kaiko. 1957 Nendo. Bessatsu: Hōritsu Jihō. Tokyo: Nihon Hyōron Shinsha, 1958.

Hasegawa Masayasu. *Kempō Hanrei Kenkyū* ("Study of Constitutional Precedents"). Tokyo: Keiso Shobō, 1956.

Kempō Chōsa Kai. *Kempō Chōsa Kai Dai Jurokkai Sōkai Gijiroku* ("Minutes of the Sixteenth General Meeting of the Commission on the Constitution"). Tokyo, April, 1958.

――――. *Kempō Kankei Hanrei Yōshi Shū* ("Digest of Precedents Relating to the Constitution"). Tokyo, March, 1958.

Kaneko Hajime. *Saibanhō* ("Trial Law"). (Hōritsugaku Zenshu 34.) Tokyo: Yūhikaku, 1959.

Miyazawa Toshiyoshi. *Kempō Kyōzai* ("Constitutional Teaching Materials"). Hanrei Kyōzai Sosho. Tokyo: Yūhikaku, Vol. I, 1952; Vol. II, 1956.

――――. *Nihonkoku Kempō* ("The Constitution of Japan"). (Horitsugaku Taikei. Konmentaaru-hen, 1.) Tokyo: Nihon Hyōron Shinsha, 1955.

Tabata Shinobu (ed.). *Hanrei Kempōgaku* ("Constitutional Cases"). Kyoto: Minerubaa Shobō, 1958.

Yunoki Kaoru (ed.). *Saikōsaibansho Minpō Hanrei Yōroku* ("Digest of Supreme Court Civil Precedents"). Tokyo: Yūhikaku, 1958.

———. *Saikōsaibansho Minpō Hanrei Yōroku. Tsuiho* (1). ("Digest of Supreme Court Civil Precedents. Supplement 1"). Tokyo: Yūhikaku, 1959.

BOOKS AND ARTICLES IN ENGLISH

Appleton, Richard B. "Reforms in Japanese Criminal Procedure under Allied Occupation," *Washington Law Review*, XXIV, No. 4 (November, 1949), 401–30.

Blakemore, Thomas L. "Post-war Developments in Japanese Law," *Wisconsin Law Review*, Vol. 1947, pp. 632–53.

Dionisopoulos, P. Allan. "Judicial Review and Civil Rights in Japan: The First Decade with an Alien Doctrine," *Western Political Quarterly*, XIII, No. 2 (June, 1960), 269–87.

General Headquarters, Supreme Commander for the Allied Powers. *Political Reorientation of Japan September 1945 to September 1948. Report of Government Section, Supreme Commander for the Allied Powers.* 2 vols. Washington, D.C.: U.S. Government Printing Office, n.d.

Ito, Count Hirobumi. *Commentaries on the Constitution of the Empire of Japan.* Translated by Miyoji Ito. Tokyo: Igirisu-Horitsu Gakko, 1889.

Maki, John M. "Japan's Rearmament: Progress and Problems," *Western Political Quarterly*, VIII, No. 4, 545–68.

Matsuda, Jiro. "The Japanese Legal Training and Research Institute," *American Journal of Comparative Law*, VII, No. 3 (Summer, 1958), 366–79.

Nathanson, Nathaniel L. "Constitutional Adjudication in Japan," *American Journal of Comparative Law*, VIII, No. 2 (Spring, 1958), 195–218.

Oppler, Alfred C. "Japan's Courts and Law in Transition," *Contemporary Japan*, XXI, Nos. 1–3 (1952), 1–37.

———. "The Reform of Japan's Legal and Judicial System," *Washington Law Review*, XXIV, 290–324.

———. "The Sunakawa Case: Its Legal and Political Implications," *Political Science Quarterly*, LXXVI, No. 2 (June, 1961), 241–63.

Quigley, Harold S. *Japanese Government and Politics.* New York: The Century Company, 1932.

Quigley, Harold S. and Turner, John E. *The New Japan: Government and Politics.* Minneapolis: University of Minnesota Press, 1956.

Steiner, Kurt. "A Japanese *Cause Célèbre;* The Fukuoka Patricide Case," *American Journal of Comparative Law*, V, No. 1 (Winter, 1956), 106–11.

von Mehren, Arthur T. "Some Reflections on Japanese Law," *Harvard Law Review*, LXXI, No. 8 (June, 1958), 1486–96.

INDEX

the Justices vividly illustrate the conflicts underlying the Japan of today.

Of interest as comparative law, *Court and Constitution in Japan* will also be of great value to political scientists, historians, and Far Eastern scholars, for it demonstrates the problems encountered in the modification of Western norms to Eastern use. In addition, these decisions debate such universal questions as the conflict between individual rights and the public welfare, and the precedence of legislative power over judicial review.

An extensive introduction by Professor Maki explains the history and philosophy of the Constitution of 1947 and describes the operation of Japan's legal system prior to World War II. The author has also edited these translations, prefacing each decision with an explanatory note and the relevant statutory and constitutional references. Both majority and minority opinions are included.

Assisting the author were three scholars — David Sissons of the Australian National University, Ikeda Masaaki of Rikkyo University, Tokyo, and Kurt Steiner of Stanford University—whose nationalities and affiliations illustrate the wide interest in this project.

John M. Maki, professor of Japanese government and politics at the Far Eastern Institute of the University of Washington, is author of *Government and Politics in Japan: The Road to Democracy*, and *Conflict and Tension in the Far East: Key Documents, 1894-1960*.